The
Battle for Christmas

The
Battle for Christmas

STEPHEN NISSENBAUM

ALFRED A. KNOPF

New York 1996

THIS IS A BORZOI BOOK
PUBLISHED BY ALFRED A. KNOPF, INC.

Library of Congress Cataloging-in-Publication Data

Nissenbaum, Stephen.
    The battle for Christmas / Stephen Nissenbaum. —1st ed.
       p.   cm.
    ISBN 0-679-41223-9
    1. Christmas—United States—History.   I. Title.
GT4986.AIN57   1996
394.2´663´0973—dc20
                                                                    96-22355
                                                                    CIP

Manufactured in the United States of America
First Edition

For
William R. Taylor
My teacher

Contents

Preface

THIS BOOK had its beginnings more than twenty years ago, when I delivered a speculative scholarly paper titled "From 'The Day of Doom' to 'The Night Before Christmas.'" In that paper I dealt with the striking parallels between the best-known American poem of the 1600s and 1700s and the best-known American poem of the 1800s and 1900s. The earlier poem was about God's wrath, the later one about the goodwill of Santa Claus—but somehow the two were engaging in a kind of dialogue with each other.

Actually, though, it is clear that the book began earlier still, with my childhood fascination for "The Night Before Christmas," whose verses I recited over and over when December came around. For me, growing up as I did in an Orthodox Jewish household, this was surely part of my fascination for Christmas itself, that magical season which was always beckoning, at school and in the streets, only to be withheld each year by the forces of religion and family. (I once decided that Christmas must mean even more to America's Jewish children than to its Christian ones.) I can remember, one Christmas Day, putting some of my own toys in a sack and attempting to distribute them to other children who lived in my Jersey City apartment house: If I couldn't *get* presents, at least no one stopped me from giving them away, and in that fashion at least I could participate in the joy of what, much later, I would come to think of as the "gift exchange."

Much later came soon enough. By the late 1980s I had been a professional historian for some twenty years, and I was also regularly engaging in the nonacademic aspects of my trade. In 1988 I found myself involved in the development of a teacher-training program sponsored by Old Sturbridge Village, the living-history museum in central Massachusetts. The theme we decided to focus on with the teachers (they taught grades 3–8) was *holidays*. Remembering that paper I had written more than a decade earlier, I figured young children might be intrigued by seeing unfamiliar things in "A Visit from St. Nicholas," that most familiar of poems. ("Mama in her 'kerchief and I in my cap . . ."? "Away to the window . . . and threw up the sash . . ."? "A *miniature* sleigh"? "Eight *tiny* reindeer"?) So I volunteered to take on Christmas myself.

Preparing for my session, I made a series of startling discoveries that precipitated me into writing this book. To begin with, in an essay by the preeminent modern scholar of St. Nicholas, Charles W. Jones, I learned that "Santa Claus," far from being a creature of ancient Dutch folklore who made his way to the New World in the company of immigrants from Holland, was essentially devised by a group of non-Dutch New Yorkers in the early nineteenth century. (This discovery tied into another new notion I was acquainted with in a different context, that of "invented traditions"—customs that are made up with the precise purpose of appearing old-fashioned: the idea, for example, that every Scottish clan had its own unique tartan plaid—which turns out to have been the product of a nineteenth-century effort to romanticize the valiant Scots.)

Second, from reading a biographical sketch of Clement Clarke Moore, the author of "A Visit from St. Nicholas," I realized that the history of his best-loved poem was intertwined with the physical and political transformation of New York City during the early nineteenth century. Moore, it turned out, was a wealthy and politically conservative country gentleman who found himself at war with the encroaching forces of New York's commercial and residential development at the very time he was writing his undying verses about the night before Christmas.

It was my third discovery that helped make sense of that curious convergence. The Christmas season itself was undergoing a change, I learned. From the writings of several obscure nineteenth-century folklorists, along with contemporary historians Peter Burke and Natalie Zemon Davis and Russian theorist Mikhail Bakhtin, I discovered that Christmas had once occasioned a kind of behavior that would be shocking today: It was a time of heavy drinking when the rules that governed people's public behavior were momentarily abandoned in favor of an unrestrained "carnival," a kind of December Mardi Gras. And I found that in the early nineteenth century, with the growth of America's cities, that kind of behavior had become even more threatening, combining carnival rowdiness with urban gang violence and Christmas-season riots. (My key guides here were essays by the great British historian E. P. Thompson and one of his American disciples, Susan G. Davis.) Given the changed historical circumstances of the nineteenth century, I began to understand the appeal of a new-styled Christmas that took place indoors, within the secure confines of the family circle.

Those discoveries became the basis of much of the first three chapters of this book. Before long, I found myself exploring other issues, issues that stemmed from what I was learning about the creation of a new-styled domestic Christmas: At what point, and in what fashion, did Christmas become commercialized? What happened to family relationships on this holiday, when children became the center of attention and the recipients of lavish gifts? (After all, before our own day, weren't parents supposed to have avoided at all costs such gestures of intergenerational indulgence?) So I began to think about Christmas in the context of the larger history of consumer culture and child-rearing practices. Once again, I came up with some rather unexpected findings, findings that drove me to the conclusion that where Christmas was concerned, the problems of our own age go back a long way. The Christmas tree itself, I discovered, first entered American culture as a ritual strategy designed to cope with what was already being seen, even before the middle of the nineteenth century, as a holiday laden with crass materialism—a holiday that had produced a rising generation of greedy, spoiled children.

Those issues became the subjects of Chapters 4 and 5. The remaining two chapters, about Christmas charity and Christmas under slavery, respectively, resulted from two very different circumstances. I had intended, from an early point, to write about Dickens's novella *A Christmas Carol*, that other classic text of the holiday season (along with Moore's poem). But when I reread Dickens's book (for the first time in many years), I was led to explore the intricate and not always proud history of face-to-face Christmas charity, especially as it related to impoverished children. As far as Christmas under slavery is concerned, it was my students at the College of William and Mary, where I taught during the 1989–90 academic year, who provoked my interest in that subject. The documentary materials several of these students brought to me proved to be something of a revelation. I glimpsed a picture of Christmas under slavery that oddly resembled the pre-nineteenth-century carnival celebration I had discovered at the beginning of my work. As I struggled to achieve a deeper understanding of the slaves' holiday, I realized that with this topic my project had come full circle and it was time to stop.

One consequence of stopping there was that my book would essentially come to a halt with the turn of the twentieth century, well before the present day. But, I decided, this was exactly where I wished to stop. By the end of the nineteenth century, if not earlier, the Christmas celebration practiced by most Americans was one that would be quite familiar to their modern descendants. Between then and now, the modifications have been more of degree than of kind, more quantitative than qualitative. The important changes—the *revealing* changes—had all taken place. And those were the only changes I really cared about.

For the real subject of this book is not so much Christmas itself as what Christmas can tell us about broader historical questions. In writing about the commercialization of Christmas, for example, or the way Christmas made children the center of attention and affection, I have always tried to remember that those changes were expressions of the same forces that were transforming American culture as a whole. But it has been equally important for me also to see Christmas as *one* of those very forces—as a cause as well as an effect, an active *instrument* of change as well as an indicator and a mirror of change. From that angle, Christmas itself played a role in bringing about both the consumer revolution and the "domestic revolution" that created the modern family.

To raise such questions in this context is new. Until recently, the history of holidays has pretty much been written in what could be called an "antiquarian" fashion, as a subject that existed in isolation, sealed off from matters of broad importance. It is largely the work of anthropologists that has provoked a new look, by showing that the holiday season has long been serious cultural business. Christmas rituals—whether in the form of the rowdy excesses of carnival or the more tender excesses that surround the Christmas tree—have long served to transfigure our ordinary behavior in an almost magical fashion, in ways that reveal something of what we would like to be, what we once were, or what we are becoming despite ourselves. It is because the celebration of Christmas always illuminates these underlying features of the social landscape—and sometimes the very "fault lines" which threaten to divide it—that the content of the holiday, its timing, and even the matter of whether to celebrate it at all, have often been hotly contested. For this reason the book I have written constitutes just a single large chapter in the history of the perennial battle for Christmas.

But if I am concerned with those larger issues, I remain fascinated by Christmas itself, as fascinated today as when I was a child in that Jersey City apartment house—perhaps even more so, in the light of what I have learned in writing this book. For if I am writing about Christmas with the larger goals of a social and cultural historian, I also aim to tell a good story in a new way. Whether I have succeeded or not, I know that I have at least (and at last) managed to make Christmas my own, and I hope I have done so without betraying either its enduring meanings or my own patrimony.

Cambridge, Massachusetts
June 1995

The
Battle for Christmas

CHAPTER I

New England's War on Christmas

THE PURITAN WAR ON MISRULE

*I*N NEW ENGLAND, for the first two centuries of white settlement most people did not celebrate Christmas. In fact, the holiday
was systematically suppressed by Puritans during the colonial period
and largely ignored by their descendants. It was actually *illegal* to celebrate
Christmas in Massachusetts between 1659 and 1681 (the fine was five
shillings). Only in the middle of the nineteenth century did Christmas
gain legal recognition as an official public holiday in New England. Writing near the end of that century, one New Englander, born in 1822, recalled going to school as a boy on Christmas Day, adding that even as late
as 1850, in Worcester, Massachusetts, "The courts were in session on that
day, the markets were open, and I doubt if there had ever been a religious
service on Christmas Day, unless it were Sunday, in that town." As late as
1952, one writer recalled being told by his grandparents that New England
mill workers risked losing their jobs if they arrived late at work on December 25, and that sometimes "factory owners would change the starting
hours on Christmas Day to five o'clock or some equally early hour in order
that workers who wanted to attend a church service would have to forego,
or be dismissed for being late for work."[1]

As we shall see, much of this is misleading or exaggerated. It is true
that the New England states did not grant legal recognition to Christmas
until the middle of the nineteenth century, but neither did most of the
other states. There *were* Christmas Day religious services in Worcester be-

fore 1850. And nineteenth-century factory owners had their own reasons for treating Christmas as a regular working day, reasons that had more to do with industrial capitalism than with Puritan theology. Still, the fact remains that those factory owners were indeed operating within a long New England tradition of opposition to Christmas. As early as 1621, just one year after the Pilgrims landed on Plymouth Rock, their governor, William Bradford, found some of the colony's new residents trying to take the day off. Bradford ordered them right back to work. And in 1659 the Massachusetts General Court did in fact declare the celebration of Christmas to be a criminal offense.

Why? What accounts for this strange hostility? The Puritans themselves had a plain reason for what they tried to do, and it happens to be a perfectly good one: There is no biblical or historical reason to place the birth of Jesus on December 25. True, the Gospel of Luke tells the familiar story of the birth of Jesus of Nazareth—how the shepherds were living with their flocks in the fields of Judea, and how, one night, an angel appeared to them and said, "For unto you is born this day in the city of David a Savior, which is Christ the Lord." But nowhere in this account is there any indication of the exact date, or even the general season, on which "this day" fell. Puritans were fond of saying that if God had intended for the anniversary of the Nativity to be observed, He would surely have given some indication as to when that anniversary occurred. (They also argued that the weather in Judea during late December was simply too cold for shepherds to be living outdoors with their flocks.)

It was only in the fourth century that the Church officially decided to observe Christmas on December 25. And this date was chosen not for religious reasons but simply because it happened to mark the approximate arrival of the winter solstice, an event that was celebrated long before the advent of Christianity. The Puritans were correct when they pointed out—and they pointed it out often—that Christmas was nothing but a pagan festival covered with a Christian veneer. The Reverend Increase Mather of Boston, for example, accurately observed in 1687 that the early Christians who first observed the Nativity on December 25 did not do so "thinking that Christ was born in that Month, but because the Heathens Saturnalia was at that time kept in Rome, and they were willing to have those Pagan Holidays metamorphosed into Christian [ones]."[2]

Most cultures (outside the tropics) have long marked with rituals involving light and greenery those dark weeks of December when the daylight wanes, all culminating in the winter solstice—the return of sun and light and life itself. Thus Chanukah, the "feast of lights." And thus the

Yule log, the candles, the holly, the mistletoe, even the Christmas tree—
pagan traditions all, with no direct connection to the birth of Jesus.[3]

But the Puritans had another reason for suppressing Christmas. The
holiday they suppressed was not what *we* probably mean when we think
of a traditional Christmas. As we shall see, it involved behavior that most
of us would find offensive and even shocking today—rowdy public displays of excessive eating and drinking, the mockery of established authority, aggressive begging (often involving the threat of doing harm), and
even the invasion of wealthy homes.

It may seem odd that Christmas was ever celebrated in such a fashion. But there was a good reason. In northern agricultural societies, December was the major "punctuation mark" in the rhythmic cycle of work,
a time when there was a minimum of work to be performed. The deep
freeze of midwinter had not yet set in; the work of gathering the harvest
and preparing it for winter was done; and there was plenty of newly fer-
mented beer or wine as well as meat from freshly slaughtered animals—
meat that had to be consumed before it spoiled. St. Nicholas, for example,
is associated with the Christmas season chiefly because his "name-day,"
December 6, coincided in many European countries with the end of the
harvest and slaughter season.[4]

In our own day the Christmas season begins as early as the day after
Thanksgiving for many people, and continues to January 1. But our culture is by no means the first in which "Christmas" has meant an entire *season* rather than a single day. In early modern Europe, the Christmas
season might begin as early as late November and continue well past New
Year's Day. (We still sing about "the twelve days of Christmas," and the
British still celebrate "Twelfth Night.") In England the season might
open as early as mid-December and last until the first Monday after January 6 (dubbed "Plow Monday," the return to work), or later.[5] But it isn't
very useful, finally, to try to pin down the exact boundaries of a "real"
Christmas in times past, or the precise rituals of some "traditional" holiday season. Those boundaries and rituals changed over time and varied
from one place to another. What is more useful, in any setting, is to look
for the dynamics of an ongoing contest, a push and a pull—sometimes a
real battle—between those who wished to expand the season and those
who wished to contract and restrict it. (Nowadays the contest may pit
merchants—with children as their allies—against those grown-ups who
resent seeing Christmas displays that seem to go up earlier and earlier
with each passing year.)

In early modern Europe, roughly the years between 1500 and 1800,

the Christmas season was a time to let off steam—and to gorge. It is difficult today to understand what this seasonal feasting was like. For most
of the readers of this book, good food is available in sufficient quantity
year-round. But early modern Europe was above all a world of scarcity.
Few people ate much good food at all, and for everyone the availability of
fresh food was seasonally determined. Late summer and early fall would
have been the time of fresh vegetables, but December was the season—
the only season—for fresh meat. Animals could not be slaughtered until
the weather was cold enough to ensure that the meat would not go bad;
and any meat saved for the rest of the year would have to be preserved
(and rendered less palatable) by salting. December was also the month
when the year's supply of beer or wine was ready to drink. And for farmers, too, this period marked the start of a season of leisure. Little wonder,
then, that this was a time of celebratory excess.

Excess took many forms. Reveling could easily become rowdiness;
lubricated by alcohol, making merry could edge into making trouble.
Christmas was a season of "misrule," a time when ordinary behavioral restraints could be violated with impunity. It was part of what one historian
has called "the world of carnival." (The term *carnival* is rooted in the
Latin words *carne* and *vale*—"farewell to flesh." And "flesh" refers here not
only to meat but also to sex—*carnal* as well as *carnivorous.*) Christmas
"misrule" meant that not only hunger but also anger and lust could be expressed in public. (It was no accident, wrote Increase Mather, that "December was called *Mensis Genialis,* the Voluptuous Month."[6]) Often
people blackened their faces or disguised themselves as animals or cross-
dressed, thus operating under a protective cloak of anonymity. The late-
nineteenth-century historian John Ashton reports one episode from
Lincolnshire in 1637, in which the man selected by a crowd of revelers as
"Lord of Misrule" was publicly given a "wife," in a ceremony led by a man
dressed as a minister (he read the entire marriage service from the Book
of Common Prayer). Thereupon, as Ashton noted in Victorian language,
"the affair was carried to its utmost extent."[7]

Episodes like these offered another reason, and a deeper one, for the
Puritans' objection to Christmas. Here is how the Reverend Increase
Mather of Boston put it in 1687:

> The generality of Christmas-keepers observe that festival after such
> a manner as is highly dishonourable to the name of Christ. How few
> are there comparatively that spend those holidays (as they are called)
> after an holy manner. But they are consumed in Compotations, in

Interludes, in playing at Cards, in Revellings, in excess of Wine, in mad Mirth. . . .

And Increase Mather's son Cotton put it this way in 1712: "[T]he Feast of Christ's Nativity is spent in Reveling, Dicing, Carding, Masking, and in all Licentious Liberty . . . by Mad Mirth, by long Eating, by hard Drinking, by lewd Gaming, by rude Reveling . . ."[8]

Even an Anglican minister, a man who *approved* of "keeping" Christmas (as it was then put), acknowledged the truth of the Puritans' charges. Writing in 1725, the Reverend Henry Bourne of Newcastle, England, called the way most people commonly behaved during the Christmas season "a Scandal to Religion, and an encouraging of Wickedness." Bourne admitted that for Englishmen of the lower orders the Christmas season was merely "a pretense for Drunkenness, and Rioting, and Wantonness." And he believed the season went on far too long. Most Englishmen, Bourne claimed, chose to celebrate it well past the official period of twelve days, right up to Candlemas Day on February 2. For that entire forty-day period, it was common "for Men to rise early in the Morning, that they may follow strong Drink, and continue untill Night, till Wine inflame them."

Bourne singled out two particularly dangerous seasonal practices, mumming and (strange to modern readers) the singing of Christmas carols. Mumming usually involved "a changing of Clothes between Men and Women; who when dressed in each other's habits, go from one Neighbor's house to another . . . and make merry with them in disguise." Bourne proposed that "this Custom, which is still so Common among us at this Season of the Year, [be] laid aside; as it is the Occasion of much Uncleanness and Debauchery." As for singing Christmas carols, that practice was a "disgrace," since it was "generally done, in the midst of Rioting and Chambering, and Wantonness."[9] ("Chambering" was a common euphemism for fornication.) It was another Anglican cleric, the sixteenth-century bishop Hugh Latimer, who put the matter most succinctly: "Men dishonour Christ more in the twelve days of Christmas, than in all the twelve months besides."

The Puritans knew what subsequent generations would forget: that when the Church, more than a millennium earlier, had placed Christmas Day in late December, the decision was part of what amounted to a compromise, and a compromise for which the Church paid a high price. Late-December festivities were deeply rooted in popular culture, both in observance of the winter solstice and in celebration of the one brief period of leisure and plenty in the agricultural year. In return for ensuring massive observance of the anniversary of the Savior's birth by assigning it to this resonant date, the Church for its part tacitly agreed to allow the holiday to be celebrated more or less the way it had always been. From the beginning, the Church's hold over Christmas was (and remains still) rather tenuous. There were always people for whom Christmas was a time of pious devotion rather than carnival, but such people were always in the minority. It may not be going too far to say that Christmas has always been an extremely difficult holiday to *Christianize*. Little wonder that the Puritans were willing to save themselves the trouble.

THE PURITANS understood another thing, too: Much of the seasonal excess that took place at Christmas was not merely chaotic "disorder" but behavior that took a profoundly ritualized form. Most fundamentally, Christmas was an occasion when the social hierarchy itself was symbolically turned upside down, in a gesture that inverted designated roles of gender, age, and class. During the Christmas season those near the bottom of the social order acted high and mighty. Men might dress like women, and women might dress (and act) like men. Young people might imitate and mock their elders (for example, a boy might be chosen "bishop" and take on for a brief time some of the authority of a real bishop). A peasant or an apprentice might become "Lord of Misrule" and mimic the authority of a real "gentleman."[10] Increase Mather explained with an anthropologist's clarity what he believed to be the origins of the practice: "In the Saturnalian Days, Masters did wait upon their Servants. . . . The Gentiles called Saturns time the Golden Age, because in it there was no servitude, in Commemoration whereof on his Festival, Servants must be Masters." This practice, like so many others, was simply picked up and transposed to Christmas, where those who were low in station became "*Masters of Misrule*."[11] To this day, in the British army, on December 25 officers are obliged to wait upon enlisted men at meals.*

The most common ritual of social inversion during the Christmas season involved something that is associated with Christmas in our own day—we would call it charity. Prosperous and powerful people were ex-

---

* If there was any point at which the two modes of celebrating Christmas—as carnival and as pious devotion—managed to intersect, if only in theory, it was here. The Gifts of the Magi, too, represented the high-in-status waiting on the low—three kings paying homage to an infant lying in squalor. (But of course that ritual simultaneously represented the low bringing gifts to the high—mere mortals paying homage to a deity.)

pected to offer the fruits of their harvest bounty to their poorer neighbors and dependents. A Frenchman traveling in late-seventeenth-century England noted that "they are not so much presents from friend to friend, or from equal to equal . . . , as from superior to inferior."[12] That may sound familiar enough. But the modern notion of charity does not really convey a picture of how this transaction worked. For it was usually the poor themselves who initiated the exchange, and it was enacted face-to-face, in rituals that would strike many of us today as an intolerable invasion of privacy.

At other times of the year it was the poor who owed goods, labor, and deference to the rich. But on this occasion the tables were turned—literally. The poor—most often bands of boys and young men—claimed the right to march to the houses of the well-to-do, enter their halls, and receive gifts of food, drink, and sometimes money as well. And the rich had to let them in—essentially, to hold "open house." Christmas was a time when peasants, servants, and apprentices exercised the right to demand that their wealthier neighbors and patrons treat them as if *they* were wealthy and powerful. The Lord of the Manor let the peasants in and feasted them. In return, the peasants offered something of true value in a paternalistic society—their *goodwill.* Just when and how this actually happened each year—whether it was a gracious offering or the forced concession to a hostile confrontation—probably depended on the particular individuals involved as well as the local customs that had been established in years past (and which were constantly being "re-negotiated" through just such ritualized practices as these).

This exchange of gifts for goodwill often included the performance of songs, often drinking songs, that articulated the structure of the exchange. These songs (and the ritual as a whole) bore a variety of names. One name that is still known in our culture is that of *wassailing,* and I shall take the liberty of using this word to refer to a whole set of similar rituals that may have had other names. Wassailers—roving bands of youthful males—toasted the patron's well-being while drinking the beer he had been kind enough to supply them. Robert Herrick included this wassail in his 1648 poem "Ceremonies for Christmasse":

> Come bring, with a noise,
> My merrie, merrie boys,
> The Christmas log to the firing;
> While my good dame she
> Bids ye all be free [i.e., with the alcohol]
> And drink to your heart's desiring. . . .[13]

The wassail usually possessed an aggressive edge—often an explicit threat—concerning the unpleasant consequences to follow if the beggars' demands were not met. One surviving wassail song contains this blunt demand and threat:

> We've come here to claim our right. . . .
> And if you don't open up your door,
> We will lay you flat upon the floor.

But there was also the promise of goodwill if the wassailers were treated well—toasts to the patron's health and prosperity. (It is the promise of goodwill, alone from this ritualized exchange, that has been retained in the modern revival of old Christmas songs.) The following wassail was sung on the Isle of Man by bands of young men who marched from house to house begging for food:

> Again we assemble, a merry New Year
> To wish to each one of the family here. . . .
> May they of potatoes and herrings have plenty,
> With butter and cheese, and each other dainty. . . .

One song that has recently been revived, the "Gloucestershire Wassail," shows the drinkers going from one well-to-do house to another ("Wassail! Wassail! all over the town"). At each stop they wish their patron a successful harvest, the fruits of which are to be shared with them ("God send our master a cup of good beer. . . . God send our mistress a good Christmas pie . . ."). Each verse amounts to a toast that ends in a fresh round of drinks ("With my wassailing bowl I drink to thee")—to the master and mistress, to their horse, to their cow, to anything at all that can be toasted.[14]

It was not enough for the landlord to let the peasants in and feed them. On this one occasion he had to share with them his choicest food and drink, his private stock. Robert Herrick included a couplet to this effect in the poem quoted above: "Drink now the strong beere, / Cut the white loaf here." (The emphasis is on the "*strong* beere," the "*white* loaf.") When the wassailers on the Isle of Man had sung their verses, they were, in the words of the folklorist who recorded their ritual, "invited into the house to partake of *the best the family can afford*." The final verse of the "Gloucestershire Wassail" opens with just such a demand for choice beer ("Come, butler, draw us a bowl of the best / Then we hope your soul in heaven shall rest"), but the threat follows quickly: "But if you draw us a bowl of the small [i.e., weak beer], / Then down will come butler, bowl, and all."[15]

In an agricultural economy, the kind of "misrule" I have been describing did not really challenge the authority of the gentry. The historian E. P. Thompson has noted that landed gentlemen could always try to use a generous handout at Christmas as a way of making up for a year's accumulation of small injustices, regaining in the process their tenants' goodwill. In fact, episodes of misrule were widely tolerated by the elite. Some historians argue that role inversions actually functioned as a kind of safety valve that contained class resentments within clearly defined limits, and that by inverting the established hierarchy (rather than simply ignoring it), those role inversions actually served as a reaffirmation of the existing social order.[16] It was all a little like Halloween today—when, for a single evening, children assume the right to enter the houses of neighbors and even strangers, to *demand* of their elders a gift (or "treat") and to threaten them, should they fail to provide one, with a punishment (or "trick").

This kind of trick-or-treat ritual is largely nonexistent today at Christmas, but vestiges of it do remain. Take, for instance, a December 1991 article in *Money* magazine, which warns its readers to "Tip Defensively" at Christmas: " 'At holiday time you must show people who work for you that you appreciate good service,'. . . . Translation: if you don't, you'll suffer the consequences all next year (Day-Glo hair tinting or sprinkler-soaked newspapers). . . . Keep in mind a kind of reverse Marxism: to each according to *your* need. That is, tip most generously those who can do you the most damage."[17]

PROSECUTING THE CHRISTMAS-KEEPERS, 1620–1750

In early modern Europe, all this postharvest behavior operated within (though at the boundaries of) the normal social order. It was part of a cultural world that went back thousands of years and involved the yearly agricultural cycle, which defined and integrated work and play, with times of intense labor followed by periods of equally intense celebration. This seasonal cycle, perhaps more than anything else, was what determined the texture of people's lives. It was even appropriated by the Church (as the Christmas season itself had been) and given a religious gloss, whereby times of celebration were associated with any number of official saints' days that were generally observed with more revelry than piety.

Here was exactly what the Puritans tried to suppress when they came to power in England, and New England, in the middle of the seventeenth century. It was this entire cultural world, with its periodic seasons of labor and festivity—and not just Christmas itself—that Puritans felt to be corrupt, "pagan," evil. It was this world that they systematically attempted to abolish and "purify." They wished to replace it with a simpler, more orderly culture in which people were more disciplined and self-regulated, in which ornate churches and cathedrals were replaced by plain "meeting-houses," in which lavish periodic celebrations—the seasonal cycle itself—were replaced by an orderly and regular succession of days, punctuated only by a weekly day of rest and self-examination, the Sabbath.

Christmas was an important (and symbolically charged) expression of this cultural world, and the Puritans attacked it with particular intensity. In England, the Puritan Parliament made a point of holding regular

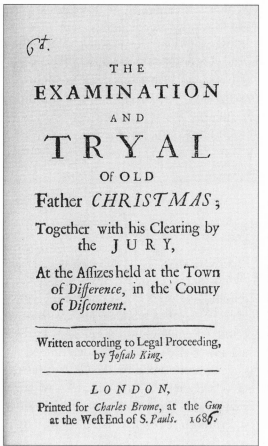

THE
EXAMINATION
AND
TRYAL
OF OLD
Father *CHRISTMAS* ;
Together with his Clearing by
the J U R Y,
At the Affizes held at the Town
of *Difference*, in the County
of *Difcontent*.

Written according to Legal Proceeding,
by *Jofiah King*.

LONDON,
Printed for *Charles Brome*, at the *Gun*
at the Weft End of S. *Pauls.* 1686.

"The Tryal of Father Christmas." The title page of a 1686 British book mocking the Puritans who had suppressed Christmas—and who had been out of power in England for some twenty-five years when this book was published. The Puritan jurors in this trial bore such names as "Mr. Cold-kitchen," "Mr. Give-little," and "Mr. Hate-good." *(Courtesy, Mark Bond-Webster)* sessions each December 25 from 1644 through 1656, and it did what it could to suppress the traditional observance of the date. (In 1644 Parliament actually decreed that December 25 was to be observed as a day of fasting and repentance—for the sinful way the occasion had been made into a time of "giving liberty to carnall and sensual delights.")[18] One unhappy Englishman referred to those delights as nothing more than "liberty and harmless sports . . . [by] which the toiling plowswain and labourer were wont to be recreated, and their spirits and hopes revived for a whole twelve month." But the Puritans had made these innocent customs "extinct and put out of use . . . as if they never had been. . . . Thus are the merry lords of misrule suppressed by the mad lords of bad rule at Westminster [i.e., Parliament]."[19]

In England the success of the Puritans was limited and temporary. Legislation banning the celebration of Christmas was contested in many places even during the 1640s and 1650s, when Puritans controlled the government (there were riots in several towns), and the policy was quickly reversed in 1660 upon the restoration of the English monarchy.[20]

But in New England the Puritans did largely succeed in eliminating Christmas, along with many of the other practices of English popular culture. David D. Hall has succinctly described the "transformed culture" of what he aptly terms a "new Protestant vernacular":

> Psalm-singing replaced ballads. Ritual was reorganized around the
> celebration of the Sabbath and of fast days. No town in New England
> had a Maypole; no group celebrated Christmas or St. Valentine's Day,
> or staged a pre-Lenten carnival![21]

TAKE THE EXAMPLE of almanacs. Almanacs had become popular in England by the seventeenth century, and they remained popular in New England as well. English almanacs generally listed Christmas, along with the bevy of saints' days that showed the commitment of the Church of England to the old, seasonally based calendar. (These saints' days were known as "red-letter days," because in English almanacs and church calendars they were printed in red ink.) But in seventeenth-century New England, almanacs were "purified" of all these old associations. (Indeed, for a time even the common names for the days of the week were purged from the almanacs on account of their pagan origins—after all, *Thursday* meant "Thor's day," and *Saturday* was "Saturn's day.") The Puritans knew that the power to *name* time was also the power to *control* it.

So it should come as no surprise that seventeenth-century Massachusetts almanacs did not refer to December 25 as Christmas Day. Instead, the date December 25 would be left without comment, or it would contain a notice that one of the county courts was due to sit that day—an implicit reminder that in New England, December 25 was just another workday.

THE SUCCESS of the New England Puritans was impressive and long-lasting. Christmas was kept on the margins of early New England society. Still, it was never suppressed completely. Take, for example, two instances that are sometimes cited to show that the Puritan authorities succeeded in abolishing Christmas. We have already encountered the first of these in the entry for Christmas Day, 1621, in the journal of Governor William Bradford of Plymouth Colony. Bradford encountered a group of people who were taking the day off from work, and he promptly sent them back to work. Here, in the first full year of the Pilgrims' life in the New World, were a group of Christmas-keepers. Nor did this group observe Christmas in a devout fashion or even by simply staying in their houses—Bradford indicated that he would have allowed them that. What bothered the governor was that these Christmas-keepers were, in his own words, out "gaming [and] reveling in the streets."[22]

The second instance is the 1659 law passed by the Massachusetts Bay Colony, the law that levied a five-shilling fine on anyone who was "found observing any such day as Christmas or the like, either by forbearing of labor, feasting, or any other way."

Such laws are not made, of course, unless there are people who are engaging in the forbidden activity. And the Massachusetts Bay law of 1659, like Governor Bradford's earlier report, suggests that there were indeed people in Massachusetts who were observing Christmas in the late 1650s. The law was clear on this point: It was designed "for preventing disorders arising in several places within this jurisdiction, by reason of some still observing such Festivals as were superstitiously kept in other countries." The wording of the law also implied that the authorities were chiefly concerned (as Governor Bradford had been) not with private devotion but with what the law termed "disorders." That point was reinforced by a provision in the law that threatened to impose a second five-shilling fine for gambling "with cards or dice," a practice, the court noted, that was "frequent in many places . . . at such times [as Christmas]."

This is not to argue that Christmas was widely "kept" in seventeenth-century Massachusetts. (For example, I have found no records of prosecutions under the 1659 law, which remained in force until 1681, when it was repealed under pressure from London.) What it does argue is that a festival with such old and deep roots in English culture could not simply be erased by fiat, and that it always hovered just beneath the surface of New England culture, emerging occasionally into plain sight.[23] When that happened, it was in ways that confirmed the Puritan nightmares of excess, disorder, and misrule.

Who were the people who practiced Christmas misrule in seventeenth-century New England? Not surprisingly, the evidence suggests that they were mostly on the margins of official New England culture (or altogether outside it). It is difficult to know for sure. There is no Christmas episode so notorious as the 1627–28 confrontation in which the Pilgrims of Plymouth Colony forcibly destroyed the maypole that had been defiantly set up on nearby Mount Wollaston by Thomas Morton and his merry men. (May Day, like Christmas, marked a seasonal celebration that resonated deeply in English popular culture.) But that is only because Thomas Morton was practically the sole New England representative of popular culture who was literate, and even literary; he actually published a satirical account of the maypole episode. The rest of New England's early Christmas-keepers were at most barely literate, and they left no records.

It was fishermen and mariners who had the reputation of being the most incorrigible sinners in New England, the region's least "reformed" inhabitants. Maritime communities such as Nantucket, the Isles of Shoals, and (especially) the town of Marblehead, were notorious for irreligion, heavy drinking, and loose sexual activity; they were also repositories of enduring English folk practices—places that ignored or resisted orthodox New England culture. It is no coincidence that Marblehead was also a site of ongoing Christmas-keeping.[24]

In 1662, for example, a fisherman named William Hoar, a 33-year-old resident of Beverly, Massachusetts, "was presented for suffering tippling [i.e., drinking] in his house by those who came to keep Christmas there."[25] That is all we know about this event, but the Hoar family itself is another story. Hoar's wife and children became notorious for their brazen defiance of Puritan authority. They carried on a long-term vendetta against the local minister, the Reverend John Hale, even to the point of regularly invading his house while he was away, in order to consume his food and loot his goods. Hoar's wife, Dorcas, was a fortune-teller (she specialized in palmistry), and she cultivated the rumor that she was also a practicing witch. Indeed, Dorcas Hoar's reputation finally brought her down. In the dark year of 1692, she was convicted of witchcraft and sentenced to hang on Gallows Hill, a victim of the Salem witchcraft outbreak.[26]

The Miser and the Sots: A Salem Village Wassail

The single incident of Christmas-keeping in seventeenth-century Massachusetts that can be described in any detail took place in 1679, and it is wonderfully revealing of the persistence of English seasonal folkways on the margins of Puritan New England.

At about 9 p.m. on Christmas night, 1679, four young men from Salem Village invaded the house of 72-year-old John Rowden, who lived with his wife, Mary, and their apprentice—and adopted son—Daniel Poole. (John Rowden was a farmer who owned an orchard that apparently included pear trees, from the fruit of which he and his wife had prepared a stock of pear wine, commonly known as perry.) In the testimony he gave three months later, old John Rowden provided a detailed account of what happened that night. First, the four men entered his house and sat down by the fire, and two of them "began to sing." When they had completed two songs, one of the men asked John Rowden, " 'How do you like this, father? Is this not worth a cup of perry?' " Rowden answered them, " 'I do not like it so well, pray be gone.' " But the men would not leave, telling Rowden "it was Christmas Day at night and they came to be merry and to drink perry, which was not to be had anywhere else but here, and perry they would have before they went."

Rowden again refused to offer them perry, and "told them they should have none there." The four visitors still would not take no for an answer. This time they tried to cajole Rowden into offering them the perry by promising payment at a later time: " 'Call for your pot [of perry] and mine and I will pay you again,' " said one. This time it was Rowden's wife who replied, saying, " 'We keep no ordinary [i.e., tavern] to call for pots.' " (A *pot* commonly referred to alcohol, as in the still-current usage *potted*.)

So the four men left. Or so it seemed—for fifteen minutes later three of them returned, saying they had managed to borrow some money and could pay for the perry on the spot. Apparently the Rowdens would actually have sold them the drink at this point, but the couple demanded to see the money in advance. One of the men shoved a "coin" in Goodwife Rowden's face; it proved to be "nothing but a piece of lead."

At this point the Rowdens, assisted by their young apprentice, managed to cajole (or push) the visitors out the door and into the December night. But once again the respite was brief. The visitors stopped about forty feet from the house and began to harass the Rowdens. They bellowed out sarcastic cries of "hello." One of them, Samuel Braybrooke by name, began to taunt the Rowdens' apprentice, demanding that he give them directions to the town of Marblehead (where alcohol could surely be had, especially on Christmas night). The apprentice, Daniel Poole, replied that " 'he had better be at home with his wife.' " Braybrooke continued to taunt young Poole, asking him "if he wanted to fight, if so to come out." Braybrooke's companion Joseph Flint renewed the dare, this time suggesting that they make a bet out of it: "Flint said if he [Poole] wanted to box, he would box with him for a pot of perry." Finally, when it became clear that despite all this bravado the apprentice could not be pressured into leaving his doorway, the dares and taunts turned into actual violence—violence that was directed not directly at Poole or the Rowdens but at their house. Here is John Rowden's account of what happened:

> [T]hey threw stones, bones, and other things at Poole in the doorway and against the house. They beat down much of the daubing in several places and continued to throw stones for an hour and a half with little intermission. They also broke down about a pole and a half of fence, being stone wall, and a cellar, without [outside] the house, distant about four or five rods, was broken open through the door, and five or six pecks of apples were stolen.[27]

Quite a scene. But one that is wholly recognizable from the English and European sources; for this was a wassail gone bad. The four young men came to the old man's house and sang for their gift of perry. When refused, they pretended that they were willing to pay for the perry (even though making the exchange a financial transaction represented a violation of the wassail ritual, in which the drink would have been a gift offered in return for the songs). But the visitors could (or would) not pay; the "coin" they brought turned out to be a fake, and their offer of payment seems to have been intended merely as a sarcastic comment on the Rowdens' refusal to play their expected role in the gift exchange. Finally, the wassail turned into what the French call a "charivari" (loud noise, mocking taunts, and stone-throwing), which lasted for more than an hour. There was no gift and therefore no goodwill—no "treat," but only a "trick" in turn.

Typically, all four of the wassailers were young men (one was seventeen, another about twenty-one; only one of the four was married). Typically, too, all of them stood near the low end of the economic hierarchy, and none would ever achieve any great degree of prosperity.[28] Finally, thirteen years later, three of the four men were peripherally involved in the events surrounding the Salem witch trials of 1692. Two of them (Braybrooke and Flint) were among the signers of a 1695 petition urging the dismissal of the Reverend Samuel Parris, the Salem Village minister who played a central role as a supporter of the trials and an accuser of the witches. And a third, Benjamin Fuller, was one of thirty-six Salem Village residents who refused to pay their taxes in support of Samuel Parris's ministerial salary when Parris first arrived (amid controversy) in Salem Village in 1689.[29]

The "Salem wassail" (as I have come to call it) surely represented no threat to the social or cultural fabric of Massachusetts, just as more frequent but similar incidents in Europe of misrule and charivari were hardly revolutionary acts. This was a trivial event, and the only harm it did was to the family of one elderly man (possibly a stingy and ill-tempered individual). Still, the episode suggests something of the animosities engendered by the cultural fault lines that continued to divide "official" Massachusetts culture from the lingering traditions it tried so hard (and on the whole with such great success) to eradicate.

A Window on Popular Culture:
The Dominion of New England

Once, for a few strange years, the curtain of Puritan suppression was lifted, and not by choice. By 1680 it was becoming clear that the Restoration government in London would not continue to tolerate the Puritan political culture that had been established in New England. Knowing that its official charter of incorporation might be abrogated, in 1681 the Massachusetts General Court reluctantly revoked several of the colony's laws that were most obnoxious to the English authorities. (One of the laws thus revoked was the act banning the celebration of Christmas.) But this was not enough to save the charter. It was abrogated in 1684, and during the three years from 1687 through 1689, Massachusetts was governed directly from London, as part of a short-lived entity known as the "Dominion of New England."

What happened during these three years was deeply humiliating to the Puritans. The hated governor of the Dominion, Sir Edmund Andros, ruled most of New England (along with New York). From his headquarters in Boston, Governor Andros attempted to impose English law and custom in the very seat of Puritan power. On Christmas Day, 1686, for example, two religious services were performed at the Boston Townhouse, and Andros attended both of them, with "a Red-Coat [soldier] going on his right hand and Capt. George on the left."

But Governor Andros did not simply impose Anglican practices on a populace that was universally resistant to them. One effect of his rule was to permit the public expression of a set of seasonal practices that were associated with the popular culture of seventeenth-century England. Those expressions of the popular culture could not have surfaced openly without the legal protection offered by the Andros regime. Under its protective mantle, during this brief period, it was possible for the first time in Massachusetts to act out heterodox rituals in public. A few Bostonians celebrated Shrove Tuesday (Mardi Gras) by dancing in the streets, and a maypole was erected in Charlestown.

Christmas-keeping apparently began even in advance of the Andros regime. On December 25, 1685, the magistrate Samuel Sewall noted that "Some somehow observe the day," but he added, as if to reassure himself, that "the Body of the People profane it, and blessed be God no Authority yet to compel them to keep it." (Sewall also offered himself the reassurance that there was "less Christmas-keeping [this year] than last year, fewer Shops Shut up," but that reassurance implicitly ceded the point that in 1684 an even greater number of persons had "observed" Christmas.) A year later, on December 25, 1686, Sewall once again noted, "Shops open today generally and persons about their occasions." (Again, the key word here may have been "generally," because Sewall went on to acknowledge, "Some, but few, Carts [were] at Town with wood. . . ."[30])

Christmas-keeping even entered into print culture during the Andros regime. The most dramatic example was an almanac, written by a resident of Saybrook, Connecticut, named John Tully and published in Boston during each of the three years of Dominion government, 1687–89. We have already seen that the Puritans purged New England's almanacs of all reference to Christmas and the various saints' days of the English church calendar. But Tully boldly labeled December 25 in capital letters, as "CHRISTMAS-DAY," and he also added every one of the red-letter days recognized by the Church of England. December 21 thereby became "S. THOMAS," December 26 was "S. STEVEN," and December 27 was "INNOCENTS." (In all likelihood, Tully used capital letters simply because his Boston printer did not have any red ink.) The following year,

Tully's almanac was published with the official imprimatur of Andros's deputy, Edwin Randolph, on the title page.[31]

That same year, Tully made an even more dramatic gesture to signify his incorporation of English popular culture. At the end of his 1688 almanac Tully added a series of monthly "prognostications," all of them satirical and most of them bawdy or scatological. For example, he concluded his prognostication for the month of March by announcing that if it failed to come true, the reader should "light tobacco, or make bumfodder with our Observations" (in other words, use the pages of his almanac to wipe their asses). For February, Tully wrote:

> The Nights are still cold and long, which may cause great Conjunction betwixt the Male and Female Planets of our sublunary Orb, the effects whereof may be seen about nine months after, and portend great charges of Midwife, Nurse, and Naming the Bantling.

Tully's prognostication for December was a verse that opened by referring to the feasting that would take place during the Christmas season:

> This month the Cooks do very early rise,
> To roast their meat, & make their Christmas pies.

And it went on to associate this feasting with the social inversion of rich and poor.

> Poor men at rich men's tables their guts forrage
> With roast beef, mince-pies, pudding & plum porridge.

In prose, Tully added: "This month, Money & Rum will be in great request; and he that hath the first shall not need fear wanting the latter."[32]

THE OVERTHROW of the Dominion of New England in 1689 put a stop to this flurry of popular culture, and it ushered in two decades in which there is little in the public record about Christmas. That changed in 1711, when the Reverend Cotton Mather of Boston recorded some disturbing news in his diary for December 30: "I hear of a number of young people of both sexes, belonging, many of them, to my flock, who have had on the Christmas-night, this last week, a Frolick, a revelling feast, and Ball [i.e., dance]. . . ." The very next year Mather denounced the holiday in a sermon, published immediately after its delivery under the title *Grace Defended*. The biblical text on which he based his sermon, drawn from the

Christmas in a New England Almanac. The December page from John Tully's notorious 1688 Boston almanac. Along with weather predictions, Tully brazenly (and in capital letters) named Christmas and the Anglican saints' days. *(Courtesy, American Antiquarian Society)*

Epistle of Jude, showed what was on Mather's mind: The text he chose was an attack on certain early Christians who had deceitfully "crept into" the early Christian church, using religion as a cover for sexual license, "giving themselves over to fornication"—"ungodly men, turning the grace of our God into lasciviousness." (Mather substituted the word "wantonness.")[33]

Mather returned to the same topic in 1713, in a treatise titled *Advice from the Watch-Tower*. This new treatise cut a broader swath than *Grace Defended*. It dealt with a whole battery of practices that were threatening to subvert New England culture from within. The treatise ended by presenting "a Black List of some Evil Customes which begin to appear among us." Along with Christmas—and gambling with cards and dice—

Mather's "black list" included partying on Sunday evenings (and even during the intermission between the two Sabbath-day sermons); running horse races on such solemn occasions as funerals, training days, and public lectures; turning weddings into drunken "revels"; and holding cornhuskings that were little more than excuses for "riot."[34]

There was a pattern here: All these practices involved young people who were appropriating serious social occasions as opportunities for bouts of drinking and sex. (In his section on cornhuskings, Mather warned young people: "Let the Night of your Pleasure be turned into Fear.") It was in just such a context—positioned between the drinking of toasts and riots at cornhuskings—that Mather placed the subject of Christmas. "Christmas-Revels begin to be taken up," he reported, "among some vainer Young People here and there in some of our Towns."[35] It was bad enough, Mather argued, that Christmas was not divinely ordained, but what was "offensive" about it "most of all" was that it was being abused just as the weddings and the cornhuskings were abused—an occasion on which, as Mather put it, "Abominable Things" were done. Clearly, those abominations had mostly to do with sex.

Mather's charges are confirmed by demographic data. Social historians have discovered that the rate of premarital pregnancies in New England began to climb early in the eighteenth century, and that by mid-century it had skyrocketed. (In some New England towns almost half the first children were born less than seven months after their parents' marriage.) What makes the demographic data especially interesting is that this sexual activity had a seasonal pattern to it: There was a "bulge" in the number of births in the months of September and October—meaning that sexual activity peaked during the Christmas season.[36]

Misrule in New England Almanacs

Mather's charges are also buttressed by—once again—the evidence of almanacs. Almanac makers sometimes included monthly verses along with aphorisms (in prose or verse) that were interlineated at particular dates, along with the astronomical and astrological data, and the tides and weather observations. The December page sometimes included implicit references (occasionally explicit ones) to the Christmas season, and much of this material dealt with food and drink. In his notorious 1688 almanac John Tully wrote that in December "Money and Rum will be in great request." But even as early as 1682, a Boston almanac written by the thoroughly orthodox William Brattle contained a verse for the December page that referred to all the drinking that went on during that month ("sack" refers to sherry, and "tubs" to kegs):

> This month, 'twill rain such store of sack (each night)
> That any man that tubs doth empty quite,
> And leave abroad [i.e. outdoors], and then the next day view,
> He'll find them full of pure good sack: It's true.[37]

(In other words, if people drink up all their sherry each day and leave the cask outside overnight, the next morning it will be magically full.) Brattle's verse may have referred to a popular belief about magical rebirth and renewal at the time of both the solstice and Christmas, but what matters more is that he seems to have assumed that December was indeed a month of heavy drinking. The same double allusion to intoxication and solstice can be found in an almanac printed in Boston in 1714, placed by the dates December 28–31: "By strong Liquor and Play / They turn night into day." And here, from that same almanac, is the verse that heads the month of December:

> Strong-Beer Stout Syder and a good fire
> Are things this season doth require.
> Now some with feasts do crown the day,
> Whilst others loose their coyn in play. . . .[38]

In 1702 the Boston almanac-maker Samuel Clough reported (disapprovingly, to be sure) that December was a time when men of the lower orders—"Coasters and Boat-men"—gathered in taverns to gossip and drink:

> Some ask a Dram when first come in,
> Others with Flip or Bounce begin;
> Tho' some do only call for Beer,
> And that i' th' morn is but mean chear.

And in 1729 Nathaniel Whittemore warned simply: "Extravagancies bring Sickness."[39]

New England almanacs occasionally addressed the sexual barriers that were breached by the license (and the cold temperatures) of the Christmas season. Thus in 1749 Nathanael Ames wrote (at December 15–17):

> This cold uncomfortable Weather,
> makes Jack and Jill lie close together.

On a similar note, George Wheten's almanac for 1753 noted in a quadruple rhyme: "The weather that is cold[,] that makes the maid that is old for to scold for the want of a Bed-fellow bold."[40]

But most common of all were the references to interclass eating and drinking—the familiar social inversion in which the low changed places with the high. At one extreme was John Tully's 1688 verse that Christmas was a season when "poor men at rich men's tables their guts forrage." Another Boston almanac, this one by Nathaniel Whittemore for the year 1719, contains an interesting piece of advice interlineated at the dates December 18–21. It warns householders about a practice we can recognize as another familiar element of the wassail ritual (once again, "abroad" means outside): "Do not let your Children and Servants run too much abroad at Nights."[41]

A Warning for Late December. Christmas is not named in this December page from Nathaniel Whittemore's 1719 Boston almanac, but between the dates December 18 and 21 can be found, in italics, an admonition to householders: "Do not let your Children and Servants run too much abroad at Nights." *(Courtesy, American Antiquarian Society)*

Several decades later, Nathanael Ames's almanac for 1746 put at the dates December 20–23 a concise but rather cynical description of inter-class merriment (the words recall the 1679 Salem Village wassail, when old John Rowden was visited by four young men who came "to call for pots"):

> The Miser and the Sot
> together they have got,
> to drink a Pot.[42]

A "Yankee Doodle" Christmas

Finally, even closer to the center of New England popular culture, there is the eighteenth-century song that can almost be regarded as the first American national anthem. "Yankee Doodle" was not a single song but a variable cluster of verses, all composed in a meter that could be sung to a version of the still-familiar tune. What all the verses have in common is that they are about backcountry manners.[43] (Most of these verses are un-known today, but all are written in the same meter, the meter of the line *Yankee Doodle goes to town, riding on his pony*.) Several of the verses dealt with sexual antics:

> Two and two may go to Bed,
> Two and two together;
> And if there is not room enough,
> Lie one a top o'to'ther.[44]

A number of "Yankee Doodle" verses refer to such seasonal events as election day or cornhusking (a "frolic" at which "[t]hey'll be some as drunk as sots").[45] One of these seasonal verses is about Christmas. "Christmas is a coming Boys," the verse begins:

> Christmas is a coming Boys,
> We'll go to Mother Chase's,
> And there we'll get a sugar dram [i.e., rum]
> Sweetened with Melasses.

And the verse continues by shifting from alcohol to sex:

> Heigh Ho for our Cape Cod,
> Heigh ho Nantasket,
> Do not let the Boston wags
> Feel your Oyster Basket.[46]

Cotton Mather himself could not have stated the issue more tellingly.

CHRISTMAS ENTERS
THE CULTURAL MAINSTREAM, 1730–1800
A Temperate Christmas

Christmas was becoming respectable, too. Even orthodox Congregationalists were beginning to concede that the observance of Christmas would be rendered less obnoxious if the holiday were celebrated with piety and moderation, purged of its seasonal excesses. The first New England clergyman to make such a concession, at least implicitly, may have been Cotton Mather himself. In his 1712 anti-Christmas sermon Mather paid only token attention to the purely theological arguments against the holiday—that it was man-made and not divinely ordained.[47] "I do not now dispute," Mather said, "whether People do well to Observe such an *Uninstituted Festival* at all, or no." And he continued with a statement that shows how far he had moved from a position of strident Puritanism: "Good Men may love one another, and may treat one another with a most Candid Charity, while he *that Regardeth a Day, Regardeth it unto the Lord,* and he that *Regardeth not the Day,* also shows his *Regard unto the Lord,* in his *not Regarding* of it . . ."[48] In other words, live and let live: On the issue of observing Christmas, there was room for legitimate differences among people of goodwill.

What Mather went on to emphasize was the *manner* in which Christmas was commonly observed—as a time of drunken revels and lascivious behavior. (*That* was "a thing, that there can be *no doubt* about.") Cotton Mather's father, Increase, would have readily agreed with his son's angry warning about the bad things that went on at Christmas. But he would never have gone along with Cotton Mather's idea that it was possible for good Christians to differ in "candid charity" about observing the holiday at all. For Increase Mather, as for other seventeenth-century Puritans, the licentious fashion in which Christmas was commonly practiced was just an intrinsic expression of its non-Christian origin as a seasonal celebration; the holiday was "riotous" at its very core. For Cotton Mather, writing a generation later in the early eighteenth century, the essence of the holiday could be distinguished, at least in principle, from its historical origins and the ordinary manner of its celebration.

From a modern perspective, the difference between Mather *pere* and

Mather *fils* may seem trivial. The young people whom Cotton Mather addressed in 1712 may not have noticed the difference themselves. But it mattered nonetheless. Cotton Mather's concession, small as it was, left little room to contest the legitimacy of any movement that managed to purify Christmas of its seasonal excesses. And such a movement was not long in coming about.

Signs of change began to emerge in about 1730. Once again, some of the best evidence comes from almanacs. In 1733 James Franklin printed the following couplet on his almanac's December page: "Now drink good Liquor, but not so, / That thou canst neither stand nor go." Of course, the most famous of all eighteenth-century American almanac-makers was James Franklin's younger brother Benjamin. Raised in New England (and trained as a printer by James), Benjamin Franklin became the century's preeminent exponent of moderation, sobriety, and self-control. In 1734, in the second number of his almanac, *Poor Richard,* Franklin applied that philosophy to the Christmas season. The December verse, written in the voice of "Poor" Richard Saunders's wife, Bridget, chastised a husband who "for sake of Drink neglects his Trade, / And spends each Night in Taverns till 'tis late." But on the same page, in an interlineation placed at the dates December 23–29, Franklin made it clear enough (in a rhymed but characteristically Franklinesque piece of advice) that he was no hater of Christmas: "If you wou'd have Guests merry with your Cheer, / Be so yourself, or so at least appear." And similarly in 1739: "O blessed Season! lov'd by Saints and Sinners, / For long Devotions, or for longer Dinners."[49]

The emphasis on *temperate* mirth intensified at mid-century, when Nathanael Ames (New England's most popular almanac-maker) began to mix calls for charity and cheer with admonitions against excess. In 1752 Ames offered his first warning: "Bad times, Dull-Drink and clouded Minds make heavy, listless, idle bodies." And in the 1760s similar warnings came thick and fast. Ames's verse for December 1760 was a warning against getting drunk. His 1761 almanac included a similar piece of advice: "The temperate man enjoys the most delight, / For riot dulls and palls the appetite." And in 1763: "The temperate Man nor ever over feeds / His cramm'd Desires with more than Nature needs." In 1764 dietary strictures actually took over Ames's entire almanac, constituting the subject matter for the accompanying material in all twelve months of the year.[50]

What Benjamin Franklin and Nathanael Ames were calling for was a Christmas that combined mirth and moderation. Both of these men were shopkeepers—versatile, thrifty, and self-made.[51] What they were trying to do was actually similar to what the Puritans had done a century earlier: to restructure people's work habits by having them do away with periodic binges. But unlike the Puritans, their strategy did not entail the elimination of Christmas. Instead, they were spreading the idea—a new idea—that Christmas could be a time of cheer without also being a time of excess.

Christmas in the Household of Martha Ballard, 1785–1811

The single best personal account of what such a "moderate" Christmas season may have been like can be found in the diary of Martha Ballard, the Maine midwife whose social world has been painstakingly and brilliantly reconstructed by the historian Laurel Thatcher Ulrich. For twenty-six years, between the ages of 50 and 76, Martha Ballard recorded her daily activities as wife, mother, midwife, and resident of the Maine community of Hallowell. During the twenty-six years between 1785 and 1811, Ballard chose seven times in her diary to name December 25 as *Christmas.* In six other years, she had reason to omit such a reference: She was occupied in delivering someone's baby; December 25 was just another working day for her.

But Martha Ballard's diary also makes it clear that December 25 was just another working day in *any* case, even when she was not delivering babies—and even when she named the day as Christmas. In 1788, for example, Martha's husband, Ephraim, was away from home on business; Martha herself stayed home, finishing "a pair of Stockins" for one of her daughters. In 1807 ("it is Chrismas day"), she noted laconically, "I have done a fortnit's wash." And on December 25, 1811, the final Christmas of her life, the 76-year-old woman reported simply: "I have done hous wk & knit Some."[52]

The younger generation in Hallowell observed Christmas more actively than Martha Ballard herself did. In 1801 Martha reported nothing special for herself on December 25, but she wrote that her two unmarried children celebrated the day in the company of two members of the opposite sex: "Ephm & Patty kept Christmas at Son Lambards, his partnr [was] Polly Farewell [and] hers [was] Cyrus."[53] (Sure enough, a couple of years later Ephraim Ballard, Jr. and Polly Farwell got married.) Some years earlier, two of the Ballards' young live-in servants likewise took Christmas as an opportunity for courtship: On December 23, 1794, "Dolly & Sally went to a daunce [dance] at mr Capins, were atended by a mr Lambart and White." (The previous day they had prepared for this event by purchasing at the local shop "a pair Shoes & other things.") But

Martha Ballard quickly reasserted her control over this frolicsome pair: On Christmas Day itself, she reported, "Dolly & Sally have washt, Scourd my puter & washt the Kitchen."[54]

Christmas may have been a time of work for Martha Ballard, but what is equally striking is how often that work involved the preparation of special meals for the season. It is on this very point that her diary is most revealing. On December 24, 1788: "Dan'l Bolton & his wife Dined here. we made some mins Pies." Three years later, Ballard spent the entire week from December 21 to December 27 staying at the home of one Mrs. Lithgow, a young woman who was waiting to deliver her first baby (which would be born on Christmas Day itself). But on December 23, the pregnant woman and her midwife turned to other tasks: "I helped mrs Lithgow make Cake & Pies. . . ." On December 31, 1802, New Year's Eve, Martha was at home and "made pumpkin and apple pies." A year later she recorded that her son Jonathan (together with his wife, Sally, and their six children) dined at their parents' house on "puding and roast spare rib."[55]

On two occasions Martha Ballard actually went shopping for her New Year's dinner, and she recorded her purchases in such detail as to make it clear that she was planning to cook a special holiday meal. On December 31, 1791, she shopped in three places and came home with what are unmistakably the ingredients for special cakes and pies: almost ten pounds of sugar, one pound of raisins, a pound of ginger, "2 half muggs," and a pint and a half of rum. And in 1808 Ballard reported on December 28 that her husband went shopping for almost the same ingredients: "[M]r. Ballard went to the Settlement, brot home 1 gl'n Molases, ½ [gallon] N E rhum, ½ do Ginger, ¼ lb Allspice, a bottle of Slolens Elxr." Ballard spent the next two days cooking with what were almost certainly these very items: "I Bakt mins pies" on December 29; and on December 30: "I have Bakt Mins and Apple Pies. . . ." (On New Year's Day she reported, "Sons Jona, Ephm & wife Supt with us . . . *at home. Childn here. . . .*")[56] We can probably assume that the family consumed at least part of what Ballard—she was then in her mid-seventies—had spent the previous two days preparing for them.

During Martha Ballard's old age, such feasts may have been occasions of reconciliation within this family (as Laurel Ulrich has shown, the Ballards had gone through a period of intergenerational alienation and conflict). It appears that in the last five years of their mother's life, Martha's children began to bring her New Year's presents—presents that invariably took the form of special food for the dinners in which they themselves partook. It was in 1807 that this ritual seems to have taken place for the first time: "Son Ephm made us a present of 12½ lb Beef, Son Town [a present] of a fine Goos & 2 wings; they both sleep here [in other words, they stayed to eat]."[57] A year later the ritual was repeated, and this time Martha concluded her entry for the day with a clear expression of her own reaction: "Jan. 1, 1808: Son Lambard Conducted his wife and Henry to See me . . . they made me a present of a Loin of muttun, Some Sugar, Butter and Bread. Son Ephms wife Came here, Jona[than']s wife also. She brot me 2 Pumkin pies. O happy has this year began and So may it proceead. . . ."[58] On at least one occasion during this period, Martha appears to have reciprocated. On December 23, 1808, she "bak't apple & Squash pies & brown bread," and sent a couple of the pies to one of her daughters, along with "a Stake of fresh Pork."[59]

What Martha Ballard's entries make strikingly clear is that for the Ballard family the celebration of the Christmas season was deeply embedded in the normal rhythms of seasonal activity. In any traditional rural society, late December was ordinarily the time when animals were slaughtered, when there was food and drink aplenty and (for men, at least) the opportunity to relax after the labors of the harvest. Martha Ballard and her neighbors might very well have been baking "mins pies" at this time even if there were no special holidays to mark the occasion. A supply of mince pies, if properly stored, would last through much of the winter. Even the "presents" (of food) that her children brought her after 1806 were part of a normal, ongoing exchange of goods and services that characterized life in communities of this sort.

There was nothing about those presents that marked any real departure from the ordinary dynamics of life in Hallowell. Above all, the presents were not intrinsically commercial. The goose, beef, and mutton, the bread and butter, the pumpkin pies—these were nothing more than the things that Hallowell families raised or produced in the normal course of events. Only the special ingredients that went into making cakes and pies—the sugar, ginger, allspice, and rum—involved a commercial transaction. But this suggests only that Martha Ballard's Hallowell community had links to the broader Atlantic world and was not some isolated backwater whose economy operated at a level of subsistence production.

The Transformation of New England Almanacs and Hymnals

Martha Ballard's diary records a single present of a commercial nature. On December 29, 1796, she noted that "Daniel Livermore made a present of an Almanack to my Son Cyrus."[60] We cannot know what prompted Livermore to make such a gift, or just which almanac he chose (there were many), but of one thing we can be sure: The almanac would have noted that December 25 was Christmas.

There is a story here. As far back as the seventeenth century, and even among devout Puritans, there had never been complete unanimity about the need to deny that Christmas could be an occasion for legitimate religious observance. In England, in 1629, no less prominent a Puritan than John Milton wrote a Christmas poem, "On the Morning of Christ's Nativity." The poem began by announcing (almost defiantly, given the political context in which it appeared), "This is the month, and this the happy morn. . . ."[61] In Boston itself, on December 18, 1664, the young minister Increase Mather felt it necessary to deliver a sermon reinforcing the colony's official policy. The day after Mather delivered it, he was confronted by three of the wealthiest members of his own church, who demanded that he discuss the subject further with them. In his diary Mather recorded the argument with tantalizing brevity: "Discoursed much about Christmas, I Con, they Pro."[62]

Such evidence is scarce. But there is another kind of record that is much easier to come by and has broad implications—once again, the printed almanac. As we have seen, seventeenth-century almanacs were purged of all the traditional red-letter days that marked the seasonal calendar in English society (except, of course, for the countercultural almanacs that John Tully produced in the period of direct English rule from 1687 to 1689).

But there was a pair of exceptions to the ordinary rule. In the almanac for 1669, quietly placed at this date, in small italic letters, can be found the Latin phrase "*Christus Natus*" [i.e., Christ born]. And exactly ten years later, the 1679 almanac indicated, in English, "*Our Savior born.*"[63]

These two almanacs, like every book published in New England during the period, were printed on a press owned by Harvard College. The authorities must have noticed the insertions and allowed them to be made. A small notation in an almanac or diary may not seem very important today. But in the context of seventeenth-century New England, this gesture would have been charged with meaning. It was such small things that signaled to contemporaries the shifting lines between what was open for public debate and what was not.

Those lines shifted more clearly after 1700. During the 1710s, several almanacs named Christmas (one of them written by Edward Holyoke, a future president of Harvard). And in the 1720s James Franklin published several more.*[64] By 1730 the hegemony of the government of Massachu-setts in the matter of almanacs was fading. From that point on, the dom-inant role in determining whether the holiday was named was played not by official preferences but by the forces of the market, in concert with the personal predilections of individual almanac-makers. Before 1730 or so, it was not wholly safe to publish an almanac that named Christmas or the Anglican saints' days. After 1730, it *was* safe. Over the next thirty years, some writers chose to name Christmas in their almanacs, and others chose not to.

But after 1760 it was exceptional *not* to name Christmas. The last major holdout, Nathanael Ames, named Christmas in 1760, and when he did so he added an explicit religious verse ("This is a Time for Joy and Mirth / When we consider our Saviour's Birth"). Ames went further still that year: He incorporated all the saints' days in the Anglican Church cal-endar. It was a major change, and the newspaper advertisements for the 1760 Ames almanac made a point of noting that it contained, "besides what is usual, *The Feasts and Fasts of the Church of England.*"[65] The year 1760 was also when Ames began his systematic campaign—described ear-lier—to take the gorging and drunkenness out of the Christmas holiday. The timing of Ames' decision to name Christmas thus provides still an-other indication that the holiday became accepted into mainstream New England culture only as it was purged of seasonal excess.

The change is confirmed by the experience of Connecticut almanac-maker Roger Sherman. Sherman published a series of almanacs from 1750 to 1761. Every one of these almanacs listed Christmas and the saints' days. But in 1758 Sherman felt obliged to publicly defend his practice. He had learned, as he wrote in the preface to that year's almanac, "that some good

---

* James Franklin was often a thorn in the side of the Massachusetts authorities. In 1722 he featured a front-page poem in praise of Christmas in his newspaper, the *New England Courant* (the legislature's efforts to suppress the *Courant* a decade earlier are reported in Benjamin Franklin's autobiography). In his 1729 almanac, James Franklin included a belief originating deep in popular lore—that Christ-mas was a season when witches and evil spirits could do no harm, when bad spells would have no ef-fect: "This month [December] is a great Enemy to *evil Spirits,* and a great Dissolver of *Witchcraft,* without the help of *Pimpernal,* or *Quicksilver* and *Yellow Wax* [these were supposed to be counterspells that would protect against witchcraft]. . . . Some Astrologers indeed confine this Power over evil Spirits to *Christmas Eve* only; but I know the whole Month has as much Power as any Eve in it: Not but that there may be some wandering Spirits here and there, but I am certain they can do no Mis-chief, nor can they be seen without a Telescope." In fact, William Shakespeare reported a similar be-lief in *Hamlet* (Act I, Scene 1), where a minor character speaks the following lines upon hearing a cock crow: "Some say that ever 'gainst that Season comes / Wherein our Saviour's birth is celebrated, / This bird of dawning [i.e., the cock] singeth all night long; / And then, they say, no spirit dare stir abroad, / The nights are wholesome, then no planets strike, / No fairy takes, nor witch hath power to charm, / So hallow'd and so gracious is that time." (To this, Hamlet's friend Horatio responds non-committally, "So have I heard and do in part believe it.")

People in the Country, dislike my Almanack, because the observable Days of the Church of England are inserted in it." Sherman, a good Congregationalist, denied that he had Anglican leanings. He insisted that his almanac was not intended as an expression of personal belief; rather, "my Design in this Performance is to serve the Publick." Everybody was free to observe such days or not, and no harm would be done as long as the physical space in the almanac taken up by naming the red-letter days "does not crowd out any Thing that might be more serviceable."[66]

Sherman's words concealed his real point. After all, the "good People in the Country" who "disliked" the practice were themselves members of the "Publick." What Sherman was really alluding to was not religious freedom but market demand. His words suggest that the old Puritan preference for a "reformed" almanac remained just important enough to warrant a rhetorical response, just as his actual practice reveals that such an old-fashioned preference was no longer widespread enough to require anything *but* a rhetorical response. "Reformed" almanacs were still being published in 1758, but only four years later they would be gone, gone for good. By the 1760s the naming of Christmas and the saints' days seems to have offended such a small group that it would not pay to produce even a single almanac for them. The Puritan buying market seems simply to have evaporated.

WHAT WAS true of almanacs was equally true of another immensely popular form of culture in early New England, the hymnal. During the seventeenth and well into the eighteenth century, most New England congregations used the so-called Bay Psalm Book, a rhymed version of the Old Testament Psalms, with additional hymns taken from various biblical sources (this was the first book published in New England). None of these hymns dealt with the Christmas story.

But by the 1750s the Bay Psalm Book had largely been replaced in New England churches by a pair of new verse translations of the Psalms, both of which contained Christmas hymns. The first of these had been written late in the seventeenth century by the English poets Nicholas Brady and Nahum Tate. (Tate was then England's poet laureate; he is best known today as the librettist of Henry Purcell's opera *Dido and Aeneas*.)[67] Brady and Tate's *New Version* of the Psalms contained a hymn that told the story of the Nativity. (Written by Nahum Tate, this hymn is still popular today. It begins with the lines "While Shepards watch'd their Flocks by Night, / All seated on the Ground, / The Angel of the Lord came down / and Glory shone around.") The *New Version* was first printed in Boston in 1713. It was reprinted three times between 1720 and 1740, and some forty times more between 1754 and 1775.[68]

The other version of rhymed psalms and hymns that replaced the old Bay Psalm Book was written by the great English hymnist and religious poet Isaac Watts (1674–1748). Watts published not one but *two* Christmas hymns; both (like Tate's) were rhapsodic accounts of the Nativity. Each was called "The Nativity of Christ," and each placed the Nativity "today"—which would have made the hymns almost impossible to sing at any time other than the Christmas season.[69] Watts's religious verse became the steadiest of what David Hall has termed "steady sellers." One New Englander who grew up toward the end of the century later recalled that as a youth "I could recite Watts' version of the Psalms from beginning to end, together with many of his Hymns and Lyric Poems."[70]

After 1762 no Congregationalist hymnal published in New England failed to include a hymn for Christmas. What makes the change especially suggestive, of course, is the way it parallels the transformation of New England almanacs. In both cases, Christmas was hardly to be found before 1720; after 1760 it could not be avoided.

THESE HYMNALS were printed with texts only, and they could be sung to any tune that fit the meter. In fact, the earliest religious *music* to be printed in New England first appeared in 1698. Thereafter a familiar pattern emerged. In the first half of the eighteenth century, none of the religious "tune books" published in New England had texts that referred to the Nativity. But in 1760 (that year, again!) a tune book published in Boston included the music and words to a "Hymn on the Nativity," composed by Englishman William Knapp to the familiar text of Nahum Tate. Other Christmas music composed by Englishmen appeared throughout the decade. In all, during the 1760s nine different Christmas songs were published in New England.[71]

Beginning in 1770, a new set of Christmas songs began to appear—songs written by native New England composers. The most famous of these Yankee composers, William Billings of Boston, composed Christmas music for each of the tune books he published between 1770 and 1794; there were eight such Christmas pieces in all, several of them extended contrapuntal "anthems."[72] Three of these pieces (and part of a fourth) were settings for the hymns by Isaac Watts and Nahum Tate. The texts of the others were written by Billings himself.

William Billings, "An Hymn for Christmas" (1770). The first of Billings's eight Christmas pieces. The words, taken from Isaac Watts's hymn "While Shepherds Watched Their Flocks by Night," are indicated only by the opening phrase of each line—perhaps the singers were already acquainted with the text. The hymn's subtitle, "Charlston" (i.e., Charlestown), probably names the congregation for which Billings first wrote the piece. *(Courtesy, American Antiquarian Society)*

Billings was hardly alone. All told, during the last two decades of the eighteenth century, seven different New England composers published original Christmas music. And Christmas pieces by English composers continued to be routinely included in the anthologies of sacred music that appeared with accelerated frequency in the 1780s and '90s. One of the most important of the new tune books, Isaiah Thomas's 1786 *Worcester Collection of Sacred Harmony,* even contained the "Hallelujah Chorus" from Handel's *Messiah!* And another composer, Daniel Read, published an unattributed arrangement of a second chorus from *Messiah,* "Glory to God in the Highest," together with his own version of the several recitatives that precede this chorus (beginning with "There were angels abiding in the fields").[73] Between 1760 and 1799 at least thirty different Christmas songs were published in New England. It is safe to say that the decades after 1760 saw a veritable explosion of Christmas music in the region.

A Devotional Christmas

Beginning in about the middle of the eighteenth century, even some or-thodox Congregationalist ministers began to confess their desire to ob-serve Christmas, along with their regret that it carried too much unacceptable baggage, social as well as theological. (Their ambivalence is similar to the feelings about this holiday experienced by many contempo-rary American Jews.) One of these ministers, the Reverend Ezra Stiles, reflected on the quandary that would be faced over the coming years by an increasing number of Congregationalist clergymen (Ezra Stiles himself would later become president of Yale). On December 25, 1776, Stiles con-fided to his diary:

> This day the nativity of our blessed Savior is celebrated through three quarters of Christendom . . . ; but the true day is unknown. On any day I can readily join with my fellow Christians in giving thanks to God for his unspeakable gift, and rejoice with them in the birth of a Savior. Tho' [i.e., if] it had been the will of Christ that the anniver-sary of his birth should have been celebrated, he would at least let us have known the day. . . .[74]

In 1778 Stiles specified the nature of his own reservations: "*Without superstition* for the day I desire to unite with all Christians in celebrating the incarnation of the divine Emmanuel."[75] In fact, as president of Yale, Stiles permitted his students to attend Christmas service (as Edward Holyoke had done at Harvard a generation earlier).[76]

Ezra Stiles was a theological liberal. But there were several more conservative Congregational ministers who left records of their attraction to Christmas in their private diaries. The Reverend Ebenezer Parkman of Westborough, Massachusetts, was one of these. For twenty years Parkman had been going about his ordinary business each December 25; he had even been chiding his neighbors for attending Christmas services in a nearby Episcopal Church. But suddenly, in 1747, Parkman revealed that he himself was tempted to join them: "God grant that I and mine may be happy partakers this Day with all those who Sincerely celebrate the Na-tivity of Jesus Christ!" Eight years later, in 1755, Parkman expanded on his earlier entry: He wrote that he had once again "had some serious

Thoughts on the Day, as kept by many in Commemoration of our Lord's Nativity." And he expressed the "desire to be one with all of them that are one with Christ, *and who avoid the Superstitions and Excesses of this Day, and Serve the Lord in sincerity* [italics added]." The caveat was crucial: Like Ezra Stiles, Ebenezer Parkman wished to celebrate Christmas with those people who did so "in sincerity," not with those who did so with "Superstitions and Excesses."[77]

The Reverend David Hall was minister to the central Massachusetts community of Sutton for sixty years, from 1729 until his death in 1789. Born in 1704, Hall was a "New Light," an evangelical supporter of the Great Awakening during the 1740s. Hall began to keep a diary in 1740, but it was not until 1749 that he chose to refer to Christmas. When he did so, it was with enthusiasm: "[T]his day, as tis apprehended, the Saviour was born[,] w[hic]h was to be glad tidings of Great Joy to all people. . . . I'll join to sing a Saviours love for there's a Saviour Born." And he added, in a further indication of what it was that really worried all these New England ministers, "Would to God more notice was taken of the day *in a suitable manner* [italics added]."[78]

In a suitable manner . . . Without superstition . . . The excesses of this day . . . We should not assume that these were merely the prim phrasings of unworldly clergymen. Consider a little episode that took place on the night of December 22, 1794, in the rural western Massachusetts town of Deerfield (now the site of Historic Deerfield). It is the kind of incident that rarely leaves any mark in the written record. We know about this one only because it appeared in the account book of a disgruntled local shopkeeper, John Birge by name. What Birge reported was a charivari of sorts. "Just before two of the Clock in the morning," he wrote, "my house was assaulted by sum Nightwalkers—or rather blockheads." These wassailers demanded entry: They "assaulted the house very bould by knocking or pounding as if they meant to force the house." When Birge refused to let them in, the intruders shattered one of his windowpanes "all to slivers." They may even have broken in and carried something away—the shop sold foodstuffs and clothing—because Birge ended his account with the comment, "I cannot see why it was much better than Burglary."[79]

WHAT DOES it all add up to? The answer must be that when Christmas returned to New England in the second half of the eighteenth century, it was embraced by different groups with different cultural agendas. Then as now, there was no single "Christmas." For some it was probably little more than the name for a day in the year. For others it was a time of pious devotion, devotion that could range all the way from mirthful joy in the Savior's birth to angst over personal failings, and from stately prayers to ecstatic hymns. For others still it was a time of feasting—accompanied or not by a supply of alcohol. Finally, Christmas might mean misrule and carnival, in which alcohol could lead to sexual liberties, social inversion, or even violence.

But not one of these ways of celebrating Christmas bore much resemblance to the holiday that most of us know today. All of them were public rituals, not private celebrations; civic events, not domestic ones. In none of them would we have found the familiar intimate family gathering or the giving of Christmas presents to expectant children. Nowhere would we have found Christmas trees; no reindeer, no Santa Claus. Christmas in late-eighteenth-century New England—or anywhere else—was not centered around the family or on children or giving presents. It was neither a domestic holiday nor a commercial one.

FROM HOUSE OF ALE TO HOUSE OF GOD: CHRISTMAS IN BOSTON, 1750–1820

The House of Ale: A Masonic Holiday

Nowhere is the variety of forms in which New Englanders celebrated Christmas, and their occasional intersection or even conflict, better revealed than in the region's major urban center, the town of Boston. We have already encountered Christmas in eighteenth-century Boston, in the 1711 Christmas "frolic" that moved Cotton Mather to deliver his sermon "Grace Defended." Mid-century Bostonians witnessed a far more open display of Christmas revelry, performed by some of the town's most prosperous merchants and tradesmen. These were the members of the Boston lodge of Freemasons. The Masonic lodge had been organized in 1730, and it held a festive banquet each 27th of December, the name-day of St. John the Evangelist.

As it happens, the lodge's 1749 banquet was described by one of the participants in a long and comic poem published several weeks after the event. (The poem constitutes the sole extant record of any of these Masonic festivities.) It begins by promising to "regale" its readers "with a diverting christmas tale."

The "tale" went like this. First, the Freemasons assembled at a tavern, then they attended a church service, and finally they marched back to the tavern in a formal procession that gathered along its route an "apron'd throng" of curious workingmen. It was the eating and drinking that formed the center of the story, and it was this that bound the masons together in mutual brotherhood. As the poet put it (in what amounts to a stunning parody of both Masonic culture and Puritan social theory, with its insistence on the need for mutual love):

> 'Tis Love, pure Love cements the whole.
> Love—of the BOTTLE and the BOWL.

The interval of religious service ("Masons at church! . . . / Such folk as never did appear / So overfond of coming there") is treated simply as an ironic interlude, showing "how they came

> To house of God from house of ale
> And how the parson told his tale:
> How they return'd, in manner odd,
> To house of ale from house of God.

Even the clergyman who preached on this occasion ("told his tale") acknowledged that it was the feast, and not the sermon, that made up "the weightier business of the day." His "sermon" is reported in aphoristic verse modeled on that of the English poet Alexander Pope:

> For eating *solid sense* affords,
> Whilst nonsense lurks in many words.
> Doubting does oft arise from thinking,
> But truth is only found in drinking.
>
> This having said, the reverend vicar
> Dismiss'd them to their food and liquor.[80]

These verses are funny today (and would have been shocking in 1749) for their deliberate juxtaposition of the sacred and the profane. And the event they described must have made for quite a scene in mid-eighteenth-century Boston. But in the context of older Christmas traditions one point stands out: The Freemasons' banquet was limited to the lodge members themselves, all of whom were prosperous men. The "apron'd throng" that collected on the streets to watch the procession was not invited to participate in the feast itself. Even so, it may have been part of the ritual. The British historian E. P. Thompson has argued that in England, too, the eighteenth-century elite no longer performed the requisite paternalist rituals of the season, but Thompson adds suggestively that the English elite still continued to "perform" in front of the poor, in a kind of disdain-ful "theater of the streets."[81] That may have been what the Boston Freemasons were doing when they chose to march to their feast in a for-mal procession. The poet even suggests that the "apron'd throng" put on something of a performance of its own in response to the march—"shoul-dering close," they managed to "close, press, stink, and shove" around the marchers." In an aside, the poet reveals that the Grand Master of the lodge, a wealthy Boston merchant, decided not to attend the banquet—ostensibly because he had caught a cold, but in fact because he had fore-seen "that the jobb / Would from all parts collect the mob."[82] An interesting reason: Could it be that the Grand Master was not wholly comfortable with the implications of this performance?

Carriers' Addresses: Wassailing in the Streets

It is difficult to know how the poorest residents of eighteenth-century Boston observed the Christmas season. But the limited evidence that does exist suggests a reemergence of Christmas misrule, reminiscent of what was happening in European cities. In its more innocent form this involved a ritual that is still with us today: giving Christmas tips to the paper car-rier. Newspapers were delivered door to door in eighteenth-century Boston. During the Christmas season these newspaper carriers expected a tip. Unlike their modern successors, the colonial carriers were not mem-bers of prosperous families who took on a paper route to earn a little extra spending money; they were the sons (very likely the teenage sons) of the poor.

By the 1760s these Boston carriers were going on their begging rounds armed with little printed verses that they presented in turn to each of their patrons. Such "carriers' addresses" were usually written and printed by the editor of the newspaper and distributed on or about New Year's Day. (The custom originated in Philadelphia during the 1730s and had been picked up in Boston by 1760.) But there were at least four Boston carriers' verses (printed between 1764 and 1784) that referred to Christmas as well as New Year's. The 1764 verses in the *Boston Evening Post*, for example, was headed "The News-Boy's Christmas and New Year's Verses." It begins:

> The Boy who Weekly Pads the Streets,
> With all the freshest News he meets,
> His Mistresses and Masters greets.

Christmas Begging Broadside. This Boston "Carrier's Address" was delivered during the 1770 Christmas season. The final verse asks patrons to bestow a "few shillings on your lad." Similar broadside pleas were used by other "plebeian" residents of Boston. One, dating from the mid-1760s, was from a blacksmith's apprentice: "This is unto all Gentlemen who shoes [sic] here, / I wish you a merry Christmas, a happy New Year: / For shoeing your Horses, and trimming their Locks, / Please to remember my New-Years Box." *(Courtesy, American Antiquarian Society)*

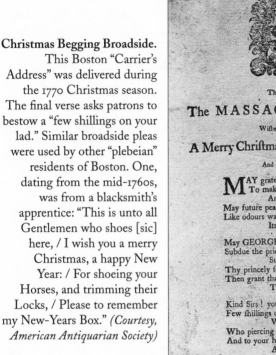

The LAD who carries

The MASSACHUSETTS SPY,

Wifhes all his kind Cuftomers

A Merry Chriftmas, and a Happy New Year!

And prefents the following:

MAY grateful omens now appear,
　　To make the New a happy Year,
　　　　And blefs th' enfuing days:
May future peace in every mind,
Like odours wafted by the wind,
　　　　Its fweeteft incenfe raife.

May GEORGE in his extenfive reign,
Subdue the pride of haughty SPAIN
　　　　Submiffive to his feet.
Thy princely fmiles our ills appeafe;
Then grant that harmony and peace
　　　　The dawning year may greet.

Kind Sirs! your gen'rous bounty fhow,
Few fhillings on your Lad beftow,
　　　　Which will reward his pains,
Who piercing Winter's cold endures,
And to your hands the SPY fecures,
　　　　And ftill his tafk maintains.

Bofton, January 1, 1771.

And it goes on:

> Christmas and New-Year, Days of Joy,
> The Harvest of your Carrier Boy,
> He hopes you'll not his Hopes destroy. . . .
>
> [That] His generous Patrons may inspire,
> By filling up his Pockets higher![83]

Three other carriers' addresses wished their recipients "a Merry Christmas and a Happy New Year," and asked, respectively, for a "few shillings," "some pence," and a "lib'ral hand."

To be sure, this ritual was a far cry from the boisterous begging we have encountered in European popular culture (and will reencounter shortly in Boston itself). The paper carrier approached his patrons individually, not as part of a gang. As far as we know, he did not demand entry into his patrons' houses or threaten damage if refused a gift. Above all, the verses that the carrier handed to his patrons were written by his employer. This was a ritual that was largely controlled and regulated from above—and perhaps that was its point. Nevertheless, it *was* a form of door-to-door begging, in which poor and youthful clients approached older and more prosperous patrons. It involved the exchange of gifts for expressions of goodwill, and the exchange was mediated by a "performance"—the token gift of a verse that expressed the essence of the exchange. The ritual's roots in wassailing are clear, and they were probably in the back of the participants' own minds. (And if the newsboy was not tipped, he was always capable, like his modern descendants, of leaving water-soaked newspapers at his patrons' doors.)

The Anticks: Mumming in the Houses

As begging goes, the "Carriers' Addresses" may have been pretty tame stuff. But that is not to say that other forms of begging, more aggressive or threatening, did not take place. Evidence of such activity is hard to come by. Generally, the only public disorders reported by eighteenth-century Boston newspapers were those occasional crowd actions that had serious and overt political meaning (such as the Stamp Act riots of 1765). Episodes of a more ordinary nature—including the less politicized rituals of the Christmas season—did not make it into print.

With one vivid exception. Several sources, taken together, make it clear that a tradition of aggressive Christmas mumming (a variety of wassail) was practiced by some of Boston's poorer inhabitants over a period of at least thirty years, beginning no later than the early 1760s and continuing at least into the mid-1790s. These groups called themselves the Anticks, masked troupes who demanded (or forced) entry into the houses of respectable Bostonians at Christmas. Once inside, they engaged in a dramatic "performance" and demanded gifts of money in return.

The first piece of evidence of the existence of the Anticks is sketchy, taking the form of an oral report given to a folklorist late in the nineteenth century by a man whose mother—born in about 1752—had told it to him.[84] It serves chiefly to date the origin of the Anticks at least as far back as 1760 or so. The second report, too, is from the later recollection of a Bostonian who recalled their visits from the years of his childhood. But his is a detailed account of the Anticks' actual "performance." The man, Samuel Breck, belonged to a very wealthy family. He was born in 1770 and lived in a mansion in central Boston during the years when the Anticks paid their holiday visits (his recollections presumably date from the years around 1780). Breck recalled the Anticks as "a set of the lowest black-guards" who were "disguised in filthy clothes and ofttimes with masked faces." They "went from house to house in large companies, and *bon gre, mal gre,* obtruding themselves everywhere, particularly into the rooms that were occupied by parties of ladies and gentlemen." There they "would demean themselves with great insolence."

Breck's account makes it amply clear that the Anticks were indeed Christmas mummers, and that they would actually perform an old mummer's play, "St. George and the Dragon":

> I have seen them at my father's, when his assembled friends were at cards, take possession of a table, seat themselves on rich furniture and proceed to handle the cards, to the great annoyance of the company. The only way to get rid of them was to give them money, and listen patiently to a foolish dialogue between two or more of them. One of them would cry out, "Ladies and gentlemen sitting by the fire, put your hands in your pockets and give us our desire." When this was done and they had received some money, a kind of acting took place. One fellow was knocked down, and lay sprawling on the carpet, while another bellowed out,
>
> > "See, there he lies,
> > But ere he dies
> > A doctor must be had."
>
> He calls for a doctor, who soon appears, and enacts the part so well that the wounded man revives.[85]

This often went on for half an hour. Breck remembered that even after the men finally left, "the house would be filled with another gang." (Apparently there were multiple bands of Anticks.) Breck concluded by recalling an especially significant cultural point, that the victims of such visitations did not feel entitled to expel the Anticks from their houses: "Custom had licensed these vagabonds to enter even by force any place they chose." ("What should we say to such intruders now?" Breck asked rhetorically in the very different culture of his old age. "Our manners would not brook such usage a moment.")

The third and final report about the Boston Anticks reveals that at the century's end the customary "license" to which Breck referred was coming under challenge. This third report, dating from 1793, is firsthand evidence. On December 20, 1793, a Boston newspaper printed an anonymous letter to the Boston Police Inspector, warning of the Anticks' imminent annual appearance and demanding that something be done to stop them. The letter specified in outraged detail the threat these mummers posed to respectable Bostonians:

> The disadvantages, interruptions, and injuries which the inhabitants sustain from these gangs, are too many for enumeration, a few only must suffice. When different clubs of them meet in the street, noise and fighting immediately commences. Their demands for entrance in house, are insolent and clamourous; and should the peaceful citizen (not choosing to have the tranquillity of his family interrupted) persevere in refusing them admittance, his windows are broke, or the latches and knockers wrenched from his door as the penalty: Or should they gain admittance, the delicate ear is oftentimes offended, children affrighted, or catch the phrases of their senseless ribaldry. [In other words, the Anticks used bawdy language.][86]

Aggressive, indeed. But the behavior of these mummers can also be seen as a kind of symbolic "counter-theater," their response to the refusal of "peaceful citizens" to perform *their* allotted Christmas role. In any event, the Police Inspector responded with a letter of his own. Such gangs had been performing for years, he noted, though he agreed that they caused "inconveniency and frights" by "disturbing families and *begging a Copper.*" But it was difficult to identify the participants, because they went around in disguise. The Inspector also implied that they came from the town's poorest classes (the kinds of people who "seldom if ever read the public papers"). In conclusion, the Police Inspector urged Boston's respectable citizens to take into custody any Anticks who harassed them, promising that such persons would be prosecuted as criminals. (When William Bentley of Salem read this item, he considered it worth noting in his diary that "[t]he inspector of Police in Boston has forbidden the 'Anticks,' as they are called, by which the resemblance of this Christian feast to the Saturnalia has been so admirably maintained."[87])

A final note about this episode. The exchange of letters about the "Anticks" never once mentioned Christmas *by name*, even though the connection would have been clear enough to anyone (as it was to Bentley). But the same issue of the newspaper that contained the Police Inspector's notice also contained a pious poem about the mystery of the Nativity—and it took *Christmas* as its title. The presence of *this* word in the poem, and its complete absence in the discussion of the "Anticks," suggests something of a rhetorical contest over the meaning of the word itself—whether it signified pious devotion or disruptive misrule. Back at the beginning of the eighteenth century, the people who "spoke for" New England culture associated Christmas so profoundly with misrule that they needed to suppress it altogether. By the end of the eighteenth century, the descendants of those same people had discovered an alternative (and more acceptable) meaning of *Christmas*. Now they could wrest the word—if not the thing itself—away from the Anticks and their ilk, to redefine (and reclaim) it as their own.

The House of God: Reviving Christmas as a Public Holiday

With the turn of the nineteenth century, the reappropriation of Christmas took on a concerted form—a move to hold church services on December 25. This move was led by both evangelicals and liberals. In the forefront of the evangelicals were the Universalists. Largely a rural sect, Universalists openly celebrated Christmas from the earliest stages of their existence in New England. The Universalist community in Boston held a special Christmas Day service in 1789, even before their congregation was officially organized,[88] and in the early nineteenth century it was this denomination that proselytized for Christmas more actively than any other.

The Unitarians were close behind. Compared with Universalists, Unitarians were more genteel, and (for all their theological liberalism) more socially conservative. And there were also more of them, especially in Boston. As a formal institution, the Unitarian movement was not organized until 1825. But by the early 1800s ministers who were inclined to doubt the trinity of the Godhead (and, by implication, the divinity of Christ) had come to dominate the Congregational churches in Boston. In fact, for most of the first decade of the nineteenth century, not a single church within Boston's town limits remained in Trinitarian hands. So bad was the situation from an orthodox point of view, that in 1809 a group of theologically conservative ministers from neighboring communities found it necessary to establish a new church in the heart of Boston that would serve as a beachhead of orthodoxy, a kind of mission church on hostile turf. (The new Park Street Church was soon dubbed "Brimstone Corner," after its first minister preached a sermon titled "The Use of Real Fire in Hell.")[89]

Unitarians were calling for the public observance of Christmas by about 1800. They did so in full knowledge that it was not a biblically sanctioned holiday, and that December 25 was probably not the day on which Jesus was born. They wished to celebrate the holiday not because God had ordered them to do so but because they themselves wished to. And they celebrated it in the hope that their own observance might help to purge the holiday of its associations with seasonal excess and disorder.

In 1817 a concerted two-pronged effort got under way to transform Christmas Day in Boston: by holding services in the local churches and by closing down its businesses. Within three years that effort would fail, but for the moment it was waged hard and with the support of influential citizens. The local press helped out, blanketing the town with publicity. The following report was typical:

> Many Christians of the Congregational denomination in this town, have for a long time been desirous, that the anniversary of the nativity of our blessed Saviour should be marked by some religious observance of the day, and by a general abstinence from secular concerns. In consequence, some of the churches of that denomination will be open for public worship. . . .

That was one prong of the campaign. A second local paper described the other prong, announcing that "Gentlemen of business in State-street" had "circulated a paper" to their colleagues. Those who signed the paper pledged themselves "to close their places of business, provided the same engagement should be signed by the principal part of the gentlemen on that street." The circulators of this paper had received "the signatures of about seven eighths of the gentlemen on the street, and of nearly all to whom it was offered, including all who have the government of public offices."[90]

The businessmen appear to have kept to their pledge. One rural merchant who was in town on a buying trip noted in his diary that "[t]he inhabitants of Boston introduced the suspension of business for the first time, with a view to commemorating this day in Religious Exercise." He added that "but little business could be done," and that he had been forced to reload the goods he had brought in to sell that day.[91]

The crusade was renewed the following year. For a week before Christmas, the newspapers were filled with letters and editorials calling for the general observance of the day as a religious holiday.[92] One woman pointed out an additional reason. "Christmas is *now* generally observed as a holiday," she wrote (i.e., a holiday in the de facto sense). "Our children and domestics claim it as such." She added that "[s]chools and public places are closed . . . and generally the day is spent in idleness, and with regret I may add, by many in revelry and dissipation." Opening the churches, she implied, would help reduce both the idleness and the dissipation. Another citizen turned the same point on its head, arguing plausibly that if Bostonians abandoned their regular business on December 25, "it would become only another reason for dissipation, for frolic and insobriety."[93]

Services were held in five reformed churches on Christmas Day, 1818 (in addition to the Catholic and Episcopal churches). These included three Congregational churches as well as a Universalist and a Methodist one. Services were held in the central Massachusetts town of Worcester as well, in the Congregational church led by Aaron Bancroft (father of historian George Bancroft). That same year one Boston newspaper published, without comment, the 1659 Puritan law banning the celebration of Christmas in Massachusetts.[94] No comment was needed, since everyone would have caught the point: *We've come a long way since those days.*

A long way, indeed. That year, 1818, even the staunchly Trinitarian Congregationalist paper in Boston, the *Recorder,* indicated its approval. The *Recorder* was the organ of the Park Street Church—"Brimstone Corner." But its editorial began: "We are happy to learn that it is the intention of many persons to observe Christmas day, this year, in a more solemn manner than they ever yet have done. . . ." It even went on to imply that the Park Street Church itself should join in: "We are . . . decidedly in favor of the measure, and hope divine service will be performed in *all* our churches."[95]

And so again in 1819. A letter to one newspaper declared that "all the banks, public offices, &c. will suspend business," and expressed the hope that "every merchant and liberal minded man will also follow the example, and observe Christmas *more universally,* if possible, than Bostonians did the last year." By this time the movement had reached as far as the rural New Hampshire town of Amherst, whose newspaper printed an impassioned editorial arguing that Christmas was more important than Thanksgiving.[96]

But the movement ran out of momentum that very year (religious services were held only at the two Universalist churches and at the Old South Church). Many businesses did remain closed that year, although by 1823 one paper reported with amusement that several shops only *appeared* to be closed—their window shutters were fastened, but "their doors kindly opened to all who would take the trouble to lift the latch." The newspaper that reported this development went on to express its pleasure that "no law, either civil or divine," actually *required* "the observance of the feasts of the papal and episcopal churches," and to deplore the fact that Boston's businessmen felt unable to "pursue their occupations openly."[97]

Actually, this movement seems to have been part of a larger counterattack. Early in 1820 a religious magazine published in Boston assaulted the idea of making Christmas a public holiday. But its argument had nothing to do with theology, with the dating of Christ's birth. The magazine acknowledged that December 25 was a time of "rejoicing, and of religious ceremonies" for many Christians. The problem lay with other kinds of behavior: "an immense majority of those, who celebrate the day, make it an occasion of indulgence and profane mirth, and of almost every species of licentiousness." In any case, within only a few years the movement to close the shops and open the churches was dead. In 1828 the *Boston Statesman* noted with regret that "few places of business were closed yesterday, and none but the churches of the Episcopal order, we believe, were opened. . . ."[98]

As it turned out, the years 1817–19 were to represent a historical high-water mark in the religious celebration of Christmas in Boston. To this day New England's Unitarian, Baptist, and Methodist churches are ordinarily closed on Christmas Day, along with its Congregational and Presbyterian ones.

What happened was that in New England, as elsewhere, religion failed to transform Christmas from a season of misrule into an occasion of quieter pleasure. That transformation would, however, shortly take place—but not at the hands of Christianity. The "house of ale" would not be vanquished by the house of God, but by a new faith that was just beginning to sweep over American society. It was the religion of domesticity, which would be represented at Christmas-time not by Jesus of Nazareth but by a newer and more worldly deity—Santa Claus.

CHAPTER 2

Revisiting
"A Visit from St. Nicholas"

*T*HE CHRISTMAS SEASON was always an important occasion in the life of John Pintard, a prominent New York City merchant and civic leader of the early nineteenth century. As Pintard went to bed on the evening of December 31, 1820, he was looking forward to the schedule he had carefully laid out for the celebration of New Year's Day, the season's end. First he would get up early for a private chat with his daughter, who was married but still lived in the household. Next there would be a devotional morning service at a nearby Episcopal church. The middle hours of the day would be devoted to an extended round of "ceremonial and friendly visits" with acquaintances and colleagues around the city. Finally, in midafternoon Pintard would return to his Wall Street home, where the entire household would, as he put it, "assemble round our festive boards" for a "little family party"—a meal of venison and other holiday dishes that had been prepared weeks in advance, and punctuated by a series of toasts "drunk with all affection and old fashioned formality."

Pintard managed, the next day, to get through most of the activities he had planned, but only after his night's sleep had been interrupted—not once but twice. First, in the middle of the night, with the household sound asleep, Pintard's daughter was awakened when she heard "someone take [a] key and deliberately open the door." The family knew that New

49

Year's Eve marked the peak of rowdy Christmas revels in New York, so Pintard had reason to fear the presence of an intruder. He roused his wife ("mama," as he referred to her in a letter written very early the next morning). "I threw on my clothes in haste, and down we sallied [to investigate,] found the back parlor door ajar, but nothing out of place." As it turned out, the noise was only a false alarm—the family's black servant had merely arisen early in order to light a fire in the study. So Pintard returned to bed. But no sooner had he fallen asleep than he was roused again, this time by bands of loud revelers marching down Wall Street and directly outside his house, banging on drums, blowing fifes and whistles, and all the while loudly proclaiming the New Year. The revelers did not leave, and in fact kept Pintard up for the rest of the night: They "interrupted all repose until daylight, when I arose, leaving mama . . . to take a little rest till nine, when I shall call [her]."[1]

What this little episode reveals is two incompatible styles of celebrating the holiday season. One of them, that of John Pintard, was a daytime affair, genially formal, and quiet. The other, that of the revelers in the street, was nocturnal, aggressively public, and just as noisy as they could make it. It was, in short, carnival. The two styles came into conflict in Pintard's household only two years before Pintard's friend Clement Clarke Moore wrote his poem "A Visit from St. Nicholas"—the account of a rather different kind of nighttime visitation during the Christmas season. The connection is not artificial, for John Pintard himself played a role in the development of Christmas as we know it today. One might even say that his role was that of John the Baptist to the figure of Santa Claus that Moore would soon perfect.

MISRULE AND CAPITALISM IN EARLY-NINETEENTH-CENTURY NEW YORK

A generation earlier, in 1786, a newspaper in a nearby community pointed out the same contrast between the different fashions in which New Yorkers celebrated the season: "Some good people religiously observe it as a time set apart for a most sacred purpose," some by "decently feasting with their friends and relatives." But others observe the holiday by "revelling in profusion, and paying their sincere devotion to *merry Bacchus*." The newspaper went on to rephrase the contrast in metaphoric terms: "in several churches divine service [was] performed," while "the temples dedicated to the service of *merriment, dissipation* and *folly,* were much crouded [sic];

where the *sons of gluttony and drunkenness* satiate their respective appetites."

> The scene with these gentry generally concludes about midnight, when they sally forth into the streets, and by their *unmeaning, wild, extravagant noise*, disturb those citizens who would rather *sleep* than *get drunk*.[2]

Chapter 1 of this book argues that traditional Christmas misrule did not ordinarily pose a significant threat to the social order or to the authority of the gentry class. In fact, it actually served to reinforce the existing order of things by providing a sanctioned opportunity for the poor to let off steam; it was a safety valve that allowed them to express resentments in a fashion that was generally apolitical. Indeed, the form that misrule commonly took—that of *inverting* the ordinary social structure rather than simply ignoring it—may have served to confirm the legitimacy of the status quo. After all, what the patron received from his clients in return for his gifts was their goodwill—something that had a great deal of value, indeed, in the dynamics of a paternalist order.

But this would change as paternalism itself came to wither away as a dominant form of social relations. In England much of the change took place during the eighteenth century. E. P. Thompson has argued that in eighteenth-century England it was the upper classes themselves who severed the paternalist bonds that allowed the rituals of misrule to operate as a safety valve. Both the gentry and the established church abandoned their control over holiday rituals; these now became purely "plebeian" cultural expressions. (The Boston Anticks discussed in Chapter 1 offer a good example of what Thompson had in mind.) In this new setting, rituals of misrule began to assume a more clearly *oppositional* form. Thompson describes these eighteenth-century protests as a kind of political "theater," directed at the gentry "audience" before whom it was "performed"—something less than a full-fledged radical movement but more than sheer, unfocused rowdiness.[3] For example, in eighteenth-century England there appeared a kind of late-night serenade on New Year's Eve known as the "callithumpian band"—possibly derived from the Greek word *calli-* (for "beautiful"). But the music these bands played was hardly beautiful. It was meant to be loud and offensive, characterized by "beating on tin pans, blowing horns, shouts, groans, catcalls," and it was performed as a gesture of deliberate mockery; the general term in England for such things was "rough music." (This was not wholly new; "rough music" is simply the

British term for what in France was called "charivari." But the calli-thumpian bands seem to have directed their "rough music" against those who seemed to be claiming too much dignity or abusing their power.)[4]

By the early nineteenth century, with the spread of wage labor and other modes of capitalist production in England and the United States, what I have chosen to call the "battle for Christmas" entered an acute phase. For some urban workers, the Christmas season no longer entailed a lull in the demand for labor; their employers insisted on business as usual.[5] (It was this impulse that Charles Dickens would caricature in his character Ebenezer Scrooge.) For other urban workers, the coming of winter brought the prospect of being laid off, as the icing-up of rivers brought water-powered factories to a seasonal halt. December's leisure thus meant not relative plenty but forced unemployment and want. The Christmas season, with its carnival traditions of wassail, misrule, and cal-lithumpian "street theater," could easily become a vehicle of social protest, an instrument to express powerful ethnic or class resentments. Little won-der, then, that the upper classes displayed little interest in making the sea-son a major holiday. Before the mid-1820s the holiday was mentioned only cursorily in British and American newspapers.[6] The turn of the nine-teenth century may have marked a historic low point in the celebration of Christmas among the elite.

LET US return, then, to New York City, where John Pintard's neigh-borhood was subjected to the rough music of a callithumpian band in 1821, and where our modern American Christmas was invented, the following year, with the composition of Clement Clarke Moore's poem "A Visit from St. Nicholas." New York in the early nineteenth century was a fast-growing place. As late as 1800, the urbanized part of the city covered only a small area at the southern tip of Manhattan Island, well to the south of what are now the numbered streets. But the size of the city's population had begun a rapid, almost geometrical increase—from 33,000 in 1790 to 200,000 in 1830 and 270,000 just five years later. In order to accommodate the rapid increase in population, the city in 1811 started implementation of a plan to construct a regular grid system of numbered streets (and av-enues) that would crisscross the entire island. (As we shall see, this plan would have an effect on Clement Clarke Moore.)

The numerical growth of the city's population was accompanied by a change in its composition: an influx of immigrants, especially Irish Catholics, and the appearance of an impoverished underclass that was living for the first time in its own poor districts (generally divided up by ethnicity and race), along with a wealthy upper class that took up residence in its fashionable ones.[7] In the second decade of the nineteenth century, New York underwent an explosion of poverty, vagrancy, and homelessness. That was followed in the third decade by serious outbreaks of public violence. In the eyes of New York's "respectable" citizens, to quote a recent historian on the subject, "the entire city appeared to have succumbed to disorder. . . . [It] seemed to be coming apart completely."[8] Many well-to-do New Yorkers began to move out to new uptown estates, which they enclosed with fences or hedges. In turn, those fences were sometimes pulled down, and the hedges uprooted, by poor and homeless people who persisted in regarding the new estates as "common land" open to everyone. As a result, by the 1820s these estates were commonly being guarded by watchmen, drawn from the same underclass as the rioters themselves.

The city's streets became the center of a different version of the same conflict. As Elizabeth Blackmar has written, the city's poorest residents—"peddlers, ragpickers, prostitutes, scavengers, beggars, and . . . criminals"—depended for subsistence on the freedom of the streets, and the unregulated opportunity to accost strangers at will, whether for legal or illegal purposes. But by the 1820s, the propertied classes had begun to make systematic efforts to protect themselves from such "unwanted intrusions from the streets."[9]

John Pintard was one such propertied man. He was deeply troubled by the increasing visibility of poor people and by the danger their aggressive behavior posed to respectable New Yorkers.[10] Pintard was the moving force behind the establishment, in 1817, of the Society for the Prevention of Pauperism, an organization designed to put both a cap on the skyrocketing costs of poor relief and a stop to the public begging and drinking of the poor in order to make the city streets a safe place for people like himself.[11] Needless to say, all these efforts failed. By 1828 Pintard was acknowledging that the problems of poverty, drinking, and street crime had, "I confess, baffled all our skill. . . . The evil is obvious, acknowledged by all, but a sovereign remedy appears to be impossible."[12]

It should come as no surprise that all of these developments were reflected in the transformation of the Christmas season. As early as 1772, a New York newspaper complained that the absence of "decency, temperance, and sobriety" at Christmas was so serious a matter that it belonged in the courts. The problem was caused by "[t]he assembling of Negroes, servants, boys and other disorderly persons, in noisy companies in the streets, where they spend the time in gaming, drunkenness, quarreling, swearing, etc., to the great disturbance of the neighborhood." The behavior of these rowdies was "so highly scandalous both to religion and civil government, that it is hoped the Magistrates will interpose to suppress the enormity."[13]

By 1820 Christmas misrule had become such an acute social threat that respectable New Yorkers could no longer ignore it or take it lightly. What Susan G. Davis has demonstrated in her study of Philadelphia in this period holds equally true of New York. By the 1820s bands of roaming young street toughs, members of the emerging urban proletariat, were no longer restricting their seasonal reveling to their own neighborhoods; they had begun to travel freely, and menacingly, wherever they pleased. Often carousing in disguise (a holdover from the old tradition of mumming), these street gangs marauded through the city's wealthy neighborhoods, especially on New Year's Eve, in the form of callithumpian bands, which resembled (and may have overlapped with) the street gangs that were now vying for control of the city's poorer neighborhoods. Throughout the night these bands made as much noise as they could, sometimes stopping deliberately at the houses of the rich and powerful.[14] In 1826, for example, such a gang stopped in front of the Broadway house of the city's mayor; there they "enacted" what a local newspaper termed "a scene of disgraceful rage."[15] The next year another newspaper sarcastically described these same gangs as "a number of ill-bred boys, chimney sweeps, and other illustrious and aspiring persons" whose sole purpose was "to perambulate the streets all night, disturbing the slumbers of the weary . . . by thumping upon tin kettles, sounding penny[whistles] and other martial trumpets."[16] John Pintard would have understood.

In 1828 there occurred an extensive and especially violent callithumpian parade, complete with the standard array of "drums, tin kettles, rattles, horns, whistles, and a variety of other instruments." This parade began along the working-class Bowery, where the band pelted a tavern with lime; then it marched to Broadway, where a fancy upper-class ball was being held at the City Hotel; then to a black neighborhood, stopping at a church where the callithumpians "demolished all the windows, broke the doors [and] seats," and beat with sticks and ropes the African-American congregants who were holding a "watch" service; next, the band headed to the city's main commercial district, where they smashed crates and barrels and looted at least one shop; still unsatisfied, they headed to the Battery (at the southern tip of the city), where they broke the windows of several of the city's wealthiest residences and tried to remove the iron fence that surrounded Battery Park; finally they headed back to Broadway for a second visit. This time a group of hired watchmen were waiting for the callithumpians; but the band stood down the watch force, and, in the words of a local newspaper, "the multitude passed noisily and triumphantly up Broadway."[17]

What are we to make of scenes like these? Once again, E. P. Thompson makes a convincing case that it would be misleading to interpret them either as wholly conscious political protest *or* as mere revelry that got out of hand, a kind of nineteenth-century frat party. Historians of American cities have agreed with that assessment. One of them puts it like this: " Riotous disorder, racial violence, and jolly foolery for neighbors and audiences existed side by side . . . for decades. . . . Customary Christmas license combined with seasonal unemployment made the winter holiday a noisy, drunken, threatening period in the eyes of the respectable." And another historian suggests that New York's callithumpians can be considered "a bridge between the traditional youth group misrule of the English village . . . and a more direct challenge to authority."[18]

KNICKERBOCKER HOLIDAY

Let us return for a few minutes to our friend John Pintard, if only because at one point, in December 1823, Pintard offered his own interpretation of the situation—and it is both interesting in itself and germane to the question of Christmas. Pintard mused that it might be the culture of Protestantism itself that was to blame for New York's problems. Protestants, he argued, unlike Catholics and even pagans, had systematically suppressed the kind of "religious festivals" at which "mechanics and laborers" could find officially sanctioned and organized "processions" that would allow them to release their "pent-up" energies in satisfying but orderly ways.[19] (Pintard might almost seem to be referring to *Puritans* in particular rather than to Protestants in general.)

In fact, John Pintard himself was drawn almost compulsively to ceremonies, rituals, and traditional practices—for himself and his family, for New York City, and even for the United States as a nation. And when he could not find such things, he devised them. (One of the nation's first antiquarians, Pintard was the founder of the New-York Historical Society in 1804; and he played a role in the establishment of Washington's Birthday, the Fourth of July, and even Columbus Day as national holidays.[20]) In fact, it was John Pintard who brought St. Nicholas to America, in an ef-

fort to make that figure both the icon of the New-York Historical Society
and the patron saint of New York City. In 1810 Pintard paid for the publication of a broadside, sponsored by the Historical Society, that featured
a picture of St. Nicholas bringing gifts to children during the Christmas
season (actually, on St. Nicholas' Day, December 6). The picture was accompanied by a short poem that began, "Sancte Claus goed heylig man."[21]

In his letters Pintard regularly expressed nostalgia for what he called
the "old customs" and "ancient usages" of New York, and particularly for
the forgotten spirit of the old Christmas season, when rich folk and poor,
old and young, would mingle together in genial harmony in the streets of
the city.[22] But Pintard never managed to discover or devise any way of observing the Christmas holidays that actually involved working-class people. All of his own carefully planned seasonal rituals were restricted to the
members of his own social class (for example, the formalized New Year's
Day described at the beginning of this chapter). The reason for this nar-
rowing down was clear: It had simply become impossible for New York's
respectable citizens to continue participating in the rowdy old cross-class
celebrations that Pintard recalled fondly from his own youth, when he and
a family servant traveled together around New York in "boisterous" fashion, drinking a "dram" at every stop and "coming home loaded with sixpences." As Pintard put it in 1827, "since staggering through the streets on
New Years day is out of fashion [now], it is impossible to drink drams at
every house as of old." And while Pintard sorely regretted the disappear-
ance of the goodwill that had characterized such occasions of public
drinking in the olden days—he referred to this as "the joyous older fashion"—he also understood that the social price to be paid for that goodwill
had become impossibly high. He noted that "intemperance, among the
higher classes of our city, is no longer the order of the day. Among the
hospitable circles . . . , a man would be marked who should retire intoxicated; indeed, convivial parties are all decent and sober."[23]

Sobriety had become a necessity. "It is well," Pintard acknowledged
with a kind of sigh—"It is well, for formerly New Years was a riotous day."
And he quickly added, as if suddenly recalling that the *real* problem was a
present-day one, that "the beastly vice of drunkenness among the lower laboring classes is growing to a frightful excess. . . . Thefts, incendiaries,
and murders—which prevail—all arise from this source."[24] After all, that
was why he had founded the Society for the Prevention of Pauperism.

Since there existed no Christmas rituals that were socially acceptable
to the upper class, Pintard took on the responsibility of inventing them—
characteristically enough, in the name of restoring something that had

been forgotten. For more than twenty years—roughly between 1810 and 1830—he tried almost every year to come up with the perfect holiday. (Before the late 1820s these holidays did not involve Christmas Day itself; until 1827 Pintard always observed December 25 in simple fashion, as a time of prayer and private religious devotion.)

In the 1810s, Pintard organized and led elaborate St. Nicholas' Day banquets for his fellow members of the New-York Historical Society, held at the society's office in City Hall. But in 1820 his celebration of St. Nicholas' Day was interrupted: "At six [p.m.] I attended [a meeting of] the Pauperism Society, for even festivity must not interfere with works of benevolence." That, as it happens, is the last mention of St. Nicholas' Day in Pintard's published correspondence. By this time, and with an increasing intensity of commitment throughout most of the 1820s, he had turned to New Year's Day—holding lavish dinners for his extended family, and making formal visits to old friends and relatives around the city. On January 1, 1821, Pintard engaged, apparently for the first time, in what he called "the good old custom of mutual visitings and cordial greetings." For the rest of the decade he devoted each year to efforts to establish New Year's as a day of mutual visitation in New York, describing it (as he did in 1822) as "the custom of the simple Dutch settlers." Pintard sometimes referred to this custom with the phrase "open house," but his use of the phrase is clear: Houses were "open" only to old friends and kin—to members of his own class. And in 1828 he ruefully admitted that the phenomenon was fading away in New York: "[T]he joyous older fashion [of visitation] has declined gradually." Two years later he explained why: The practice was becoming "irksome" because "our city grows so extensive, and friends so scattered."[25] But by then, as we shall see, Pintard had discovered Christmas.

IN FACT, Pintard was not the only New Yorker who expressed an interest in restoring the old customs of the Christmas season. In 1819 and 1820 there appeared a book written by a fellow member of the New-York Historical Society—Washington Irving. Irving had actually written parts of *The Sketch Book,* as he titled his new publication, at one of the tables in the Historical Society. The book was a smashing success, one that propelled Irving into sudden transatlantic celebrity. *The Sketch Book* contained two stories that were destined to become classics: "Rip Van Winkle" and "The Legend of Sleepy Hollow." But it also included five stories about Christmas. Unlike "Rip Van Winkle," those Christmas tales were not about the Dutch heritage of New York but were set on a gracious estate in the modern British countryside, Bracebridge Hall. In these stories Irving used Christmas as the setting for a culture in which all the classes joined together in paternalist harmony.

Irving's narrator is hosted at Christmas by old Squire Bracebridge, an antiquarian-minded gentleman who is obsessed with the past, and who wields so much social authority that he is able to recruit the neighboring peasantry to join him in a reenactment, under his direction, of "the holyday customs and rural games of former times." Irving's narrator waxes eloquent as he contemplates "the quaint humours, the burlesque pageants, the complete abandonment to mirth and good fellowship with which this [Christmas] festival was celebrated." The occasion "seemed to throw open every door, and unlock every heart. It brought the peasant and the peer together, and blended all ranks in one warm generous flow of joy and kindness."

At the climax of the "Bracebridge Hall" stories the squire presents a Christmas banquet at which are displayed, along with "brawn and beef, and stout home brewed," all the archaic customs of the season, including a wassail bowl, a Lord of Misrule, and a group of peasants—the old squire's trusty dependents—who perform an old dance and then mingle gratefully with the squire's household:

> There is something genuine and affectionate in the gayety of the lower orders, when it is excited by the bounty and familiarity of those above them; the warm glow of gratitude enters into their mirth, and a kind word, and a small pleasantry frankly uttered by a patron, gladdens the heart of the dependent more than oil and wine.

It is, of course, an invention—"the invention of tradition," as the historian Eric Hobsbawm has dubbed this kind of self-conscious re-creation of ostensibly old-time customs[26]—and Irving knows that. In fact, he not only knows it, he even takes pains to let us in on the secret. The narrator's description of the squire's Christmas celebration is larded with such terms as "odd and obsolete," "quaint," "ancient," even "eccentric," and in a later edition of *The Sketch Book* Irving admitted that at the time he wrote the "Bracebridge Hall" stories he had never actually seen the kind of Christmas he described in it. Even the Lord of Misrule is fictive: The role is taken by a real gentleman.

Nor is this all. As Squire Bracebridge drives home from church just before his great dinner party, he engages in a bit of nostalgic commentary.

He begins by lamenting

> the deplorable decay of the games and amusements which were once prevalent at this season among the lower orders, and countenanced by the higher. When the old halls of castles and manor houses were thrown open at daylight; . . . and when rich and poor were alike welcome to enter and make merry.

As the squire continues, his nostalgia spills over into a confession of his inability to re-create the genuine rituals of Christmases past. And at precisely this moment, he moves from antiquarianism into political theory—*Tory* political theory:

> "The nation," continued he, "is altered; we have almost lost our simple true-hearted peasantry. They have broken asunder from the higher classes, and seem to think their interests are separate. They have become too knowing, and begin to read newspapers, listen to ale house politicians, and talk of reform. I think one mode to keep them in good humor in these hard times, would be for the nobility and gentry to pass more time on their estates, mingle more among the country people, and set the merry old English games going again."

At this point Irving's own narrative voice takes over from Squire Bracebridge's. "Such," Irving continues, "was the good Squire's project for mitigating public discontent; and, indeed, he had once attempted to put his doctrine in[to] practice, and a few years before had *kept open house during the holidays in the old style*" [emphasis added]. But the open-house experiment failed:

> The country people . . . did not understand how to play their parts in the scene of hospitality: many uncouth circumstances occurred [these Irving does not choose to describe]; the manor was overrun by all the vagrants of the country, and more beggars [were] drawn into the neighborhood in one week than the parish officers could get rid of in a year.

So the squire was forced to back off his original project. Nowadays, Irving tells us, he "contented himself with inviting the *decent part* of the neighboring peasantry to call at the hall on Christmas day" [emphasis added]. It is that select group, rather than the entire neighborhood, that comes to Bracebridge Hall (at the stipulated time) to entertain and mingle with the squire's *real* guests.

But so self-conscious is this scene—so close to the edge of silliness—that Irving himself suspected it might ring false to contemporary readers. For as the squire "mingled among the rustics, and was "received with awkward demonstrations of deference and regard," Irving's narrator observes (and reports to us) something that escapes the notice of his host: "I perceived two or three of the younger peasants, as they were raising their tankards to their mouths, when the Squire's back was turned, making something of a grimace, and giving each other the wink, but the moment they caught my eye they pulled grave faces, and were exceedingly demure." Irving surely wrote this little scene to protect his credibility with an 1820 audience, and his meaning would have been clear enough to the knowing reader: Despite all the precautions Squire Bracebridge had taken to do the job right, he had been unable to keep even the "decent part" of the local peasantry in "good humor" on Christmas Day.

The "Bracebridge Hall" stories were immensely popular, and they played an important part in restoring the interest of "respectable" Americans (and Britishers) in celebrating Christmas. Indeed, it was these sketches, together with the stories of Charles Dickens, that provided much of what a recent book terms the "enduring imagery of Christmas which is annually reiterated in Christmas cards and festive illustrations, where jovial squires entertain friends and retainers by roaring fires, and stout coachmen, swathed in greatcoats, urge horses down snow-covered lanes as they bring anticipatory guests and homesick relations to their welcoming destinations."[27]

When the "Bracebridge Hall" stories were published in 1819, they set off something of a debate about whether reviving the old rural Christmas rituals would be enough to restore the fading authority of the English gentry. The issues were understood in just these terms. One essay, published in 1825, summarized them by asserting bluntly "that the merry-makings of the times of Elizabeth and the Stuarts originated solely in an instinctive [i.e., paternalist] understanding between master and man; that the rich encouraged them [i.e., the merrymakings] as a means of patronage and superiority, and that the poor accepted them as an oil to their chain, or a happy rivet of their dependence." On those points, the essay argued, conservatives and reformers agreed. Where they differed was in their response: Conservatives believed "that the old times were the best because they were least free"; while reformers argued "that a merry season is dearly purchased by servility all the rest of the year."

This particular writer (he remains anonymous) was a skeptic. He maintained that a revival of the old rituals was unlikely to have any effect, simply because the times themselves had changed. In former days, when "people believed any thing because a magistrate set his hand to it, the case was different;"

> but now-a-days, bring rich and poor together as we please, roast as many oxen as there are villages to do it in, and let one general wassail-bowl set the hearts of great and small dancing all over England; and [still,] as long as there are Mechanics' Magazines [i.e., to educate the poor] . . . , there is no fear that people will be too thankful for a sirloin of beef, or melt with maudlin souls into the overflow of a beer barrel. There is, in fact, no necessity for [their] accepting either.

"Sports may be revived," this man concluded; "wassail bowls may abound; the poor may cultivate their strength and spirits with gymnastic exercise, and the rich assuredly be no nearer an undue influence."[28]

In any event, Washington Irving's vision of Christmas did not exactly offer a practical model for anyone who was tempted—and many must have been—to celebrate Christmas in this fashion. How could John Pintard, say, reproduce a ritual that Washington Irving himself found it difficult even to *imagine* for his readers? It is easy to sympathize with Pintard, who almost certainly read *The Sketch Book* and felt the power of Irving's vision. But it was easier for Irving to imagine such a scene than for John Pintard to duplicate it, even though it may have been the "Bracebridge Hall" stories that inspired—and finally frustrated—Pintard's elaborate efforts during the 1820s to re-create an old-time New Year's Day. Pintard would not be satisfied until he discovered what had happened, in the hands of his friend Clement Clarke Moore, to a figure that he himself had originally introduced—that is, of course, the figure of St. Nicholas.

As LATE AS 1826, Pintard did not associate Christmas itself with St. Nicholas (or with anything at all except attending church and what Pintard termed "solemni[ty]" and "devotional feelings"). Pintard went to church on Christmas in 1827, too; but there was something new that year: "We had St. Claas in high snuff," Pintard noted, and he referred briefly to the "bon bons" his grandchildren had received. The following year, 1828, Pintard's description was more elaborate:

All due preparations having been made by the children the preceding evening, by placing hay for his horses [!] and invoking "St. Claas, Gude Heylig Man," he came accordingly during the night, with most elegant toys, bon bons, oranges, etc., all which, after filling the stockings suspended at the sides of mother's chimney, were displayed in goodly order on the mantle, to the ecstatic joy of [the children] in the morning, whose exhaltations resounded through the house.[29]

Pintard's letters from each of the years 1830 through 1832 contain descriptions that were at least as extensive as this one. By 1831 he characteristically referred to the ritual as an "ancient usage," adding that "St. Claas is too firmly riveted in this city ever to be forgotten." And in 1832 Pintard concluded a very lengthy account of the children's reactions to Santa's visit with these words: "Happy golden age. All was joy and gladness."[30] That was all there would be; Pintard lived for another dozen years (dying at age 85), but he was becoming blind and seems to have stopped writing letters.

DURING THE TWO DECADES from 1810 to 1830, while Pintard shifted his energies from December 6 to January 1, then from January 1 to December 25, this much remained constant: The season was to be celebrated with members of his own social class. But one thing had changed nevertheless, and it was more important than the simple date of the celebration. Pintard had gradually moved from a celebration that took place in public (first at City Hall, with the New-York Historical Society, then on the city streets and in the houses of kinsmen and old acquaintances) to one that took place in private, in his own home, with his immediate family. Just as important, the new celebration focused on a single group within the family: young children.

In a very important way, such a child-centered event was a new thing. Before the nineteenth century children were merely dependents—miniature adults who occupied the bottom of the hierarchy within the family, along with the servants. But perhaps that was exactly the point, because in another way this was a very old thing. Making children the center of joyous attention marked an inversion of the social hierarchy, which meant that a part of the structure of an older Christmas ritual *was being precisely preserved:* People in positions of social and economic authority were offering gifts to their dependents. The ritual of social inversion was still there, but now it was based on age and family status alone. Age had replaced social class as the axis along which gifts were given at Christmas.

The children of a single household had replaced a larger group of the poor and powerless as the symbolic objects of charity and benevolence. It was those children who became the temporary centers of attention and deference at Christmas, and the joy and gratitude on their faces and in their voices as they opened their presents was a vivid re-creation of the exchange of gifts for goodwill that had long constituted the emotional heart of the Christmas season.

It was just such an exchange that Washington Irving had evoked in "Bracebridge Hall" when he insisted that "there is something genuine and affectionate in the gayety of the lower orders, when it is excited by the bounty and familiarity of those above them; [how] the warm glow of gratitude enters into their mirth, and a kind word, and a small pleasantry frankly uttered by a patron, gladdens the heart of the dependent more than oil and wine." During the 1820s such an exchange had particular appeal for the urban upper classes, precisely because they were still residually sensitive to the need to demonstrate noblesse, especially during the Christmas season. But Irving, who continued to place the patron-client exchange in the older context of social class, was able to imagine it only with difficulty. Clement Moore, by translating the patron-client exchange from one between the classes to one between the generations, helped to transform it into a practical, simple ritual that almost any household could perform. And eventually, as we know only too well, almost every household would.

NOWADAYS many Americans believe, as I did until recently, that there was nothing new about "the night before Christmas" described in Moore's poem—that the story it told was simply an old Dutch tradition brought to the New World in the seventeenth century and then, in the natural course of things, gradually Americanized. That is just what John Pintard would wish us to believe (and he may even have believed it himself).

But the preeminent scholar of St. Nicholas in our own day has shown that this could not have been the case. In an article published in 1954, Charles W. Jones argued forcefully that "there is no evidence that [the cult of Santa Claus] existed in New Amsterdam, or for [more than] a century after British occupation." Jones pointed out that *nobody* has ever found any contemporaneous evidence of such a St. Nicholas cult in New York during the colonial period.[31] Instead, the familiar Santa Claus story appears to have been devised in the early nineteenth century, during the two decades that ended in the early 1820s. It seems likely that a similar ritual, along with others, was practiced in parts of Holland during the mid-seventeenth century, on St. Nicholas' Day, December 6. But Charles Jones makes a compelling case that this ritual did not cross the Atlantic, and that the Santa Claus who was devised in early-nineteenth-century New York was therefore a conscious reconstruction of that Dutch ritual— an invented tradition.

This does not mean that "the night before Christmas" belongs to Clement Moore alone. In fact, it was the work of a small group of anti-quarian-minded New York gentlemen—men who knew one another and were members of a distinct social set. Collectively, those men became known as the Knickerbockers; the name comes from an immensely pop-ular book published in 1809 by the best-known member of the group, Washington Irving. Irving's book, commonly known as *Knickerbocker's History of New York,* was a brilliantly satirical allegory about life in the contemporary city that the author lived in, but it was written in the guise of a history of New Amsterdam in old Dutch times. Irving himself men-tioned St. Nicholas twenty-five times in *Knickerbocker's History,* including references to the saint's wagon, his pipe (more of that later), and a line that read: "laying his finger beside his nose." Irving even chose to have *Knicker-bocker's History* published on St. Nicholas' Day. If it was John Pintard who introduced the figure of St. Nicholas, it was Washington Irving who popularized it. In the words of Charles W. Jones, "Without Irving there would be no Santa Claus. . . . Santa Claus was *made* by Washington Irving."[32]*

The Knickerbocker set inhabited a special niche in the world of early-nineteenth-century New York. As a rule, its members were of British, not Dutch, descent. They belonged to the Episcopal Church, and, more particularly, to its ritually inclined High Church faction. They were part of the wealthy old aristocracy of the city (or at least they identified with it). And they were politically conservative, reactionary even—op-posed to democracy (which they identified with mob rule) and fearful of

---

* A fascinating equivalent to the Knickerbockers' invention of Santa Claus (and all in the guise of continuing a venerated old tradition) is to be found in an unlikely arena: the early history of the game of baseball. The American national pastime, like the American Christmas, was invented in New York—and less than a generation later. Astonishingly, the earliest extant description of a baseball match, in a press account dating from 1845, referred to this newly devised sport as a "*time-honored game*"! But a clue that may help explain that phrase is to be found in the name of the best-known base-ball club from this early period of the sport: formed in 1846, this New York team was known as the "Knickerbockers." (The account of the 1845 match, printed in the *New York Morning News,* was un-earthed only in 1990; it antedates by one year the earliest previously known report of a baseball game. The discovery was a front-page story in the *New York Times,* October 4, 1990.)

both the working class and the new bourgeoisie. Indeed, they often failed to distinguish between these two groups, sometimes lumping them together with the general, yet quite telling, word *plebeian.*

For example, in his *Knickerbocker's History,* Washington Irving disdainfully summarized in a single sentence an episode that clearly represented to his readers the Jeffersonian revolution of 1800: "[J]ust about this time the mob, since called the sovereign people . . . exhibited a strange desire of governing itself."[33] And in 1822 (the year "A Visit from St. Nicholas" appeared), John Pintard explained to his daughter just why he was opposed to the new state constitution adopted that year, a constitution that gave men without property the right to vote: "All power," Pintard wrote, "is to be given, by the right of universal suffrage, to a mass of people, especially in *this* city, which has no stake in society. It is easier to raise a mob than to quell it, and we shall hereafter be governed by rank democracy. . . . Alas that the proud state of New York should be engulfed in the abyss of ruin."[34]

In short, the Knickerbockers felt that they belonged to a patrician class whose authority was under siege. From that angle, their invention of Santa Claus was part of what we can now see as a larger, ultimately quite serious cultural enterprise: forging a pseudo-Dutch identity for New York, a placid "folk" identity that could provide a cultural counterweight to the commercial bustle and democratic "misrule" of early-nineteenth-century New York. The best-known literary expression of this larger enterprise is Irving's classic story "Rip Van Winkle" (published a full decade after *Knickerbocker's History*). But in the *History,* too, Irving pictured old New Amsterdam as a place of "filial piety" in which people thought and acted "with characteristic slowness and circumspection . . . ; who adhere . . . to the customs . . . of their revered forefathers." New Amsterdam was a serene place in which people (watched over by good St. Nicholas himself) "did not regulate their time by hours, but by [the smoking of] pipes."[35]

CLEMENT CLARKE MOORE, COUNTRY GENTLEMAN

Which finally brings me to Clement Clarke Moore, the author of "A Visit from St. Nicholas." If we have any image of the man at all, it is apt to be of a benevolent figure, a scholarly but genial professor of Hebrew who stepped, just this once, out of his ivory tower to write, for his own chil-

Clement Clarke Moore.
This woodcut was made
from one of the four
portraits painted of Moore
at different stages of his life.
Good oil portraits were
expensive, and only wealthy
people could afford even
one. This is from the last of
Moore's four portraits, done
around 1850, almost thirty
years after the writing of
"A Visit from St. Nicholas."
*(Courtesy, Harvard
College Library)*

dren, those magical verses about what happened on "the night before
Christmas." He is a man who would appear to be as distant from the wider
currents of history and politics as the figure of Santa Claus himself.

The image is not particularly misleading, and it is not my intention
to dispel it. Still, Moore did have a real existence. He was born in 1779
(during the American Revolution) and died eighty-four years later, in 1863
(during the Civil War). And he fits perfectly the Knickerbocker mold:
High Church Episcopalian, politically conservative, and quintessentially
upper-class. Moore's father was for thirty-five years Episcopal bishop of
the diocese of New York, and Moore himself, though a layman, was an active and influential figure in the Church. (In fact, Moore held his professorship in a seminary that he himself had helped to establish.)

Moore was also conservative. His parents and grandparents had
been closet Tories during the American Revolution—and open Federal-
ists afterward. Moore's own brand of conservatism took the form of an
agrarian paternalism not far removed from that of a wealthy Virginia
planter of the same generation. As a young man, Clement Moore himself
published a series of tracts attacking both Jeffersonian radicalism and

urban commerce, and to the end of his life he remained suspicious of democracy and other "reforms." For example, in middle age he opposed the movement to abolish slavery. Indeed, at the time Moore wrote "A Visit from St. Nicholas," in 1822, he himself owned five slaves.[36]

Moore's ideology was well suited to his social position. He was an old-style country gentleman, a patrician man of leisure who inherited so much land (and the income it brought) that he never needed to take a job. Moore accepted his professorship when he was past 40, and for a token salary, in a seminary constructed on land he himself had donated for the purpose.[37] He inherited his mother's large Manhattan estate, originally located well to the north of New York City. The estate, which bore the name Chelsea, extended all the way from what is now Nineteenth Street to Twenty-fourth Street, and from Eighth to Tenth Avenue. (This estate has given its name to the present-day Chelsea district of the city, just north of Greenwich Village.)

But when Moore was a young man this area was isolated and pastoral.[38] John Pintard, who knew Moore well, wrote in 1830 that his Chelsea estate alone was worth $500,000. He also acknowledged Moore as his social superior, writing that even though he and Moore "have been always on the most friendly terms, . . . I have resisted all hospitalities when sitting in [his] elegantly furnished drawing room, for *he* is *wealthy*."[39]

Still, Moore's great wealth did not prove sufficient to insulate him from the pressures that transformed New York in the first decades of the nineteenth century. In 1811, as already noted, the New York City council approved a grid system of numbered streets and avenues that would crisscross the island above Fourteenth Street. By the time Moore wrote "A Visit from St. Nicholas," New York was expanding north through Chelsea itself. In fact, late in 1818 something called "Ninth Avenue" was dug right through the middle of his estate (the land having been taken from him by eminent domain).[40] The 1821 city directory lists Moore as residing, not at Chelsea, but near the corner of Ninth Avenue and Twenty-first Street.[41] Eleven years later, in 1832, John Pintard visited Chelsea and mused about the changes that had overtaken the neighborhood, filled now (as Pintard put it) with "streets that have become regularly built up . . . where, but a few years ago, all was open country. It really surprised me to notice a dense population and contiguous buildings in what only 10 years since was merely a sparse city."[42] By the 1850s the entire hill on which Moore's house stood had been leveled to make new land and bulkheads along the Hudson River waterfront, and Moore had built new homes for himself and his family.[43]

Moore was disturbed by the transformation of his city, and the cut-

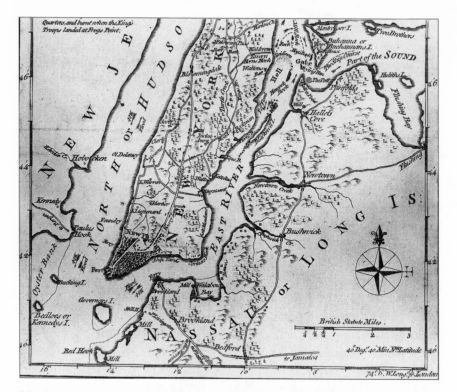

Manhattan in 1778. When this map was drawn, New York City occupied only the lower tip of Manhattan (the shaded area at the bottom). The rest of the island was rural. Halfway up the map, on the left, is an estate labeled "Clarke"—the property of Thomas Clarke, Moore's maternal grandfather. He called it Chelsea, after a district in London. *(Courtesy, American Antiquarian Society)*

ting-up of his estate. In 1818, the very year that his property was bisected by Ninth Avenue (and just four years before he wrote "A Visit from St. Nicholas"), Moore published a pamphlet that protested against the relentless development of New York. In it he expressed a fear that the city's beauty and tranquillity would be lost forever, and that its future was already in what he termed "destructive and ruthless hands," the hands of men who did not "respect the rights of property." City politics and policy were controlled by men Moore described as "mechanics and persons whose influence is principally among those classes of the community to whom it is indifferent what the eventual result of their industry may be to society." New York was being turned over to a conspiracy, and Moore named its members: "cartmen, carpenters, masons, pavers, and all their

Manhattan in 1831. Now Moore's Chelsea estate has been divided up into gridded urban terrain. Moore's property, located near the lower right-hand corner of the map, extended from Eighth Avenue to Tenth Avenue, between Eighteenth and Twenty-fourth streets. (Note that on this map the more usual north–south orientation has been reversed; the southern part of the island is at the top.) *(Courtesy, American Antiquarian Society)*

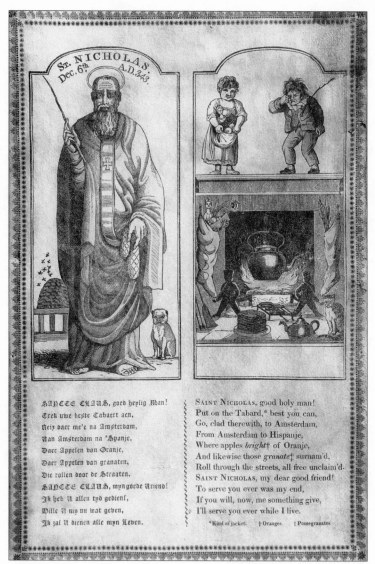

1810 **St. Nicholas.** The broadside that John Pintard commissioned at his own expense, executed by the noted illustrator Alexander Anderson. In the right-hand panel are two children: a pleased little girl who has received a present and a tearful little boy who has not (perhaps he has received a caning instead). John Pintard confirmed the reverential image in a short poem placed beneath the picture: a child's poem that begins with the words "Saint Nicholas, good holy man" and concludes: "Saint Nicholas, my dear good friend! / To serve you ever was my end. / If you will now, me, something give, / I'll serve you ever while I live." *(Courtesy, The New-York Historical Society)*

host of attendant laborers." Moore doubted that the city could (as he put it) be "save[d] from ruin." And he was pessimistic about the future of his class: "We know not the amount nor the extent of oppression which may yet be reserved for us."[44]

From St. Nicholas to Santa Claus

It was at this difficult juncture, in 1822, that Clement Clarke Moore wrote "A Visit from St. Nicholas." As we already know, Moore did not invent "the night before Christmas" out of whole cloth. In the distant background was the old Dutch ritual, and John Pintard and Washington Irving offered more immediate models. In addition, three other poems, two from 1810 and the third from 1821, would provide more materials—for example, Santa's sleigh and reindeer, and even the poetic meter that Moore would employ. Moore's own contributions may have been small, but they were crucial to the creation of a myth that suited the needs of his own Knickerbocker set—and that finally proved malleable enough to transcend those needs and to be appropriated by other groups of Americans. It is time to examine more closely the sources Moore had at his disposal.

First: Washington Irving. Yes, there *were* twenty-five references to St. Nicholas in *Knickerbocker's History*. But Irving represented St. Nicholas not as a figure who appeared during the Christmas season but rather in the way that John Pintard had originally introduced him to the New-York Historical Society—that is, as the mythic patron saint of New Amsterdam. Early in *Knickerbocker's History,* Irving wrote that "the great and good St. Nicholas . . . took . . . New Amsterdam under his peculiar patronage, and has ever since been . . . the titular saint of this excellent city." In this role St. Nicholas (he never actually appears, except once in a dream scene and, again, as the wooden figurehead on a ship) was essentially an amusing caricature of the old-time Dutch gentry who inhabited Irving's imaginary New Amsterdam: a genial yet obviously patrician saint, dressed in a broad hat and invariably smoking a long pipe.[45] (Moore would later pick that up, but with one difference.)

Next: The 1810 broadside picture that John Pintard commissioned—together with the verse that accompanied it—also influenced Moore; then the two anonymous poems, one from 1810 and the other from 1821. In all of these writings the pipe disappeared, and so did the satire, but St. Nicholas himself finally became a figure who distributed gifts to children during the Christmas season. Still, in all these sources the saint was very much a figure of majesty and authority—or at least of benevolent, kindly dignity. (The real St. Nicholas, if he existed at all, was an actual bishop, and in any case he was an official saint—the *real* patron saint of both Russia and Greece.) As a bishop, St. Nicholas was the direct representative of God and a figure of great authority as well as great charity. So it is not surprising that John Pintard would wish him to be represented in such a "serious" fashion in the broadside he commissioned, and not (as Washington Irving had irreverently done) as a humorous figure.

In this illustration (page 70) St. Nicholas has come not just to reward but also to punish. He is a figure of authority: We see him with his halo, ecclesiastical robes, and bishop's scepter. St. Nicholas retained that air of authority in a poem that appeared in a New York newspaper just two weeks after Pintard's broadside. This poem, essentially a longer, more elaborate version of Pintard's, opens in a similar fashion, with a child hailing St. Nicholas—this time not in awkward iambic but in a more tripping meter—in fact, the exact meter that Moore would employ twelve years later, anapestic tetrameter. It opens: "Oh good holy man! whom we Sancte Claus name, / The Nursery forever your praise shall proclaim." The poem goes on to catalogue the presents St. Nicholas might be expected to leave, followed by a "prayer" that St. Nicholas not come for the purpose of punishment ("[I]f in your hurry one thing you mislay, / Let that be the Rod— and oh! keep it away") And it concludes with a promise of future good behavior:

> Then holy St. Nicholas! all the year,
> Our books we will love and our parents revere,
> From naughty behavior we'll always refrain,
> In hopes that you'll come and reward us again.

The pattern of authority and judgment holds even in the poem that was Clement Moore's most immediate source. Published in 1821, only a year before Moore wrote "A Visit from St. Nicholas," this poem appeared as a little illustrated book called *The Children's Friend*. Here, for the first time, we even find St. Nicholas appearing not on December 6 but on Christmas Eve; and we also find him traveling on a sleigh that is pulled by a reindeer—a single reindeer. But he is still a bishop (a "child's bishop," perhaps), a figure who metes out punishments along with rewards, and whose visit is designed to inspire anxiety along with hope:

Old Santeclaus with much delight
His reindeer drives this frosty night,
O'er chimneytops, and tracks of snow,
To bring his yearly gifts to you.

The steady friend of virtuous youth,
The friend of duty, and of truth,
Each Christmas eve he joys to come
Where love and peace have made their home.

Through many houses he has been,
And various beds and stockings seen,
Some, white as snow, and neatly mended,
Others, that seem'd for pigs intended.

Where e'er I found good girls or boys,
That hated quarrels, strife and noise,
I left an apple, or a tart,
Or wooden gun, or painted cart;

To some I gave a pretty doll,
To some a peg-top, or a ball;
No crackers, cannons, squibs, or rockets,
To blow their eyes up, or their pockets.

No drums to stun their Mother's ear,
Nor swords to make their sisters fear;
But pretty books to store their mind.
With Knowledge of each various kind.

But where I found the children naughty,
In manners rude, in temper haughty,
Thankless to parents, liars, swearers,
Boxers, or cheats, or base tale-bearers,

I left a long, black, birchen rod,
Such, as the dread command of God
Directs a Parent's hand to use
When virtue's path his sons refuse.[46]

This kind of Christmas can be thought of as a mini-version of the Day of Judgment. Insofar as the history of gift-giving on St. Nicholas Day can be traced to Europe, it is this kind of judgmental ritual that seems to have been involved. It can be seen in a seventeenth-century painting, *St. Nicholas's Day,* by the Dutch painter Jan Steen, in which there appear both

The steady friend of virtuous youth,

The friend of duty, and of truth,

Each Christmas eve he joys to come

Where love and peace have made their home.

1821 St. Nicholas (from *The Children's Friend*). This St. Nicholas is more benevolent-looking than John Pintard's (and the label "Sante Claus" appears at the base of his hat), but he still holds a bishop's scepter. Each verse of this charming book was similarly accompanied by an illustration—in color. *(Courtesy, American Antiquarian Society)*

presents and punishments. Even today, something of this notion still lingers in the American celebration of Christmas, as, for example, in the song that begins "You'd better watch out . . . Santa Claus is coming to town," and continues: "He knows if you've been sleeping, he knows if you're awake; he knows if you've been bad or good—so be good for goodness' sake!"

To be sure, this kind of Christmas ritual was designed largely for children, while Judgment Day was for adults. Christmas took place once a year, Judgment Day once an eternity. The "judge" at Christmas was St. Nicholas; on Judgment Day it was God himself. And both the rewards and the punishments meted out on Christmas—a cookie on the one hand, or a birch rod on the other—were far less weighty than those of eternal joy or eternal damnation. But the parallel was always there, and always meant to be there. Christmas was a child's version of Judgment Day, and its ambiguous prospects of reward or punishment (like those of Judgment Day itself) were a means of regulating children's behavior—and preparing them for the greater judgment that was to come. Indeed, *The Children's*

Jan Steen, "Hes feest van Saint Nicholaas" (1666). Note the smiling little girl holding her present in the foreground and the tearful boy on the left—he is being mocked by the other children. The girl's present is a doll that represents one of the saints, which suggests that this prosperous family is Roman Catholic. The St. Nicholas ritual did not cross the Atlantic; one reason may have been that it was performed by Holland's Catholic community, while the Dutch immigration to New Netherlands was largely Protestant—and Dutch Protestants, much like the English Puritans, tried to suppress such practices as the celebration of saints' days (as well as the use of icons like the little girl's present). *(Courtesy, Rijksmuseum-Stichting, Amsterdam)*

Friend even speaks of the birch rod as a product of "the dread command of GOD."

FROM THE DAY OF DOOM TO THE NIGHT BEFORE CHRISTMAS

The threat of judgment was gone the next year, when Moore wrote "A Visit from St. Nicholas." Moore's St. Nicholas, as we all know, leaves only presents and goodwill, and he makes no threats—not even gentle ones. There is no warning of the birch rod, no hints about messy rooms or bad behavior. There is no stick to join the carrot. There is no little Day of Judgment. There is only a "happy Christmas to *all*."

This shift is all the more striking because the structure of "A Visit from St. Nicholas" (unlike that of its immediate sources) parallels the structure of a seventeenth-century American poem about the real Judgment Day. That poem, written by Massachusetts clergyman Michael Wigglesworth, was published in 1662 with the title "The Day of Doom." It was nearly as popular in its own time as "A Visit from St. Nicholas" is today, and it retained its popularity into the early nineteenth century.

Both poems begin with a scene in which people are sleeping serenely on a still night, dreaming of good things to come. It is "the night before Christmas" in the one case, "the evening before [Doomsday]" in the other:

Still was the night, Serene and
  Bright, when all Men sleeping lay;
Calm was the season, and carnal
  reason thought so 'twould last for
  ay.
Soul, take thine ease, let sorrow
  cease, much good thou hast in
  store:
This was their Song . . . the Evening
  before.

Virgins unwise . . . had closed their
  eyes . . .

Yea, and the wise through sloth and
  frailty slumbered.

'Twas the night before Christmas,
  when all through the house
Not a creature was stirring, not even
  a mouse;

The stockings were hung by the
  chimney with care,

In hopes that St. Nicholas soon
  would be there.

The children were nestled all snug in
  their beds,
While visions of sugarplums danced
  in their heads;
And mama in her 'kerchief, and I in
  my cap,
Had just settled our brains for a long
  winter's nap.

Then, suddenly, the slumbering calm is shattered by a sound that rouses the sleepers, causing them to leap out of bed and run to the window:

For at midnight brake forth a Light,
    which turn'd the night to day,
And speedily an hideous cry did all
    the world dismay.
Sinners awake, their hearts do ache,
    trembling their loins surprizeth;
Amazed with fear, by what they hear
    each one of them ariseth.

When out on the lawn there arose
    such a clatter,

They rush from Beds with giddy
    heads, and to their windows run,

I sprang from my bed to see what was
    the matter.
Away to the window I flew like a
    flash,
Tore open the shutters and threw up
    the sash.

At the window they witness the arrival through the air of an unexpected supernatural visitor, accompanied by other magical creatures:

Viewing this light, which shines
    more bright than doth the
    Noonday Sun.

Straightway appears (they see't with
    tears) the Son of God most dread;
Who with his Train comes on amain
    to Judge both Quick and Dead.

The moon, on the breast of the new-
    fallen snow,
Gave a luster of midday to objects
    below
When, what to my wondering eyes
    should appear,
But a miniature sleigh and eight tiny
    reindeer,
With a little old driver so lively and
    quick
I knew in a moment it must be St. Nick.

His winged Hosts flie through all
    coasts, together gathering
Both good and bad, both quick and
    dead, and all to Judgment bring.

More rapid than eagles his coursers
    they came,
And he whistled and shouted and
    called them by name. . . .

These parallels make the contrasts between the two poems all the more acute. In "The Day of Doom," the supernatural visitor has come as a pitiless judge; he causes everyone to come before his "throne," to separate those who can look forward to eternal happiness from those who are filled with the "dreadful expectation" of "endless pains and scalding flames." In "A Visit from St. Nicholas" he is a jolly fellow who reassures his startled company that they have "nothing to dread," and who departs from the house wishing happiness "*to all.*"

I am not sure whether Moore read "The Day of Doom." But so close are the parallels between the two poems that it is difficult to avoid speculating that the one was written with the other somewhere in mind. If so, then "The Day of Doom" constitutes another source of "A Visit from St. Nicholas."

What Moore has evoked, in any case, is Christmas without the prospect of judgment. Without such a prospect, St. Nicholas himself loses his authority—indeed, he loses his very identity as a bishop. And Moore's lengthy physical description of St. Nicholas reinforces the point (such a description is not to be found in any of Moore's sources, but here it takes up four of the poem's fourteen stanzas): Santa's eyes "twinkle," his cheeks are "rosy," his dimples "merry," his mouth is "droll," his figure "chubby and plump," his manner "jolly." He is tiny—the size of an "elf." His appearance and manner actually cause the narrator to laugh out loud "in spite of [him]self."

In every possible way, then, Moore's St. Nicholas has lost his authority, his majesty, even his patrician dignity. He carries no bishop's scepter. He is clothed not in a bishop's red robes (despite the illustrations we may recall from modern editions of the poem) but in ordinary fur. This St. Nicholas is no bishop at all. He has effectively been defrocked.

But not only has Moore defrocked St. Nicholas, he has *declassed* him, too. It is not only his authority that has vanished; his gentility is gone as well. Consider how St. Nicholas is pictured in the first illustrated edition of Moore's poem, dating from 1848 (and probably issued with Moore's approval). He looks like a plebeian, and that's also how he is described in the text. Remember that Moore says "he looked like a pedlar"—"a pedlar just opening his pack"—something, that is, between a beggar and a petty tradesman.

THE STUMP OF A PIPE

And he smokes "the stump of a pipe." Now, that little detail comes directly from Washington Irving—and from none of Moore's other sources. Irving invariably associated St. Nicholas with a pipe. But there was a difference: That pipe was always referred to as a *long* pipe (indeed, *flamboyantly* long—in Irving's word, a "mighty" pipe).

It is necessary to say something here about the history and politics of pipes, if only because Irving himself does so. Indeed, there is a chapter

Plebeian St. Nicholas. This illustration appeared in the first book-length edition of "A Visit from St. Nicholas," published in 1848 under Moore's name and almost certainly with his approval. *(Courtesy, American Antiquarian Society)*

in *Knickerbocker's History* that bears the title "Of the Pipe Plot." This chapter has nothing to do with St. Nicholas; what it deals with is the moment at which New Amsterdam (that is, New York) was transformed from a community characterized by "ease, tranquillity, and sobriety of deportment" into "a meddlesome and factious" city. Irving associated this transformation with the Jeffersonian revolution of 1800, the same political upheaval in which "the mob, since called the sovereign people . . . exhibited a strange desire of governing itself." What happened, Irving reported, was that the citizens of New York organized themselves, for the first time, into two opposing parties. The terms Irving chose to identify

Long and Short Pipes. This engraving, used as the
frontispiece to Irving's *Knickerbocker's History,* was drawn
by the well-known American artist Washington Allston.
The four men in front are gentlemen; three of them are
smoking long pipes. The plebeian tavern-keeper standing
at the far back is smoking a short pipe. *(Courtesy, American
Antiquarian Society)*

these parties are intriguing: "[T]he more wealthy and important . . .
formed a kind of aristocracy, which went by the appellation *Long Pipes,*
while the lower orders . . . were branded with the plebeian name of *Short
Pipes.*"[47]

Clearly, Irving was suggesting that short pipes were associated with
working-class radicalism in the early nineteenth century. Not surprisingly,
his suggestion seems to have been accurate. A recent paper delivered by a
historical archaeologist who has been studying artifacts from the board-

ing houses of the cotton mills in Lowell, Massachusetts, bears the improbable subtitle "Clay Pipes and Class Consciousness." It seems that by
the early nineteenth century, gentlemen smoked long pipes (some as
much as two feet in length) known as "aldermen" or "church wardens";
workers smoked short pipes (or "cuddies"). It was not from economic
necessity—that is, because short pipes happened to be cheaper—that
working-class men (and women) smoked them; rather, they did so as a
public gesture of class identity. In fact, the archaeological evidence (in the
form of numerous broken-off pipe stems) suggests that workers often
purchased longer pipes and then proceeded immediately, before smoking
them, to break off the stems. The evidence seems compelling: Few of the
broken-off stems recovered from the Lowell mills bear any telltale tooth
marks.[48] Workers *chose* to smoke "the stump of a pipe."

Which finally brings this excursion into literary history back into
connection with social history, and the analysis of genteel mythology into
connection with the social changes that helped to generate it. Remember
what was actually happening in the streets of early-nineteenth-century
New York during the Christmas season: the presence there of marauding
bands of revelers who threatened peace and property, whose revelry often
turned into riot, who used this annual opportunity to reclaim for themselves (if only symbolically) the fashionable residential territory that had
recently become the private preserve of the well-to-do. Remember the example of John Pintard's unsettling experience on New Year's Eve in 1821,
when he was kept awake until dawn by the noise of a callithumpian band
that stayed outside his door. Remember Clement Clarke Moore's own
anxiety, during the same period, over the slicing up of his pastoral estate
into city streets for rapid development, the result of a plebeian conspiracy
of artisans and laborers. Remember that Moore wrote "A Visit from St.
Nicholas" in 1822, when the streets had just been dug and the development
begun.

Viewed from this angle, there is something resonant about the
choices Moore made in writing his little poem. And especially about his
decision to both "defrock" St. Nicholas and "declass" him, to take away his
clerical authority and his patrician manner, and to represent him instead
as a "plebeian." Moore's decision meant that his St. Nick resembles, after
all, the kind of man who *might* have come to visit a wealthy New York patrician on Christmas Eve—to startle him out of his slumber with a loud
"clatter" outside his door, perhaps even to enter his house, uninvited and
unannounced.

But there was one dramatic difference: The working-class visitor feared by the patrician would come in a different way, for a different purpose. Such a visitor would have inhabited that murky ground between old-style village wassailing and the new urban political violence. He would have been youthful and full-sized, not a tiny "old elf." He would very likely have been part of a roving gang (perhaps a callithumpian band), not a single individual. He would have come to make all the noise he could rather than to speak "not a word"; to *demand* satisfaction, not to *give* it; to harass or threaten his host, not to *reassure* him that he "had nothing to dread." And, if he had finally departed in a genial spirit, wishing (in familiar wassail fashion) a "happy Christmas to all, and to all a good night," it would have been because he had *received* satisfaction, not because he had *offered* it.

By contrast, the household visitor Moore portrays has come neither to threaten his genteel host nor to make any demands on his generosity. The narrator of "A Visit from St. Nicholas" is openly fearful when St. Nicholas first appears, but his fears have been assuaged by the time St. Nicholas departs.

There is another real-life variation on this theme. The houses and shops of well-to-do men in large urban centers were guarded, as we have seen, by night watchmen, a kind of private police force. As it happens, these watchmen, like other menial workers of the period, took the Christmas season as a time to ask their wealthy patrons for tips. We know this because the watchmen's ritual sometimes took the form of a printed broadside (much like the carriers' addresses discussed in Chapter 1). A few of these broadsides—watchman's addresses, as they were known—have survived. All of them remind their wealthy readers of the sense of security their nocturnal vigilance has managed to provide, and all go on to beg a reward for their efforts. A particularly resonant watchman's address was circulated in 1829 by the watchmen of the Philadelphia suburb of Southwark. Headed "Southwark Watchman's Address for Christmas Day," it went in part like this:

> . . . [W]hile you're reposing in sleep's fond embrace,
> Upon your rich soft downy bed,
> The Watchman, who's one of your own fellow race,
> Sees clouds gathering thick o'er his head.
>
> This doth not affright him, his pathway is clear,
> To serve you, he's ne'er seen to stray;
> To shield you from danger, and guard you from fear,
> Propels him alone on his way. . . .

Watchman. The watchman is guarding a fenced-in New York estate at night. This illustration appeared in *Cries of New-York,* published in 1822, the same year that Clement Moore wrote "A Visit from St. Nicholas," and was the work of Alexander Anderson, the illustrator who also executed John Pintard's 1810 St. Nicholas broadside. *(Courtesy, American Antiquarian Society)*

> The *ruffian* at midnight is drove from your door,
> By the watch that is faithful and true;
> And this keeps in safety your house and your store;
> To him, then, is gratitude due.

Here the watchman has reminded his patrons that he is protecting them in their "rich soft downy bed"—protecting them, indeed, from the "ruffian" who tries to enter in the middle of the night (and in the context of the Christmas season it is surely significant that the watchman has chosen to speak of a "ruffian" and not of a thief). He shields his prosperous patrons from danger and fear, to be sure. But he also makes demands of his own, demands that take the classic form of a wassail:

> Now to close, he wishes you health, to fare well;
> And your mite from him hope you won't spare.[49]

On such occasions the watchman in effect turned the tables on his ordinary role, symbolically becoming the very personage from whom he is supposed to offer protection. As with any wassail there was always a veiled edge of threat behind the good wishes—and in this instance a miserly patron would surely be risking far more than a wet newspaper!

But if "A Visit from St. Nicholas" spoke to the physical *fears* of its upper-class readers, it also addressed their moral *guilt*. What it suggested was that Santa Claus was one Christmas visitor to whom the patron owed no obligations, not even tips. This visitor asks for nothing, and by implication his host owes him nothing—an important point, if one is willing to believe that even as late as the 1820s many patrician New Yorkers still felt a strong, if inchoate, obligation to be generous to the poor during the emotionally resonant holiday season.

If Moore's upper-class readers were to be comfortable at Christmastime, they needed to have at their disposal a class of dependents whose palpable expressions of goodwill would assure them that they had fulfilled their obligations after all. They did this in part by substituting their own children for the needy and homeless outside their household. In that way, as we have seen, they managed to preserve the *structure* of an older Christmas ritual, in which people occupying positions of social and economic authority offered gifts to their dependents. The children in their own households had replaced the poor outside it as the symbolic objects of charity and deference, and the gratitude those children displayed at present-opening time was a re-creation of the old Christmas exchange— gifts for goodwill. The ritual of social inversion was still there, but it now remained securely within the household.

Still, that change could easily have been implemented without transforming St. Nicholas from a bishop and a patrician into a plebeian (indeed, it could have been achieved without introducing St. Nicholas into the picture at all). By representing him as a plebeian, Moore allowed something else to happen, and it's a fascinating transformation. Without losing his role as the bringer of gifts, St. Nicholas has taken on an additional function: that of a grateful, nonthreatening old-style dependent. In the first of these roles (as gift-bringer), St. Nicholas is purely imaginary— a fiction devised for children, a private joke among adults (more about that in a moment). In the second role (as grateful dependent), he is imaginary in a different way, and only in part—a fiction devised for adults, and hardly as a joke; and imaginary only to the degree that, say, the old Dutch yeomanry nostalgically described by Washington Irving in "Rip Van Winkle" or *Knickerbocker's History* were imaginary, or the loyal peasants that Irving presented in his "Bracebridge Hall" stories. Like those fictional characters, Moore's St. Nicholas may not have existed; but (in this second role) he, too, was based on a real-life prototype that meant a great deal to the upper-class New Yorkers who very much wished to believe that he did still exist.

In this way, Moore managed to evoke what had eluded his fellow Knickerbockers, Washington Irving and John Pintard, in their own efforts to recapture the spirit of Christmas past: that is, the integration of the social classes in a scene of shared festivity where the poor posed no threat and gratefully accepted their place. Moore did this by replacing the cheerful poor of cherished memory not just with the children of the household but also with the magical figure of St. Nicholas himself. With this tricky maneuver Moore managed to transform what had been merely archaic and sentimental (and also patronizing to the poor) into something that can be called mythic.

In order to negotiate that transformation, to create that myth, Moore had to make the two simple yet crucial changes I have described: He had to present St. Nicholas as a figure who would evoke in his hearers and readers a working-class image (and not a patrician one) and also as a figure who would act the patrician's part (and not the worker's). He had to present St. Nicholas in the *role* of a bishop, but without a bishop's authority to stand in judgment. In short, Moore had to present St. Nicholas as both a bishop and a worker—but without either the power of the one or the animosity of the other.

He had to devote fully one-third of his poem to offering the reassurance that the people who received visits from this figure of the night would have "nothing to dread." St. Nicholas first offers that reassurance by giving "a wink of his eye and a twist of his head." And a little later, when he has filled all the stockings and is about to depart, he turns abruptly to face the narrator—the head of the household, or, in other words, us, the reader—and places his finger "aside of his nose." This is a meaningless phrase today, but in the late eighteenth and early nineteenth century the gesture seems to have represented the equivalent of a secret wink—a visual way of saying something like "Shh! I'm only kidding" or "Let's keep it between the two of us."[50] In the illustration on page 80, the man seated on the left is making this very gesture to the man on the right, who is laughing so hard at the other man's joke that he has dropped his long pipe. In fact, the source of Santa's gesture in "A Visit from St. Nicholas" was a passage in Irving's *Knickerbocker's History,* a passage in which St. Nicholas appears in a dream to a character named Van Kortland. The dream concludes with these words: "And when St. Nicholas had smoked his pipe, he twisted it in his hat-band, and *laying his finger beside his nose,* gave the astonished Van Kortland *a very significant look,* then, mounting his wagon, he returned over the tree-tops and disappeared" [italics added]. Since Moore was obviously alluding to this very passage, St. Nicholas' gesture in his poem, too, can be understood as a signal to the narrator (and to all *adult* readers of the poem): *This is all a dream.* As if to say: "*We* know I don't exist, but let's keep *that* between you and me!"

1863 Santa. In this, the first of many pictures of Santa Claus drawn by noted American cartoonist Thomas Nast, Santa still looks rather plebeian, and he is smoking a short pipe. *(Courtesy, Harvard College Library)*

1881 Santa. Thomas Nast drew this, his most famous Santa Claus picture, in 1881. Now Santa is holding a very long pipe, and he has grown fat and avuncular—imagine this Santa trying to fit into a chimney! This is pretty much the way Santa Claus has remained to the present day. *(Courtesy, Harvard College Library)*

BACK TO THE FUTURE

All a dream. For the upper-class New Yorkers who collectively "invented" Christmas, Moore's quiet little achievement was especially resonant. It offered a Christmas scenario that took a familiar ritual (the exchange of generosity for goodwill) and transfigured it with a symbolic promise to release them from both the fear of harm and the pressure of guilt. A generation earlier, one might argue, the parents of these men were sufficiently in control of their social world not to require such a catharsis. A generation later their children were sufficiently purged of a sense of direct social obligation not to require it any longer.

By then, in any case, "A Visit from St. Nicholas" would be taking on new meanings. Santa Claus himself would lose his plebeian character as time passed, and as the poem (and the new kind of holiday it helped create) was taken over by the middle classes and even by the poor themselves. In the years to come, even the visual image of Santa Claus would change. Still "plebeian" in the 1840s, Santa and his "team" soon cease to be portrayed as a miniature ("eight tiny reindeer," a "miniature sleigh," and a "jolly old elf"). He becomes full-sized, even large. His beard turns into the full gray beard of the late-Victorian bourgeoisie. He appears increasingly avuncular. And, in the hands of Thomas Nast, the famous cartoonist who was responsible for much of this change, over a period of eighteen years even his pipe grows long once again. Still, for all these changes, Santa Claus recovers none of the episcopal dignity that Clement Moore took from him in 1822. Between being a jolly plebeian elf and a jolly fat uncle, the real St. Nicholas would surely have found it difficult to choose.

The versatile saint would be put to other uses, too. The late nineteenth century was a period of vexing religious doubt for many middle-class Americans, and one characteristic solution was to think that God must exist simply because people so badly needed Him to; without God, human life would be simply unendurable. It should not be too surprising that this rather elegiac Victorian argument came to be applied to Santa Claus as well: In 1897, in reply to an inquiry posed by a young reader whose "little friends" had told her that Santa Claus did not exist, the *New York Sun* printed what was destined to become a classic editorial. "Yes, Virginia, there is a Santa Claus," the editorial began. It was written by the newspaper's religious-affairs reporter, and its language and tone self-consciously mirror that of late-Victorian popular theology. "Virginia, your little friends are wrong," the reporter insisted, explaining that "[t]hey have been affected by the skepticism of a skeptical age." And he went on to stake out terrain that many of his adult readers would have found familiar from sermons they heard in church: "Alas! how dreary would be the world if there were no Santa Claus," the reporter argued. "There would be no childlike faith then, no poetry, no romance to make tolerable this existence." And he concluded: "No Santa Claus? Thank God, he lives and he lives forever."[51]

CLEMENT MOORE WROTE "A Visit from St. Nicholas" on what might be called the cusp of his life. The expansion of New York affected him in a direct way, breaking up his estate into city blocks. Before around 1820 he viewed this change as a threat, and protested it accordingly. But thereafter Moore adopted a different strategy. He stopped protesting the new conditions and began instead to protect his economic and social position by systematically controlling the development of the Chelsea district. As early as 1818, he donated an entire city block adjacent to his own house for the construction of an Episcopal theological seminary (the institution in which he later became a professor of Hebrew and ancient languages). And he gave another large parcel for a new and very elegant

Episcopal church, St. Peter's.[52] By doing this, Moore was able to protect the value of his remaining holdings in Chelsea. And during the following years he consciously controlled the development of those holdings, by leasing lots rather than selling them and by including restrictive covenants in the deeds he gave to builders.[53] Under Moore's careful direction, Chelsea became for a time a fashionable district, an oasis of respectability on New York's West Side.

As a great Manhattan landowner, Clement Moore played a part in the emergence of a new urban landscape, a landscape that stratified and segregated the city by wealth and class, and in which housing itself became a commodity.[54] What I have tried to suggest in this chapter is less easy to prove: that Moore helped to bring about a parallel change on the American cultural landscape, in the role for which he is best known to most Americans today—as the poet of Christmas Eve. If such a reading is correct, it was *that* which constituted his most important contribution to the history of American capitalism.

Chapter 3

The Parlor and the Street

The Battle for Santa Claus
Santa Claus and Alcohol in New York

*D*URING THE 1822 Christmas season, the very season during which Clement Moore was writing "A Visit from St. Nicholas," a New York newspaper editor proposed that one aspect of the local holiday celebration be reformed. As we have seen from the experience of John Pintard, many respectable New York men during the 1820s spent part of their New Year's Day in paying visits to the homes of their circle of acquaintances. There they were received by the women of the household, who were expected to serve them food and drink—alcoholic drink. For example, that same season another New York newspaper published without comment a notice from an anonymous group of "unmarried gentlemen," noting their expectation that the ladies they visited would serve them "large quantities of cake and wine, rum jelly and hot punch."[1]

The reforming editor, a Federalist named William Leete Stone, called for a stop to the serving of alcohol in the course of these New Year's Day visits. "A cup of good coffee" would be an "excellent substitute," he suggested, a token of hospitality that would serve to "tranquilize the excesses of the young."[2]

Stone's suggestion met with a barrage of public ridicule. (This was several years before the emergence of a temperance movement in the

United States.) One man—he did not provide his name but identified himself as a former sheriff of the county—wrote an especially pointed rejoinder. This sheriff embroidered a lengthy account of his usual sequence of visits, visits to homes where he had always counted on being greeted with "gaiety and hospitality"—but at every stop he was now greeted only with a cup of coffee. When he declined one such offer by telling his hostess that he had " 'breakfasted already,' " he was told that " 'this is not intended as breakfast—Mr. Stone, of the Commercial, recommends coffee as a substitute for wine or cordial.' " And so it went throughout the morning. " 'Oh, sir,' " said one of his hostesses, " ' 'tis all the rage now—wine and cordial heat the blood, while coffee warms and stimulates without producing deleterious effects.' 'So it does, ma'am, at breakfast, but at this hour I would prefer a glass of raspberry [cordial] and a cooky, vulgar as it may appear.' " Even at the house of a good friend, a house "where gaiety and hospitality were ever united," the sheriff encountered only "a neat gilt china cup, filled with coffee, presented to me by a beautiful young lady." " 'Surely you will not refuse any thing I offer you,' said the lady, with a bewitching smile, and with some tenderness in it. . . ." When he continued to protest, she added: " 'But, sir, 'tis recommended in the newspapers by Mr. Stone.' . . ."

At last the sheriff gave up and decided instead "to visit some of the Hotels—the landlords having thrown open their doors with their usual hospitality." At one of these—"our old friend Niblo's"—there was, "as usual, good fare and a hearty welcome." Another hotelier provided "such a display of wines and delicacies [as] has never been surpassed in this city." At length the sheriff entered a third hotel, and there he encountered an unexpected guest: "[W]ho should I see seated at the table, and up to his elbows in good things, but my coffee-drinking friend Stone." The sheriff looked around the table, "and thank heaven not a cup of coffee was to be seen. Stone was so intent on eating cold round [of beef] and turkey, and washing it down with large draughts of old Madeira, that he saw nobody, and if it had not been cruel to have check'd this terminal gratification of his appetite, I certainly should have been tempted to have gone up to him, and said, 'Stone, how are you off for coffee?' "

The sheriff took pains to show that he knew all about holiday rowdiness, too, and that it did not bother him very much. Indeed, he wrote with more affection than anger about the antics of working-class men on New Year's Eve. Such behavior was nothing more than part of the standard "ceremonies and jolifications [*sic*]" of the occasion. It was hardly surprising that those New Yorkers sometimes chose to go on "what they called a spree." Some of them "went forth with bands of music to serenade their friends, but the most mischievous amused themselves by knocking on doors, displacing signs, knocking down the watchmen, firing crackers and pistols, and snow balling the frail fair ones of the city. . . ." About twenty of the revelers were jailed for the night, but even incarceration failed to dampen their spirits: In the jailhouse itself "[t]hey snapped their fingers, danced waltzes, whistled loud and shrill, and sang glees and catches." Nor did the magistrate who tried their case early the next morning seem troubled by their offenses, for, as the sheriff concluded, "in consideration of the day, [he] discharged them all, with suitable admonitions, and without requiring any fees [i.e., fines]."

It was an interesting account. The sheriff presented himself as a man who reached easily across class lines and was equally at ease in the drawing room of a "splendid mansion," a boisterous public house, and even a jail. Actually, the only people who seemed to bother him were reformers (like Colonel Stone) and fashionable women. In that sense, his little story is about gender and class. Women are the purveyors of fashion who portend the decline of real hospitality in the form of good food and drink; the sheriff must go to a "public house" (run and attended by men) in order to eat and drink properly. He takes pains to let his readers know that he is not bothered by working-class drinking and rowdiness. The real social threat (however humorously it is posed) comes from emerging middle-class reforms, represented by Stone's editorial appeal for coffee instead of alcohol—and it is *women* who read and act on this advice, turning even the homes of old friends into cold comfort. (As the decades passed and the temperance movement emerged and spread, other newspaper editors tried to rally women to the antidrinking cause. Almost every New Year's during the 1840s, for example, Horace Greeley used his paper, the *New York Tribune,* to persuade women to remove alcohol from their tables.)

Resistance to the reform of the Christmas season thus came from above as well as below. Men of a similar stripe to the sheriff actually tried to claim Santa Claus himself as an ally in the cause of old-fashioned hospitality. Two years earlier, in 1820, a New York newspaper printed a poem about Santa in which the "good St. Nicholas" had "just come from Amsterdam / To give the New-years maids their cakes, / And Pinester lads their drams." The poem then proceeded to address the "lads" directly:

> Much to this Saint you owe
> For eggs, and nuts, and pies, and crulls,
> And whyskey's jovial flow.[3]

Nor was this all. On January 4, 1828 (five years after Clement Clarke Moore had written "A Visit from St. Nicholas," and during the very Christmas season in which his poem began to be widely printed in newspapers around the nation), at least two New York newspapers printed another poem, this one bearing the title "Ode to Saint Claas, Written on New Year's Eve."[4] The author of this 1828 poem signed himself "Rip Van Dam" (a sure indication that he was *not* of Dutch ancestry) and insisted, in an introductory note, that he had written his poem only because, "[s]o far as I know, nothing in the way of honourable commendation hath been sung in this city of honest Dutch Burghers, to the thrice-blessed Saint Nicholaas—the saint of all saints, and king of good fellows." That claim may have been a dig at Moore's poem, because the figure of "Saint Claas" he presented—"king of good fellows"—was a far cry from Moore's. To be sure, "Rip Van Dam's" figure is chubby and jolly, and he, too, "fills every stocking" with little treats: "Apples, and nuts, and sugar-plums, / Grateful to little urchin's gums . . . new suits for girls and boys, / Pretty books and prettier toys."

But that was not all *this* St. Nicholas brought. The very next verse promised other treats of a very different order: "Mull'd cider, cherry bounce, [and] spic'd rum, / Jolly Saint, O hither come!" And the poet went on to fantasize about joining Santa in a drunken orgy:

> Come then with thy merry eye,
> And let us bouse it [i.e., *booze it*] till we die!
> Come and o'er my thirsty soul
> Floods of smoking glasses roll!

This Santa Claus was an "imp" who would "frisk about" and encourage his charges (no doubt emboldened by drink) to dance and perform "merry pranks." (Only one such "prank" is named, but it suggests what this writer had in mind: "[M]aidens" would approach their male companions to "seek" a "kiss.") This Santa Claus was no other than the Lord of Misrule, master of the Christmas carnival:

> A little short, thick, lusty, "whoreson,"* rover,
> Rolling about the room full half seas over.[5]

---

* The term *whoreson* meant "bastard" (or "coarse fellow") but, as here, it could be used affectionately between men, as for example, in the modern usage "you old bastard."

"Rip Van Dam" himself acknowledged that this lusty and drunken "whoreson" of a Santa was on the way out, a figure of the past, merely a nostalgic symbol. "Fashions" were changing, he lamented:

> And all the good of olden times
> Is lost, save in old fashioned rhymes;
> While cold hard-hearted revelry
> Usurps the place of heartfelt glee. . . .

Only a faithful few had kept to the old traditions:

> Though good old customs long have flown,
> And few *thy* honest sway will own,
> Still will I bow the reverent knee,
> And shout Saint Claas, all hail to thee!

Of course, it was Clement Moore and not "Rip Van Dam" whose representation of Santa Claus carried the day. Nor, given the new patterns of holiday violence, should that be surprising. Indeed, the very day that the "Ode to St. Claas" appeared, the same newspaper carried a shocked report about an especially violent callithumpian New Year's Eve parade in which more than a thousand "persons of all ages" marched down "many of the principal streets of the city" committing "outrageous" acts. The mob

> moved from one end of the city to the other, making the most hideous noises, committing many excesses, and for several hours in succession, disturbing neighborhoods where they thought proper to become in some measure stationary, to such a degree that sleep and rest, for the sick or for the well, were entirely destroyed. No nocturnal tumult or disturbance that we have ever witnessed, was in any measure equal to this. We understand that wherever the watch offered to interfere for the purpose of preventing mischief, they were either overpowered, or intimidated by numbers, and the mob had undisputed possession of the streets until a very late hour in the night.

The newspaper demanded that the authorities take aggressive action to prevent any recurrence of such "outrages." And it asserted that alcohol was the proximate cause: "Such a multitude of persons, assembled together for an unlawful purpose, when maddened with liquor, and conscious of their force, will, after a very few more experiments, be guilty of the greatest atrocities." Most important of all, the account concluded, the public should not dismiss these events by viewing them through the lens of seasonal ritual, as high jinks that had to be tolerated. "It is in vain to wink at such excesses, merely because they occur at a season of festivity. A license of this description will soon turn festivals of joy, into regular periods of fear to the inhabitants, and will end in scenes of riot, intemperance, and bloodshed." What had taken place was not a matter of letting off steam at Christmas; it was a criminal mob, and—here the editor hinted at the presence of underlying economic issues—a mob not only "stimulated by drink" but also "enkindled by resentment." Left to itself, it would soon commit "the most outrageous offenses without reflection, and without remorse."[6]

Remember that this report appeared in the same newspaper that simultaneously printed "Rip Van Dam's" ode to the drinking Santa Claus. But by now an alternative was beginning to emerge. The other newspaper that printed Van Dam's poem that year also began to deal with Christmas in a new way, as a family holiday. (In previous years that paper had casually printed verses about Christmas revelry.) The paper published two holiday items in its December 28, 1827, issue: an editorial that termed Christmas "a festival sacred to domestic enjoyments" and a reprint of a passage from Washington Irving's "Bracebridge Hall" sketches that described how Christmas evoked "the pure element of domestic felicity."[7] And the following year, in 1828, the same paper carried an account of the Christmas celebration in New York, an account that stressed sobriety, and associated it with Santa Claus himself: " 'Merry Christmas' was celebrated yesterday joyously and *soberly* in our goodly Dutch city," this account began. But it continued by acknowledging that New York was "Dutch no longer" and had become a multiethnic city with "new houses and new names." Even so, the report insisted, the ancient Dutch Christmas traditions had managed to remain in place among the new immigrant groups: "[T]he olden festivities retain their hold, and the good St. Nicholas is adopted into the calendar of all the nations that congregate in this, his faithful city; and makes glad the hearts of merry urchins of the various tongues and kindreds that now call New-York—*home.*"[8]

It is no coincidence that the previous year's callithumpian riot had been perpetrated largely by immigrants. It is no coincidence that the editor now chose to associate the Santa Claus ritual with a "sober" Christmas, and made that ritual serve as an instrument of cultural assimilation for "the various tongues and kindreds that now call New-York—*home.*" It is no coincidence that the same newspaper had previously recognized that heavy drinking was an integral part of the holiday season, and that in 1829 it would demand that alcohol be eliminated. It is no coincidence, in short, that Clement Clarke Moore's Santa Claus beat out Rip Van Dam's.

This is not to say that the rowdy Christmas season simply disappeared or even diminished. A domestic Santa Claus did not obliterate
other modes of celebrating the holiday (indeed, it still has not). On New
Year's Eve, 1839–40, one ailing visitor to the city was kept awake by "revelers, making frightful noises." This visitor, Eliza Follen, reported that the
lights in her sickroom "attracted the attention of some rioters in the street;
they stopped under the window and screamed 'Happy New Year!' with
what seemed to me the voices of fiends, the sound was so frightful."[9] For
that matter, a domestic Santa Claus did not wholly extinguish other versions of St. Nicholas himself. Just a week before Follen's unpleasant experience, a New York theater advertised a Christmas-night performance of
a "new pantomime got up for the occasion, called 'Santiclaus, or the orgies
of St. Nicholas.' "[10]

To read the city's newspapers at mid-century is to encounter upbeat
editorials about Christmas shopping and the joyous expectations of children juxtaposed with unsettling reports of holiday drunkenness and rioting. A couple of examples will tell the story. On December 26, 1840, a
party of German-Americans (they were "engaged in fiddling, dancing,
and making night hideous with their discordant din") engaged in a serious street battle with the police in which twenty-five people were arrested.
But on the same day, the paper announced that "the holidays are at
hand—the merry days to which childhood and youth look forward
throughout the year with such anticipation and delight. . . ." The "holidays," as this report defined them, were domestic and child-centered:
"*Santiclaus* is about making his annual visit to our world-renowned Dutch
city." And the holidays were commercial: "[T]he display of all sorts of
presents is striking," the paper boasted. "The various shops and establishments, whose special province it is to minister to the supply of Christmas
wants, exhibit no lack of accustomed temptations."

In 1839 the *New York Herald* made it clear that this was the only decent choice: "Let all avoid taverns and grog shops for a few days at least,
and spend their money at home." In that way men would be sure "to make
glad upon one day, the domestic hearth, the virtuous wife, the innocent,
smiling, merry-hearted children, and the blessed mother." "Christmas,"
the editorial concluded, "is the most hallowed season of the whole year."[11]

Not for everyone. In 1848 George Templeton Strong was able to note
casually that Christmas was "essentially an indoor and domestic festival,"
but when he took an omnibus to go shopping that same day, he noted that
"[t]he driver was drunk and the progress of the vehicle was like that of a
hippopotamus."[12] Two years later, with accounts of Santa Claus and

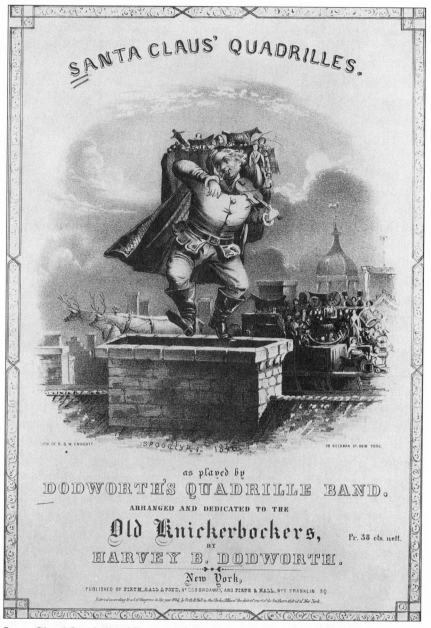

Santa Claus' Quadrilles. The cover to a piece of sheet music published in
New York in 1846. This Santa Claus is beardless and youthful, apparently a merry
bachelor. He is playing the fiddle as he dances on a New York chimneytop.
(The picture was drawn by an artist who went by the name "Spoodlyks.")
(Courtesy, American Antiquarian Society)

Christmas shopping plastered lavishly throughout the pages of the *Tribune,* gangs of youths were still roaming the streets at Christmas, making trouble wherever they went. By this time the gangs even had names, such as "[t]he Short Boys, Swill Boys, Rock Boys, Old Maid Boys, Holy Ch—s, and other bands of midnight prowlers [who] should have been in state prison long ago."[13] New Year's Eve, 1851–52, was ushered into the city by what the *Tribune* termed "a Saturnalia of discord, by Callithumpian and Cowbellian bands, by musketry and fire-crackers, by bacchanal songs and noisy revels, which for two hours after midnight made sleep not a thing to be dreamed of." One man was arrested "for entering, uninvited, the house of Philip Herring, during his absence, and insulting his wife." And a group of about 150 men (most of them apparently Irish, and all of them drunk) invaded a fashionable Broadway restaurant and systematically destroyed the furniture, threw food and dishes around the place, and finally (before the police arrived) assaulted the owner, his wife, and their staff. All in all, upwards of one hundred men were arrested that night "for entering residences in which they never were before, and where they knew not a soul, and after eating and drinking without molestation to their hearts' content, maliciously breaking decanters, dishes, scattering the provisions about the premises, and not content with that, in many instances breaking windows, doors, and behaving more like fiends than like men."[14]

At the heart of all this disorder, the *Tribune* reiterated, was the prevalence of alcohol during the Christmas season: "In the Eleventh Ward an unusual number of men were arrested for drunkenness, creating a mob, exciting a riot, insulting females, and other offenses to which men of low breeding, when intoxicated, are addicted." Such behavior was abetted by certain business establishments; local bars actually served drinks gratis on Christmas Day, in a holdover from the old English custom demanded of innkeepers (which was itself a variant of the tradition by which the gentry held "open house" for their dependents). The results, Horace Greeley reported, were obnoxious:

> The first flash of morning discovered the liquor shops in full operation, with wassail bowls of smoking punch, and "medicine" of all sorts, free as water. This dangerous and wicked temptation was the means of setting a great many *young men and boys* in a state of crazy intoxication long before noon. As early as 10 o'clock we saw, in Broadway, between the Park and Broome-st., about a dozen parties of boys, each numbering from four to ten persons, nearly every one

grossly drunk, and four fellows, in as many parties, entirely helpless, and being dragged along by neck and heels by their hardly less drunk companions.[15]

What had changed, then, was not that the rowdier ways of celebrating Christmas had disappeared, or even that they had diminished, but that a new kind of holiday celebration, domestic and child-centered, had been fashioned and was now being claimed as the "real" Christmas.[16] The rest of it—public drunkenness and threats or acts of violence, "rough music"—had been redefined as *crime*, "making night hideous." In part, this was accomplished through institutional means (in 1828 New York introduced a professional police force to replace the private "watch" that had failed to control the previous year's callithumpian riot). And in part it was accomplished through the manipulation of language itself. Henceforth, newspaper stories about Santa Claus would appear under the heading "Christmas," while stories about callithumpian activities would be relegated to the police column. In the terminology of a later age, those activities would be *marginalized*.

Belsnickles and Burlesquers in Philadelphia

Santa Claus came to Pennsylvania, too, in the 1820s. But there he encountered a rival figure, a somewhat scarier personage associated with the Germanic culture that pervaded much of the state. That figure, whose features are already familiar to us, was commonly known as the Belsnickle. (The term is a variant of the German phrase *Pelz-nickle*—that is, "St. Nicholas in Fur.") I do not know when or how the term was first used (it may not have come into usage until the 1820s, when Santa Claus himself was emerging). But it was almost certainly based on an older German figure, commonly known as Knecht Ruprecht (that is, "Rupert the Servant"). The British writer Samuel Taylor Coleridge encountered Knecht Ruprecht during a 1798 visit to Ratzeburg, a village in the northern part of Germany. Knecht Ruprecht was a man outfitted in "high buskins, a white robe, a mask, and an enormous flax wig"—in other words, he was burlesquing the dress of a gentleman. On Christmas night this figure

goes round to every house and says, that Jesus Christ his master sent him thither—the parents and elder children receive him with great pomp of reverence, while the little ones are most terribly frightened—He then enquires for the children, and according to the character which he hears from the parent, he gives them the intended present as if they came out of heaven from Jesus Christ.—Or, if they should have been bad children, he gives the parents a rod, and in the name of his master recommends them to use it frequently.[17]

In contrast to Santa Claus, who was never actually seen, the roles of both Knecht Ruprecht and the Belsnickle were performed by real people—generally men of the lower orders, who went around town in disguise. (The disguises varied, but they were always ornate and often involved wearing a wig.)

What Coleridge encountered resembles only the most carefully regulated form this practice took in Pennsylvania. Here the Belsnickle would offer small gifts (usually of food) to good children and intimidate ill-behaved children by threatening to hit them (or actually doing so) with a rod or a whip as they reached for the gifts he had brought. A Philadelphia newspaper reported one such appearance in 1827—by which time the Belsnickle was already being compared to Santa Claus. It is interesting to note that this Belsnickle was made up in blackface:

> Mr. Bellschniggle is a visible personage. . . . He is the precursor of the jolly old elf "Christkindle," or "St. Nicholas," and makes his personal appearance, dressed in skins or old clothes, his face black, a bell, a whip, and a pocket full of cakes or nuts; and either the cakes or the whip are bestowed upon those around, as may seem meet to his sable majesty.[18]

In this form the Belsnickle, although an intruder, would serve to reinforce the authority of the householders he visited. (Indeed, at least one father assumed the role himself.[19]) But it is clear that Belsnickling, like most rituals, was profoundly malleable. The Belsnickle might snap his whip at a child who had behaved well, or a whole group of Belsnickles might visit a house together. Often the Belsnickle frightened the parents as well as the children.[20]

In fact, Belsnickles frequently struck those they visited as unsavory (perhaps because they were frequently played by men of the lower orders). James L. Morris, a shopkeeper from Morgantown, Pennsylvania, described them in his diary in 1831 as "horrid frightful looking objects." In 1842 Morris recorded his impressions at greater length:

> Christmas Eve—a few "belsnickels" or "kriskinckles" were prowling about this evening frightening the women and children, with their

uncouth appearance—made up of cast-off garments made parti-
colored with patches, a false face, a shaggy head of tow, or rather wig,
falling profusely over the shoulders and finished out by a most patriarchal beard of whatsoever foreign [material] that could possibly be
pressed into such service.[21]

Belsnickles could wreak mischief, as they did in Pottstown, Pennsylvania, in 1826, where for several nights running one or more of them left
a "wreck of lumber that is strewed through our streets and blockading the
doors generally every morning":

a complete bridge built across the street, principally composed of old
barrels, hogsheads, grocery boxes, wheelbarrows, harrows, plows,
wagon and cart wheels. It is reported that he nearly demolished a
poor woman's house in one of the back streets a few nights ago. . . .

Despite the damage this Belsnickle did, the phrasing of this report
suggests that he was seen as a mere prankster:

He performs these tricks *incog*, or otherwise he would be arrested
long since by the public authorities, who are on the alert; but it will
take a swift foot and a strong arm to apprehend him while he is in full
power of his bellsnickelship, as he then can evade mortal ken. . . .[22]

Like wassailers and mummers, Belsnickles often took on the role of
beggars, visiting houses (and shops) to *demand* rather than offer gifts. This
may very well have been the reason that four or five of them visited James
L. Morris's store in 1842 and once again in 1844, when Morris noted that
"[s]ome 4 or five hideous and frightful looking mortals came into the store
dressed out in fantastic rags and horrid faces." These Belsnickles were
probably coming for gifts. In 1851 several "processions" of them in Norristown, "arrayed in all their fantastic costumes, . . . paid their annual visit to
the shopkeepers and citizens, soliciting the 'good things' and rendering an
equivalent in caricaturing the sable sons of our soil" (in other words, they
too were performing in blackface). They were still begging in the 1870s.
This was the case in Lancaster, for instance, where "[t]he old custom of
playing 'Bellsnickle' was renewed in our midst, and we heard perhaps half
a dozen parties, dressed in hideous disguise, going about on Christmas eve
from house to house, and entering without so much as 'by your leave'"; or
in Carlisle, where in the same year "[t]here were numbers of bell-snickles

going from house to house in quest of cakes, wine, apples, or whatever else the good housewife might place at their disposal, large boys and small boys. . . ." (In the latter instance they were dressed in women's clothes, "burlesquing the ruling fashions among the ladies.")[23]

The examples above make it clear that youths and boys were playing the Belsnickle role themselves, thus reverting to the "original" structure of the ritual. In Reading, in 1851, "juvenile harlequins were running from house to house, scattering nuts, confections, consternation, and amusement in their way." Or in Norristown, where in 1853 "[s]illy children parade[d] the streets dressed in hideous masks." Or in Easton, in 1858, where "[t]he 'bell-snickels' were . . . a most attractive feature on the streets . . . as there seemed to be a general feeling among the juveniles . . . to participate. . . ."[24] But these youthful Belsnickles were frequently a source of annoyance rather than amusement, as in Pottstown, where the local newspaper was not amused in 1873:

> Pottstown was full of "bell-snickles" on Christmas Eve, young chaps with their faces blacked, with masks, and dressed in all kinds of outlandish styles. These fellows, with their ugly mugs, visited the hotels, stores, shops, and in many instances private dwellings, and went through their monkeyish grimaces, and annoyed people with their horrible attempts at singing, making themselves odious throughout the town generally. This "bell-snickle" business, which is becoming more of a rough and rowdyish observance of the Christmas season each year, might as well be omitted altogether.[25]

A malleable ritual, as I have said. But there is a pattern behind it all. Whether the part was played by a grown man or a child, and whether he acted as the donor of gifts or as a beggar, the Belsnickle always used his costume and his manner as a means of intimidating those he visited, a way of taking on an air of mock authority over the rest of the community. Young people had traditionally been just another part of the lower orders, so that it was socially natural for them to step outside the constraints of their normal roles by imitating what other plebeians were doing. And it was a thin line—and probably more of a terminological distinction than a historical one—that divided a Belsnickle from a mummer, a callithumpian, or simply a hoodlum. (On the other side of the cultural ledger, Belsnickles were frequently referred to as "Christkindle," "Kriss Kringle," or even "Santa Claus.") The particular term may have been a matter of local or even personal preference. But whatever he was called then, or termed now, the Belsnickle remained a Lord of Misrule.

There seem to be virtually no records of Belsnickles in Philadelphia itself. But this too may be partly a matter of terminology, since the city (in contrast to much of the Pennsylvania backcountry) was not dominated by German-Americans. And in Philadelphia, as in New York, the disorder that was associated with figures of misrule took on a tone of greater menace.

Susan G. Davis, who examined this aspect of Christmas in Philadelphia in an important 1984 article, observes that people arrested there for disorderly behavior at Christmas "were uniformly young and male," and she attributes this to "the breakdown of the apprenticeship system and the decline of craft skills"—the general economic problem besetting youths and young men in a period of rapid industrialization. Rowdy Christmas revelry "crystallized the city's year-round youth problem." Davis observes that "In the street Christmas, rowdy youth culture reached its apotheosis; concern over riotous holiday nights was constant from the 1830s on. The mid-1840s were especially uproarious, but tumult and commotion seemed ominous for decades."[26] As early as 1833 the *Philadelphia Daily Chronicle* reported:

> Throughout almost the whole of Tuesday night—Christmas Eve— riot, noise, and uproar prevailed, uncontrolled and uninterrupted in many of our central and most orderly streets. Gangs of boys and young men howled and shouted as if possessed by the demon of disorder. Some of the watchmen occasionally sounded their rattles; but seemed only to add another ingredient to the horrible discord that murdered sleep. It is undoubtedly in the power of our city police to prevent slumbering citizens from being disturbed by the mad roars of such revelers.[27]

The problem, in Philadelphia as well as New York, was that this kind of rowdiness had been transformed in an urban capitalist setting into something that respectable people found threatening, as they did in 1839, when a riot broke out on Chesnut Street, opposite the state capitol. The participants, one newspaper reported with disgust, "could not have chosen a more public place; throngs of persons were passing on both sides of the street, viewing all the sights that were to be seen; but . . . a street fight was one of the entertainments that did not please a majority of them. . . ."[28] Susan Davis reports that gangs of young men from the working-class communities that surrounded Philadelphia were deliberately invading the downtown business and theater districts, "where playgoers and promenaders thronged to view shop-window illuminations."[29]

In Philadelphia as in New York, respectable people placed the greatest measure of blame on alcohol. Drinking itself, as we have seen in Chapters 1 and 2, had been an interclass ritual at Christmas, but now it was becoming a way of *distinguishing* the classes from one another. In 1839 a newspaper pointed out, in a Christmas Day editorial, that "there are certain modes of rejoicing which are appropriate to Christmas, and other modes of doing the same thing, which are quite unbecoming and reprehensible." But the editorial went on to acknowledge that this was a recent development, and even to analyze how it had come about:

> Some years ago, every housekeeper thought it incumbent on himself or herself to provide a bowl of egg-nog or spiced toddy for the celebration of this day. Persons who were usually of temperate or sedate habits, seemed to think that the return of Christmas justified a slight degree of intoxication. Friends and acquaintances, who called to tender the compliments of the season, were urged to partake of these liquid preparations, the seductive taste of which frequently overcame the most sober resolutions. On such occasions, it may be supposed that there were many evidences of joy and hilarity; but it was properly questioned by some considerate persons whether that kind of joy and hilarity became [i.e., suited] a day set apart to commemorate the origin of Christianity.
>
> When this subject was duly considered, the customs spoken of, fell into disuse, and soon became ranked among the barbarisms of a former age. We are happy, therefore, to find that *one* incorrect mode of celebrating Christmas is no longer *general;* though particular instances may be noted wherein the relics of these absurd practices are still preserved.[30]

By the late 1840s that attitude had come to be backed by force of law. Philadelphia simply banned the sale of alcohol—it became a "dry" community (by that time the temperance movement had gained widespread support). But that did not stop people from buying drinks in the neighboring towns, where, following an old Christmas tradition, "as usual . . . the proprietors of . . . groggeries that fill the bystreets on either side of the boundaries of the city . . . treated their motley customers with egg-nog."[31]

But if geographic dividing lines were hard to draw, so were psychological ones. Even the newspapers themselves sometimes betrayed a lingering ambivalence toward rowdy behavior at Christmas. An 1844 editorial started out by describing the new domestic Christmas as "religion in each man's house . . . a celebration of the spirit of the universe, humanized and domesticated." But the same editorial went on to acknowledge that the day also had a long tradition of "high rejoicing, eating, drinking (and getting drunk, we presume . . .)."[32] Or take the headlines that one Philadelphia newspaper employed to report the arrest of men charged with inciting riot and similar forms of behavior. One such report, from 1836, was headed "CHRISTMAS GAMBOLS." Others in subsequent years were headed "CHRISTMAS FESTIVITIES" (1840); "FUN ON CHRISTMAS DAY" (1841); "CHRISTMAS SPREES" (1846); and "CHRISTMAS SPORT" (1850). These headings reveal an acute uncertainty about what to make of such behavior. The phrasing may be sarcastic, but it also betrays a residual understanding that rowdy behavior was to be *expected* at Christmas.

In Philadelphia the matter was made more complicated by another Christmas ritual, one that seems to have been unique to that city. In Philadelphia, during the late 1830s and 1840s, even respectable people observed Christmas Day in part as a public occasion. Each year thousands of people would spend the afternoon promenading in the downtown streets, attracted in part by the sheer sociability of the proceedings and in part by the prospect of doing their Christmas shopping, an activity that many Philadelphians (in common with residents of other cities) engaged in on Christmas Day itself. (Downtown shops generally remained open on both Christmas Eve and Christmas Day.)[33]

The scene attracted notice nationally. *Nile's National Register* reported that on Christmas Day, 1841,

> Chesnut street [the main commercial street] was crowded with a dense mass of human beings. The entire population of the outer districts seemed gathered there, eagerly gazing at the sights in the shop windows and enjoying the excitement of the moving panorama. It is estimated that there were 40,000 people on Chesnut street most of the afternoon.[34]

It is clear from such reports that the "moving panorama" itself was part of the show: People went to see and be seen, dressed in their best outfits— outfits presumably purchased in local establishments. This was the Philadelphia equivalent of New Year's visiting in New York.

The Christmas Day promenades always bore an edge of menace, and by tracing local coverage after 1840 through a single newspaper, the *Public Ledger*, we can see that edge grow sharper year by year. In 1840 the promenade was described as an impressive scene: "We never before saw Chesnut street so thronged, from morning to night, in passing and re-passing—indeed, one to make any progress, was obliged to take the centre of the street." (But the report added defensively, "This is right.") The tone was still quite positive in 1841, even though the crowds on Chesnut Street were so dense that people were "struggling and jostling their way through the mass of humanity that well nigh blocked the great thoroughfare of fashion." In 1842, from early afternoon until midnight, "the whole city seemed to have emptied into Chesnut street, which . . . was filled with a dense mass of human beings, young and old, male and female, great and small, black and white." This report went on to describe the promenaders as "a rude and noisy crowd."[35]

In 1843, after describing the promenade as an impressive display of fashion, the writer of the article acknowledged that "[a] number of arrests were made for disorderly conduct and breaches of the peace, and no small number were taken up for being intoxicated. There were more drunken men and boys in our streets, than we have witnessed for many a day before." And again the 1844 article indicated that some portions of the crowd had chosen to dress in bizarre style, "tricked out in burlesque garb," and that they were making cacophonous music with instruments "from the trumpet to the penny whistle." A further report commented that "[a]n easy, carnival-like, practical joking air pervaded the moving crowd," and noted ambiguously that "[m]any young men, individually and collectively, paraded the streets dressed in fantastic attire, ready for all kinds of sport. . . ." It is not clear what kinds of "sport" these young men were ready for, but the fact that they were young and male links them with the one demographic group that had long been most closely associated with Christmas misrule. In any case, the reporter went on to condemn all the drunkenness, and to recommend that "[o]ur temperance friends should increase their zeal to counteract this fresh attack by the enemy."[36]

The tide was turning. In 1845 there was no coverage at all of the promenade, only a brief notice that "Christmas was duly celebrated on Thursday," followed by a very lengthy report headed "Rowdyism." In 1846 there was, once again, only a very brief item (four sentences), noting that Christmas Day witnessed "the usual festivities," and followed by another report of rowdy behavior: "There was, undoubtedly, more drunkenness visible in the streets . . . than has occurred for years before. . . ."[37]

Finally, in 1847, a severe snowstorm on Christmas Day forced most Philadelphians to give up the promenade and spend the day at home. The result was almost an epiphany for the writer of an editorial that appeared in the *Public Ledger*. It was as if he had discovered that Christmas could best be celebrated without leaving one's house after all. He suggested that the poor weather actually made for "a merrier Christmas than we've had for several years":

> The ladies could not leave their houses, it is true, and we missed their pretty faces and winning smiles from Chesnut st.; but looks were brighter and smiles were sweeter, where they are most valued, *at home*. It is no wonder, then, that the streets were comparatively deserted, for husbands, sons, brothers and lovers deemed themselves the happiest within the family circle. . . .

It was true, this writer continued, that not everyone stayed at home. Some persisted in maintaining the old ways:

> Those who were in the streets defied the uncomfortable weather with rude revelry, and occasionally the ear was attracted to their shouts, as they circulated from one tavern to another, imbibing at each another quantity of vinous excitement.

But such people were not partaking in the real spirit of Christmas. The only pleasures that qualified as true holiday mirth were those of home and hearth: "We have said that the day was a merry one—it was so, at home. Those who were out were merry also; but it was [only] the forced merriment which bacchanalian libations bring."

CREATING CHILDREN

It was during the 1820s that the Philadelphia press first began to take notice of Christmas as a family event. Before the middle of the 1820s Philadelphia's newspapers, like those in New York and other cities, had acknowledged the coming of Christmas only by printing a religious poem or an occasional admonition to remember the poor. The absence of a special notice should not be taken to mean that Philadelphians did not celebrate the holiday, only that their celebrations did not require comment.[38]

The change began with the 1824 Christmas season, when no fewer than four new almanacs—all published in Philadelphia—printed Clement Clarke Moore's poem "A Visit from St. Nicholas." This marked the first appearance of the poem anywhere after its initial publication, just a year earlier, in a newspaper in Troy, New York. (A copy of one of these almanacs recently sold at auction for nearly $30,000.) Two years later, in 1826, the same poem appeared in a weekly Philadelphia paper, the *Saturday Evening Post*. In 1827 another local paper followed suit, and a third paper published an extract from Washington Irving's "Bracebridge Hall" sketches.[39]

The rush was on, in Philadelphia as well as other American cities and towns. More than any other text, it was Moore's poem that introduced the American reading public to the joys of a domestic Christmas. In Philadelphia itself, in 1828 "A Visit from St. Nicholas" appeared in *Poulson's Daily Advertiser,* and the *National Gazette* published another "antiquarian" Christmas poem, "Old English Christmas," written by Walter Scott. And in 1829 *Poulson's* reprinted a piece from a New York paper that gave a detailed explanation of the Santa Claus ritual. The following year, 1830, the *National Gazette* editorially explained the *inner* meaning of the new Christmas: That paper would not be appearing on December 25, readers learned, because it was a day to forget business in favor of domestic pleasures—and domestic pleasures were the most important thing in life, more important even than social standing, poverty, and "external disappointments or calamities." The Christmas season, the paper noted, brings to mind "the culture and value of *the social and domestic affections,*" just as it reminds us of "the comparative insignificance, for private happiness, of all that is beyond them."[40]

Children and Servants

In Philadelphia as in New York, then, the period from the 1820s to the 1840s was one in which the carnival form of Christmas was essentially "read out" as a legitimate part of the holiday, and in which the "real Christmas"—indeed, everything that really mattered most in life itself— came to be seen in domestic terms that centered around family and children. That process actually involved two elements. Thus far we have dealt with the first of these, which might be summarized as *keeping the poor away from the house.* But it now became necessary not only to keep the poor *outside* the house but to keep one's own children *inside.*

Much of the rowdy behavior indulged during the Christmas season had been ascribed, simultaneously and indistinguishably, to youths and workers. Evidence of this abounds from the colonial period well into the nineteenth century. A 1719 Boston almanac warned householders in late December: "Do not let your Children and Servants run too much abroad at Nights." A 1772 New York newspaper referred to "[t]he assembling of Negroes, servants, boys and other disorderly persons, in noisy companies in the streets." An 1805 letter written from Albany, New York, reported that on account of "the holydays, a considerable number of pennies has been given to the boys & servants. . . ." In 1818 a Boston woman noted that "Christmas is now generally observed as a holiday. Our children and domestics claim it as such." (And she went on to complain that the children as well as the domestics often spent the day "in idleness and dissipation.")

It was this same social mix that John Pintard himself fondly recalled from his own childhood days in the latter 1700s, when he and a family servant traveled together around New York in "boisterous" fashion, drinking a "dram" at every stop and "coming home loaded with sixpences." And as late as 1854, when the New York situation had turned ugly, a local newspaper complained that "at almost every corner gangs of *boys and drunken rowdies* were seen amusing themselves by throwing snowballs, using vulgar and blasphemous language, and otherwise desecrating the Sabbath [emphasis added]."[41]

Children and servants; boys and drunken rowdies. Why this improbable linkage? To answer that question is to probe a much broader historical issue—the changing historical relationship between age and social class. I have been arguing that what happened during the nineteenth century was that age replaced class as the axis along which the Christmas gift exchange took place. But it would be useful now to modify that point. Until the nineteenth century, children did not make up a distinct social category; they were not a separate social group, as they are in modern Western societies. Nor did they act as if they were. Instead, children were lumped together with other members of the lower orders in general, especially servants and apprentices—who, not coincidentally, were generally young people themselves.[42]

From this perspective it becomes clear that giving Christmas gifts to children was not new, after all. Young people did receive gifts at Christmas—but in their role as servants or apprentices (or newspaper carriers) and not because they were children. Both children and servants were at the bottom of the hierarchy in the households in which they lived, linked to the larger household as much by bonds of labor and subordination as by those of affection. (For example, the term "maid" was used to refer not to a cleaning lady but to an unmarried girl or a young woman [i.e., a "maiden"]. But the household tasks generally assigned to such females were ordinarily menial ones—the kind of work that was later associated with the term "maid" in its more recent usage.) Conversely, servants and apprentices were treated as members of the household in which they worked and lived. Before the nineteenth century, in other words, *class* and *age* were thoroughly intermingled.

What happened in the early nineteenth century was that age ceased to be associated with social status. Youth no longer connoted "meniality." It no longer made sense to refer to girls as "maids," or, conversely, to speak of those of lowly status as "boys"—except in a vestigial fashion, as in the term "bellboy" or "cowboy"—or, notably, whenever the color line was involved. (But just as black men commonly continued to be addressed as "boys" in order to connote their lower status, so, too, women of any race continued to be addressed as "girls" to connote *theirs*. And, of course, the term "maid" has come to refer *only* to household service.)

Only from the perspective of our own culture, in which age and class bear no significant relationship to each other, does it appear as if Christmas rituals of class were replaced by those of age. It would be more accurate to say that in the early nineteenth century, *age alone* was coming to replace a more general kind of status as the primary axis along which presents were given. The domestication of Christmas was thus related (as both effect and cause) to the creation of domesticity and of "childhood" itself, even to the novel idea that the central purpose of the family was to provide not simply for the instruction of its children but for their happiness as well.

From Christmas Box to Christmas Present

We can glimpse something of this process by tracing changes in the very *terminology* of the Christmas gift exchange. As we have seen, Christmas presents had their origin in wassailing and other forms of Christmas begging, in which the poor demanded gifts from the neighboring gentry— generally gifts of food and drink, to be consumed on the spot. An urban version of the same ritual, known as the "Christmas box," was developed in seventeenth-century London (and probably in other cities) by young tradesmen's apprentices and other low-level workers, who kept earthenware boxes—the ancestor, really, of the piggy bank—into which, during the Christmas season, they asked those who employed their services to put money. (The purpose of this box was to ensure that none of the money could be appropriated by a single individual, and that it would be distributed collectively within the shop when the box was broken open.) Men of means regarded their contributions to Christmas boxes as a necessary expense. Samuel Pepys referred to them in 1668: "Called up [i.e., waked up] by drums and trumpets; these things and boxes having cost me much money this Christmas already. . . ." And Jonathan Swift wrote sardonically in 1710: "I shall be undone here with Christmas boxes. The rogues at the coffee house have raised their tax. . . ."[43]

During the course of the eighteenth century, the term "Christmas box" came to be applied not to the box itself but to the donation that was placed into it—and, soon, to any such gift. By century's end, the term was being used colloquially to refer to Christmas presents per se, even when those presents were commercial products given by parents to their children. Thus a children's book published in New England in 1786 was titled *Nurse Truelove's Christmas Box*. And in Virginia, in 1810, Mason Weems announced that he would sell his biography of George Washington at a deep discount to buyers "who take several copies . . . for Christmas Boxes to their young relations."[44]

Unlike the term "Christmas box," the word *present* did not signify something that was given as a tip or an obligation but rather something that was given freely. But this term, too, was often used to name a gift offered by patrons to their dependents. It is striking that before 1780 the only two books published in America bearing the word *present* in the title were guidebooks for servants: *A Present for an Apprentice* and *A Present for a Servant-Maid*. These works, which were reprinted frequently until about 1800, consisted of a series of short admonitory essays warning apprentices of the dangerous temptations they were apt to encounter in their position.[45] These were "presents" given down across class lines—but apprentices and maidservants also happened to be young people themselves, so these presents were also given across lines of age. (We have no way of knowing whether any of them were ever actually given during the Christmas season.)

The three decades following 1780 saw the appearance of a spate of books with the word *present* in the title. But now there was a change: All of these books were specifically intended for young people. *A Present to Children* (1783); *Present for Misses* (1794); *A Present for a Little Boy* (1802) and its mate *A Present for a Little Girl* (1804).[46] At first these books, too, contained rules for behavior (children, like servants and apprentices, were household dependents whose behavior could not be wholly trusted and thus required careful regulation). The first five editions of *A Present to Children*, for example (all published before 1800), contained nothing but catechisms and "moral songs." One actually warned against playing with toys.[47]

But the subtitle of the sixth edition of this same work, printed in the year 1800, promised to introduce a new genre—"entertaining stories." The change had begun—the change from books designed for training young people to books designed for *amusing* them. Just as age alone was coming to replace status in general as the primary axis along which presents were given, pleasure was coming to replace discipline as the primary purpose of those presents.

It seems that Christmas "presents" slowly replaced Christmas "boxes" as gifts given within the household at a time when the household itself was coming to exclude servants from real membership. It was the isolation of children from other dependents at Christmas that produced—that *was*—the domestication of the holiday.

CHILDREN'S GAMES

But in the early nineteenth century Christmas had not yet become a child-centered domestic ritual. Nor did children instinctively know that they were being created as "children." Indeed, there were no Christmas activities for children other than making noise or making trouble. "Christmas is now generally observed as a holiday," a Boston woman said in 1818, noting that "[o]ur children and domestics claim it as such." And she went on to complain that it was generally spent in "idleness" or else "in revelry and dissipation." (The same woman also proposed that the local churches hold Christmas services—not for religious reasons but so that "families, children, and domestics, can attend public worship" instead of making trouble.[48])

It is interesting to learn that Christmas was "generally observed as a holiday" by Boston's schoolchildren in the mid-1810s. But what is also interesting is the casual observation that children were taking the day through their own initiative rather than by virtue of an official policy ("our children . . . claim it as such"), and there is the implication, too, that their actions were informally sanctioned by those in authority. There is a story behind this, one that reveals something about the nature of youth culture in the era before the invention of childhood.

Barring Out the Schoolmaster

School was one place, perhaps the only place before the nineteenth century, where young people (particularly boys) were physically separated from their peers in the lower orders. But at Christmas schoolboys devised their own version of carnival misrule, a ritual practice that "turned the world upside down" every bit as much as aggressive peasant wassailing had done. Here the figure of authority was the schoolmaster, and it was on him that the tables were turned.

This ritual, which became known as "Barring Out the Schoolmaster," originated in England toward the end of the sixteenth century. A modern historian describes it this way: "As Christmas drew near the boys gathered together weapons, ammunition and a store of provisions. Then one morning they seized the school premises and barred the doors and windows against the master." The most important goal of the "barring out" was to force the schoolmaster to grant his pupils a holiday vacation.[49] (In addition to the threat posed to their authority, schoolmasters had a reason to attempt to reclaim the schoolhouse: They were generally paid by the day, and would lose their stipend if they were not able to teach.)

Barring-out came to America early, and rather violently. The year was 1702, and the place was a grammar school in Williamsburg, Virginia. On that occasion students not only barricaded the schoolhouse but actually fired pistols at the schoolmaster when he responded by trying to break down one of the doors. He reported what took place:

> About a fortnight before Christmas 1702 . . . , I heard the School boys about 12 o'clock at night, a driving of great nails, to fasten & barricade the doors of the Grammar School. . . . I made haste to get up & with the assistance of 2 servant men . . . I had almost forced open one of the doors before they sufficiently secured it, but while I was breaking in, they presently fired off 3 or 4 Pistols & hurt one of my servants in the eye with the wadd . . . of one of the Pistols[.]
>
> [W]hile I pressed forward, some of the boys, having a great kindness for me, call'd out, "for God's sake sir don't offer to come in, for we have shot, and shall certainly fire at any one that first enters." . . . [I then] resolved to let them alone till morning, and then getting all the other masters together & calling for workmen to break open the doors.[50]

The practice of barring-out continued through the eighteenth century and into the nineteenth, and extended into other regions of the United States. A letter to a Philadelphia newspaper written in 1810 objected to the practice but acknowledged that it was commonplace there:

> A very absurd and wicked practice has long prevailed in this country, namely, that of Scholars barring out the Schoolmasters a little before the 25th of December, commonly called Christmas day, in order to extort permission from him to spend a number of days called the Christmas holidays in idleness or play. A scene of this kind took place last year in our school in this place: a few of the scholars took posses-

sion of the school-house, and so completely fortified it, that it was impossible to reduce it except by a regular siege, and the caitiffs [*sic*] had provided against this also by laying in a large quantity of provisions. Thus was not only the Teacher shut out, but also all those who wished to occupy their time in learning, and not in idleness and riot.

In this instance a group of parents (including the writer of this letter) went to the schoolhouse to negotiate with the rebellious children. First they "prevailed" on the rebels "to raise one of the windows a little." Then, when they inquired about the purpose of the rebellion, the answer was clear: "One of them, who seemed to be the commander in chief, replied they wished to have ten days of Christmas-play."[51]

The practice even penetrated into rural New England. Horace Greeley later recalled that barring-out was common during his childhood in early-nineteenth-century New Hampshire:

> There was an unruly, frolicsome custom of "barring-out" in our New Hampshire common schools, which I trust never obtained a wider acceptance. On the first of January, and perhaps on some other day that the big boys chose to consider or make a holiday, the forenoon passed off as quietly as that of any other day; but, the moment the master left the house in quest of his dinner, the little ones were started homeward, the door and windows suddenly and securely barricaded, and the older pupils, thus fortified against intrusion, proceeded to spend the afternoon in play and hilarity. I have known a master to make a desperate struggle for admission; but I do not recollect that one ever succeeded,—the odds being too great. . . .[52]

Greeley went on to indicate that the practice was informally sanctioned by adults. If a persecuted schoolmaster "appealed to the neighboring fathers" for assistance, Greeley remembered, "they were apt to recollect that they had been boys themselves, and advise him to desist, and let matters take their course."[53]

"Snowballing" and the Battle for Children

In whatever fashion it might be gained, the young people's holiday generally took the form of what its critics, such as the 1818 Boston parent mentioned above, termed "idleness and dissipation." Young boys went around the neighborhood firing guns and "squibs," making noise, playing tricks.

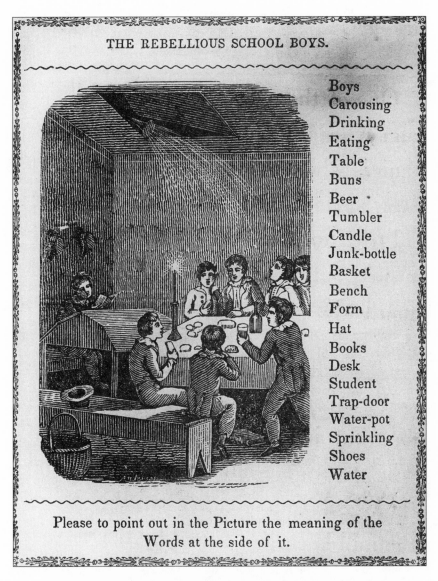

THE REBELLIOUS SCHOOL BOYS.

Boys
Carousing
Drinking
Eating
Table
Buns
Beer
Tumbler
Candle
Junk-bottle
Basket
Bench
Form
Hat
Books
Desk
Student
Trap-door
Water-pot
Sprinkling
Shoes
Water

Please to point out in the Picture the meaning of the Words at the side of it.

Barring Out the Schoolmaster. These boys have brought a supply of food and drink to last them through the anticipated siege (the words printed on the right in this primer include "carousing," "drinking," and "beer"). But the rebels' plans are about to be foiled: The schoolmaster is pouring water through a secret trapdoor in the ceiling, so as to douse the schoolboys' candle prior to his invading the schoolhouse. This illustration was included in a child's primer published in 1850, but it had appeared earlier in the same publisher's 1822 Boston edition of an English novella, Maria Edgeworth's *The Barring Out. (Courtesy, American Antiquarian Society)*

Children of both sexes drank and played kissing games.[54] In its most innocent form, Christmas games meant having snowball fights, but even these could lead to disturbance and damage. Snowballing could become especially vicious in urban areas, where, during the Christmas season, respectable citizens associated it with the kind of menacing behavior they feared from working-class youth gangs at Christmastime. Remember, for example, the language in which the *New York Tribune* described the city streets during the Christmas season in 1854 (the emphasis is mine): "[A]t almost every corner *gangs* of *boys and drunken rowdies* were seen amusing themselves by *throwing snowballs.*"

That was how respectable adults saw it. But the issue was surely more complicated for many of the boys themselves, who must have been drawn in two directions at once—an old pull, toward carnival in the streets, and the new one, toward the quieter rewards that were promised at home. That double pull would have been especially salient in families that were positioned anywhere near the vulnerable lower borders of middle-class respectability. Youths who belonged to such families constituted a major battleground in the transformation of Christmas.

Young people do not often leave direct records of their inner experience. But a hint of what this inner battleground might have meant in human terms can be found in a careful reading of one rather sensitive Christmas story published in 1838 under the title "Snow-Balling." The author of this story, Eliza Leslie, was a popular writer of the time. Set in Philadelphia on Christmas Day, the story tells of the adventures of a young boy whose father gives him a "Christmas dollar" and sends him downtown to buy himself a present. Left on his own, young Robert Hamlin encounters trouble. Unable to choose from the plethora of tempting items for sale in the shops, Robert becomes confused and begins to wander about the streets.[55]

In his wanderings, Robert comes upon an alleyway where he sees "some rude boys engaged in snow-balling." ("Rude boys" is a phrase that may require some explanation for modern readers: The word *rude* was a reference to these boys' social class as well as to their manners. A "rude boy" was a working-class youth, the sort of person who might be expected to engage in forms of rowdy activity even more threatening than throwing snowballs.)

Robert is tempted to join these youths, especially after one of them throws a snowball at him and proceeds to laugh. But he is saved by luck from succumbing to this temptation. One of the boys throws a snowball at a woman who is observing the scene from the entrance to her house;

the snowball hits her in the nose and hurts her badly, causing her husband to run out of the house and chase the youths away by brandishing a pair of fireplace tongs. Witnessing this scene, Robert feels "glad that he did not belong to them."

At this point the author of the story is engaging in a significant gesture of evasion. For, as we shall see in a moment, young Robert gets into a snowball fight after all. In real life, as opposed to a work of fiction, someone like Robert would probably have joined the "rude boys." But Eliza Leslie does not wish to have the fictional Robert become involved with such a crew. She has taken pains to let us know his social class. He is the son of an artisan, a "respectable mechanic," which means that he is not so far in origin from the "rude boys." While not a proletarian, he is not securely middle-class, either. If a real Robert Hamlin had joined those boys he might have ended up in serious trouble, causing damage or injury, and his snowball fight might have been the first step in his descent out of respectability and into permanent proletarian status. Such a descent was far from uncommon among urban artisans in the middle of the nineteenth century, a period when independent artisanship itself was being subverted by industrial capitalism. Joining a gang of "rude boys" in a Christmas game of snowballs was thus a small but potent symbol of the larger dangers faced by the son of a "respectable mechanic."

If the fictional Robert is to get into trouble, then, it cannot be with the "rude boys." But get into trouble he must, or there is no point to the story. Eliza Leslie manages to devise a clever solution: the fictional Robert ends up getting into trouble with youngsters *above* his class.

Turning a corner away from the "alley" of the "rude boys," young Robert comes upon "a row of very handsome new houses." And in front of these houses he sees "a party of rather genteel looking boys, engaged also in snow-balling." The earlier scene now repeats itself: One of these "genteel looking" boys hurls a snowball at Robert. But this time Robert joins in. He makes a "very hard snow-ball," and throws it at the boy who has just done the same to him. But Robert's aim is poor, and his snowball smashes through a windowpane of one of the handsome new houses. Fortunately, no one is injured, though the snowball nearly hits "the head of a pretty little girl" who has been sitting quietly "engaged in reading one of the new annuals [i.e., a Gift Book she has presumably received as a present that very day]." The girl screams loudly, and Robert hides. But the family's black servant rushes outside and confronts the other boys, threatening them with the wrath of the owner: " 'Ah! you young nimps— only wait till the gentleman comes home—I'll be bound Mr. Cleveland

will give you enough of snow-balling, for smashing his rights and property in this way, without leave or license.' "

Robert overhears the threat, and he quickly runs off and returns to
his own house, where his parents are just sitting down to the family's
Christmas dinner, having planned a domestic Christmas for their children: a festive dinner followed by a "juvenile party" at his aunt's house. But
Robert, beset by guilt, is hardly capable of eating his turkey and mince pie,
or looking forward to the party. After a while he gets up from the table,
leaves the house, and goes back to the scene of his recent crime. There he
confesses to having been the culprit who broke the window and offers the
owner the dollar he had been given for Christmas (the same dollar he
could not make up his mind how best to spend). Now he feels better, and
returns home again, this time to enjoy the turkey and mince pie—and the
praise of his parents when he finally tells them what he has just done.

As I have said, the dangers presented in this story were very real in

Snow-Balling. This engraving appeared as an illustration for
Eliza Leslie's 1838 short story of the same title. It vividly
conveys the menace that could be associated with that sport.
(Courtesy, American Antiquarian Society)

households like Robert Hamlin's. We can assume that respectable boys *did* sometimes join "rude boys" in Christmas sport, and that snowballing was not the worst of their games. With snowballing as a partly symbolic act, Eliza Leslie's little story can be read as offering the same kind of warning to younger boys that older boys heard in the 1830s about the dangers of alcohol—or that girls heard about the dangers of sexual seduction. In all these cases, the ultimate risk was that of a serious decline in social status, the loss of respectability and independence itself.

But if the dangers were real, so, too, were the alternative lures that were now being offered to the Robert Hamlins of America: Christmas dinner at home, tempting presents to play with, and even children's parties—such as the "juvenile party" that young Robert could look forward to at his aunt's house. Such activities posed no social risk; and some of them (for example, reading the Gift Books that were frequently given as Christmas presents, and in one of which Eliza Leslie's story "Snow-Balling" was itself published) even promised harmless amusement along with cultural enhancement. In the words of an 1840 newspaper editorial, "Good books are good gifts for good children."[56]

DOMESTICATING GAMES

The story "Snow-Balling" ends before the "juvenile party" gets under way. But other stories published in the same period give us an idea of what such parties may have been like. For one thing, it is clear that they would have taken place indoors, usually in the family parlor and under the immediate or general supervision of an adult. In addition, the participants would have been young cousins and/or trustworthy friends—children who had been picked and invited by the parents, and not by the children themselves. We can be sure that there would be no "rude boys" in attendance—not even the children of household servants. Lower-class people were to be kept away on these occasions, and the children of the household were kept inside.

The literature of the decades after 1820 is filled with Christmas scenes in which parents arrange parties for their children. These are invariably indoor parties, and the games are indoor games. In the fictional literature, Christmas has become a controlled children's "frolic," sometimes wild enough to recall the rowdiness of an interclass carnival Christmas, but always under complete control. One story, published in 1850, begins with a Christmas Eve party for twenty preteen children. There are "cakes and candies . . . lemonade ice-cream," music (a piano), and games. "The windows rattled and the very walls were shaken, by the bounding and leaping—the racing and tumbling—of the half-dancing and half-romping youngsters." The twin parlors had been set up "to give room for the frolic of Christmas Eve, and most fully did the children avail themselves of the license of the season." Before the party was over, "scarce a chair or a table was to be found in its proper place and posture half an hour after the revel [had] begun."[57]

But this was "frolic," "license," and "revel" only in quotation marks. It was limited to blood relatives, and to preadolescents at that. The writer of the above-mentioned story could not be clearer on this point: "All the little Thompsons, and all their relatives by blood or marriage, even to the third degree of cousinship, who had not reached their 'teens,' were there . . ." The room had been carefully childproofed in advance; and the party ended early—it was at its height as early as 8 p.m. And an adult was always present.

And that was one of the wilder scenes in this literature. More often the parties were described as sedate affairs. It was common for them to culminate in "a great call for games." But the games seem to have been talking games, role-playing games, sometimes even board games. In one 1827 book a mother organizes a quiet Christmas Eve party for her children, a group of cousins, and other children who are known to the parents. For entertainment she has devised moral games: "puzzles, which had enfolded in them [i.e., the solutions to which involved], some moral or religious precept." The mother never leaves the children alone during the party, lest they "romp and disturb the neighbors with their noise." Instead, she stays with them "to moderate the buoyancy of their spirits." She even plays teacher with them. Here, too, the party ends early: "Nine o'clock was the hour she fixed, for the young people to separate, and they seldom infringed on these limits . . . [for her word] was a law to them."[58]

Perhaps so. But the lesson taught in this book was not necessarily taken to heart by the children who read it—a fact that comes across clearly in some lines handwritten on the flyleaf to one copy of that very book that is now owned by the American Antiquarian Society. These lines serve to remind us that books were not always used by readers in quite the way their authors intended. The lines read as follows: "Touch not this book / For if you do / The owner / Will be after you. Punch. Punch you. —Touch not this book / For fear of shame. / For you will find the owner's name. Punch. —Touch not this book / For fear of life. / For the owner has / A big Jack knife."

*　　*　　*

PARENTS DID NOT have to invent their own games for children to play on such occasions. By the 1830s a spate of Christmas books were available that consisted mostly of suggestions for children's games and puzzles. These books were generally published during the Christmas season, and they were intended to be purchased as Christmas presents. Lydia Maria Child published such a book, *The Girl's Own Book*, in 1831. The preface makes the purpose of the book clear. It concludes: "To all my readers, little ones especially, a merry Christmas and a happy New-Year."[59] Like other such books, this one, too, contained several activities intended specifically for Christmas. *The American Girl's Book*, also a popular collection of harmless but entertaining games, appeared in the same year. (This book was authored by Eliza Leslie, the woman who would a few years later write the cautionary tale "Snow-Balling.") And while there is no printed evidence that this book was intended as a Christmas present, a copy of a later (1859) edition, also owned by the American Antiquarian Society, is inscribed by a father to his daughter with the date "Christmas 1860."[60]

But children (and grown-ups, too) did not have to rely on the Christmas-party games featured in books; ready-made games were widely available for purchase at bookshops and other stores. As early as 1817, one Broadway merchant advertised (under the heading "Amusement for the Holydays") a "complete assortment" of children's games: "Different games with tetotums, such as Panorama of Europe, Heathen Mythology, Who Wears the Crown. . . . The celebrated Chinese Puzzle, and Philosophical & Mathematical Trangrams . . . is one of the most curious and entertaining amusements ever contrived . . . Price \$2." Seven years later, in 1824, another Broadway store advertised

> a large assortment of Juvenile Pastimes, all of which are calculated to improve as well as amuse the youthful mind, viz: Geographical Games. The Traveller's tour through the United States, performed with a tetotum and travellers [also The Traveller's tour through Europe and The Traveller's tour round the world]. They are put up in three different modes—on pasteboard and double folded on cloth, with a case, and dissected [i.e., jigsawed]. Dissected Maps. Vernacular Cards, Geographical Cards, The Cabinet Of Knowledge Opened, PHILOSOPHICAL Cards, Astronomical Cards, Scriptural Cards, Botanical Cards, Dissected Pictures. . . . In addition, [the store has] a good assortment of Juvenile Books, in plain and elegant bindings. Also, Pocket Books, Chess Men, Backgammon Boards, Pen-Knives, and Ladies' Work Boxes.[61]

By the 1840s these games had reached flood proportions. The largest selection I have encountered comes from a Cincinnati, Ohio, shop that in 1845 advertised "A Great Variety of Games." Heading the list was a game that actually seems to have been about the process of Christmas shopping itself: "The laughable game of 'What d'ye Buy.' " This amounts to an ironic comment on the list that followed:

> The Oracles of Fortune, The Game of Heroes, The Game of Characteristics, Shakespeare in a New Dress, The Christmas Cards, Robinson Crusoe and His Man Friday, The Strife of Genius, The Game of Cup and Ball, Jack Straws, The Pickwick Game, The Game of Kings, The Mansion of Happiness, The Game of Pope and Pagan, Dr. Busby's Cards, The Game of Graces, Master Rodbury and his Pupils, The Game of the American Eagle, The Devil on Sticks, &c. &c.[62]

But these indoor games had not replaced more traditional forms of Christmas revelry. In 1844, a Cincinnati confectionery concluded an advertisement that featured "Sugar Plums" and other sweets with the added note that the store "also" offered a "splendid assortment of Fire-works, for both little and big Pyrotechnists." That same day the Cincinnati press carried an admonitory reminder from the local mayor: "The city ordinances impose a fine for discharging fire-arms, or firing squibs, crackers, &c., 'in the streets, alleys, market spaces, and public commons' in the city proper. The Holidays are not made an exception."[63]

THE PARLOR OR THE STREET: BOOKS VERSUS THEATERGOING

The battle for children extended to another form of popular Christmas amusement: attending the theater. Before the 1820s American theaters did not offer performances on Christmas Day, either in a gesture of respect for the holiday or, more likely, because the actors refused to work on that day. But on the two adjacent days they did offer performances, and these were specially designed for the season. Thus in 1821 a Cincinnati theater offered performances on both December 24 and 26 of "a comic Pantomime Ballet, called CHRISTMAS FUN; or, The Village in an Uproar." When Boston's Haymarket Theater was first established back in 1796, it deliberately settled on December 26 for its opening night. A Boston newspaper remarked disdainfully in 1823 that the theatrical productions of the Christmas season were "of a mixed nature and not of a high intellectual order." The reason was that those productions had to compete with the local Circus (which was "thronged every evening"). In response, the theater managers "have thought it expedient to introduce rope-dancers and tumblers, as adjuncts to the drama."[64]

By the 1820s pressure was building to hold performances on December 25 itself. In 1825 the *New England Galaxy* praised the managers of the local theater for remaining closed that day, and thereby "sacrificing the profits of [their] ordinary business." The article noted that if the house had been open on Christmas evening, its receipts would have approached the record $800 chalked up on the previous Thanksgiving Day. (The Circus had an audience of 1,600 on Christmas evening, and another 500 had been turned away.)

The Boston theater soon succumbed to this pressure; beginning in 1826 it held yearly Christmas-night performances. Once again, Boston was typical. Christmas performances began during the mid-1820s in New York, Philadelphia, and Cincinnati as well. By the 1830s they were being advertised as special Christmas productions; and by 1840 the Christmas special had become part of every theater's stock-in-trade. In the 1840s, for example, the Boston Museum offered "Christmas pantomimes" that were "built around the characters of Harlequin, Columbine, old Pantalon, and Clown . . . [performed] without conversation." And in 1843, Christmas week at the Boston Museum opened with "The Christmas Gift, or The Golden Axe." The following year's Christmas pantomime was "The Busy Bee, or Harlequin in the Hive of Industry."[65]

These were wild affairs on *both* sides of the curtain. Going to the theater in early-nineteenth-century America did not mean sitting passively through the performance; audience behavior resembled that seen at modern rock concerts. As at rock concerts, the audience at these events thought of themselves as an active part of the performance, shouting back responses to the lines delivered onstage—sometimes they even threw objects at the actors. (This was especially true in the cheapest seats, known as the Gallery.) All in all, attending the theater was not very removed from participating in "street theater," and it was the same group of people who were most likely to engage in both.[66]

That was particularly true at Christmas. Christmas productions tended to be especially exaggerated, burlesque affairs. And audiences behaved correspondingly. In 1837 the *New York Herald* reported that the theaters attracted "a considerable portion of the Christmas revelers." One house especially, the Bowery Theater, was "more peculiarly a holiday theater than [any other]." "The audience here, [even] upon most occasions, performs as much before the curtain as the actors do behind it; but on Christmas eve . . . the acting on the stage is altogether secondary to the acting in the body of the house." By 1844 things had become even wilder: "In the noisy theaters, nothing was heard of the performances; and the actors and actresses might as well have gone through their parts in dumb show." In one place, the play itself "was neither seen nor heard, the fun all being this side the foot-lights. . . ."[67]

Worst of all that year was the Chatham Theater, where several hundred newsboys had assembled to witness—of all things—a musical play based on Charles Dickens's novel *A Christmas Carol,* which had been published in book form only a year earlier. Here's how the *New York Herald* described the scene:

> Some three hundred news boys, sharp set for relaxation in the shape of theatrical criticism, were engaged throughout the earlier part of the evening in an animated contest with the police officers, and several "stirring scenes," and peculiarly animated exits and entrances were enacted, to the uproarious delight of the gods and goddesses of the gallery, who cheered on the combatants with the various slogans and war-cries of the tribe, known only to the initiated, and altogether untranslatable. Several of the noisiest and most unmanageable of these amateurs, were, at length, snaked out by the police, and the scene of their exploits changed to the Tombs [the city jail]. . . .

Even after "comparative quiet" had been restored, the "clamor" of a noisy youngster "quite drowned the bass drum, in the melo-dramatic music which ushered the ghost of old Jacob Marley through the trap."[68]

Newsboys, the source of all this disorder, were themselves a new phenomenon on the urban scene. The development of cheap newspapers in the 1830s (the "penny press," so called because that was now the price of a daily paper) had helped create the need for street vendors who would hawk the afternoon papers on street corners. (In contrast, their predecessors in the trade—the "carriers" we encountered in Chapter 1—delivered newspapers only to the houses of those who had subscriptions.) Newsboys were drawn from the poorest classes of large cities; often they were homeless—in fact, the word *newsboy* was sometimes used interchangeably with *homeless boy* or *street arab.* Their love of theatergoing was notorious; everyone agreed that they attended "night after night." They used the theater as a gathering place and even as a place where they could sleep. But above

GREAT ANNUAL PROCESSION OF THE NEW YORK NEWS BOYS,

Newsboys at Christmas. This picture appeared in the 1844 Christmas edition of a New York newspaper, *Brother Jonathan*. These were the same newsboys who would end up disrupting several of the city's theatrical performances later that evening. *(Courtesy, American Antiquarian Society)*

all, newsboys loved theatrical performances and responded interactively to events onstage just as if they were witnessing real life. The presence of police officers in the theaters was a standard precaution against newsboy excesses.[69]

Newsboys may have been a new phenomenon in the late 1830s, but they fit a social and demographic profile that had long been associated with rituals of Christmas misrule: They were poor and youthful males. So it is no wonder that they took to acting up with particular intensity during the holiday season. This was as true in Philadelphia as it was in New York. An 1844 advertisement for one Philadelphia theatrical production ended with a notice assuring other prospective theatergoers that "[e]fficient Police have been engaged to preserve order; boys will be prevented from congregating in front. . . ."[70] Just a year earlier, in 1843, the Christmas-evening theatrical scene suggests the reason:

> The Arch Street [theater] was also crowded, where as well as at the National [theater], the boys amused themselves by tossing each other, as well as they could in the crowd, over each other's heads and jostling the weak under foot, to the great discomfiture of their apparel.[71]

To put all this in context, consider the program presented at two theaters on that occasion. The matinee performance at the National Theater opened with a drama, "George Barnwell," continued with a blackface show, the "Original Virginia Minstrels," and ended with another drama,

"King of the Mist." The Arch Street Theater matinee opened with "Hunter of the Alps," continued with "a Comic Song," and concluded with "the Colored Music Festival, by the Virginia Minstrels." The evening show at that same theater opened with a drama, followed once again by the Virginia Minstrels, and concluded with "a new Pantomime, entitled 'Sante Claus'—Old Krisskingle [played by] Mr. Winans."

Old Krisskingle. By 1843 this figure had become the lead character of a Christmas pantomime performed in concert with a minstrel show. (This would not be the only occasion on which Santa Claus converged with blackface minstrelsy. In about 1840 a collection of minstrel songs was printed in New York under the authorship "by Santaclaus." And remember, too, the Belsnickles who went wassailing in blackface in areas of Pennsylvania.) Two years later Kriss Kringle would once again appear at the theater, this time in front of the lights, in the form of a costumed actor distributing gifts to the children who attended the show: "KRISS KRINGLE will deliver Presents of Toys, &c. to all his Juvenile Visiters [sic]. . . . KRISS KRINGLE will positively appear, in propriae personae, and present Toys, Sweetmeats and Fruits to the juvenile visitors. . . ."[72]

By this time Kriss Kringle was a ubiquitous presence in Philadelphia, and several places were announcing themselves as his "headquarters." One of these places advertised that " 'KRISS KRINGLE' has determined to make the Assembly Building his Head Quarters over the Holidays. . . ." He would be appearing there with a ventriloquist for six performances on Christmas Day (every two hours from 10 a.m. to 8 p.m.) But on that same day a bookstore, too, advertised itself as "KRISS KRINGLE'S HEAD QUARTERS FOR CHRISTMAS BOOKS":

> Come and choose—come one, come all—he has laid a great variety on the counter for you to choose from. Parents bring your children. Children don't forget to ask your parents, and remember that it is at JOHN B. PERRY'S, No 198 Market street."[73]

Bookstores and theaters represented two different cultural worlds. If theatergoing was part of the rowdy world of Christmas carnival, reading books was part of the world of quiet domestic pleasures. By the mid-1840s Kriss Kringle had entered the world of books, and he was urging his youthful readers to do the same. In 1842 a Philadelphia publisher brought out *Kriss Kringle's Book,* a gift book for children that explained the ritual of St. Nicholas (it even included Clement Clarke Moore's poem, "A Visit from St. Nicholas") and urged its youthful readers to "prepare" for his visit

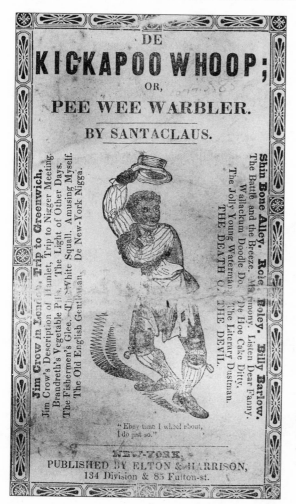

Santa in Blackface. The cover page of a collection of minstrel songs published in New York in about 1840. The songs were written and performed by one of the best-known American minstrels, Thomas Rice, who performed onstage as "Jim Crow." The exact reason for attributing the authorship of this pamphlet to "Santa Claus" is obscure. *(Courtesy, American Antiquarian Society)*

by acting "obedient to their parents, studious, respectful to their teachers, gentle to their play-fellows, and attentive to their religious duties." If they did so, such children would be certain to receive "numerous tokens" of Santa Claus's goodwill. And among these tokens there were sure to be books: "Saint Nicholas . . . loves to give the children nice little story books, such as will teach them to be good, and at the same time afford them a good deal of innocent amusement. . . ."[74]

In 1845 two other Philadelphia publishers entered the Kriss Kringle market. One came out with *Kriss Kringle's Christmas Tree,* which contained a poem in which a boy chooses a book as his present, passing over the rowdier options of a "sword or drum." The other publisher produced a book called *Kriss Kringle's Raree Show, for Good Boys and Girls.* This, too,

Santa Claus as Theater Manager. This illustration, from the title page of *Kriss Kringle's Raree Show* (1845), shows Kriss Kringle in the role of a theater manager, collecting tickets from the eager boys shoving to get into the show on Christmas Day. Kriss Kringle is depicted as a plebeian here, and he even smokes a short pipe! *(Courtesy, American Antiquarian Society)*

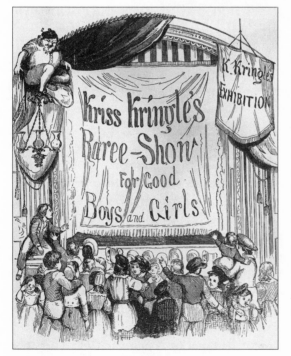

Theater Interior with Curtain Down. Kriss Kringle is now seated atop the chandelier at the top left, his pipe tucked into his cap. From this position he will draw the curtain for each change of scene. The audience itself suggests elements of misrule: One boy is sitting on the stage; the little girl in front of him is crying; and another little girl (at the right) is blowing a tin horn. *(Courtesy, American Antiquarian Society)*

Theater Interior with Curtain Raised. Only the scene onstage has changed here—the rest of the setting remains the same (as it does in every single illustration in this book). The dramatic scenes, this one showing Indians battling Conquistadores, are all represented as merely drawings on an inner curtain. This is a low-budget operation even in fantasy! *(Courtesy, American Antiquarian Society)*

was a gift book. Its text consisted of a series of history lessons—thirty-eight very brief stories (two pages each), most of which were accounts of famous battles in American or European history.[75]

But the text of *Kringle's Raree Show* is the least interesting thing about this book. What is more intriguing is the way the book was organized around the conceit implied by its title. A *raree show* meant either of two things.[76] Its first meaning was "a show carried about in a box," such as an exhibition of pictures, viewed through a magnifying lens inserted in a small opening at one end of the box (this would later become known as a "peep show"). Indeed, each of the thirty-eight historical accounts contained a full-page picture—and instead of being divided into chapters, each account was labeled a "sight" (thus "Sight the Twenty-First" was "the Capture of Stony Point" during the American Revolution; and "Sight the Thirty-Eighth" was "the Battle of Lake Erie" during the War of 1812).

The second meaning of the term *raree show*, by extension, was large-scale and theatrical: "a spectacle of any kind," or a "spectacular display," especially a theatrical spectacle (often, apparently, one related to pantomime). *Kriss Kringle's Raree Show* fit this definition because it pretended to offer the experience of going to the theater—specifically, the experience of a group of children attending a theatrical "exhibition" at Christmas. On the title page is pictured the arrival of the children at the theater (page 128, top). Kriss Kringle plays the role of theater manager in this picture. Standing at the entrance, he takes the children's tickets as they attempt to press into the hall. He is pictured much as Moore described Santa Claus—a plebeian, short and plump, bearded, holding "the stump of a pipe" in his teeth. (But that is also, I suspect, very much the way an actual theater manager of the time might have looked.)

The book's brief introduction sets the scene and also describes the interior of the theater. This description is accompanied by a full-page illustration of the interior of the theater, with the lowered curtain at its center (page 128, bottom; the inscription on the curtain is the title of the book). Kriss Kringle, the manager, now magically sits poised atop a candelabrum at the left side of the proscenium, where he will presumably manipulate the curtain for each of the "sights" in the show (or book). In the foreground we see the children who will be the audience (or readers). These children may not exactly resemble the real Philadelphia children who had disrupted theatrical performances two years earlier by "tossing each other . . . over each other's heads and jostling the weak under foot." But they aren't exactly quiet or passive, either. One boy has already climbed onto the stage; several are laughing and talking, and waving (apparently to Kriss Kringle). The little girl on the extreme left is crying, and the little girl at the right is blowing a tin horn (presumably she has received it as a Christmas present; tin horns were such notorious noise-makers that they were later banned in the city of Philadelphia). Finally, several youthful couples appear to be taking the opportunity to do some flirting. I suspect that the artist drew the scene this way because he wanted to convey at least a semblance of how such a theatrical audience would have looked and behaved on an occasion like this—to provide, perhaps,

just enough verisimilitude to evoke in the young readers of the *book* something of the vivid sensation of actually *being there.*

On with the show. At the signal of a ringing bell, the curtain rises
abruptly, and the performance begins. Kriss Kringle is still present, again
in the role of theater manager: "He is enjoying the astonishment and delight of the children at the scene which presents itself on the rising of the
curtain."[77] In each of the scenes that follow—the thirty-eight "sights"—
the same full-page background illustration I have just described appears
(see page 129); the only thing that changes is the "sight" itself (i.e., the historical scene behind the curtain). The purpose of this repetition was presumably to save money and time on the book's artwork; but it also
inadvertently suggests what we already know from other sources: that a
real audience would not have quieted down when the curtain went up.

In *Kriss Kringle's Raree Show* we see in action the battle between the
two cultures of Christmas—going out into the loud streets and staying
quietly at home. But the battle is not really joined. Reading is presented
here not so much as an attractive alternative to misrule as a mini-version
of it, one in which the rowdy adventure went on inside one's head. Here
the two forms of behavior, the two cultures of Christmas, seep into each
other. Reading the book promised the adventure of theatergoing, and
even showed it, and a little of its misrule, led by plebeian Kriss Kringle. It
was possible to experience the excitement of the theater without leaving
home—and without posing (or risking) any real danger. But that, perhaps,
has always been the promise of reading itself.[78]

By the 1840s the police in Philadelphia and other American cities
were regularly on the lookout for gatherings of unruly boys, and ready to
throw them in jail. That was one prong in the assault against Christmas
misrule. *Kriss Kringle's Raree Show* is a very poor book, but it does show us
something of the second prong in that same assault—something that
other, better books did far more effectively. One of those was the famous
Christmas story "The Nutcracker," authored by the German writer
E. T. A. Hoffmann and first published in 1816. Here a proper young girl
has an extended fantasy of misrule in which her world turns crazily upside
down. "The Nutcracker" ended up becoming, in the hands of Peter
Tchaikovsky, a brilliant and popular theatrical spectacle, while *Kriss
Kringle's Raree Show* was quickly forgotten. But both the trite Philadelphia book and its far more ingenious German counterpart shared a single
purpose: to offer youthful readers a secure yet exhilarating Christmas
treat—a carnival of the mind.

CHAPTER 4

Affection's Gift:
Toward a History of Christmas Presents

"Christmas won't be Christmas without any presents."
—Opening line of Little Women *(1868)*

A COMMERCIAL CHRISTMAS

AKING CHRISTMAS an indoor family affair meant enmeshing it in the commercial marketplace. As long as the Christmas gift exchange was still a matter of wassailing from peasants to landlords, from poor folk to rich ones, the gifts themselves most often took the form of food and drink—the landlord's best food and drink, served within his house. Such gifts were not "presents" in the modern sense of being purchased in the commercial market. Oftentimes, indeed, they were manufactured within the household itself, and from grains cultivated by the same peasants who were now receiving them back in the form of "cakes and ale."

When the gift exchange was brought inside and limited to the family circle, such gifts no longer made sense. The wife and children of a prosperous man already ate the household's best food; they were already living in the family manor. What made Christmas special for *them* had to be a different sort of gift, the sort of gift that soon became known as a Christmas "present." And that was precisely the kind of gift that could most conveniently be procured through a *purchase*.

The actual change was not that simple, of course. In the latter part of the eighteenth century, as we have already seen, ordinary households sometimes held special Christmas dinners, dinners that might include (as they did for the Maine midwife Martha Ballard—see Chapter 1) a few special ingredients—sugar, spices, rum—that were purchased in local shops. Or shopkeepers might provide some finishing touch for a hand-made Christmas present: In 1769, for example, Joseph Stebbins paid a shopkeeper in Deerfield, Massachusetts, for "coolering [dyeing] a pare of Mitt[en]s for [his] wife." Presumably the mittens themselves had already been knitted, probably at home, perhaps by Mrs. Stebbins herself. (We can infer that the newly dyed mittens were probably intended as a Christmas gift because the transaction took place on December 22.)[1] We might think of such transactions, in which shops played a small but crucial role, as "semi-commercial." They may have been commonplace, though evidence on this score is extremely difficult to come by—buried in manuscript account-books. But things would begin to change soon after 1800.

IT IS COMMONPLACE, nowadays, to hark back to a time when Christmas was simpler, more authentic, and less commercial than it has become. Even professional historians have tended to write about the pre-twentieth-century Christmas in that way. Generally when people muse along these lines it is to associate the noncommercial holiday with the years of their own childhood, or perhaps the childhood of their parents or (at most) their grandparents.

As it happens, such musings have been commonplace for a long time—for more than a century and a half. Consider the theme of a short story dating back to the middle of the nineteenth century, a story that commented on the profusion of presents bought and sold during the holiday season—and the trouble many comfortably-off Americans had in finding something meaningful to give their loved ones at Christmas. The author of the story was soon to become America's best-known writer—Harriet Beecher Stowe. When Stowe wrote her Christmas story in 1850, she had not yet written *Uncle Tom's Cabin*, although that great novel was beginning to take shape in her mind. But what was also in her mind that year were the problems posed by Christmas shopping.

" 'Oh, dear!' " sighs one of the characters in the opening lines of this story. " 'Christmas is coming in a fortnight, and I have got to think up presents for everybody! Dear me, it's so tedious! Everybody has got everything that can be thought of.' "This character goes on to declare that even though " 'every shop and store is glittering with all manner of splendors,' " it was impossible to decide what presents " 'to get for people that have more than they know what to do with now; to add pictures, books, and gilding when the centre tables are loaded with them now, and rings and jewels when they are a perfect drug!' " When she was a child of 10, explained Stowe (or the character who stands in for her in the story), " 'the very idea of a present was so new' " that a child would be " 'perfectly delighted' " with the gift of even a single piece of candy. In those days, " 'presents did not fly about as they do now.' " But nowadays, things are different: " 'There are worlds of money wasted, at this time of year, in getting things that nobody wants, and nobody cares for after they are got.' "[2]

Just as many people do today, Harriet Beecher Stowe seems to have believed that this change took place within her own generation (she was born in 1811). But the difference is that Stowe was substantially correct. Commercial Christmas presents did start to become common when she was a child, and especially during the decade of the 1820s. This chapter will explore the process by which that came to happen and the implications such a development had for the meaning of the gift exchange.

Advertising for Presents

If the domestic reform of Christmas began as an enterprise of patricians, fearful for their authority, it was soon being reinforced by merchants, who needed the streets to be cleared of drunks and rowdies in order to secure them for Christmas shoppers; by shoppers who in turn needed to feel secure in the streets; and by newspaper editors whose success depended on their mediating between other businessmen and their own readers (who were shoppers, too).

Advertisements for Christmas presents actually began to appear as early as the first signs of interest in St. Nicholas emerged, although they did not become common for several more decades. The first explicit ad for Christmas presents I have found anywhere in the United States comes from a New England community, Salem, Massachusetts. Dating from 1806 and headed "Christmas Gifts," the advertisement was placed by a local bookseller. (Salem was a major port at this time, and a prosperous one.) Boston and New York had their first Christmas advertising two years later, in 1808, when two such ads appeared in the *New York Evening Post*. One of these was for a shop offering "four hundred and fifty kinds of Christmas presents and New-year's gifts, consisting of toys, childrens

[sic] and school books, Christmas pieces, Drawing books, Paint, Lead Pencils, Conversations and Toy cards, Pocket Books, Penknives, &c."[3]

The advertising began to proliferate after 1820. By 1823 Christmas was already becoming so commercial that one Boston magazine was able to make a joke of it:

> "[There] is a time to give," says Solomon, and had [that] preacher lived in these days, he would have acknowledged, that there was no time like the *present,* and never a better assortment of *gifts.* Could he [just] peep into the Bookstore of Munroe & Francis, . . . he might find a book for each of his wives [and] concubines, and each of their children, without purchasing duplicates.[4]

A decade later, in 1834, a letter printed in a Boston Unitarian magazine suggested that the available choice of presents, and the aggressiveness with which they were being advertised, had reached the point where Christmas shopping was becoming a source of confusion. "The days are close at hand when everybody gives away something to somebody," this letter began:

> All the children are expecting presents, and all aunts and cousins to say nothing of near relatives, are considering what they shall bestow upon the earnest expectants. . . . I observe that the shops are preparing themselves with all sorts of things to suit all sorts of tastes; and am amazed at the cunning skill with which the most worthless as well as most valuable articles are set forth to tempt and decoy the bewildered purchaser.

The same letter warned shoppers to "put themselves on their guard, to be resolved to select from the tempting mass only what is useful and what may do good," and to avoid "empty trifles, which amuse or gratify for the day only."

> The very multitude bewilders most purchasers; and often have I been pained to observe the perplexity of some kind parent or friend, who wished to choose wisely, but knew not how, and after long balancing took something at random, perhaps good, perhaps worthless.[5]

Only too familiar. Even in a small town in rural New Hampshire, in 1835 a local newspaper printed a cautionary tale titled "Reflect Before You Buy"—a story written for young children![6] Similar examples abound from following years. By the time Harriet Beecher Stowe published her 1850 lament, the sentiment she expressed had become a commonplace.

Most commercial presents were manufactured for children. The very first advertisement I have found for Christmas presents, the 1806 one from Salem, Massachusetts, was for "a large assortment of Youth's and Children's Books." The first ad from Boston, in 1808, was for "Books for Children." The first New York ad, also in 1808, was for children's books and toys.[7] Over the years, children remained the primary target of Christmas ads, but they ceased to be the *exclusive* targets. In 1809, for example, four of the five ads for holiday presents that appeared in one Boston newspaper were for the entertainment of children, but the remaining one focused on the decoration of women: "a general assortment of elegant and fashionable JEWELLERY [sic], consisting of Fine pearl set Brooches; Ear Rings; Finger Rings; Bracelets, &c., with rich carnelian and topaz Centers; . . . carnelian Necklaces; Ear Knobs; Tops and Drops; tortoise-shell Combs of all descriptions; gold Watch Chains. . . ." (Women, like children, were dependent members of the household. Only later were adult men included as appropriate recipients of Christmas presents.)[8]

A thorough examination of early-nineteenth-century American newspapers might well yield slightly earlier dates for such minor milestones as the first complaint about consumer confusion or the first Christmas advertisement. But the pattern itself seems clear enough: Commercial Christmas presents were first publicly advertised in the first two decades of the nineteenth century, and the advertising became pervasive during the following decade, in the 1820s. And through the "country editions" printed by many urban newspapers for their rural readers, word that Christmas presents were available (and fashionably appropriate) spread throughout much of the United States.

In the early 1840s advertisements for Christmas presents became more numerous, ornate, and sophisticated, and newspapers began to organize them into a separate category titled "Holiday Advertisements." These columns were typically placed on the front page, at the very beginning of the advertising section (one New York paper noted in 1841 that they held "the post of honor").[9] Christmas advertisements began to appear earlier and earlier, into the second week of December.[10] On December 23, 1845, Horace Greeley's *New York Tribune* announced that the paper would be "compelled to issue a [special] supplement" the following day so as "to make room for the matter which the pressure of Holiday Advertisements has crowded out for a few days past." ("By the way," it added, "our readers who think of making Christmas Presents will find our advertising columns unusually interesting. Almost every thing worth buying is offered there. Read and make your selections.") Finally, Santa Claus himself began to be used in advertisements, and of course in shops themselves, as a way of attracting the attention of children (more about this later).

It was probably no accident that these aggressive advertising tactics were devised in hard economic times. The depression that set in at the end of 1839 was the deepest the United States had yet experienced. But merchants, abetted by newspapers, openly used Christmas as a way to attract shoppers even in the depths of the depression. One Philadelphia paper announced on December 24, 1841, that "Christmas is at hand," and tried to persuade its readers to ignore economic conditions for a while by opening their purses to buy holiday gifts. The newspaper represented the depression as "Old Hard Times," an unpopular monarch. But readers were assured that he "has abdicated for the present," to be replaced by a more benevolent figure: "Old Santa Claus is expected tonight, and gaily are the windows of the fancy, fruit, cake, and other stores decorated to receive him—and puzzled will the old fellow be to make a selection from the thousand curiosities, delicacies, and elegancies which are spread before him." The newspaper itself was prepared to come to Santa's assistance: "In consideration of the many duties that he has to perform at this time, we will endeavor to lighten his labors; and in order that he may make the best choice to be found in the city, we are determined to send him a copy of the Ledger, where he will find every thing that is worthy of his notice judiciously advertised under the proper head. . . ."[11]

Most Philadelphia shopkeepers emphasized the variety of gifts they had in stock and—in a tacit acknowledgment of the hardness of the times—the wide range of prices for which they could be bought. A jeweler made the point as well as anyone: He had rings as costly as $25 each, but also as cheap as 25 cents (the same was true of his earrings, breast pins, gold and silver pencil cases, and so on). This jeweler even offered violins for sale—at anywhere from "$1 to $40."[12]

Businessmen went to great lengths to persuade Philadelphians to visit their shops. Beginning with the 1840 Christmas season, a fierce competition developed among the city's confectioners, who devised the idea of baking immense cakes that would be displayed in their shop windows on December 23—"mammoth cakes," they were termed. Customers could purchase pieces of the cake to take home. One of these cakes weighed in at 250 pounds; another was twice that size. The following year the stakes went up: One confectioner titled his ad "LARGE AND EXTRA MAMMOTH FRUIT CAKE—NEARLY 1000 POUNDS."[13] Another confectioner concluded his ad with a verse:

My cake is of a giant size,
Form'd to delight your tastes and eyes;

Lastly, to name a case in point,
The *Times* being sadly out of joint [i.e., the depression] . . . ,

My *Prices* shall be very small,
To meet my patrons, one and all.

Confectioners also created an even more widespread fad: caramel-ized sugar and chocolate molded into a variety of improbable shapes, and crafted to appear real. One report, from Philadelphia, referred to lavish Christmas displays of candied "mutton chops, sausages, boiled lobsters, pieces of bacon, cabbages, carrots, loaves of bread, &c. all made of sugar, and colored to the life."[14] More common shapes included various kinds of animals as well as oversize insects such as beetles, spiders, and—for some reason these were a special favorite—cockroaches.

LUXURY AND THE LURE OF CHRISTMAS

There is a paradox here. Christmas presents were almost by definition lux-ury items—and luxuries are the first things that people give up when times are hard. But there was also another side to the same coin, a coun-tervailing impulse that made many people vulnerable to splurging at Christmas, even in hard times. Businessmen knew that Christmas was the one time of the year when people had long expected to buy and consume things they did not need, even if they could not really afford to. A New York newspaper, the *Herald,* had played on this point two years earlier, when the depression was just coming on. Despite the state of the econ-omy (what the writer of one article coyly termed "the rumored hardness of the times"), Christmas presents were readily available, and everyone should purchase something—at the very least, a present for the "one being that they love." Forget the depression for a little while, this writer coun-seled: "Who is there, that is not ground into the very dust by biting poverty, that would hesitate, at this hallowed season, to bestow a souvenir upon this one beloved object—this cherished flower of affection?"[15] This writer was well aware of how vulnerable his readers were to the call for spending even beyond their means "at this hallowed season."

It was potent fuel. Christmas had long been a special ritual time when the ordinary rules of behavior were upended. It was a time when people let strange things happen to their sense of what was acceptable behavior, their sense of limits. Christmas was (and still is) a time to let go of ordinary psychological restraints, to shift into an inner state in which it became possible to do what was otherwise unthinkable. What made that sort of indulgence objectively possible in an agricultural society was, as we have seen, the cycle of the seasons, in which December was a time of leisure and a season of plenty—plenty of food and drink. It was a time when consumption—overconsumption—was expected. It was a time to gorge on the best food and drink—not just bread and beer but "cakes and ale." It was a time to splurge, until the hard freeze of winter, and with it the constraints of ordinary existence, set in once again.

For many people living in America (and Western Europe) in the second quarter of the nineteenth century, that seasonal rhythm was less powerfully imposed, less all-defining, than it had once been. Urbanization and capitalism were liberating people from the constraints of an agricultural cycle and making larger quantities of goods available for more extended periods of time. But that change was very recent; and memories of the behavioral rhythms of the old seasonal cycle were still fresh. Late December was still associated with letting go, with splurging, with overindulgence in luxuries that were hardly available at all during the rest of the year.

In early-nineteenth-century America, however, Christmas had to contend with another countervailing force. This had to do not with seasonal rhythms but with cultural predisposition. Most Americans of the Jacksonian period were predisposed to distrust luxury and excess. Even where buying luxury goods was economically possible, it was ideologically suspect. During and after the War for Independence, Americans had been taught that indulging in luxury was frivolous—that it was a vice associated with the decadent aristocratic nations of Europe. The American Republic had to be more abstemious than that if it was to survive and prosper. Buying luxury goods amounted, therefore, almost to a subversive political act, the kind of small gesture that could jeopardize the future health of the Republic. Consumer capitalism and civic virtue were not commonly associated with each other in early-nineteenth-century America.

Once again, Christmas came to the rescue. For this was one time of the year when the lingering reluctance of middle-class Americans to purchase frivolous gifts for their children was overwhelmed by their equally lingering predisposition to abandon ordinary behavioral constraints. Christmas helped intensify and legitimize a commercial kind of consumerism.

Producers and merchants were not slow to grasp these connections. They recognized that it was possible to exploit the season by offering a plethora of "fancy" goods, luxury items of precisely the kind that few people were willing to purchase at any other time of the year: books, toys, jewelry and fancy clothes, candy and cake. After all, one of the defining characteristics of an effective Christmas present was that it *was* a luxury, not something that satisfied a practical need. As Horace Greeley put it in an 1846 editorial, a Christmas gift should never be "a matter of homely necessity."

A commercial Christmas thus emerged in tandem with the commercial economy itself, and the two were mutually reinforcing. On the one hand, the new economy made possible that now-familiar development—the commercialization of Christmas. On the other, Christmas itself served to fuel the general process of commercialization. It was the thin end of the wedge by which many Americans became enmeshed in the more self-indulgent aspects of consumer spending. (To be sure, it has recently become clear that the "consumer revolution" was actually a long process, one whose beginnings historians now place back in the colonial period, even before the American Revolution.[16] But the process accelerated sharply around the beginning of the nineteenth century.) Christmas was used to lubricate the "demand side" of a dynamic commercializing economy. Much as Christmas alcohol helped release one sort of ordinarily forbidden behavior, so Christmas advertising helped release another sort. In this way Christmas became a crucial means of legitimizing the penetration of consumerist behavior into American society.

Affection's Gift

Books as Gifts

As it happened, publishers and booksellers were the shock troops in exploiting—and developing—a Christmas trade. And books were on the cutting edge of a commercial Christmas, making up more than half of the earliest items advertised as Christmas gifts. (The very first commercial Christmas gift I have encountered was the almanac that Martha Ballard's son-in-law received from one of his acquaintances. See Chapter 1.) In fact, even before books were actually labeled as Christmas presents in the newspapers, they were being marketed for that purpose.

Mason Locke Weems ("Parson" Weems), a bookseller and writer who is remembered today for inventing the legend of young George Washington and the cherry tree, distributed his own books as Christmas presents in 1810—including the popular biography of Washington in which the cherry tree story first appeared. That year he advertised that he would offer a deep discount to buyers "who take several copies of Washington and Marion [another biography] for Christmas Boxes to their young relations."[17]

Even in New England, and as early as 1783, the publisher Isaiah Thomas inserted on Christmas Day in his Worcester, Massachusetts, newspaper an ad titled "Books for little Masters and Misses, proper for NEW YEAR'S GIFTS." A year later Thomas ran a similar ad, headed "CHILDREN'S BOOKS. . . . Very proper for parents &c. to present to their children as New-years gifts, &c." (He inserted these ads on December 25, probably because the term "New Year's" covered the two holidays together.)[18] Then, in 1789, Thomas went a step further: He published a little children's book, *Nurse Truelove's Christmas Box* ("Christmas box" was a term for a Christmas gift). The text of this book actually concluded with a promise from "Nurse Truelove" herself—she was something of a cross between Mother Goose and Santa Claus—"to make a present of another book by way of *New Year's Gift*, (which will be published soon after *Christmas*)." As a parting shot, "Nurse Truelove" added an explicit ad for Isaiah Thomas's Worcester bookshop: "In the mean time, if you should want any other little Books, pray send to Mr. *Thomas's*, where you may have the following" (what followed was a list of children's books that Isaiah Thomas had on hand). Thomas was using the special associations of the Christmas season with luxury spending to get children (and their parents) into his shop.[19]

Gift Books

It was in the 1820s that publishers began to cultivate the Christmas trade in a systematic fashion. In 1826, for example, the Boston booksellers Munroe and Francis printed a special Christmas flyer—207 children's books, ranging in price from 6¼ cents to 40 cents each. Two years later the same booksellers circulated another flyer; this one was headed "Christmas and New-Year . . . Presents for the Coming Season." Four densely printed pages in length, it listed the better part of a thousand items.[20]

But it was not just by heavy advertising that the book trade acted as the shock troops of a commercial Christmas during the 1820s. The most important step it took in that direction was to invent a new kind of product, in the form of a new literary genre that was specifically linked to the Christmas season. The genre was the "Gift Book"—a mixed anthology of poetry, stories, essays, and (frequently) pictures. Gift Books were always published at the very end of the year, just in time for sale as Christmas presents. Whenever one of them sold well, a new number bearing the same title would be brought out a year later (giving rise to an alternative name for the genre, "literary annuals").

Gift Books first appeared in Europe at the beginning of the decade and were taken up in the United States in 1825, when the Philadelphia publishers Carey & Lea brought out *The Atlantic Souvenir.* The preface to this volume defined the new genre as a specific combination of sentiment, season, and content:

> Nothing would seem more naturally to suggest itself, as one of those marks of remembrance and affection, which old custom has associated with the gaiety of Christmas, than a little volume of lighter literature, adorned with beautiful specimens of art.

Of course, the genre had no more suggested itself "naturally" than was the practice of buying Christmas presents really an "old custom." Still, within a very few years American Gift Books had proliferated wildly. And their proliferation followed a clear pattern, one that was unprecedented in the history of American publishing. Gift Books were available at every price range and for every conceivable market—demographic, religious, political, and cultural. Some Gift Books consisted entirely of poetry; others were humorous (*The Comic Annual*). There were Gift Books for children (in fact, for boys and girls separately), young men, mothers, Jacksonian Democrats, proponents of temperance and abolitionism, even members of men's clubs (*The Masonic Offering* and *The Odd Fellows' Offering*). In other words, publishers had managed to divide the market for Gift Books into highly specialized niches—identified by class, age, ideology, and cultural temperament. They had managed to achieve an astonishing degree of what modern economists now refer to as *market segmentation.*

And an equally high degree of market *penetration.* From the time they were introduced in 1825, Gift Books were sold in almost every corner of the nation and advertised in newspapers throughout the American hinterland. What was especially remarkable about this market penetration was the way it was organized: Virtually every American Gift Book was published in one of only three places, in the cities of Boston, New York, and Philadelphia. And this was in an era when the publication of other kinds of books was still being carried out on a strikingly decentralized basis. (In fact, books were often printed in towns so small that nowadays they would not even support a local newspaper.)[21] Gift Books had a nationwide distribution that was based on a highly centralized mode of production. Here again, they were on the cutting edge of economic change in the United States.

Many Gift Books were ornate, with gilt edges, lavish bindings, expensive engravings, and colored "presentation plates." But they came at all price levels. James Gordon Bennett's *New York Herald* noted in the depression year 1840 that Gift Books "come within the range of the means of most persons, varying in price from $3 to $15"; and it added pointedly: "There are few that would wish to give a lady a present of a less value than $3."[22]*

Gift Books were compiled whenever possible by a popular author whose name on the title page could be expected to guarantee added sales. They could be put together fast, in a matter of weeks if necessary. In 1837, one apologetic editor publicly acknowledged that the decision to compile his Gift Book "only suggested itself to the Publisher a fortnight before the last sheet was put to press," and that the work had to be completed so quickly because the publisher wished it to "appear at the season when the annuals and other similar publications are most in request."[23] Nowadays such books are called quickies.

Gift Books have been studied to show their influence in disseminating literature and art to the American public. They have also been studied, more than any other genre of printed matter, as physical objects, examples of the "materiality" of literary culture: to show that books were not only read but also gazed at, fondly handled, and proudly displayed. What I wish to add here is a point that it is easy to overlook: Gift Books were marketed as *presents,* purchased only to be given away. Indeed, as far as I can determine, Gift Books were the *very first* commercial products of any sort that were manufactured specifically, and solely, for the purpose of being given away by the purchaser. And, of course, they were to be given away during the Christmas season. The overwhelming majority of Gift

---

* In a sense, Gift Books picked up where almanacs left off, as popular reading for Americans. There are some striking parallels. Both genres were annuals: They appeared each year as part of a series, with the same title, format, and organization; in both cases the only thing on the title page that changed from one year to the next was the year itself. Almanacs themselves were often filled with "literary" material (though this was usually more "oral" and "folk" in nature than the literary material found in Gift Books), and they even contained illustrations. Finally, both genres were sold during the Christmas season. (Indeed, the first commercial Christmas present I have encountered was an almanac.) But for all that, the differences between the two genres were even more striking (which is why Gift Books are not ordinarily linked with almanacs). First, almanacs were produced primarily for adult male readers, while Gift Books were more often produced for female or youthful readers. And second, almanacs were intended to provide not just entertainment but also information that was of "public" use (e.g., dates of court sittings, a calendar, even weather predictions), while Gift Books were intended to provide "culture": literature, art, moral values—bourgeois values. Those differences suggest transformations far more significant than the term *genre* might suggest.

Books bore as their subtitle the phrase "A Christmas and New Year's Gift" (or "Present"). That is why they were often so physically ornate: Christmas was the appointed time for luxury spending. Once again, the case of Gift Books suggests the manner in which Christmas was consciously used by entrepreneurs as an agent of commercialization, an instrument with which to enmesh Americans in the web of consumer capitalism.

For at least one major publishing house (and probably others), Gift Books represented the single-largest venture of the business year. The Philadelphia firm of Carey & Lea invested heavily in the production of *The Atlantic Souvenir.* In 1829 and again in 1830, the firm printed 10,500 copies of this very popular Gift Book, at a cost of more than $12,500 each year; in 1830 this sum came to more than 30 percent of their *total* production costs for the year. (The $12,500 included printing costs and payments to the book's editor and its contributors, but the single most expensive item, easily exceeding all the authors' payments combined, was the book's engravings.) But Carey & Lea hoped for a substantial return on their investment: if the press run sold out, they would take in $17,386, for a net profit of almost 40 percent.[24]

Gift Books were marketed with aggressive new techniques. For example, they commonly contained their own advertisements—not tucked away in the back pages but inscribed within the literary matter itself. (This was especially true of Gift Books that were intended for children.) Sometimes this self-advertising took the general form of a story or poem in which a character insisted that books (and especially Gift Books) made the best presents. Take *The Violet* for 1837 (edited by Eliza Leslie, whom we have encountered before as the author of the story about young Robert Hamlin's Philadelphia shopping excursion). This volume contains a poem in which four young siblings discuss the Christmas presents they would like to receive. Three of the four indicate that they are hoping for toys. But the fourth child, an older sister, knows that children will quickly lose interest in toys. What she wants instead are books—and a Gift Book most of all:

> For me, of books I should not tire
> Were hundreds on my shelf;
> I'll tell you now my chief desire—
> An "Annual" for myself;
> With cover handsomely emboss'd,
> And gilded edges bright;
> With prints to look at, tales to read,
> And verses to recite.

Often poems such as this named the very Gift Book in which they appeared. The 1840 preface to a children's Gift Book, *The Annualette*, contained this typical verse:

> Annuals for every taste, for every age,
> Lie scattered round, decked in their covers gay. . . .
> Then choose, and neither old nor young forget—
> Each child, at least, must have the ANNUALETTE.[25]

Sometimes such verse even advertised other volumes on the publisher's list. For example, *The Pearl* was published by the Philadelphia firm of Ash and Anners, which also published a periodical named *Parley's Magazine*. Sure enough, a poem in *The Pearl* for 1836 has a father who tells his children, as he is handing them their presents:

> Here's Parley's Magazine, my boys,
> And for my little girl
> Here is a very pretty book,
> Whose title is "The Pearl."

And in the very next number of *The Pearl*, for 1837, one story ends with a group of children opening their Christmas presents. " 'I am so glad that I have got *The Pearl*,' " one says, and a second chimes in after opening another holiday book brought out by the same publishers: " 'I have *The Boys' Week-Day Book*—I have wanted it so much.' "[26]

Even Santa Claus got into the act. The preface to a Gift Book first published in 1842 as *St. Nicholas's Book* conveyed the point that it had been put together directly on the personal instructions of St. Nicholas himself, who desired to have a book "made exactly to his mind for the Christmas of this year" and who therefore "applied to the author to make one, to be called 'St. Nicholas's Book for All Good Boys and Girls.' " The preface noted, simply, "Here it is." And it continued:

> Each of those children whom Saint Nicholas . . . most highly approves, will be sure to find a copy of this book, with all its stories and pictures, and its nice binding, safely deposited in his stocking in the chimney corner, on the morning of next Christmas, or at farthest, next New Year's Day.[27]

When they were manufactured as presents for adults, Gift Books were often ornate and luxurious to the eye and hand. Commonly, they were named to suggest their resemblance to other kinds of beautiful luxury objects, notably jewels or flowers, both of which were also popular as

Christmas presents (the latter were newly available in winter through commercial hothouses). Thus, for jewelry, there were the *Amaranth, Amethyst, Amulet, Brilliant, Coronet, Diadem, Gem, Gem of the Season, Jewel, Literary Gem, Lyric Gem, Opal, Pearl,* and *Ruby.* For flowers, there were *Autumn Leaves, Bouquet, Christmas Blossoms, Dahlia, Dew-Drop, Evergreen, Floral Offering, Flowers of Loveliness, Garland, Hyacinth, Iris, Laurel Wreath, Lily, Lily of the Valley, Magnolia, May Flower, Moss-Rose, Primrose, Rose, Rose Bud, Violet, Winter-Bloom, Wintergreen, Woodbine,* and *Wreath.*

Gift Books were probably among the most expensive books many Americans had ever purchased. Take the experience of a rather prosperous man, John Davis of Worcester, Massachusetts. (A future governor of Massachusetts, he was then serving in the U.S. Congress.) On December 26, 1826, Davis wrote to his wife that he had visited a Washington bookstore and bought her a "very beautiful" Gift Book:

> I went into a bookstore to see what was the price of a souvenir [i.e., a Gift Book] that I might send you a new year's present. I saw them advertised as very beautiful and found them so as you will judge by the price $5. This bookstore is one of the best . . . the most pleasant I ever saw. The proprietor . . . seems to spare nothing to get the most rich and costly collections of books, of prints, maps and everything else. The shop is not large but elegant. I saw many things I wanted to buy but they cost too much.[28]

Davis admitted here that he had been tempted to buy "many things" that were more expensive than he was used to purchasing. But he did spend $5 on a single book for his wife—and he let her know it (which suggests that he was not used to spending so much money on books).

IT WOULD be unfair to conclude that these books were purchased and given away simply as a display of conspicuous consumption. Christmas gifts had to be (or appear to be) expressions of personal sentiment, designed to signify or enhance intimate personal bonds—bonds between parents and children, husbands and wives, suitors and those they courted. And that is surely what parents, husbands, and suitors wanted them to be. Such Christmas presents were intended above all to represent an *expression of feeling.* This meant that they were to be given freely, out of affection, and not as part of an old-fashioned gift exchange offered in fulfillment of an obligation. The *Herald*'s new rival, Horace Greeley's *New York Tribune,* put this point quite clearly in 1846: "The season approaches when Good Wishes take visible, palpable form, becoming active in the shape of Gifts. . . . To give and receive the free will offerings of Friendship and Affection are among the purest pleasures permitted to this state of being. . . ." Greeley stressed that such "free will offerings of Friendship and Affection" had nothing in common with the traditional exchange of gifts for goodwill:

> A present given to create a sense of obligation, even to a dependent or child, becomes at the best a Charity, humiliating rather than inspiring the receiver. Charity is well in its place . . . : but a Gift of Affection is quite another matter.

That was why it was so important for the gift to stand outside the realm of ordinary day-to-day needs, to be a luxury item and never what Greeley called "a matter of homely necessity or mere mercantile utility." "In short, it should not so much satisfy a want as express a sentiment, speaking a language which if unmeaning to the general ear, is yet eloquent to the heart of the receiver."[29]

Greeley knew that spouses and lovers often presented such Gift Books to each other. And an editorial puff in the *New York Herald* in 1839, describing the "splendid volumes" of Gift Books on sale at the local bookshops, suggested that they would make the best possible present for the "one beloved object," the "cherished flower of affection" in their lives. The notice concluded pointedly: Such presents say, "in language not to be mistaken, 'Forget me not.' "[30]

In other words, the presentation of a Gift Book could be used as part of the courtship process, as a way of deepening a personal relationship or signaling a willingness to do so. That often meant treading a delicate line—to be personal and sincere yet not *too* intimate. As the preface to one Gift Book phrased the matter:

> In the festive season of the year, when kind feelings flow forth in gifts, tokens, and remembrances, nothing . . . is more appropriate as a souvenir, than a handsome book. It can be given and received without a violation of delicacy. . . .[31]

There was a problem here. Whether Gift Books were used by suitors or by affectionate parents, there was an inherent tension between the message they were intended to convey and the fact that they were actually mass-produced and mass-marketed commodities. Given the personal weight such gifts were meant to carry, that was hardly appropriate. It was crucial that they be able to conceal the facts of their own production and distribution—to disguise their origins, in other words.

One reason that Gift Books made such successful Christmas gifts is that they managed to do that job very well. (In the antebellum years, as now, both jewels and flowers seemed to do the job, too, since they were not only beautiful luxury goods but also objects that could be represented as the creations of nature. This was another reason so many Gift Books were named for jewels and flowers.) Sometimes the very title of a Gift Book indicated the sentiment it was meant to carry: thus *Souvenir* itself (meaning something to be remembered), but also *Affection's Gift, Forget Me Not, Friendship's Offering, Gift of Friendship, Keepsake, Leaflets of Memory, Memento* (subtitled "A Gift of Friendship"), *Remember Me, Token,* and *Token of Friendship*. Both *The Pearl* and *The Rose* were subtitled "Affection's Gift," and in that way associated jewelry and flowers, respectively, with personal feelings—with the world of domestic affections, not the world of commodity production.

The publishers of Gift Books took pains to give their products a personalized look. Of course, *any* book given as a present could be personalized by means of an inscription on the flyleaf, giving the name of the giver and the recipient (and their relationship), and adding the date on which the book was presented. But Gift Books went further than that. Ironically, the very techniques of mass production were employed to make Gift Books appear personal and unique, to convey the impression that they were customized, even handmade, products. At the frontispiece of each volume, there typically appeared a special introductory page known as a "presentation plate"—an engraving expressly designed to be written on by the buyer of the book, to personalize it and make the presentation itself an intrinsic part of the book.

Some presentation plates contained room for the purchaser not only to fill in his name and the name of the person who was to receive the book but even to compose a phrase that indicated the precise degree or quality of affection he wished the present to convey. Thus the presentation plate in *The Token* for 1833 (a Gift Book that also happened to include three newly published stories by Nathaniel Hawthorne) left an empty line in which the purchaser was to fill in just what the book was a token of. (In the copy of this volume owned by the American Antiquarian Society, a man named Waldo Flint has written that his present to Rebekah Scott

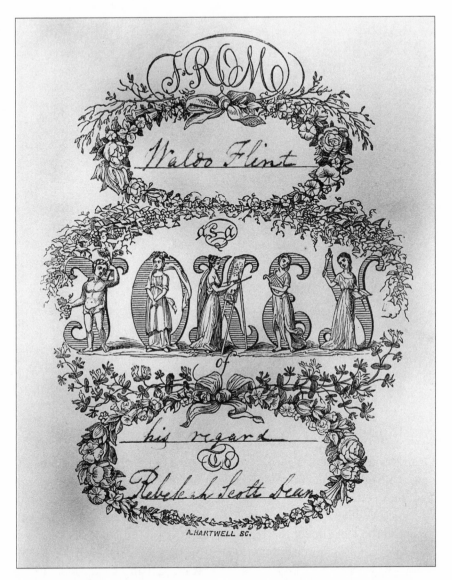

Presentation Plate. The printed part of this plate (from a Gift Book called *The Token*) leaves only three phrases to be filled in by the book's purchaser. It reads: "From ———— as a Token of ———— to ————." This particular number of *The Token* happened to contain the first publication of three stories by Nathaniel Hawthorne. *(Courtesy, American Antiquarian Society)*

Courtship at Christmas. The young Cupid in the foreground of this presentation plate has just shot an arrow into the heart placed in the background at the right. There is little ambiguity here as to the point being made by anyone who purchases this Gift Book as a Christmas present! *(Courtesy, American Antiquarian Society)*

Dean was to be taken as a token of "his regard.") In other Gift Books the nature of the relationship was already embedded in the design of the presentation plate, as it was in an 1837 design showing a picture of a Cupid who has, William Tell–like, just shot an arrow into the heart that sits perched atop a pediment located to his right.

Gift Books might be said to represent the "commercialization of sincerity." As a genre, they flourished for little more than a single generation, between 1825 and 1860. Perhaps they held a special appeal for this particular generation, which was the first to be overwhelmed by the world of commodities and thus the only one that needed to disguise commercial transactions when they threatened to intrude on an intimate setting. A generation earlier, one could argue, such transactions had not been possible; a generation later, they would be so commonplace that the violation would have seemed virtually invisible.

Bibles as Christmas Gifts

Most American families owned a Bible if they owned no other book. But before the nineteenth century these were *family* Bibles, large and durable folio volumes meant to be used in family devotions and to be passed down through the generations. But early in the nineteenth century Bibles became "personal" books as well, books meant to be the property of the individual who owned them.

Such Bibles—especially editions of the New Testament—were heavily marketed at Christmas. Booksellers frequently advertised their selection of Bibles as heavily as they did their Gift Books—and right beside them. Here is a selection of ads placed in a Philadelphia newspaper by five different booksellers on a single day, December 24, 1844:[32]

> —[B]eautiful annuals [i.e., Gift Books], bibles, and prayer books, and other publications, suited to all ages and inclinations.

> —[A]n elegant assortment of juvenile books, religious books, miniature books for gift books, bibles, prayer books and testaments.

> —[A]nnuals, prayer and hymn books, pocket bibles, &c.

> —[H]andsome hymn books, annuals, prayer books, and bibles.

> —[A]nnuals, bibles, prayer books, &c.

Even more self-evidently than with Gift Books, giving Bibles must have felt like a gesture suffused with sincerity, far removed from the world of commodity production and commercial exchange. But from a publisher's perspective, Bibles were commercial products. And as the market for Bibles expanded, so did the competition between editions. They came big and small, fancy and plain, fat and thin. Like Gift Books, too, Bibles came in a great variety of sizes, shapes, cover styles, and colors. Personal Bibles, especially, were often small in size—"pocket Bibles," as they were known. There were even illustrated Bibles for young children.[33] Booksellers advertised such Bibles as they advertised Gift Books, emphasizing their elegant bindings and illustrations. Personal Bibles were marketed with special vigor during the Christmas season, along with booksellers' other wares, as another kind of "elegant" Christmas present. As early as 1818, a bookseller in Portsmouth, New Hampshire, printed such an advertisement on December 22 (and headed it "*Christmas and New Year's Day*"):

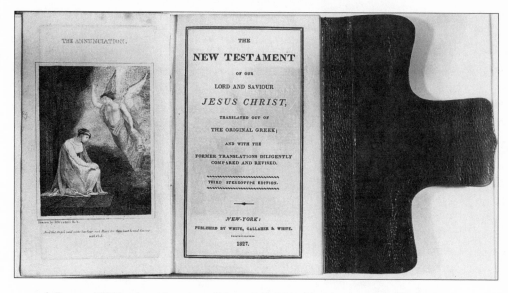

A Personal Bible. A pocket-size edition of the New Testament, printed in 1827. As this illustration shows, the binding included a leather clasp (shown at the right), the handle of which would be inserted into a slit on the front cover when the book was closed. This particular volume was inscribed to "Mrs. Dean," the mother of Rebekah Scott Dean, whose Gift Book's "presentation plate" is shown on page 149. *(Courtesy, American Antiquarian Society)*

His shop was offering "Elegant diamond type Pocket Bibles, superbly bound in morocco, full gilt"—though he would also sell "Common [i.e., plain] Pocket Bibles." In 1821, in Worcester, Massachusetts, Isaiah Thomas managed to spend the enormous sum of $30 on "elegant Bibles" for his granddaughters.[34]

By the 1820s Bibles were competing with one another for market share even in their content. One might think that all Bibles were the same on the inside, but this was not the case. Take illustrations, for example. The pictures printed in various illustrated editions of the Bible often emphasized one or another element of the text (divine wrath or divine mercy, for instance), presumably to appeal to readers of varying theological preferences or aesthetic sensibilities—once again, a form of market segmentation. And many Bibles were published with end matter appended to make the book more accessible or alluring; these included chronologies and tables of pronunciation, etymology, geography, scriptural weights and money, as well as colored maps. Several Bibles published in the 1820s contained an ingenious foldout "Key," designed to make the meaning of many of the verses easier to ponder.

But Bibles were able to disguise their identity as commercial products, even more effectively than Gift Books. The divine authorship of the
Bible, and its role as an infallible guide to the conduct of human life, rendered any clever sleight of hand quite unnecessary, especially when a Bible
was intended as a present—and even when its physical packaging was
used as a marketing device. Horace Greeley's *New York Tribune* made the
point quite clearly in 1846. After arguing that holiday gifts had to be "the
free will offerings of Friendship and Affection," objects that would "express a sentiment," Greeley went on to suggest that Bibles were the
"fittest" holiday present he had "ever yet beheld." But Greeley was not referring to just *any* Bible: "We speak of THE ILLUMINATED BIBLE, published by Harper & Brothers in a superb royal quarto of some 1500 pages,
profusely illustrated by Adams from designs selected from the most superb European editions." This edition contained "a Chronological Index,
a General Index of Subjects, a Concordance, an Alphabetical List of
Proper Names, with their significations, Tables of Weights and Measures,
&c." Most impressive of all was the physical package itself; the press work
was "glorious" (there were usually three or four illustrations on each page)
and the binding "rich and durable" (the book was leather-bound, hand-
tooled, and embossed with gold, and its pages were gilt-edged). For those
reasons, Greeley predicted that "many thousands of copies are destined to
be treasured as tokens of Affection from and after the Holydays."[35] And
indeed, the Harpers *Illuminated Bible* opened with a presentation plate of
its own, an inscription page that read only "A Sacred Token, From———
To———," leaving two blank spaces for the names of giver and intended
recipient to be filled in. In other words, the *Illuminated Bible* was deliberately marketed as a Gift Book.

The *Illuminated Bible* was a commercial triumph, selling enough
copies in its first dozen years to earn the publishers a staggering $500,000
in retail receipts.[36] But tiny personal Bibles sold well, too, and they seemed
better suited to fulfill Greeley's own stated criterion, as objects that would
"express a sentiment." Like Gift Books, again, these small volumes were
often purchased to be given as a present by one family member to another:
by a parent to a child, a husband to a wife, or a lover to his affianced. Here
are several examples, taken from the American Antiquarian Society's
holdings of Bibles published in the single year 1827—a randomly selected
year:

—"Henry Cheever, From his affectionate brother George—A
   Thanksgiving present, November 14, 1828."

—"This little volume is a New Year's Gift to Horace James, by his affectionate Mother. . . . Jan. 1, 1828."

—"Mrs. Dean with the sincere love of her affectionate daughter Rebekah. December 21st, 1827." (This is the same Rebekah Dean who would in turn be presented with a Gift Book six years later, by Waldo Flint in token of "his regard" for her—see illustration on page 149.)[37]

There is a classic literary example of all this, and one that occurs in a very famous book—Louisa May Alcott's 1868 novel *Little Women*. When the four young sisters who inhabit this novel awaken on Christmas morning, each one finds a "little" illustrated copy of the New Testament under her pillow, inscribed with "a few words by their mother." The four presents are of the identical edition (each contains "the same picture inside"); but the colors of the covers are different, and Alcott specifies just what they are: Jo's copy is "crimson-covered," Meg's is "green," Beth's is "dove-colored" (i.e., beige), and Amy's is "blue." (Beth was "very much impressed by the pretty books," Alcott tells us; and Amy says " 'I'm glad mine is blue.' ")[38] The gift of these Bibles is an effective gesture of emotional intimacy (their mother, "Marmee," knows her daughters' precise individual tastes). But at the same time they are part of a process by which Marmee is training her daughters to make informed decisions of their own in the confusing world of consumer preferences.[39]

In fact, another popular fictional heroine of the period is simply overwhelmed when she is forced to select her own Bible. Near the beginning of Susan Warner's runaway best-seller of 1851, *The Wide, Wide World*, the young heroine, Ellen Montgomery, is taken by her mother to visit a book shop. As mother and daughter enter the shop, Ellen senses "a delicious smell of new books" (starting with "[c]hildren's books, lying in tempting confusion near the door"—that is, placed right at the entrance). And when Ellen heads for the Bibles, her "wits were ready to forsake her":

> Such beautiful Bibles she had never seen; she pored in ecstasy over their varieties of type and binding. . . . "Now, Ellen," said Mrs. Montgomery, "look and choose; take your time, and see which you like best."

Ellen looks the Bibles over intensely: "[A]s though a nation's fate were deciding, she was weighing the comparative advantages of large, small, and middle-sized; black, blue, purple, and red; gilt and not gilt; clasp and no clasp." First, Ellen selects for herself "a large, royal octavo Bible, heavy enough to be a good lift for her." But her mother persuades her that it would be too bulky "for everyday use." So she chooses again, this time "a beautiful miniature edition in two volumes, gilt and clasped, and very perfect in all respects, but of exceeding small print." (Ellen says, " 'Isn't it a beauty? I could put it in my pocket, you know, and carry it anywhere with the greatest ease.' ") This time Mrs. Montgomery warns Ellen that reading the fine print in such a book would soon cause her to require eyeglasses—and so presumably to lose her beauty.

Ellen is bewildered. She has "lost the power of judging amidst so many tempting objects. . . ." Finally, rejecting "all that were decidedly too large, or too small, or of too fine a print," she chooses among three Bibles "of moderate size and sufficiently large type, but different binding." Her mother approves of all three; Ellen finally picks "the red one."[40]

This was the best-selling novel of its day. Susan Warner's point is clear, and her scores of thousands of avid readers must have responded to it: There was simply *too much stuff.* The very choices buyers faced made them feel helpless. Middle-class America was consumer heaven, but consumer heaven was also consumer hell. The Bible itself—the Book of Books, the one book that offered a certain guide through the labyrinth of human existence—had become a part of the labyrinth, another overwhelming commodity.

THE SEDGWICKS:
HOW ONE FAMILY DISCOVERED CHRISTMAS

The commercial and domestic Christmas did not enter American culture in some abstract fashion, through some impersonal force called *consumer capitalism.* It was actively pressed, as we have seen, by actual producers and sellers and their cultural allies. And on the other side it was actively embraced, person by person and community by community. To show something of that embrace, I have chosen to focus in detail on a single American family. What makes this family—the Sedgwicks of western Massachusetts and New York City—such a rewarding case study is the richness of the private papers they left behind. The Sedgwicks were more numerous, and their papers cover a longer period of time, than any of the scores of other families whose Christmas practices I have traced. The extant Sedgwick family correspondence, housed in several hundred manuscript boxes at the Massachusetts Historical Society, is filled with detailed and interlinked descriptions of domestic events, including holiday rituals. The family letters give us a good picture of the way a prosperous New England family made the transition to a child-centered Christmas focused on the exchange of commercially produced presents. Some of the letters were actually written by children. And there is a final touch, though it will receive its due attention only in the next chapter: One member of this family, the writer Catharine Maria Sedgwick, herself played a small role in the larger history of this holiday—for it was she who wrote the first fictional account of an American Christmas tree, in a story published in 1835.

THE SEDGWICK CLAN was the leading family in Stockbridge, Massachusetts, a small town located in the Berkshire Hills in the rural western part of the state. The family patriarch, Theodore Sedgwick (1746–1813), moved to the area from Connecticut before the Revolutionary War, and afterward he became an imposing political presence, serving first in the Massachusetts legislature and later in the U.S. Congress, where he advanced from the House of Representatives to the Senate. In 1799 Theodore Sedgwick moved back to the lower house, to be elected its Speaker. In 1802 he was appointed to the Massachusetts Supreme Court. Always a staunch political conservative, Sedgwick was a leading opponent of Shays's Rebellion, the populist uprising that swept through Massachusetts in 1786–87, and he became an active member of the Federalist Party under the new constitution of 1787.

Theodore Sedgwick had ten children, born between 1775 and 1791, and seven of the ten lived to reach adulthood. His four surviving sons entered adulthood between 1800 and the early 1820s. Three of these sons became lawyers; two of them moved to New York City to pursue their practice. None of the children achieved anything like their father's power, although Theodore, Jr., did get himself elected to the Massachusetts state legislature (he also became a Democrat and an antislavery reformer during the 1830s). The most prominent and influential of Theodore Sedgwick's children, though, was not any of his sons but his youngest daughter, Catharine Maria Sedgwick (1789–1867). Catharine Sedgwick became a professional novelist and short-story writer—indeed, one of the most popular American authors during the 1820s and '30s.[41] Along with all her siblings, she rejected Calvinist orthodoxy and became a committed Unitarian.

Sedgwick Family Genealogy

(includes marriages and surviving children born to 1830)

THEODORE SEDGWICK I (1746–1813), m. 1774 PAMELA DWIGHT (1753–1807)

I. Elizabeth Mason (1775–1827), m. 1797 Thaddeus Pomeroy:
1. Theodore Sedgwick Pomeroy (1798–1845), m. 1822 Huldah Hopkins:
   a. Theodore Sedgwick II (b. 1824)
   b. Mary Jane (b. 1825)
   c. Frances Hopkins (b. 1829)
2. George William (1799–1856)
3. Egbert (1801–25)
4. Pamela Dwight (1803–04)
5. Elizabeth Pamela (1805), m. 1827 Judge Horatio Byington
   a. Eliza Sedgwick (b. 1829)
6. Ebenezer Watson (1806–61)
7. Frances Susan (1807–53)
8. Catherine Eliza (1809–80)
9. Julia (1812–?)
10. Charles Sedgwick (1813–50)
11. Mary (1815–72)
12. Thaddeus (1817–51)

[II. Unnamed child, died at birth, 1777]

III. Frances Pamela (1778–1842) m. 1801 Ebenezer Watson of Hartford:
1. Theodore (1802–1820)
2. Ebenezer Henry (1804–50), m. 1829 Elizabeth Knapp
3. Catherine Sears (1806–48)
4. Robert Sedgwick (1809–88)
5. Frances Pamela (1811–?)

IV. Theodore II (1780–1839), m. 1808 Susan Livingston Ridley:
1. Theodore III (1811–59)
2. Maria Banyer (1813–1883)

[V. Catherine (1782–1783)]

[VI. Henry Dwight (1784–1785)]

VII. Henry Dwight (1785–1831), m. 1817 Jane Minot (1795–1859):
1. George Minot (1818–21)
2. Jane (b. 1821)
3. Frances (b. 1822)
4. Henry Dwight II (b. 1824)
5. Louisa (b. 1826)

VIII. Robert (1787–1841), m. 1822 Elizabeth Dana Ellery:
1. Elizabeth Ellery ["Lizzy"] (b. 1824)
2. William Ellery ["Ell"] (b. 1825)
3. [Robert (1826–27)]
4. Susan Ridley (b. 1828)
5. Henrietta Ellery ["Haddie"] (b. 1829)

IX. Catharine Maria ["Kitty"] (1791–1856), the author

X. Charles (1791–1856), m. 1819 Elizabeth Dwight:
1. Katherine Marie ["Kate"] (b. 1820)
2. Charles (b. 1822)
3. Elizabeth Dwight (b. 1826)

Source: Hubert M. Sedgwick, *A Sedgwick Genealogy: Descendants of Deacon Benjamin Sedgwick* (New Haven: New Haven Historical Society, 1961)

The Sedgwicks were hardly a typical American family. But as patrician as they may have been, they were not terribly wealthy (not in the same league as a man like Clement Clarke Moore, for example). In financial terms, the children of Theodore Sedgwick could best be described as belonging to the prosperous upper-middle classes. Furthermore, their fundamental conservatism (and their rural base) acted as something of a brake on the family's temptation to enmesh themselves in a consumerist Christmas.

The correspondence of the original family patriarch, Theodore Sedgwick, covers almost exactly the same period as Martha Ballard's diary (see Chapter 1). Except for a single letter from 1776, the holiday-season letters begin in the mid-1780s, and Theodore himself died only months after Martha Ballard did. Despite the differences in the social status of the Sedgwicks and the Ballards, the pattern of holiday rituals observed by the two families turns out to be somewhat similar. Christmas and New Year's are mentioned casually in the correspondence, in the form of seasonal salutations, especially in letters Theodore Sedgwick received from his friends. Theodore's wife, Pamela Dwight Sedgwick, noted the holidays more frequently than did Theodore himself, wishing her husband a "joyful Christmas" in 1792 and opening a letter to him two years later by noting that "It is a most beautiful Christmas morning."[42] Domestic presents do not enter the picture.

Theodore Sedgwick preferred to observe the season with alcohol. On January 2, 1784, his old friend and political crony Henry Van Schaack wrote him a characteristically jocular letter centering on a cask of wine. Van Schaack called Sedgwick a "drinking devil" and promised that when the two men met "We will eat & drink & be merry."[43] In fact, during the Christmas season Sedgwick and all his old friends characteristically wrote to one another in this fashion, under the guise of "good old boys." The convention endured well into Sedgwick's middle years, even though by then he was a member of the U.S. Congress and claimed to have forsworn such behavior. On January 9, 1795, he thanked another friend for his "New Years wishes" and inquired, "Where did you eat your beef stake? I suppose you gluttonized at the Tavern, and drank a little, and swore a little and gambled a little. But with all these wicked things I should have been glad to have participated not in them but in your mirth and good humour." And on December 23, 1799, Henry Van Schaack wrote to Sedgwick: "We dined at Judge Silvesters this day and demolished 3 bowls of the wine you sent."[44]

As much as anything else, Sedgwick and his friends used such festivities as a male ritual, implicitly based on the exclusion of women. When Sedgwick served in Congress during the 1790s, he wrote frequently and disdainfully of the "ladies' parties" that he was invariably pressed to attend during Christmas week in Philadelphia.[45] But along with women, it was children who were excluded from Theodore Sedgwick's holiday festivities. In all the scores of surviving letters written during this season over the years between Theodore and his wife and their seven children, there is no indication until the very end that the Sedgwicks observed the season with any special domestic celebration at their house in Stockbridge. It was Pamela Sedgwick who would write to her husband—enviously, it seems— "This is a season of great festivity to *you.*" But for her own part she had nothing to report.

Before 1804, Theodore never once so much as mentioned the holidays in his letters to his children. In that year, he finally wished them all "many happy new years." Apparently such greetings were more appropriate for Sedgwick's old friends than for his own children. (By this time Sedgwick's youngest child was 13 years old, and the others ranged in age from 16 to 28.) In any case, each year from 1804 until his death eight years later, Sedgwick invariably used the approaching New Year to lecture them about the need for critical self-reflection. On December 24, 1804, he wrote his sons a long moralizing letter warning them of the dangers of dissolute behavior, especially gambling at cards, an activity that had long been associated with the Christmas season. But nowhere in all this correspondence is there any hint of domestic celebration. Nor do such hints appear in the surviving letters written in these years by second-generation Sedgwicks themselves, whether to their father or to one another.

It was not for lack of interest. Theodore Sedgwick's children (along with their mother) keenly felt the absence of holiday festivity, at least when they were in their teens. But what they yearned for, it seems, was parties and dances, not domestic rituals—for precisely the kind of activities that Theodore Sedgwick experienced (and scorned) as a congressman in Philadelphia. As early as 1798, Pamela Sedgwick wrote about the loneliness of being in Stockbridge during the holiday season:

> We have little Matter to communicate as we live without seeing much company and know very little of what passes in our Neighborhood. The girls generally find amusement in conversing upon and scaning [scanning] the characters of their male acquaintances[.] [T]hey have very few Parties and have had but two Balls this winter. They think this want of amusement [is] the dearth of all Pleasure.

They think Stockbridge the most Intolerable Place in the world and would Prefer Greenland or Zambly[?] to staying here.[46]

The holidays did not go wholly unacknowledged in Stockbridge. On New Year's Day, 1805, Catharine M. Sedgwick (then 16 years old) used the bulk of her morning "to discharge my domestic duties, and greet my neighbors with the salutations of the New Year." And that afternoon her privacy "was interrupted by the most unwelcome and vexatious visitors." Although we have no way of knowing why these particular guests seemed so "vexatious," the Sedgwicks were the squires of Stockbridge, and it should come as no surprise that Catharine accepted such holiday visits from the townsfolk as part of her "domestic duties."[47]

December 1805 found Theodore Sedgwick's 20-year-old son Henry in Albany, New York. He reported to his father the public rituals of the season there, rituals that openly embraced the kind of interclass begging rituals that may not have characterized Christmas in rural New England:

> The holydays, our great season of festivity have this day com-
> menced. . . . It is an undoubted fact that a considerable number of
> pennies has been given to the boys & servants, and I am credibly in-
> formed that this liberality has sometimes amounted to the sum of six-
> pence. Astonishing if true![48]

But Theodore Sedgwick responded to his son's letter merely by noting that "another year has passed," and the occasion was a fit one to "retrospect."[49] Only in the final year of the patriarch's life does any sign of change appear. On January 1, 1812, Theodore Sedgwick's married daughter Eliza S. Pomeroy wrote to her brother Henry D. Sedgwick that "Pappa . . . gives a New Year feast" for some guests, and that she and her seven children would participate. And she added, "The little ones are as happy and playful as lambs."[50]

By decade's end, the tide had begun to turn. Theodore Sedgwick's children were beginning to wish one another a merry Christmas and a happy New Year, and to report Christmas dinners and New Year's parties.[51] In the mid-1810s two of the Sedgwick sons, Henry and Robert, had moved to New York City, where they set up a joint law practice. Their sister Catharine, now an aspiring writer, lived with them. But it was not on account of their departure from New England that things were beginning to change. Henry Dwight Sedgwick was married by this time, into a distinguished Boston family (his wife, Jane Minot Sedgwick, was the daughter of a prominent Boston judge). During their courtship, in 1816, he wished her a "merry, merry Christmas," confident that this would cause his New England fiancée no offense. Indeed, Jane Minot's Congregationalist family had been celebrating Christmas in Boston for years. In December 1817, the first year of her marriage, Jane's brother wrote to her that "[o]ur Christmas was a merry one," adding that he had dined "with some young people." And three years later Jane Sedgwick herself wrote to her sister Louisa Minot of her nostalgia for the "mince pies and plum puddings" they had all formerly dined on "at this merry season."[52] In the same letter she conveyed a New Year's greeting to her sister-in-law—and included Louisa's children in the greeting: "A happy New Year to you dear Louisa, & William, & to all yr good little children." This was the first time a member of the Sedgwick family had incorporated young people into their holiday wishes.[53]

S T I L L , no presents were involved in any of these interchanges. The first evidence that any of the Sedgwicks received (or offered) a holiday present was in January 1823, when Catharine M. Sedgwick received in the mail a gift from one of her friends (sent as a "little token of my affections"). The first present involving family members came a year later, and in the third generation of the family, when the two children of Theodore Sedgwick, Jr. (the eldest Sedgwick son, and the inheritor of the family manse in Stockbridge), wrote their father a charming note—entirely in French—apologizing for not having bought a present for *him*.[54]

It was two holiday seasons later, in 1825, that we find the first direct evidence of a commercial gift exchange within the Sedgwick family. For that evidence we can thank Catharine M. Sedgwick, who was living in New York with her brothers Henry and Robert and their families, and who had recently achieved acclaim as an author. Catharine had published her novel *A New England Tale* in 1822, and she was already taking on a role that would endear her to the rest of the family, that of the affectionate aunt who reported in vivid detail all the goings-on within the clan, and especially among its children, all of whom loved her dearly. Catharine Sedgwick took great pleasure in making her nieces and nephews happy, and she was very good at it. And it was to her that all her siblings would invariably turn for advice or comfort.[55]

Unmarried herself, Catharine Sedgwick spent much of her free time in devoted attention to other people, and in passing along news to other members of the Sedgwick clan. On December 28, 1825, she reported to her

5-year-old niece and namesake Katherine that "Jane and Fanny both got dolls from their Aunt Speakman for a Christmas gift." She described the scene vividly: "Jane's was a wax doll with eyes that open and shut—and it looked so much as if it was alive that Jane thought it really was and screamed 'It is alive! It is alive!' "[56]

With this gift we suddenly find ourselves hurled into the orbit of a modern Christmas. The doll is ornate, high-tech, designed to impress, and was obviously purchased at a shop (and, just as obviously, it is *expensive*).[57]

In the second half of the 1820s, Christmas came on in a rush. In 1827 little Kate Sedgwick's parents (they lived in Lenox, a village several miles from Stockbridge) "kept Christmas . . . in Episcopal style." In Stockbridge itself, on New Year's Day the rest of the family gave presents to the children, who "received with the most entire satisfaction the simplest offerings, finding in their own happy hearts the best New Year's gifts."[58] The two teenage children of Theodore Sedgwick, Jr., were in New York that same day, visiting their city kin. Their mother reported the presents they had received, along with details of the prices paid (and even a suggestive hint about the shopping excursion during which the gifts had been purchased):

> Theodore's present [i.e., her present to their son Theodore III] . . . consisted of some very ornamental things for the table, to the amount of $11. I got them [at] a great bargain, the first price asked was $16. Sister Catharine [Catharine Sedgwick], who was with me, thought them as beautiful & cheap as any thing she had ever seen. I wish you could have seen how much they were admired. Sister Catharine presented Theodore with a beautiful cameo breast pin, & decorated Maria [Theodore's sister] with flowers, & Sister Elizabeth [Robert's wife] had kindly provided a very pretty present for both Maria & Theodore, a little article combining a purse, card-case, & tablet—a convenient affair which they both wanted.[59]

Finally, that same year (1827), Robert Sedgwick and his wife, Elizabeth, set up an elaborate new ritual for their two young children (ages 2 and 3), complete with stockings—and Santa Claus. The year 1827 was the very year that Clement Clarke Moore's 1822 poem was finding its way into print in newspapers published in New York and other American cities. It is striking how quickly the Sedgwicks adopted this ritual (and we can be sure that their children would later assume that it went back forever!):

Nothing could exceed the joy of the children on New Year's morning, when awakening with the first dawn of light, they jumped up eagerly to examine their stockings, which, certain of "*Santa Claas*[']" bounty, they had had suspended the evening before from the bed post—and which, according to their anticipations were full to overflowing.[60]

The next Christmas season these same children (now ages 3 and 4) received an even more elaborate bounty, which their mother characteristically described in loving detail:

They received a great many beautiful presents, among which Lizzy had a Mahogany bedstead and Bureau, and a wax doll, whose eyes would open and shut. The Bureau, which is a gift from her father, is really a curiosity. It is more than half a yard square, and has three drawers[,] which are sufficiently deep to hold all her dolls clothes now. And to be useful as she says for her ornaments and Curiosities hereafter[,] ["]when she is a big lady."[61]

By the next year, 1829, Santa Claus had managed to reach the Massachusetts branch of the family. In the little village of Stockbridge, Henry and Jane Sedgwick's children "were awake before day light to feel for their stockings & examine what Santa Clas [sic] had put into them—& I have heard but one [ongoing] peal of merriment from them ever since."[62]

Santa Claus reached the Lenox Sedgwicks, too, that year, but there his bounty was disappointing to Catharine M. Sedgwick's favorite niece Kate, now 9 years old, who conveyed to her aunt the hope "that Santa Claus has given you at least as many presents as he has me, for he only gave me four." (Kate's four presents included a pair of books, a "neat brown pocket book which mother gave, & sixty-eight cents from father.")[63]

In New York, that same day, Elizabeth E. Sedgwick was able to note casually to her father that her two children "had *as usual* a quantity of beautiful presents at New Years [emphasis added]."[64] And the next year, 1830, she used the same phrase, but went on to include some details:

New Years day as usual was a most joyous day to the children. They were loaded with presents from all their friends—whips, tops, dolls, guns, books, tea cups, &c. Never was any thing like it. And never was such happiness.[65]

The implication here was that each year's bounty had to outdo all preceding ones. As it happens, there exists a wonderfully charming account of the excesses of gift giving, in the form of a description of that same scene, taken literally out of the mouth of one of the very children who were on the receiving end of those gifts. For this account we are indebted to Lizzy's aunt, Catharine M. Sedgwick. On January 2, 1831, Catharine Sedgwick penned a document that purported to transcribe the exact words of her little niece Lizzy Sedgwick (now 6 years old, and the oldest of five children). The transcription took the form of a letter from Lizzy herself to her cousin Kate—Catharine Sedgwick's favorite niece. It is a charming account, worth quoting in full (and diligent readers will be rewarded with a passing reference to a cockroach made out of sugar).

> When I went to bed New Year's eve I felt inclined to jump up & run about but I was afraid of waking Haddy [her infant sister, Henrietta]. I moved continually and wanted to jump. I didn't have much sleep that whole night. When we were all dressed we prepared to go into Mama's room to get our New Year's presents & Aunt Kitty [i.e., Catharine Sedgwick] came down to see us. I had mine in a bag & it felt pretty heavy. First I took out something tied in a paper. I found it was a candlestick snuffer & extinguisher. I then took out a box & opened it & found some sugar-men, some candy a cockroach-sugar also & some cherries (sugar!). I then pulled out a case & asked Papa to open it for I found it difficult. There was a microscope in it—*larger than yours*. ([Here Catharine Sedgwick interrupts in her own words:] I was going to add the italicised words when Lizzy with great delicacy said 'No I should not like to say that Aunt Kitty.') Then came the Token for 1831 [a Gift Book], from a gentleman I never saw nor heard of (Mr. Collins, a friend of her father) a large beautiful French box from Mama I forgot to mention, & some sugar-plums. Afterwards I went upstairs & Aunt Kitty gave me a chocolate lamb, very pretty. As we were looking over [her 2-year-old sister] Sue Ridley's basket we heard a squeaking noise[.] I was frightened for I tho't it was one of the children—it was doleful & funny too! I turned round & found it was Ell [her brother Ellery, age 5] blowing a trumpet. He had besides a magic lanthorn[,] sugar men, a whip, candy, a corn-[stick?]. Then for Sue's basket—tea-things & a sauce-pan, a beautiful doll stiffly & fashionably dressed (& I dressed her[:] CMS)[,] a cunning mouse & a French bag of sugar.
>
> In the course of the day George [a friend] came in & Ellery blowed his trumpet. George went out & came in with a gun which he pointed at us. We ran away trembling & George gave the gun to Ellery, then he held out the other hand to me & I grasped it & found a book called The Pearl—beautiful. Next came sister with a snake for

Ellery. I forgot a superb humming-top which Joseph [another friend] bro't Ellery. Then came some play-things from Cousin Roderick's[:] one cavalry-officer whose head took off & on & turned about, & the rider got off the horse. . . . Is not this a pretty good long letter[?][66]

It is all there: the indulgent treatment of young children; the plethora of toys, many of them expensive and ornate (that toy soldier "whose head took off & on & turned about, & the rider got off the horse"); the eager anticipation; the hard-to-open packages; the showing off; even the little edge of competitiveness (the microscope that was *"larger than yours"*). After 1830, then, it is hardly necessary to report year by year on the Sedgwick families' holiday celebrations. It is enough to say that over the next half decade the presents they gave and received became even more elaborate and numerous. And as the presents themselves became more extravagant, expectations rose with them, and so did problems and disappointments. Indeed, over the course of the ten-year period from 1825 to 1835, one or another of the Sedgwicks encountered virtually every problem that besets the Christmas shopper in our own day. Here, organized into some familiar modern categories, are a few examples (all taken from the years 1825–35):

Forgot to buy presents. On Christmas Eve, 1832, Charles Sedgwick wrote in embarrassment that he had returned to his house in Lenox only to find, to his dismay, "the whole house quite gay with Christmas presents." As for himself: "I am in consternation for I doubt not expectation is on tiptoe for presents from me & I have not as yet got one for any body." And he concluded, "Indeed the presentees are so thick I am discouraged."[67] (That last line may suggest still another category of problems: *too many people to buy presents for.*)

Presents that soon break. We have already encountered the doll that little Jane Sedgwick received from her "Aunt Speakman" in 1824, the wax doll that looked so real that Jane "screamed 'It is alive! It is alive!'" It was Catharine Sedgwick who reported this anecdote. But Sedgwick went on to note dolefully that Jane's doll soon "got a dirty mark on her forehead— a little piece broken off her beautiful fat bosom—and all the color kissed off one of her cheeks." Nine years later, a similar fate befell a wooden dog (a dog that actually barked) given to a 2-year-old toddler:

We were so successful with Willie as to protract his pleasures for at least an hour during which time his little wooden *dod* [presumably Willie's pronunciation of *dog*] kept up a merry barking; but alas how fleeting are all worldly pleasures—one untimely blow scattered his disjointed member. He gave a howl of despair as his limbs were torn asunder & Willie poor Willie's notes chimed with those of his de-parted *dod.*[68]

Not received in time, or lost in the mail. Perhaps an even more com-mon problem then than now, given the logistical problems faced by the postal system. In 1834 the gifts sent to Lenox from the New York Sedg-wicks failed to arrive until late on New Year's Day, so the family decided to repeat the entire ritual for the children the next morning. Two years later the presents from New York arrived as late as January 6 (once again the opening ceremony was held the following day); but even then a num-ber of expected gifts appeared to be missing, as Mrs. Elizabeth Sedgwick anxiously wrote to her daughter (then living in New York):

> The things have not all come, as I find . . . by allusions in your letters. There is no present as you mentioned to Bess from her Aunt E. and no box of things (bonbons) I suppose to be distributed by Bessie. . . . I will tell you, for your satisfaction, what we did receive. My parcel from you. Bessie's from you. Charley's book. Ell's book, and his pres-ent from you. Hun's parcel. 1 large parcel of bonbons. 1 ditto almonds. 1 sweets ditto lozenges. Grace's presents from Aunt Lizzy, from you and from Aunt C. Your Aunt Lizzy speaks of a guard chain for Ell which was not to be found among the parcels.[69]

Hard to find the right present . . . "Your stockings are horridly ugly but they are the only *tolerable* ones I could find." . . . *At the right price:* "I hope she will like the ring—it was very cheap. The enamel [ones] like it else-where & *very* little larger were $6, & your Aunt Lizzie preferred this size as a matter of taste—I confess I did not, but like your father I have always rather a hankering for the *best* priced article."[70]

The wrong gift. "The game you sent marked HDS [Henry D. Sedg-wick] is I presume a substitute for the one I asked you to get."[71]

The grass is always greener . . . "The children have had a merry morn-ing, although their New Year's wealth would seem very meagre, in com-parison with the piles of treasure which bless the eyes of the little folks in New York."[72] Or again: "My dearest Aunt, I hope . . . that Santa Claus has given you at least as *many* presents as he has me, for he only gave me four."[73]

What is it? "They [the children] are delighted [with your gifts]—but do explain the use of Bessy's present from Aunt Kitty—we none of us know."[74]

Useless trifles. (It was Catharine Sedgwick who usually made this point.) "The children had their usual harvest of . . . dolls, tea-sets[,] soldiers, horses, & furniture of every description—every useless thing. . . ."[75]

Hint, hint. "If you are at a loss for something to bring Sara you may get her a copy of 'Drake's Poems.' I see them advertised, & I heard her express a wish for it. But perhaps you have thought of something else. I only mention this lest you be at a loss."[76]

Keeping accounts straight. "Will you tell your mother I gave $2.50 for the port-folio, & $3.25 for the ring[,] ⅛ for the candy so that I have of the $8, 2.04 subject to her order. I can't send your acc't for the knives were bo't by my agent & he has not rendered it but the expenditure will not exceed the am't you sent. Your candy is ⅛."[77]

Guess who gets to do the shopping? Here Catharine Sedgwick is writing to her sister Frances Watson: "I meant to have written you a longer letter, but Robert has just given me some money to buy toys for the children & you know what an arduous affair that is."[78] And here is Catharine Sedgwick writing to her niece Kate: "I had enough to do buying my own presents & your Aunt Lizzy's for our own bevy—the Sedgwicks, the Wares, Eben's wife, &c.—but it is worth some trouble to light up a smile of pleasure even if it be as transient as the moment that gives it birth."[79] And Jane Sedgwick writing to Catharine Sedgwick with a request for help: "I will divide with you the N[ew] Years gifts to Roderick's children to the amount of $3 if you will take the trouble to get things."[80]

Finally, here in a single letter are seven different problems, some familiar, some new. The letter was written in 1830 by Catharine Sedgwick to accompany (and to explain) the gifts she was exchanging that year with the Lenox branch of the family (I have numbered and named each of the problems as they cropped up). 1. *Not what she asked for:* "Your friend Joseph got the music for me but he made a mistake in the Swiss Waltz & I hope will change it in time. . . ." 2. *Did it arrive in time?* "Do let me know if you rec'd. your merino in time for Albany." 3. *Don't open it before you're supposed to:* "I hope you will not open your little N[ew] Year matters till 1831." 4. *Already has it, probably:* "Nelson I know is one of Charley's heroes, but I am afraid he already has the book. If so let me know it, & send it to the library at S[tockbrid]ge." 5. *Implicit apology for conventional presents:* "I got the cravat for your father because I know he partic[ularl]y likes black cravats of no. 1 quality—& what can be more appropriate to your mother who is the very personification of modesty—the queen of all the bees—than a work-basket." 6. *Be careful opening it:* "You must unpack the basket carefully, or you will break the sugar toy: there is some of Mrs. S's candy at the bottom for you & Charley." And *7. What do you do with it?* "The beautiful toy which your Aunt E. sends to you & Charley you will have to *study out.* The figures must be placed in the little blocks & bro't on the scene according to the book. . . ."[81]

ENOUGH, then. It is time to ask what we can make of all this. Clearly, things had come a long way in a very short time. One change was economic: It is difficult to imagine any of this happening even a couple of decades earlier, because before the early 1800s there were few commercial children's toys available for purchase in the United States. The other change was psychological: Surely the Sedgwick children had always been loved, but until 1820 they had not been indulged during the holidays (nor presumably at any other time). Indeed, Catharine Sedgwick expressed lingering ambivalence about the new treatment through the 1820s and even beyond; that was why she described most of the 1833 presents as "every useless thing," with the exception of "some such solid articles as an umbrella to Ell', & solid books of solid History." That was also the meaning of her little homily about the decay of the wax doll.

Taken by itself, the experience of the Sedgwick family would be merely provocative. This was, after all, just a single family, and a prosperous one at that. But the Sedgwicks' collective experience mirrors exactly the pattern that we have seen in the data provided by urban newspaper advertisements and the history of the book trade. The key decade for the Sedgwicks was the 1820s, and especially the years from 1825 to 1829. At the beginning of the decade, the holiday season meant, at most, festive semipublic dinners in which children might participate (this feasting is reminiscent of what had been happening in the Ballard family of rural Maine only a few years earlier). At the end of the decade, the typical Sedgwick Christmas entailed an elaborate set of rituals, centered on giving lavish purchased gifts to the children of the family. These rituals were part of a new world of consumerism, a world that had hardly existed before but which had now sprung up with sudden urgency. To read a letter describing any one of the Sedgwick Christmas holidays after 1825 is to read a letter that might have been written in our own time.

SANTA CLAUS AND THE
MYSTIFICATION OF CONSUMPTION
Santa Claus as Commercial Icon

It was the figure of Santa Claus that permitted the Sedgwicks, and many other Americans, to enter the world of commercial gift-giving so quickly and completely. As early as the mid-1820s, Santa Claus was beginning to be employed to sell Christmas goods. The first such usage I have encountered comes from the proprietor of a New York jewelry shop, in the form of an advertising flyer composed in elaborate verse form. The scene is set on Christmas Eve (shops were generally open then, and often on the morning of Christmas Day itself). The narrator is a prospective customer seeking a present for a lady friend:

> And as I priced a pin
> Which caught my raptured eye,
> St. Nicholas came in! . . .
>
> He instantly commenced
> Selecting trinkets rare,
> As Christmas compliments,
> From lovers to the fair;
>
> He rummaged every shelf,
> The choicest gems to buy—
> I saw the Saint myself!
> What will you lay [i.e., bet] it's a lie? [82]

But it was during the early 1840s that Santa Claus became a common commercial icon, a figure used by merchants to attract the attention of children to particular shops. Santa Claus was barely twenty years old by then, and he had been a figure of national scope for fewer than fifteen years. In fact, the first popular visual image of Santa Claus was published in 1841, in a New York paper. But in 1842 that very picture was appropriated by a shop in Albany, which used it as part of a newspaper advertisement. The picture, in double column, was labeled "Santa-Claus in the act of descending a chimney to fill the children's stockings, after supplying himself with fancy articles . . . at Pease's Great Variety Store, No. 50 Broadway, Albany." Three years later the same picture was being used to accompany the ad of a confectioner's in Cincinnati. [83]

SANTA CLAUS, OR, ST. NICHOLAS, IN THE ACT OF DESCENDING BROTHER JONATHAN'S CHIMNEY ON NEW-YEAR'S EVE.

Santa Claus, 1841. This handsome woodcut, from 1841, was the first visual representation of St. Nicholas to be widely distributed (an earlier picture had appeared in 1830 in the *Troy Sentinel,* the same newspaper in which Clement Moore's poem first appeared). *Brother Jonathan,* into whose chimney this Santa is about to descend, was a weekly New York paper. According to the caption, the scene is set on New Year's Eve. *(Courtesy, American Antiquarian Society)*

Back in 1841, a shopkeeper in Philadelphia managed to attract thousands of children to his shop by adding a life-size model of Santa Claus that was apparently based on that same picture. One newspaper reported the delight this figure caused among youthful passersby:

> Much as our young readers have heard or imagined of this worthy character as the bountiful patron of good children on Christmas Eve, they probably never expected to behold the real personage in the very act of descending a chimney, as our friend Parkinson has shown him over his well thronged shop door in Chesnut street. He was decidedly the attraction yesterday and last evening, and monopolized more than his share of the attention of the young folks, which is usually bestowed with undivided attention on the bon bons in the windows.[84]

Another local paper fleshed out the picture, noting that "his hand [was] full of toys and his face covered with a broad smile—just that benevolent expression that those who love children ever wear." In fact, the fig-

Commercial Santa. In 1842, just a year after the publication of the woodcut shown opposite, the picture was appropriated for commercial purposes by an Albany merchant named Pease, whose name and address have been added to the bottom of the sack of toys that Santa is carrying on his back (at right, above). Two years later, a newspaper in Cincinnati carried a redrawn version of the same picture (at left), which was printed sideways simply because the merchant in question had paid for only a single-columned advertisement. The text of his advertisement read, in part: "Come at last! Important Arrival. The little people of this big city will doubtless be rejoiced to learn that the sterling old Dutchman, Santa Claus, has just arrived from the renowned regions of the Manhattoes, with his usual annual budget of Nick-Nacks for the Christmas Times. Look upon his back and shoulders, and you will get some idea of the curiosities and niceties that he has brought out this year; and in addition to all these, he has some altogether superior, hidden in his wallet, not to be seen till day before Christmas. The old gentleman has taken up his head-quarters this year at LOUDERBECK's, on 4th street, between Main and Sycamore. . . ." *(Both illustrations: courtesy, American Antiquarian Society)*

ure was so lifelike that "no lad who sees it, will ever after accuse pa or ma of being the Kriss-Kringle who filled his stocking. That such a person exists will be most indelibly fixed upon their memories." [85]

Santa Claus as Anticommercial Icon

Accusing Pa or Ma of being Kriss Kringle! From the beginning, it seems, parents found it difficult to convince their children that it was truly Santa Claus who brought their presents. But what matters just as much is that (then as now) they found it necessary to work so hard to do just that. What was it that made the pretense so important? Why did parents need to pretend that Santa Claus was real, and to deny that the presents really came from family members themselves? The answer is that Santa Claus had an extraordinary ability (in spite of his early commercialization) to disguise the fact that most of the presents he brought were commodity productions.

Like other Americans, writers, editors, and advertisers in the second quarter of the nineteenth century liked to pretend, or even believe (as most Americans nowadays continue to do), that Santa Claus represented an old-fashioned Christmas, a ritual so old that it was, in essence, *beyond* history, and thus outside the commercial marketplace.

We now know that this was mostly a myth, and that Santa Claus was all but invented in the early nineteenth century (and that the world of seventeenth-century Holland in which he had previously appeared was itself prosperous and highly commercialized). But the very people who chose to adopt the Santa Claus ritual, from the 1820s on, were willing to believe that he was a figure of great antiquity, and that in introducing him into their own households they were carrying on an authentic, ancient, and unchanging Dutch folk tradition. That was what they read, year after year, in the newspapers and magazines. Such people knew in one way, of course, that Santa Claus was not real. But in another way they did believe in his reality—his reality as a figure who stood above mere history. In that sense, it was adults who needed to believe in Santa Claus.

But if Santa Claus was new in the 1820s and '30s, so too was the ideology of domesticity itself, by virtue of which he entered so many American households. Domestic ideology placed children at the very center of family life, and assumed that families existed more to provide emotional gratification than to engage in economic production. In one sense, of course, it is true to say that the new domestic Christmas was an expression of that new ideology—a veritable celebration of domesticity.

But the obverse is true as well: The new domestic Christmas also helped to *create* that ideology. Even more than today, the exchange of Christmas gifts in the 1820s and '30s was a ritual gesture intended to generate the sense that sincere expressions of domestic intimacy were more important than matters of money and business.

That was a heavy burden to place on Christmas presents—especially since most of them were produced, advertised, and sold as mass-market commodities. The personal feelings that Christmas presents were intended to engender actually hinged on a process that enmeshed those presents in the same commercial nexus that the gift exchange promised to transcend. The result was one of the most basic internal contradictions of our modern world: Marketplace commodities were given the job of generating intense, and intensely private, emotions.[86]

It should not be surprising, then, that the nineteenth-century Americans who began to celebrate the new domestic Christmas needed, just as much as our own generation, to believe that the holiday gift exchange was rooted in something deeper and more "authentic" than the dynamics of the marketplace. To do their job, Christmas presents had to obfuscate their commercial origins.

Some presents—Gift Books and Bibles, for instance—had their own ways of accomplishing that. And for other presents the practice of gift-wrapping could be an effective technique. One newspaper tried an appeal to ancient history, claiming that even "Greek and Roman babies" had been given "expensive toys" by their parents, so that it was unnecessary to think of fancy commercial presents as a recent invention, a raw product of the modern economy—they were burnished by the sands of antiquity.[87]

But it was Santa Claus who was able to provide this kind of reassurance best of all. Santa was even more effective than ancient history; he stood *outside* history. And from a parent's perspective, the mystery of St. Nicholas effectively short-circuited any childish queries about where all the presents came from. We might say that Santa became an anticommercial symbol at the very moment he was used for commercial purposes. Better yet, we might say that it was precisely *because* he was such an effective anticommercial icon that he could become such an effective commercial icon. The two roles were quite compatible with each other. In fact, they were different sides of the same coin. Both the commercial and the anticommercial Santa were functions of the new domestic Christmas. (Here they stand in glaring contrast to *another* Santa Claus—the carnival Santa explored in Chapter 3, that "whoreson" who "boused it" and flirted

Santa's Workshop. This picture was one of several colored illustrations that Thomas Nast prepared for book-length editions of "A Visit from St. Nicholas." Notice that Santa's workshop contains only hand tools, and no machinery. This picture appeared in 1869. (Another Nast portrayal of Santa's workshop, from the early 1870s, shows the old fellow using needle and thread to make a hand-sewn stocking—at a time when almost every middle-class household had a sewing machine.) *(Courtesy, American Antiquarian Society)*

with the girls, and with whom the domestic Santa Claus was not comfortable at all.)

The domestic Santa did the job in several different ways. His old "Dutch" origin was one of these, of course. The very fact that the Santa Claus ritual could be seen as ancient and unchanging offered a powerful symbolic link to an earlier and seemingly noncommercialized folk culture.

Just as important were the actual details of the Santa Claus ritual itself. To begin with, the presents came from Santa Claus, not from the parents—and therefore not from shops. Santa mediated magically between parent and child—between the buyer and the recipient of the gifts. His presence was what took the gift out of the realm of commerce—in the eyes of parents, perhaps, as well as children. To phrase this in a more contemporary fashion, we might say that Santa "mystified" consumption.

He also mystified production and distribution. One of the great mysteries of Santa Claus was that he managed to provide presents for *all* children, everywhere. And he made them all himself—he was the producer of his own gifts. Finally, of course, he was the distributor, a distributor who managed to disburse his presents one house at a time. How Santa managed to do this was often the first skeptical question that children asked; but that he did so (and that the *how* of it all is a great mystery) must be a part of the parents' answer.

And Santa's presents are as good as handmade. Clement Clarke Moore's poem "A Visit from St. Nicholas" never described the actual manufacture of Santa's presents—nor did the structure of the poem leave any space in the text that would invite professional illustrators to do so. But illustrators found the room anyway. Beginning in the late 1860s, the most popular illustrated editions of "A Visit from St. Nicholas" began to provide pictures of "Santa's workshop," pictures that always presented it as a place of household production, where only old-fashioned hand tools were in evidence. Even though this was the very apogee of the Industrial Revolution, Santa's workshop was never violated by the presence of machinery.

In short, Santa Claus managed to reconcile opposites. He customized mass production. He maintained a personalized relationship with his enormous mass market—after all, his clientele was all but universal. And he did it all from motives that were in no way entrepreneurial. Santa Claus magically combined what in reality had now become a series of separate roles: He was simultaneously the gifts' producer, distributor, seller, purchaser, and giver. In a new age of commodity production, what Santa Claus was able to offer—what he offered to *grown-ups*—was the moral equivalent of a world that had never wholly existed in the first place. It was the fading world of the household economy.

CHAPTER 5

Under the Christmas Tree: A Battle of Generations

INTRODUCTION: FROM DISORDER TO SELFISHNESS

$\mathcal{E}$ VERY SOLUTION generates its own problems, and the child-centered consumer Christmas was no exception—particularly for people who found such a celebration most appealing. The concern those people came to feel was actually rooted in broad issues of child-rearing within the new middle-class family, but it came to a head in their fears about what a child-centered consumer Christmas might do to their children's character. This chapter will examine the intersection of a new way of celebrating the holiday with just those broader cultural issues. It will suggest that the introduction of Christmas trees represented an effort to cope with the problems posed by the child-centered Christmas.

In about 1830 the literature of Christmas in America began to change. Before that date it dealt chiefly with questions of social disorder. Afterward a new concern emerged, an anxiety about private selfishness and greedy consumerism, especially as those issues affected children. Young people themselves had previously been seen as a source of disorder at Christmas, along with the poor ("Do not let your Children and Servants run too much abroad at Nights," as that 1719 Boston almanac had warned). As part of the process by which middle-class young people were separated from the "lower orders" of society, they were created as "children" (a process explored in Chapters 3 and 4). But consequently they now began to be seen as easy prey to materialism, superficiality, and selfishness. Middle-class Americans were becoming concerned that the holiday season was an infectious breeding ground for juvenile materialism and greed. Consumerism was coming to supplant chaos as the new problem of the holiday season. The battle for Christmas was beginning to change from a physical struggle that pitted the classes against one another into a moral one that divided the generations.[1]

That is the context in which the Christmas tree became an American holiday tradition. In fact, it was what lay at the heart of the emerging middle-class interest in the rituals of Christmas in Germany, of which the Christmas tree was the preeminent example. As we shall see, these rituals were associated with children who were *not* selfish, and for whom Christmas was an opportunity to give as well as to receive.

There is a belief among those who care about such things that the Christmas tree was spread throughout American culture by German immigrants. There is some truth to this. But, much like the notion that Santa Claus was brought to these shores by the Dutch settlers of New Amsterdam, such a belief also conforms to our desire to see our Christmas customs as rooted in something old-fashioned and authentic, in ancient folkways untainted by the marketplace. But Christmas trees became widely known in the United States during the mid-1830s, almost a decade earlier than any broad-based immigration from Germany can be said to have occurred.

As it turns out, the most important channels through which the ritual was spread were literary ones. Information about the Christmas tree was diffused by means of commercial literature, not via immigrant folk culture—from the top down, not from the bottom up. It was by reading about Christmas trees, not by witnessing them, that many thousands of Americans learned about the custom. Before they ever saw such a thing, they already knew what Christmas trees were all about—not only what they looked like, but also how and why they were to be used.

I shall deal, one by one, with each of the sources through which Christmas trees were introduced into middle-class American culture during the 1830s. Each source, as we shall see, reveals in turn a different element with which this ritual was associated: first, the element of *surprise;* second, that of *folk authenticity;* third, *unselfish children;* and finally, *parental control.*

Who were the writers who introduced the Christmas tree into American culture? The evidence suggests that, much like the Knickerbockers who devised Santa Claus, these writers constituted something of

a distinct set. Like the Knickerbockers, the members of this set were genteel and cultured. But they were part of an emerging upper middle class
that laid no claim to preserving an aristocratic social order. In contrast to
the Knickerbockers, too, they lived mostly in New England and Philadelphia, not New York, and the church of their choice was Unitarian rather
than Episcopal. And instead of being politically reactionary, they tended
to stand somewhere on the progressive, reformist side of the issues that
were coming to divide Americans in the 1830s. This is not to say that the
members of this set were of a single mind on every matter. After 1830, as
we shall see, they were divided over the emerging antislavery movement,
and also over issues of child-rearing. But in any event they used culture
rather than politics as an instrument to influence the social order. They
employed their cultural authority—a combination of literary skill and access to the most popular channels of print—in a strenuous effort to deal
with what they feared were the corruptive cultural effects of consumer
capitalism, especially on the young. The Christmas tree played a serious if
relatively minor role in that larger project.

SOME CHRISTMAS TREES
Little Charley's Christmas Tree

There is no document about the Christmas tree that corresponds to
Clement Clarke Moore's verses about Santa Claus. Instead, there are only
various legends that describe how the Christmas tree came to America.
One of these legends is about Hessian soldiers during the American Revolution (it dates the real event too early); another is about Queen Victoria and her German-born husband, Prince Albert (it dates the event too
late).

What is probably the most famous of the legends, and the one with
which we shall begin, has it that the first American Christmas tree was
set up in Massachusetts, in 1835, by Charles Follen, a German immigrant
who had become an American citizen and a Harvard professor. The
source of that legend is a popular book written by a very famous British
visitor to the United States, a woman named Harriet Martineau, who
happened to witness the Follens' tree while she was touring New England. As Martineau wrote, "I was present at the introduction into the new
country of the German Christmas-tree." Though this was not the *first*
American Christmas tree, it is certainly true that Charles Follen set up a
Christmas tree in Martineau's presence for his son and namesake, an en-

dearing 5-year-old whom everybody called "little Charley." It is time to visit the scene.

The tree (actually the top portion of a fir or spruce) had been placed in the front drawing room of the house. A toy hung from every branch, and when Martineau arrived Charles Follen and his wife were just adding the seven dozen little wax candles. As little Charley and two older companions approached the house, the adults quickly closed the door to the front drawing room and moved into an adjacent room, where (as Martineau put it) they sat around "trying to look as if nothing was going to happen." After the visitors were served tea and coffee, a round of parlor games was played in an effort to distract the children's attention from the front drawing room, where Charley's parents were now busy lighting the candles. (The element of *surprise* was crucial here, and as we shall see it was something that distinguished the Christmas tree ritual from other modes of presenting children with their gifts.)

Finally, the double doors were thrown open and the children poured in, their voices instantaneously hushed. "Their faces were upturned to the blaze, all eyes wide open, all lips parted, all steps arrested. Nobody spoke, only Charley leaped for joy." After a few moments the children discovered that the tree "bore something eatable," and "the babble began again." The children were told to take what they could from the tree without burning themselves on the candles. (Martineau reported that "we tall people kept watch, and helped them with good things from the higher branches.")

After the children had eaten their fill of the edibles, the evening continued with dancing and mugs of "steaming mulled wine." By eleven, all the other guests had gone home; little Charley was in bed; and Harriet Martineau herself was left alone with the boy's parents, Charles and Eliza Follen. It had been a delightful evening, and Martineau concluded her account by predicting that the Christmas tree ritual would surely become an established American tradition.[2]

KARL FOLLEN'S STORY

Harriet Martineau's story of little Charley Follen's Christmas tree was accurate enough, even if this was not the first American Christmas tree. But in an important way the story was misleading. For when Martineau reported the episode, she placed it in a context that implied that she had simply stumbled upon it during the course of her travels. The episode appeared as part of a catchall chapter in Martineau's book, a chapter she called "Hot and Cold Weather," about seasonal phenomena in New England.

Martineau's evening with the Follens was anything but an accident of travel, and it hardly took place as part of the ordinary New England seasonal cycle. Martineau and the Follens had met only a few months earlier, but in the course of those few months they had become fast personal friends and political allies in a cause that was changing the course of their lives. Harriet Martineau had gone to visit the Follens that evening to chart their mutual plans at a moment of crisis, a crisis that was forcing them to make a difficult choice between their personal principles and their professional careers. The issue that precipitated the crisis was nothing less than the movement to abolish slavery in America. It is a story that bears telling in some detail.

IF CHARLES FOLLEN HAD not died in 1840 at the age of 43 (in the explosion of a steamship), he would in all probability be remembered today in connection with something more important than the American Christmas tree. Even as it stands, however, Follen's career is fascinating. Somewhat like Thomas Paine before him, he was a radical on two continents. Even before coming to America in 1825 in his late twenties, Follen had been exiled from Germany, and then from Switzerland, for his revolutionary activities.

Karl Follen, as he was named at birth, was no simple product of German folk culture. He was a scion of the German elite, the son of a respected judge—almost the German equivalent of Clement Clarke Moore. But early in his life Follen moved in a very different direction than Moore. He became a youthful revolutionary, a representative of the emerging liberal nationalist movement in Germany. As a university student, Follen authored an incendiary political song and was actually arrested for complicity in a political murder (he was acquitted). Appointed a member of the faculty at the University of Jena in 1820 (at the age of 24), Follen continued his political activities and was forced into exile in Switzerland, where he received another professional position; but four years later he was compelled to flee once again (in the face of new charges that he had organized a revolutionary cell). This time Follen found refuge in America. He arrived in New York, having learned English during the voyage and bearing letters of introduction from another European revolutionary, the aged Marquis de Lafayette, who suggested that he try to find employment in the Boston area. Follen followed that advice, and headed for Cambridge.[3]

Even before he arrived on New England soil, Follen stopped off in New York to meet a woman we have already met, the writer Catharine Maria Sedgwick, whose novel *Redwood* was the first book he had read in the English language. Catharine Sedgwick obviously admired Follen's intelligence and culture, his gentility, and his republican principles. The following summer she invited him to Stockbridge, Massachusetts, to meet the rest of the Sedgwick clan. Then, that fall, Sedgwick introduced Follen to one of her oldest and most intimate friends, Eliza Cabot of Boston. Two years later Follen and Cabot married, and in 1830 they had a child, who was christened Charles after the English version of his father's name.[4]

Charles Follen (as he was now being called) had fallen in love with the United States, a nation that promised to fulfill the republican values for which he had been striving vainly in Europe. He worked hard to make a new career in his new home, and in this he was eminently successful. Living in Cambridge, Follen authored books on the German language (as yet little studied in the United States) and taught German part-time at Harvard. He even established and ran a gymnasium in the Harvard area. Above all, he formed close ties with the liberal Unitarian establishment that dominated Harvard and Boston. Follen was a deeply religious man as well as an enlightened republican, and he found Unitarianism wholly compatible with his own progressive Christian beliefs.

In 1830, five years after his arrival in America, Follen reached what would prove to be the pinnacle of his new life. That year he was made a minister in the Unitarian Church, and he became a U.S. citizen. Most important of all, he was appointed to a full-time faculty position at Harvard, a new professorship of German literature that had been given five years' funding by a group of his admirers, with the expectation that Harvard would pick up the tab thereafter. Little Charley was born in 1830, too, and the next year the family moved into a new house. Follen was flying high.[5]

But within less than five years, the radical commitments that had brought him to America in the first place brought him down once again. This time the issue was slavery, a subject that was just beginning to arouse feelings of urgent intensity in a handful of Americans. In 1831 William Lloyd Garrison began publishing his abolitionist journal, *The Liberator,* in Boston, where, that same year, he organized the American Anti-Slavery Society. Follen quickly sensed the parallels between the antislavery movement and the principles he had stood for in Germany; by 1834 he had become one of the most dedicated of Garrison's followers. He even helped

CHARLES FOLLEN.

Charles Follen. This engraving, the only known likeness of Follen, appeared as the frontispiece to the biography that Eliza Follen published in 1841, just a year after her husband's tragic death in the explosion of the steamship *Lexington*. *(Courtesy, Harvard College Library)*

organize a Cambridge Anti-Slavery Society, based at Harvard. But radical abolitionism did not sit well with most Northerners, even with the Boston Unitarian establishment, whose members were offended by what they regarded as its vulgar style as well as its constant insistence that abolition be *total* and *immediate*. William Lloyd Garrison was regarded by most of Follen's acquaintances as a crazy man, and a rather uncouth one at that. (Even Follen himself was occasionally critical of Garrison's style, though never of his principles.)[6] Charles Follen was warned that becoming an active abolitionist would surely jeopardize his professional prospects, but he was too much a man of principle to let that get in the way. Anyway, he had been through it all before, back in Europe.

His fall was heroic. In early 1834 Follen became an active member and officer of the New England Anti-Slavery Society. He did so against the urgings of his Harvard colleagues, who warned him that it would cost him his position. (The professorship would expire in 1835, and only at that point would it be made permanent—or else terminated. In effect, Follen would be coming up for tenure.) Follen's friends were of course correct. Early in 1835 he learned that his appointment would terminate at the end of the spring semester.[7] He and his family (little Charley turned 5 that year) would be left high and dry, with no source of income. (Eliza Follen may have been born into the prominent Cabot family, but she had few resources of her own, and the family did not come to her assistance on this occasion.)

For the moment, though, Follen was rescued by his remaining admirers, who arranged for him to have what appeared to be an ideal position. He would oversee the education of the two children of a wealthy Boston merchant, James Perkins, who had recently died (and whose widow was emotionally incapacitated). In return for this part-time work, Follen was to have the use of the Perkinses' house, and he would be paid the comfortable annual salary of $2,000. "The fortune of the Follens seems like a Fairy-tale," Catharine Sedgwick wrote when she learned the good news.[8]

This time it was Follen's educational principles that got him into trouble. Follen took the teaching of children seriously indeed. He was committed to a progressive pedagogical strategy, derived largely from the work of the Swiss reformer Johann Pestalozzi. Pestalozzi assumed that children were intrinsically perfect creatures to begin with, and that education should therefore consist in the cultivation of those attributes that were already present in their young souls. Follen wrote (in what amounted to his job proposal) that he intended to "study their natures," so as to "awake every dormant energy" the two boys already possessed.[9] This was the kind of approach that struck many people (including many Unitarians) as leading inevitably to an indiscriminate parental indulgence of children in their immature desires and whims.

What happened next is not wholly clear. But it appears that Follen's political enemies used his progressive educational ideas against him, and when Follen, predictably enough, refused once again to retreat from his principles, he learned that he was once again out of a job. The bad news arrived in mid-December 1835, just a couple of weeks before Christmas.[10]

As if that were not enough, Follen's personal crisis was part of a larger crisis in the abolitionist movement. The last months of the year 1835 witnessed a series of verbal and physical attacks on the abolitionist movement (abolitionists later referred to this period as a "reign of terror"). In October, William Lloyd Garrison was physically assaulted by a mob which dragged him through the streets of Boston with a halter around his waist. Most Bostonians were convinced that Garrison's own behavior had brought on such treatment, and indeed that additional steps had to be taken to prevent the abolitionists from provoking further public disorder. With additional pressure coming from Southern quarters, the Massachusetts legislature was soon considering a law that would effectively ban most abolitionist activities.

Charles Follen played a role in that episode, too. Early in 1836 he testified against the proposed antiabolitionist bill at a public legislative hearing. On that occasion he was silenced by the committee chairman and threatened with charges of contempt. Through these trying hours, as always, Follen maintained his characteristically calm, patient demeanor, but he did not retreat a single inch.[11] He was a man of extraordinary principle and tenacity, an intellectual who was above all an effective moral leader—a genteel counterweight to William Lloyd Garrison. But he was also a man without a job. And it was in connection with all these troubles, just in time for the end of the Christmas season, that Harriet Martineau came to visit.

HARRIET MARTINEAU'S STORY

Her visit was no coincidence. Martineau herself had been born (in 1802) into an English Unitarian family, though one less distinguished socially than the Sedgwicks or the Boston Unitarian establishment. By the time of her American tour Martineau had become a famous writer. She had arrived in the United States in mid-1834, coming (with a publisher's travel advance) with the express intention of writing a book about life in the new nation.[12]

At first, as she traveled around the country, Martineau was welcomed and feted everywhere. Because of her connection with the Unitarian community, one of the Americans to whom Martineau received an introduction was Catharine Sedgwick (whose literary renown made her one of the best-known American Unitarians), and Stockbridge was the first place Martineau visited outside the New York City area. The two women quickly became friends. Martineau was offering her "love" to Sedgwick as early as December 1834, and urging the American writer to join her the following summer on a trip to the western states. (Sedgwick initially agreed, but had second thoughts and backed out because she was seeing a new book through the press.[13])

Harriet Martineau spent part of the summer of 1835 in Stockbridge, where the Sedgwicks once again were her hosts.[14] Returning to Boston during the autumn, she met and quickly befriended Charles Follen. It was in some measure in response to Follen's urging that Martineau attended an abolitionist women's meeting, held in Boston on November 19, in the midst of the "reign of terror." She came to this meeting in the role of a reporter, but by the time she left she had become an avowed abolitionist. In the course of the meeting a note was passed to Martineau, asking her to express her opinion of what she had heard. Martineau did so, but only with great reluctance, because she found that she was in agreement with the abolitionists' principles and knew that making a public gesture of solidarity with them would have the effect of alienating her from most of her American acquaintances—and thereby cutting off her access to most of the contacts on which she depended for the book she was writing. As Martineau later put it: "I foresaw that almost every house in Boston, except those of the abolitionists, would be shut against me; that my relation to the country would be completely changed, as I should suddenly be transformed from being a guest and an observer to being considered a missionary or a spy. . . ." As she would acknowledge twenty years later, "[t]he moment of reading this note was one of the most painful of my life."[15]

Martineau's foreboding was correct. The Boston papers reported (and ridiculed) her avowal of abolitionist sympathies, and those reports were quickly reprinted throughout the United States. By the following spring she was forced to change the itinerary of her postponed western trip in order to avoid the prospect of encountering personal danger. (As it turned out, she ended up taking this trip in the company of the Follens themselves—and using it not simply as a professional tour but also as an opportunity to engage in abolitionist activities.) Martineau had transformed herself from a journalist into an activist. She would always recall her American sojourn as a profoundly transforming episode in her life. For a time, she seriously considered returning permanently to America to engage in abolitionist work. She regarded Charles Follen as her "very nearest friend, guide, and guardian," and to the end of her life she kept his portrait (next to one of William Lloyd Garrison) in her parlor.[16]

In the meantime, soon after her political coming-out in November 1835, Martineau returned to Boston (she had meanwhile taken a brief tour of some nearby communities) in order to spend New Year's with the Follens.[17] Both of them were under heavy pressure just then; Martineau had just lost her social credibility, and Charles Follen had just lost his post as tutor to the Perkins children. The visit would be a time for mutual commiseration, and also a chance to plan a strategy for what would be (it was now clear) the abolitionist focus of the rest of Martineau's American visit, including the western trip that she would take several months later in the Follens' company.

A few days before their holiday reunion (it actually took place on New Year's Eve), Follen wrote to Martineau in mock-conspiratorial lan-

guage: "I rejoice in the prospect of having you with us next Friday, to set-
tle the affairs of this nether world at least, at this Congress of our Holy
Triple Alliance [i.e., Charles and Eliza Follen and Martineau herself]." A
week or so earlier, Follen sent her a more serious letter, deeply personal in
tone. In that letter Follen articulated to Martineau what the two of them
had recently done. They had each "stepped out of the safe vessel of selfish
indifference, and ventured to walk on troubled waters of philanthropic enterprise." As a result, both of them were suffering the fate of principled
radicals of all ages and cultures, being either "shunned with silent con-
demnation as abolitionists, democrats, agrarians, or hailed with the cries
of 'Crucify! crucify!' as fanatics and incendiaries." Follen went on, however, to assure Martineau that in their own deepening friendship they
could both find an oasis of intimate serenity: "But if the world separate itself from us, it leads us to find a world in ourselves and each other. . . ."[18]

At their reunion, Charles Follen went out of his way to seal his intimacy with Martineau, and also to offer the promised oasis of serenity, by
setting up little Charley's Christmas tree in her presence. (The Follens
had postponed the ritual until New Year's Eve in order to accommodate
Martineau's schedule.) The tree was a success, a time of joy for the grown-
ups as well as for little Charley and his friends (these friends were in fact
none other than the Perkins children; indeed, the whole event took place
in the Perkinses' house, where the Follens were still living). The rest of the
agenda—the commiseration and the political planning—could presumably wait until the next morning.

IN HER PUBLISHED ACCOUNT, Harriet Martineau took pains to
conceal all this, or at least to dissociate it from the story of little Charley's
Christmas tree. She did not even identify the Follens by name in her account, referring to them only as "Charley's father and mother."[19] But it
should be clear to us that Martineau's experience of what she believed to
be the introduction of the Christmas tree into America was actually embedded in a thick matrix of political controversy. Little Charley's Christmas tree was a carefully planned moment of domestic peace in the midst
of crisis and scandal.

Those connections make for an interesting story, and one that has
not been told. But from another angle they point to broader developments. First, they confirm something that historians have recently come
to notice: There were important similarities between the antislavery sen-

sibility and the new attitude toward children. Abolitionists and educational reformers shared a joint empathy for people who were powerless to resist the wrath of those who wielded authority over them—slaves and children, respectively. (Both types of reformers had a particular abhorrence of the use of the lash as a form of punishment.)[20]

Second, we can view the juxtaposition of the two stories (the Christmas tree and the political crisis) as a telling instance of another phenomenon that historians have been pointing to: the way that middle-class people in the early nineteenth century went about creating for themselves a private space, radically cut off from the pressures of the world outside and centered around the happiness of children.[21] In fact, what Charles Follen did in 1835 is similar in that sense to what Clement Clarke Moore had done more than a decade earlier, although his reasons—Moore was a reactionary, Follen a radical—were profoundly different. But both men had reason to feel alienated from their respective communities, and both responded by turning inward, to their own children, and using Christmas as the occasion for doing so.

It is no coincidence that radical abolitionists were in the vanguard of the new child-centered Christmas. Two years earlier, in 1833, the Antislavery Society had formed a children's chorus, the Boston Garrison Juvenile Choir (its members may have been African-Americans), which gave a public concert on Christmas Day. One of the numbers it performed was "The Cradle Song"; another was titled "The Sugar Plums." And beginning in 1834 (and continuing each year for more than two decades) the Garrisonians held an annual Antislavery Fair to raise money for the cause—invariably, on the days just before Christmas. In 1836 several abolitionists presented Garrison's own 10-month-old son George with shoes, stockings, mittens, and "a very beautiful gown" that had been offered at that year's fair. "Pretty well for the young fanatic!" the proud father noted privately—and with uncharacteristically self-deprecating wit.[22]

In fact, according to a report published in Garrison's magazine *The Liberator*, the very first of these Antislavery Fairs (the one in 1834) displayed an "evergreen shrub" that bore another witty message: "Persons are requested not to handle the articles, which, like slavery, are too '*delicate*' to be touched."[23] (This was a sarcastic reference to the reluctance of most respectable Americans to discuss the slavery issue.) Humor aside, if any of the articles for sale at the 1834 fair were actually attached to this evergreen shrub (or placed around it), then *it* would have the honor of being the first public Christmas tree displayed in the United States.

"**Christmas Eve**" (1836). This is the first image of a Christmas tree to be printed in the United States. It appeared in Boston in 1836, as the frontispiece to *The Stranger's Gift,* a Gift Book written by a German immigrant named Herman Bokum, a man who had taken over Charles Follen's old job of teaching the German language on a part-time basis at Harvard. The tree is illuminated by open candles. The door at the right suggests that the children have only moments earlier been allowed to enter the room. *(Courtesy, American Antiquarian Society)*

Catharine Sedgwick's Christmas Tree

Catharine Sedgwick declined to support the abolitionist ideology endorsed by Martineau and the Follens, but she continued to count them among her closest friends. And during the same Christmas season in which Martineau witnessed the Follens' Christmas tree, Sedgwick published a story of her own, written earlier that year, in which a Christmas tree played a small but distinct part. The story was titled "New Year's Day." (Like the Follens' Christmas tree, Catharine Sedgwick's fictional tree was set up for New Year's Day rather than Christmas itself.) Inasmuch as Martineau's account of the Follens was not published for another two years, it was actually Sedgwick's story that has the honor of introducing this ritual into American literature.

Sedgwick's fictional account resembled Martineau's report except that here the family that performs the ritual was not German but of old Yankee stock—Yankees living in New York City, as Catharine Sedgwick herself was doing. But this fictional tree was set up at the behest of a German immigrant, the young heroine's maidservant, Madeleine. The heroine herself has been planning to give Christmas presents to each of her younger siblings (as well as to her father), and the maidservant has "persuaded her young mistress to arrange the gifts after the fashion of her *father-land*"—that is, by hanging them on a tree secretly set up in the rear parlor, a room the children rarely enter. Together Lizzy and Madeleine hang up Lizzy's gifts:

> Never did Christmas tree bear more multifarious fruit,—for St. Nicholas, that most benign of all the saints of the Calendar, had through the hands of many a ministering priest and priestess, showered his gifts. The sturdiest branch drooped with its burden of books, chess-men, puzzles, &c., for Julius, a stripling of thirteen. Dolls, birds, beasts, and boxes were hung on the lesser limbs. A regiment of soldiers had alighted on one bough, and Noah's ark was anchored to another, and to all the slender branches were attached cherries, plumbs[sic], strawberries and peaches as tempting, and at least as sweet, as the fruits of paradise.[24]

As it turns out, the Christmas tree plays only a small role in this story, and the maidservant Madeleine does not make any further appearances. As far as I can tell (and I have carefully read the family's correspondence during these years), there was no German maidservant in Catharine Sedgwick's house, and no Christmas tree. It is possible, of course, that Sedgwick learned of the tree through a neighbor's maidservant. What is far more likely is that she learned about it from the Follens themselves.

But there was much else in Sedgwick's short story that clearly *was* based on her immediate experience. And in order to understand the story (and so to understand the meaning that Christmas trees bore at the moment of their introduction into American literature), it is necessary to make still another visit to the Sedgwicks' New York household during the Christmas season.

Catharine Sedgwick was in the habit of spending her winters in the New York home of her brother Robert Sedgwick and his wife, Elizabeth Ellery Sedgwick (see Chapter 4). This house was a fashionable place, perhaps too much so for Catharine's more understated tastes. Elizabeth Ellery Sedgwick cared intensely about accumulating both material goods and success in New York's fashionable social circuits, and she had a sense that by lavishing herself with the one she would help ensure herself the other. Each year Mrs. Sedgwick proudly reported to her father what she had been given that holiday season and also the number of visitors who had called upon her household on New Year's Day (one year she boasted that the total was "about 70 gentlemen"). In turn, she noted that her husband, Robert, "made 63 calls in five hours, so you may judge how he walked." (Such a schedule meant that each visit took less than five minutes, including traveling time.) Elizabeth Sedgwick even thought about her children's holiday gifts in the context of the fashionable world. Recalling how she had just greeted her seventy callers in the front room of her house, Mrs. Sedgwick proudly noted that the children "occupied the back parlor, and made a pretty perspective for us as we received our visitors." Nor did she fail to note that several of the children's gifts were "very valuable."[25]

Out of the sense of noblesse that governed so much of her life, Catharine Sedgwick participated fully in the fashionable ritual of receiving the gentlemen callers. But the visitations wore on her patience. In a private letter (written to a favorite young niece) Sedgwick noted that on New Year's Day, 1835, she had greeted "between 70 & 80" gentlemen, but she added that neither their names nor their fashionable witticisms (the latter presumably repeated at every stop) were worth passing along. A single example would have to do, Sedgwick confided to her niece. One of the callers had chosen to comment cleverly on the beautiful winter weather (the sun had come out on that very day) by comparing it to the seasonal appearance of Gift Books (or literary "annuals," as they were also known): "He said 'Nature has come out with *her* annual at last, & as bright as the best of them—the gentlemen find it a book of beauty.' "[26]

The following year Catharine Sedgwick took an author's revenge, in the form of a mocking fictionalized account of that same experience. Her account made up the central section of the short story in which the Christmas tree also figured. In Sedgwick's fictional rendering the woman who receives the visitors is the tale's teenage heroine, a charming and attractive girl named Lizzy Percival, the oldest child in a New York family of great wealth and prominence, and the character who obviously represents Catharine Sedgwick herself. (Lizzy Percival is sweet, caring, and sincere—a young woman who shares Catharine Sedgwick's disdain for artifice.)

Like the Sedgwicks, the fictional Percival family experienced a busy New Year's Day: "their visitors were innumerable, and a continual stream poured in and poured out," uttering in the process "the stereotyped sayings of the season." When one of their visitors referred to the New Year's ritual as a "fine old custom" created by "our Dutch ancestors," Lizzy secretly thought of him as an "interloper who had not a drop of . . . Dutch blood." (And when another asked for "whiskey-punch," Lizzy modestly reminded him that alcohol had been " 'banished from all refined society.' " Catharine Sedgwick evidently supported the detoxification of New Year's visitations.)

Every one of Lizzy's fictional visitors spoke in stock phrases, and most of them were coarse, materialistic, and competitive. One man boasted that his wife had received fully 200 visitors the previous year. Another openly compared the hospitality he had received at various houses. A third betrayed the confidence of a woman he knew—a relative of Lizzy's who had declined to receive visitors that day on grounds of ill health—by revealing that the woman was not sick at all: " ' "Say to my friends, 'I'm sick, I'm dead [she had confided]." But, between ourselves, my dear Lizzy, the draperies to the drawing-room curtains are not completed—that's all.' "[27]

The least offensive of the fictional visitors were the ones who merely attempted to be clever. Among these was a young man whose witticism will already be familiar to us. Echoing almost verbatim Sedgwick's earlier, real-life report, this young man extolled the weather "and said that nature had, last of all the publishers, come out with her annual, and the gentlemen had found it 'a book of beauty.' "[28]

This kind of extended (and autobiographical) satire provides a literary contrast that sets off the brief but important appearance of the Christmas tree in this story. Set in this new context, its meaning is simple: Catharine Sedgwick's Christmas tree is associated with everything that is absent in the fashionable visitation ritual. It is associated with children—innocent, good-hearted children—and the private space of a purely domestic ritual. In effect, Catharine Sedgwick had turned the tables on the sheriff (discussed in Chapter 3) who had identified with the world of alcohol and male culture and dismissed the world of women (and temperance) as cold comfort.

Here again, Catharine Sedgwick's fictional presentation stands in contrast to the Sedgwicks' actual experience. In real life, as we have seen, the children of Robert and Elizabeth Sedgwick were playing with their presents in the back parlor at the same time that Catharine and Elizabeth Sedgwick were receiving their fashionable visitors in the front one. In fact, the door between the two rooms remained open the entire time. Elizabeth Sedgwick chose to comment on the children's activities only by noting how they enhanced the charm of the adult ritual: "the children occupied the back parlor, and made a pretty perspective for us as we received our visitors." But in Catharine Sedgwick's fictionalized account of the same event, the two rituals appeared to be taking place in a separate time and space—and it was crucial that they did.

The central theme of Sedgwick's story is the contrast between artifice and authenticity. The holiday season functioned as a literary occasion on which it was easy to carve out a divide between the private and the public worlds, and to take the pleasures of the former more seriously than the demands of the latter. That is the point of the love story in which Sedgwick's plot is superficially framed (and which is not worth retelling here). And it is the reason Sedgwick chose to set the story at Christmas, a time when, as she saw it, the most artificial rituals were juxtaposed with the most authentic ones. Sedgwick's young heroine, Lizzy Percival, may be able to hold her own in repartee with the gentlemen visitors, but it is to the private domestic ritual that her heart belongs. Through the character of Lizzy, Sedgwick manages to establish a core of authenticity in a household that is besieged from without and within by the forces of social convention, whether "the stereotyped sayings of the season" or the equally stereotyped holiday presents the real-life Sedgwick children received.

I don't know exactly what those presents were, but the children's mother did report that they were numerous and "some of them [were] very valuable." When Catharine Sedgwick fictionalized this part of her

Catharine Maria Sedgwick. This picture shows the author as a young woman, and suggests something of the charm that helped endear her to a wide circle of acquaintances. *(Courtesy of the Fine Arts Library, Harvard College Library)*

experience she was more specific. The toys that Lizzy Percival placed on the Christmas tree consisted of things like books, dolls, animals, and a regiment of toy soldiers. At first glance these, too, would appear to be commercial toys, toys she has bought, the kind of toys that are available at any of number of New York shops. But as the children—Lizzy's younger brothers and sisters—comment on their gifts one by one, it becomes absolutely clear that Lizzy has prepared them all herself.

Consider the children's responses. One of the brothers receives "a nice book, filled with copies for him to draw after"; and exclaims pointedly, " 'how much pains you have taken to do this for me! how much time and trouble you have spent upon it. . . . !' " A sister receives a beaded bag and makes the same point: " 'O, sister Lizzy! 'I did not know when I spilt all your beads that you was knitting this bag for me . . . !' " The dolls that two other siblings receive may have been store-bought, but they come dressed in clothing Lizzy has sewn. (" 'O, Anne, your doll is dressed just like mine; sister has even worked their pocket handkerchiefs.' ") Even the toy soldiers have been hand-finished: " 'Sister, sister, did you paint these soldiers?' cried Hal; 'kiss me, you are the best sister that ever lived.' " One of the children speaks for them all when, thanking Lizzy for the hand-embroidered apron she has received, she exclaims, " 'O papa! does not sister do every thing for us?' "

Finally, we learn that Lizzy has done the same for her father, too; she presents him with "a pair of slippers . . . , beautifully wrought by her own hands," together with "several pairs of fine woolen hose which she had knit for him, in her intervals of leisure." Sedgwick hammers the point home: "They were just such as he liked, just such as he could not buy, just such as nobody but Lizzy could knit. . . ."[29]

Just such as he could not buy. As early as this story, written in the mid-1830s, Catharine Sedgwick was able to make a point of how special it was for Christmas presents to be handmade or even hand-finished. More to the point, Sedgwick chose to have all these gifts made by hand in order to reinforce further the point she had already suggested by the German Christmas tree: The true essence of the Christmas gift exchange must be forged outside the fevered crucible of market relations.

HANDMADE GIFTS, a German maidservant, and a Christmas tree—by employing such literary tactics, Catharine Sedgwick was partially able to resolve the contradiction between market relations and intimate personal ones. But there was one aspect of the contradiction that remained immune to such a literary solution: the tension between the story's message and the medium that carried it. After all, whether or not Catharine Sedgwick actually knew a maidservant like the fictional Madeleine, her story conveyed the impression that the tree really was a folk tradition observed by servant girls. But in fact it was not the German maidservant Madeleine who effectively spread the idea of the Christmas tree throughout American culture. It was the Yankee patrician Catharine Sedgwick—popular author and Unitarian daughter of a Massachusetts congressman—who accomplished that. Even more important, Sedgwick did this not by setting up such a tree but by writing a story about it—and publishing that story in a popular Gift Book read by middle-class readers throughout America, a Gift Book that went on sale just in time for the 1835 holiday season. Remember that the fashionable gentleman visitor (in both Sedgwick's story and her actual experience) had tried to construct a stylish pun by speaking of Mother Nature as if she were the publisher of just such an annual. (In fact, the particular volume in which Sedgwick's story appeared—a Gift Book called *The Token*—remains notable to literary historians for another reason entirely: It contains the first publication of two important stories by

Nathaniel Hawthorne—"The May-Pole of Merry Mount" and "The Minister's Black Veil.")

Literary annuals were hardly produced in the workshops of folk culture. They were a part of the fashionable new commercial world, a world that Catharine Sedgwick was critiquing from within.[30] Sedgwick's readers may unconsciously have assumed that they were learning about Christmas trees directly from the folk character Madeleine, but in fact the path of transmission was nothing other than the latest holiday-season commodity—a Gift Book that had been purchased as a present in a fashionable shop.

TOWARD A HISTORY OF CHRISTMAS TREES

We have happened upon an important paradox: The Christmas tree entered American society through the avenues of commercial culture, but it did so in the name of precommercial folk culture. This was exactly what happened with the figure of Santa Claus. We might go so far as to say that both rituals were part of an early "folk revival" of sorts, a revival that emerged close behind the full-blown emergence of commercial culture itself.

It is commonplace to believe that Christmas trees were transmitted to America by early German immigrants in Pennsylvania. And in all probability, American Christmas trees did, indeed, first appear in the Pennsylvania German community in the early nineteenth century. But it is unlikely that they made their appearance much before 1820. Folklorists have done their best to seek out the first tree in Pennsylvania, and it seems plain that credible evidence of actual Christmas trees dates no earlier than the 1810s. In 1819 (possibly as early as 1812), an immigrant artist from Germany drew a picture of a tree he saw during a tour of the Pennsylvania countryside, and that picture has been preserved in his sketchbooks. The first extant *verbal* reference to Christmas trees dates from the very next year, 1821 (it is an entry in the diary of a Lancaster resident, who reported that his children had gone to a nearby sawmill "for Christmas trees").[31] After that, references begin to multiply.

What this sequence suggests is that Christmas trees were first set up by Pennsylvania Germans sometime during the 1810s (the very decade during which St. Nicholas was introduced in New York). If that chronology holds, it is natural to wonder why Christmas trees were introduced in

An Early American Christmas Tree. This sketch was drawn from life (in either 1812 or 1819) by John Lewis Krimmel, a German painter who had emigrated to Philadelphia, and who drew the sketch while touring the Pennsylvania countryside. (Although Krimmel's sketch is the first picture of an American Christmas tree, it was not printed until a few years ago.) The eleven people who appear here are apparently members of a single family. Judging from the dress and furnishings, this was a relatively prosperous household—a point of some significance in tracing the way Christmas trees were diffused through the Pennsylvania German community. *(Courtesy, The Winterthur Library: Joseph Downs Collection of Manuscripts and Printed Ephemera, No. Col. 308)*

Pennsylvania at such a late date. Why didn't they appear a century or so earlier, when the first Germans emigrated to Pennsylvania? The answer to this question is intriguing. It turns out that the Christmas tree was a relatively new tradition in Germany itself, one that was still emerging there in the early nineteenth century. In fact, the story of the German Christmas tree has parallels to that of the Dutch Santa Claus. What happened in both cases was that a small group of people suddenly began to make much of what had previously been a distinctly minor tradition.

A careful reading of the German sources suggests both a chronology and a pattern to this process. Before the last third of the eighteenth century, Christmas trees had been a localized custom, largely limited to a single place—the Alsatian capital of Strasbourg—where they seem to have developed by the beginning of the seventeenth century. The Strasbourg Christmas tree was apparently used as part of a *judgmental* Christmas ritual—much like the similar St. Nicholas ritual in Holland—in which good children were rewarded with bonbons provided by the "Christkindle" (i.e., the Christchild), while "disobedient" youngsters were punished by a figure known as "Hanstrapp," the local version of the Belsnickle.[32]

The ritual began to spread to other parts of Germany—minus Hanstrapp—only after 1750. A key date in this development may have been 1771, when Strasbourg became the site of an extended visit by the young writer Johann Wolfgang von Goethe, who discovered in this city a new sense of "German" identity that transformed his larger cultural vision. Goethe came to associate the Christmas tree itself with that new awareness. In fact, a Christmas tree scene is included at a dramatic moment of the 1774 novel that established his literary reputation, *The Sufferings of Young Werther* (the scene takes place shortly before the hero's suicide).

It was largely through Goethe and his literary colleagues that the Christmas tree spread to other parts of Germany. It did so as a fashionable new ritual that was perceived—even there—as an ancient and authentic folk tradition. Christmas trees were adopted by the elite in Berlin, for example, only in the 1810s. In 1820 a young American visitor, the future historian George Bancroft, saw a tree there in the home of his local host, the distinguished jurist Baron Friedrich Karl von Savigny—a man who had married the sister of Goethe's mistress Bettina Brentano. (Bancroft reported this episode in vivid detail in a letter to his father, who was a Unitarian minister in Worcester, Massachusetts.)[33]

It was not until the 1830s that Christmas trees became a truly national practice in Germany. They were introduced to Munich, for example, only in 1830, by the queen of Bavaria. It seems fair, under the circumstances, to consider Christmas trees as something of an "invented tradition," much like Santa Claus in New York—a ritual picked up by the elite and spread via literary channels through a middle class that was interested in discovering its "authentic" national culture.

By the early nineteenth century, Christmas trees were being described as a timeless tradition. In 1820—the same year that produced the earliest evidence of an actual Christmas tree in Pennsylvania—a story of modern European authorship, but set in medieval Germany, noted that on Christmas Eve "every family assembles all its members together and fathers and mothers are surrounded by their children; they light up a number of wax lights, which they suspend to the branches of a small fir-tree, which are also hung round with the presents they mean to make them." (The same story also informs us—remember, this is the fourteenth century—that "the shops in the streets" are filled with "toys of every kind.")[34]

As it happens, that story was reprinted in the United States the same year it was published in Europe. Its American venue was *The Athenaeum*, a cosmopolitan literary magazine published in Boston by Unitarians and devoted to reprinting the latest European literary work. The story itself was trivial (even though it, rather than Catharine Sedgwick's 1835 story, may represent the first reference to Christmas trees that was published in the United States). Still, two things about it have a bearing on *our* story. What matters first is the story's plot. It deals with the redemption of a sinful mother by her selfless young child—a child who, like Jesus himself, was born on Christmas Eve (the story is titled "Christmas Eve; or, The Conversion"). The other point that matters is the place where the story was printed—in an organ of New England Unitarian culture.

UNITARIANS, CHRISTMAS TREES, AND THE CHARACTER OF CHILDREN

The two points are interrelated. By now it should be clear that the Christmas tree was spread throughout the United States in large measure by committed Unitarians. It is time to ask what their agenda was. Why did members of this group care so much about Christmas trees? Answering this question takes us along two important literary paths. The first starts with a famous British writer; the second, with a controversial Swiss educational reformer. Both paths run chiefly through the channels of Unitarian culture. And both constantly refer to the theme of selfless children.

Coleridge's Children: The Ratzeburg File

The British writer was Samuel Taylor Coleridge (1772–1834), the Romantic poet and essayist. Coleridge happened to spend the 1798 Christmas season in the German town of Ratzeburg, located near Hamburg in the northern part of Germany. He had gone to Germany three months earlier, shortly after making a professional decision that changed the shape of his career—he had just decided against pursuing a career as a minister in the Unitarian Church. (In addition, Coleridge had recently completed what would prove to be his two greatest poems, "Kubla Khan" and "The Rime of the Ancient Mariner.") The 26-year-old poet spent much of the season socializing with the local elite and fending off invitations to attend their frequent holiday dances.[35] But in the midst of these revels he witnessed a domestic Christmas tree, accompanied by a ritual that "pleased and interested" him so much that he published an account of it eleven years later, in a magazine he was then editing in England (the piece was published in time for the 1809 Christmas season).

The tree that Coleridge saw was, as we might expect, the top of an evergreen fastened onto a table in one of the parlors in the house to which he had been invited, and there were lighted candles attached to its branches. But that wasn't what most "pleased and interested" Coleridge. What really impressed him was a more important twist—for in the ceremony he witnessed, it was the *children* who gave presents to their *parents*, and not the other way around. Coleridge detailed the procedure:

> For three or four months before Christmas the girls are busy [working], and the boys save up their pocket-money, to make or purchase these presents. What the present is to be is cautiously kept secret, and the girls have a world of contrivances to conceal it. . . .

Those, then, were the presents that were placed under the Christmas tree, to be opened on Christmas Eve "with kisses and embraces," in a ceremony that Coleridge found deeply moving:

> Where I witnessed this scene, there were eight or nine children, and the eldest daughter and the mother wept aloud for joy and tenderness; and the tears ran down the face of the father, and he clasped his children so tight to his breast—it seemed as if he did it to stifle the sob that was rising within him.—I was very much affected.[36]

Coleridge did not realize it, but this ritual seems to have been a strictly local one, conceivably even limited to the single household in which he observed it. He afforded only brief mention to the more standard ritual that took place the following day—the familiar ritual in which the parents gave presents to their children.[37]

Coleridge's account left something of a wake in the United States, a wake that I have come to term "the Ratzeburg file." Coleridge originally published his Christmas recollections in 1809, in a short-lived magazine he edited called *The Friend*. The bound magazine was republished in London three times during the 1810s, and an American edition appeared in 1829 (in Burlington, Vermont). Catharine Sedgwick, for one, read the book no later than January 1836 and perhaps earlier.[38]

Actually, Coleridge's account of the Ratzeburg Christmas tree had been printed as a separate item in the United States back in 1824, in the official journal of the Unitarian Church in America, the *Christian Register*, published in Boston.[39] Six years later parts of the account reappeared, without attribution, in a children's book written by another Unitarian, Lydia Maria Child. Child, a novelist and an abolitionist, was best known at the time as the author of a cookbook, *The New England Frugal House-wife*. For the 1830 Christmas season she published a juvenile Gift Book, *The Little Girl's Own Book*. This volume contained a collection of games, puzzles, and riddles. It is the last item in the book, titled "A Custom Worthy [of] Imitation," that is of interest to us here. For it was nothing other than a paraphrase of Coleridge's report—except that Child did not refer to the Christmas tree itself but only to what we might think of as the central element in the ritual, the generational reversal in the gift exchange. (Child did not refer to Coleridge, either, or to Ratzeburg itself; instead, she implied that the ritual characterized Germany as a whole.)

> In Germany the children all make it a rule to prepare Christmas presents for their parents and brothers and sisters. Even the youngest contrive to offer something. For weeks before the important day arrives, they are as busy as little bees contriving and making such things as they suppose will be most agreeable.
>
> The great object is to keep each one ignorant of the present he, or she, is to receive, in order to surprise them when the offering is presented. A great deal of whispering, and innocent management is resorted to, to effect this purpose; and their little minds are brimful of the happy business.[40]

Another version of the same account appeared the very next year, 1832, in Keene, New Hampshire, in a children's primer authored by one J. K. Smith, *Juvenile Lessons; or The Child's First Reading Book*. One of the reading lessons in this book was titled "Christmas Presents." This lesson began: "The children in the North part of Germany, have a custom which pleases me much. It is usual with them to make little presents to their parents at Christmas time." The lesson went on to tell its young readers: "For some time before this happy day, the girls are as busy as so many bees, and the boys are careful to save every cent of their pocket money." It then added confidentially: "They are very careful to keep all their plans secret; for they do not wish to have their parents know the pleasant surprise they are preparing for them, till the time arrives."

> The evening before Christmas, they obtain leave to light one of the parlors, and here the presents for their parents are laid out with great care. When all things are ready, the parents are called in, and the dear

little creatures present their gifts. It is a delightful scene of kisses and embraces, and frolick.

Smith concluded by expressing a hope that "the boys and girls in America would make such a good use of Christmas eve, and Christmas day."[41]

The same item reemerged one last time, at the very end of the decade, in 1840, in a children's religious magazine, *Youth's Companion*. Like the earlier reprintings, this version, too, was published in New England. But whereas the earlier examples had been associated with Unitarians, the magazine in which this one appeared was published by their old opponents, the evangelical Congregationalists. This Congregationalist version actually came closest to Coleridge's original account. The Christmas tree reappeared in it, and so did the town of Ratzeburg itself. In this story a group of children are discussing a new kind of Christmas ritual they have happened upon. One of the children explains:

> "I was reading something about it in one of papa's books, the other day. . . . The person who wrote the account said that it is the custom at Ratzeburg, in Germany, to set up a branch of a yew tree near the wall, and fasten to the boughs little combustible things, pieces of candle wrapped up in colored papers. Then all the presents are tied to the branches, and all the children are called in. . . . [B]y and by they set fire to the little candles, and the branches begin to burn and crackle, which makes grand fun."[42]

With that, the Ratzeburg file comes to an end. It is intriguing to watch the way the whole process worked. First, each writer in turn learned about the ritual not from personal observation but from reading another writer's account. (The author of the 1840 version actually acknowledges as much: "*I was reading something about it in one of papa's books, the other day.*") American readers were learning that this ritual was performed in "Germany" (or at least in "North Germany"), and that it was presumably part of an old and widespread tradition. But when we actually trace the process, what we find is that the source of all the reports is what a single visitor to one small town observed on just one occasion, and in a single household.

But why was it so important for Americans to believe that this was an old and widespread German custom? The answer surely has to do with the one element in Coleridge's report that was included in every item in the Ratzeburg file: the appearance of children who were behaving unselfishly at Christmas—children who had freely chosen to *give* presents as well as to receive them. This was a point that would have struck a responsive chord in people who worried that the affection they lavished on their children at Christmas—and especially the gifts that were meant to symbolize this affection—were causing those same children to become self-centered and materialistic—in other words, spoiled.

Pestalozzi's Children: A Feast of the Feelings

To child rearing, then. This was a subject of real practical concern to many Americans in the 1830s, and it was especially acute for the very Unitarians who are the focus of this chapter. In addition, the subject was one on which, by the 1830s, they found themselves increasingly divided.

Child-rearing practices were linked to theological beliefs. Whether parents chose to beat their children, for example, or lavish attention on them at Christmas was linked to whether they believed in original sin. A central tenet of early-nineteenth-century Unitarians—and one that distinguished them from both the old-style Puritans and the majority of evangelical "New Lights"—was the belief that human beings were not born for damnation. Puritans and most evangelical Protestants, in contrast, believed that people were inevitably stained at birth by an original sin that corrupted them at their very core by causing them to be willful and selfish. Such a defect was so deep-seated that it could be removed, if at all, not by any act of will, no matter how strenuous (because the will itself was part of the problem), but only through a free gift of divine, arbitrary, and irresistible grace. To repeat: The will itself—that which a person wished to do—was corrupted; it could serve only to *resist* the process of divine cleansing. Puritan-minded parents, and their nineteenth-century successors, therefore felt that it was their obligation to break a child's will as early as possible.

Unitarians, on the contrary, believed that the will should be *trained* rather than broken; it might be imperfect, but it was not fundamentally corrupt. Unitarians strenuously believed that human beings were responsible—utterly responsible—for their own actions. Children therefore required constant and painstaking parental training that would enable them to learn to conquer their natural inclinations, and do so by the sheer force of their own will. Such training should at all costs avoid physical punishment, even outbursts of rage—which led only to fear. It had to be based, instead, on the firm, patient, and imaginative use of moral instruction, accompanied by assurances of parental love. The historian Philip Greven has written that the goal of this kind of child-rearing was "self-control rather than self-annihilation." And he quotes the Reverend Theodore Parker, himself a Unitarian minister (and a prominent abolitionist): "Men often speak of breaking the will of a child; it seems to me they had better break the neck. The will needs regulation, not destroying. I should as soon think of breaking the legs of a horse in training him, as [of breaking] a child's will." In other words, a child needs to make use of its will in order to function as an effective adult.[43]

By now it may seem almost inevitable that a member of the Sedgwick clan should have authored a story—a Christmas story—that demonstrates this very point. In 1833 Elizabeth Dwight Sedgwick of Stockbridge, Massachusetts (the wife of Catharine Sedgwick's youngest brother and, incidentally, a granddaughter of the Reverend Jonathan Edwards), published a Christmas story in a very popular Gift Book, *The Pearl.* The story's subtitle was "The Christmas Box."

In this tale a caring father decides to use Christmas as an opportunity to teach his four children to overcome their particular temperamental failings. Instead of putting presents in the stockings they have hung up, St. Nicholas leaves each child nothing except an individually composed poem that points, affectionately but firmly, to his or her characteristic failing—a readiness to lie, a quick temper, a lack of perseverance, and selfishness. St. Nicholas adds the promise that he will return the following Christmas to check up on the children's progress. (The son inclined to dishonesty grumbles, " 'I know I'll get something from old Nicholas another year, by hook or by crook.' ") After a year in which the children struggle, assisted by their father's constant reinforcement, to conquer their weaknesses, at the next Christmas St. Nicholas does, indeed, bring each child a handsome gift. But he arranges the gifts in such a fashion—this is carefully described—that they cannot be located or opened without an actual *demonstration* of the particular virtue that each of the children has spent the previous year cultivating. (For example, before the selfish child can receive his presents, he is first obliged to give them away to his siblings—and through an ingenious contrivance he actually does so of his own free will!)[44]

Elizabeth Dwight Sedgwick emphasizes that constant parental attention is required if this kind of training is to succeed. The children in her story are educated at home, by both parents; and even outside of school hours there are regular walks and periods of conversation, storytelling, and reading aloud. Each evening concludes with a children's game in which the parents themselves participate. The author puts it plainly:

"either one parent or the other was with the children nearly all the time."
A variety of tactics were employed, as needed: "Sometimes a soft answer
turned away his wrath; sometimes a word in season averted the coming
storm; occasionally a little ridicule thoroughly mortified him—and still
more the serious displeasure of his father, which, because he loved him
dearly, he dreaded more than any thing human, would put him for a time
effectively on his guard." After one especially bad outbreak of temper, for
example, the father told his child: " 'You are always wishing to grow up a
man, that you may become your own master; but your master I fear you
will never be. That temper of yours is your master, and a hard master.' "[45]

But Mrs. Sedgwick is quick to add a statement about the need to recruit a child's own will as an ally in the process of child-rearing: "All these
[tactics] together, however, would have been of little avail, had he not felt
a strong determination in his own mind to conquer his bad habits." And
to help create such an inner determination, the father's Christmas strategy played a key role: "The epistles of St. Nicholas, trifling as they may
seem, were of positive use in turning the minds of the children to the subject of improvement in a single particular." In other words, the hope of receiving their Christmas presents at the end of the year provided a strong
internal incentive for character development.[46]

To be sure, this was a "judgmental" Christmas that Elizabeth
Dwight Sedgwick proposed here. But it was not quite the old-style ritual
we have encountered earlier. St. Nicholas leaves no birch rod for the children, no pieces of coal. Nor does physical punishment have any place in
the repertoire of tactics that these parents employ to train their children.
(Physical punishment would have been far easier, and less labor-intensive,
but for these Unitarians it would have produced children who behaved
well only out of fear and not as a result of the self-control that could come
only from inner strength.)

Such child-rearing strategies involved walking a thin line. On the
one hand, they meant that children had to be taught complete self-
mastery, the overcoming of all weakness. But at the same time they made
children the constant focus of parental attention. Children raised in such
a fashion would find it inevitable to assume that they were the center of a
family's existence. Such a strategy invited the very indulgence it was intended to control.

On one occasion Elizabeth Dwight Sedgwick's own sister-in-law,
Elizabeth Ellery Sedgwick of New York (the woman who enjoyed receiving New Year's visitors), revealed that very fault line. In the summer of
1835, while on vacation in the countryside, the latter Mrs. Sedgwick mused

over the meaning of a lovely outing she had just taken with her young children. A simple ride in a horse-drawn wagon had put the children into "ecstasies" of good humor. "It is astonishing," she began (writing to her husband in the city), "that when the fresh and innocent natures of children require so little, to make them overflow, that more efforts are not made for their happiness." But this thought immediately provoked doubts: "Is it, that youthful privations fit them better for the losses and crosses of After Years? Do Indulgencies of a wise kind necessarily prepare the way for that most odious appendage of character, Selfishness?" Mrs. Sedgwick concluded by precisely articulating the Unitarian dilemma: "I wish I could determine how nicely to adjust the scales, so as to preserve the balance between restraint and indulgence—for on the due proportion of each, how much does the character depend?"[47]

The difficulty in making this kind of determination was compounded by a new strain of thinking that emerged after 1830, largely within the Unitarian community itself. This strain (more broadly considered, it was a local expression of the movement known as Romanticism) took the Unitarian argument about child-rearing substantially further than was initially intended. It suggested that the natural impulses of children were not flawed, after all, and that those impulses should not be suppressed but actually encouraged and indulged. In this new and controversial view, it was children who offered adults a model for emulation, and not the other way around. Children were not imperfect little adults; rather, adults were imperfect grown-up children. The seeds of perfection lay within each child, like the unopened buds in a plant; and the ills of society were produced by corruption and artifice within society itself, and not by the child's own natural impulses. The English Romantic poet William Wordsworth (a friend of Samuel Taylor Coleridge), put the idea in a nutshell in a classic phrase: "The Child is father to the Man."

In the United States, the most famous early expression of this new philosophy came from the pen of Ralph Waldo Emerson, himself a former Unitarian minister (he left the pulpit in 1831). In his very important 1836 essay "Nature," Emerson wrote that the best people were those who "retained the spirit of infancy even into the era of manhood." The "wisdom" of a man's "best hour" was no better than "the simplicity of his childhood." As Emerson summed it up, "the sun illuminates only the eye of the man, but shines into the eye and heart of the child."[48] (By the 1860s, when this radical notion had succeeded in transforming the way thousands of Americans treated their children, the now-aging Emerson looked back on the change with a certain irony. He opened an essay about the reformation of New England life in his own time by reporting a witty aphorism: " 'It was a misfortune to have been born when children were nothing, and to live till [adult] men were nothing.' ")[49]

These Romantic ideas of childhood had obvious implications for educational practices, implications that were most influentially articulated in the work of the European educational reformer Johann Heinrich Pestalozzi (1746–1827). Pestalozzi, a German-speaking Swiss whose name is unfamiliar today except to students of intellectual and educational history, was well known in the second quarter of the nineteenth century—as well known as, say, John Dewey a century later. In his most influential writings, *Leonard and Gertrude* (1781) and *How Gertrude Teaches Her Children* (1801), Pestalozzi stressed above all the importance of mothers in childhood education. He suggested that "feelings of love, confidence, and gratitude, and [even] the habit of obedience," are characteristics that "originate in the relationship established between the infant and its mother."[50] (In retrospect, we can view Pestalozzi's ideas as part of the larger process by which moral authority within middle-class households shifted away from the father and into maternal hands, and by which the teaching profession itself became essentially women's work.)

Hundreds of educators and tourists visited the progressive boarding school that Pestalozzi established in Yverdon, Switzerland, in 1805, and Pestalozzian schools were set up over the succeeding decades throughout Europe (especially in Germany). Pestalozzi's progressive ideas about education—and about childhood itself—had become influential late in the 1820s among upper-class liberals in Philadelphia and Boston, and several "infant schools" were set up in those cities. (In both cities, in the late 1820s, funds were raised for these schools by holding fairs at which Christmas presents were offered for sale; these fairs were the models for the antislavery fairs of the 1830s.)

Controversy over the Pestalozzian system surfaced in Boston in the mid-1830s. In 1835 Emerson's friend Amos Bronson Alcott, an educator who had absorbed Pestalozzi's ideas (and who would later test them out on his daughter Louisa May), opened a Pestalozzian school in Boston, a school in which Alcott devoted much of his energy to listening to the children and otherwise turning conventional child-rearing practices on their head. The pupils in the Temple School (so called because it was housed in Boston's Masonic Temple) were drawn from the children of Boston's well-to-do Unitarian establishment. Alcott's program was controversial from the beginning—for example, when his pupils misbehaved badly, Alcott would punish them by ordering them to whip *him!* But with the publication of *Conversations with Children, on the Gospels*, a book containing verbatim transcripts of the children's responses to passages from the New Testament (the idea was that children could teach their elders even about theology), more conservative Unitarians were scandalized. Enrollment in Alcott's school declined precipitously, and in 1839 he was forced to close it down (the last straw was Alcott's refusal to deny admission to an African-American pupil). From Stockbridge, Elizabeth Dwight Sedgwick (author of that 1833 story about the father who uses Christmas to teach lessons of self-discipline to his sons) had written a critical review of Alcott's first book about his school.[51] Even Harriet Martineau was appalled by *Conversations with Children, on the Gospels,* and she wrote almost savagely about Alcott in her book *Society in America.*

But Charles Follen subscribed to Pestalozzi's ideas, and as we have seen, it appears that the main reason he was fired from his brief tenure as live-in private tutor to the children of the deceased Colonel Perkins was that he insisted on employing Pestalozzian techniques in the boys' education. Later, when he was forced to give up his tutelage, Follen insisted that he had dealt with the boys "by imposing only such rules as their own moral sense approved," and by sharing "a ready sympathy with all their concerns and wants, and a hearty desire to gratify all their legitimate and innocent desires." (He added, "I was aware, that, to some, this mode of treating the boys might seem too indulgent.")[52]

It is interesting that Follen felt obliged to modify the term *desires* with the adjectives "legitimate and innocent." What that little gesture reveals is that the Pestalozzian wing of the Unitarians was caught up in a dilemma just as serious as that of their more conservative colleagues on the other side. Those more conservative Unitarians invoked a strategy of child-rearing that implicitly placed children at the center of the domestic universe, a strategy that could easily bring out the very selfishness it was intended to control. For its part, the Romantic wing of the Unitarians explicitly looked to children to find the roots of human perfection, and they found it difficult to acknowledge that children who had been properly raised would show any signs of corruption. They tried hard to believe that children were innately unselfish, and that it was only a corrupt society, and improper educational practices, that rendered them selfish and greedy. It was a risky assumption.

THE ISSUE came to a head at Christmas. Here was the one occasion on which even those parents who held to the more traditional idea of child-rearing tended to give up any real effort to maintain what Elizabeth Ellery Sedgwick called "the balance between restraint and indulgence." Christmas had long been the kind of occasion on which restraint (of whatever sort) was momentarily suspended and indulgence ruled. In a different culture—a world of scarcity, with seasonal cycles of plenitude—the axis along which that shift took place was one that involved a brief period of gluttonous feasting or similar forms of revelry. In contrast, for genteel Unitarian families who inhabited a world of relative abundance, that axis involved a similarly brief period of undammed affection for their children, an affection made manifest in a lavish orgy of gift-giving.

Back in 1827, Charles Follen (then a newcomer to America) had a conversation with a friend "about the celebration of Christmas in Germany." Follen lamented that there were "no feasts for the children" in the United States. "Such festivals for the feelings," he mused, "would be a great improvement of the moral state of the nation."[53] As we know, even as Follen spoke, this kind of festival was becoming more widespread—1827 was the very year that Clement Clarke Moore's poem "A Visit from St. Nicholas" was widely printed for the first time.

But even among those who, like Elizabeth Ellery Sedgwick, were ordinarily anxious about the dangers of such indulgence, Christmas functioned as a momentary release from that anxiety, a "festival for the feelings." Mrs. Sedgwick herself offers a case in point. During the second half of 1835, she was deeply concerned about her oldest child, a 10-year-old boy named Ellery. Young Ellery had been placed in the trustworthy care of his Aunt Elizabeth (Elizabeth Dwight Sedgwick, the critic of Bronson Alcott and author of the aforementioned 1833 Christmas story), but he was showing worrisome signs of moral weakness. On one occasion he asked his mother to give him a silver pencil. (Characteristically, she refused, suggesting instead that he buy himself "a wooden one—learn to take care of it—and then you shall deserve a better kind of one, and shall have it.") Far worse, his Aunt Elizabeth had caught him cheating systematically on his Latin homework and then lying about the matter when he was confronted with it. All that autumn, the boy's parents carried on an intensive correspondence about how to handle the matter. Elizabeth Ellery Sedgwick endured sleepless nights on her son's account. ("I am mortified and distressed, & fear I have been unfaithful to him, for these faults come back to the Mother.") But at Christmas the parents' pent-up anxiety was released in a torrent of affection, as both father and mother wrote letters assuring their errant son (still away at school with his aunt) of how intensely they missed him ("We miss you dreadfully dear Ell, every hour of the day") and letting him know that they had actually set up a table filled with presents for him ("to show where he would be if he was here").[54] Mr. Sedgwick even chose to let Ellery know that his mother was shedding tears over her letter as she wrote it. All this was hardly the kind of treatment that Elizabeth Dwight Sedgwick, young Ellery's aunt and teacher, had proposed in the Christmas story she had published two years earlier!

For followers of Pestalozzi, the impulse to make Christmas a child-focused "festival of the feelings" was reinforced in 1833 with the publication in Philadelphia of a biography of the Swiss reformer (he had died four years earlier). In the middle of that book the biographer, Edward Biber by name, chose to insert a chapter bearing the title "Christmas-Eve Discourse." This was simply the transcript of a talk—a passionate, rhapsodic talk—that Pestalozzi had delivered in 1810, on Christmas Eve, to the children and fellow teachers at his school in Yverdon. Judging from the context, it would seem that Pestalozzi gave the talk just before distributing presents to his pupils, and it is probable that those presents were hanging from a Christmas tree. (The editor of the English-language edition of Biber's biography felt compelled to offer a footnote for his British and American readers, explaining that in German-speaking regions the presents would be placed on " 'Christmas trees,' young fir-stems, lighted up with little wax tapers, on the twigs of which all the glittering gifts are hung." He went on to explain that when German children asked who had put their presents on the Christmas tree, they were told, " 'The Christ-child brought them.' ")[55]

It is just such a scene that we might imagine as Pestalozzi explained the holy significance of Christmas Eve. He addressed his rhapsodic words directly to the children at Yverdon, insisting that it was they who formed the core of his household: "Beloved children! it is for your sakes that we are united in one family; *our* house is *your* house, and for your sakes only is it *our* house."[56]

In a way, those words would have sounded familiar enough, at least during the Christmas season, when people in authority were used to deferring symbolically to those who at other times of the year would have owed deference to them. (It is not difficult to imagine Washington Irving's old Squire Bracebridge using the same ornate phrasing, but substituting the *poor* for the *children*.)[57]

But Pestalozzi meant something more than that. He meant that children were the center of the household not only in a symbolic fashion—not only on this ritual occasion—but that they constituted the actual and enduring center of the household. In part, that was because the training of children was what families were all about. But it was also be-cause—and here Pestalozzi's radicalism surfaced—the very training of children was ultimately designed to nurture the seeds of innocent perfec-tion with which they had been endowed at birth. In other words, children (properly raised) offered an actual model for adults to imitate. Adults, Pestalozzi felt, needed to become like children: "We know that except we be converted and become as little children, except we be elevated to the simplicity of a childlike mind, we shall not enter into the kingdom of heaven . . . !" And he continued by pleading for their childish spirit to re-deem the very imperfections of their adult teachers: "Children, let the graces of childhood elevate our souls, and purify us of all contamination of anger, and wrath, and hastiness in your education. . . ." [58]

The spirit of Christmas might help to accomplish that inner trans-formation. The presents that parents gave their children on Christmas might help them reverence the spirit of childhood in their own children.

> Oh [Pestalozzi mused] . . . that we might all be like unto our chil-dren, to whom the invisible love of God is made manifest in the Christchild under the form of an innocent babe, like unto them in appearance, but descending from heaven with pleasant gifts. . . . [59]

That we might all be like unto our children. What Pestalozzi ultimately wished to achieve was the reformation of *adults.* But in order for that to come about, children themselves had to play the role they had been as-signed. Their joy had to be innocent joy. They had to experience Christ-mas with what Pestalozzi constantly referred to with the word *simplicity.* ("And you, my beloved children, who celebrate this Christmas in the sim-plicity of your hearts, what shall I say to you? We wish to be partakers of your simplicity, of your childlike joy.")

Pestalozzi wished very deeply to believe (in fact, he committed his life to the venture) that the hearts of children were simpler and purer than those of adults. But even as he was speaking, the assembled children were waiting to receive their Christmas presents, gifts that were probably hang-ing on a Christmas tree at that very moment. I'm not sure exactly what was "innocent" about such childlike joy, but its connection with material expectations surely was (and remains) troubling—and this despite the ef-forts of parents to disguise the nature of the gifts by attributing them to such transcendent figures as St. Nicholas, or even (as Pestalozzi and Ger-man culture had it) the Christ child himself.

Whether it took a Pestalozzian form or the more conservative shape represented by Elizabeth Dwight Sedgwick, Unitarian pedagogy contained a serious internal contradiction. It attempted to teach children to be selfless, but it did so while placing them—*by* placing them—at the center of the domestic universe.

It was a heavy burden to place on children. At one point near the end of his talk Pestalozzi himself hesitated and actually urged the children in his audience to conform to his definition, to become more childlike: "[B]e ye innocent children in the full sense of the word. . . . Let this festival establish *you* in the holy strength of a childlike mind. . . ."[60] *The holy strength of a childlike mind.* Under the weight of this definition, it was surely difficult to grow up as an actual child—perhaps as difficult, in its own way, as it was to grow up as a child whose will was being broken by physical or psychological abuse.

From Belsnickle to Christkingle

As it happens, a short story that was published in the 1836 edition of a Gift Book, *The Pearl*, deals with these questions. The title of the story was "The Christmas Tree," and its author—for once, not a Sedgwick!—was identified simply as "Mrs. G." The story is about using a Christmas tree to teach children a hard lesson: how not to be selfish on the occasion of a holiday that was centered around making them happy. The author, a Philadelphian, lets us know where she got the idea for "The Christmas Tree." It came from "a book I have lately read, in speaking of the celebration of Christmas by the Germans." In a footnote, that book is identified as "Biber's Life of Pestalozzi."[61]

"The Christmas Tree" deals with a prosperous, child-centered family, the Selwyns. The author lets us know on the first page just where on the ideological spectrum this couple's hearts lay: "Mr. and Mrs. Selwyn were very affectionate parents, and nothing gave them greater pleasure than to gratify the wishes of their children." And their daughter Mary has great expectations of the Christmas holiday. The story opens almost two weeks before Christmas Day, with young Mary asking her mother how long she has to wait until the big day arrives: " 'How much I wish it was here!' " she exclaims. When Mrs. Selwyn asks why she is so eager, Mary replies without hesitation: " 'Because I expect to get a great many presents.' " Mrs. Selwyn responds noncommittally: " 'I will make no rash promises; Christmas is almost two weeks off, and, you know, many things may happen before that time.' "[62]

Of course, Mr. and Mrs. Selwyn are plotting a surprise: "They had been planning a Christmas celebration a few evenings before, and they thought of following the German custom in making it a surprise, by keeping the preparations a secret." They have made their preparations in the drawing room, which is ordinarily kept locked and off-limits to the children (who therefore "had no suspicion of the treat their kind parents had in store for them"). Young Mary is "a little disappointed that her mother had said nothing about a party, but she consoled herself by counting how many presents she expected to get."[63]

Christmas Day brings Mary one disappointment after another. The family goes through its standard rituals, but none of these yields a single present. First, Mary tries an old game: "Before sunrise . . . , Mary and her brothers were up and dressed, and ran into their parents' room, to catch them by calling out 'Christmas gift'—knowing that, according to the old custom, if they could say it before their parents, they were entitled to a present." This tactic fails to produce any results. Later that morning, the family goes to visit their grandfather's country estate, "where they always dined on Christmas day." But on their arrival the children are once again disappointed—"there were no presents on the table." Again they console themselves, this time with the thought that "they would get them after dinner," and again they are disappointed. At last, toward evening, the family sets out for home. On the way, "little Mary . . . burst into tears," sobbing that she had " 'never spent such a dull Christmas in her life. . . . Christmas is almost over, and I have not had a single present to-day.' " Finally, Mr. Selwyn chimes in: " 'I am sorry, my daughter, to see that you have so little fortitude in bearing disappointment.' " He gently but firmly expresses disappointment in her behavior: " 'every effort that has been made by your kind relatives, to amuse you and make you happy, has been entirely lost, merely because you could not have every wish gratified.' "[64]

That is the bad news. The good news begins as soon as the Selwyns reach their own house. Now the children are told to dress up. They are led to the parlor, where they are delighted to find "a little party of their young friends, who had been invited by Mrs. Selwyn." The children play party games (these include "Chair of Criticism," "Cross Questions and Silly Answers," and "Ladies' Toilet"). It is in the midst of these that the denouement is reached. Mr. Selwyn asks the children to come with him to the drawing room. The scene is just what we have come to expect: a Christmas tree.

[U]pon his throwing open the drawing-room door, an universal ex-
clamation of delight burst from their lips at the beautiful sight presented to them. In the centre of the room was a large table covered
with a damask cloth, and in the middle of this was placed a Christmas Tree, brilliantly illuminated with wax tapers, and suspended to
the branches were all kinds of beautiful gifts. . . .[65]

The trick has worked. By evening's end little Mary Selwyn has experienced the most delightful Christmas of her young life—and she has
been taught an important lesson at the same time. The key, even more
than the Christmas tree itself, is the element of surprise that accompanies
it. The Selwyns, we are told, were "following the German custom in making it a surprise, by keeping the preparations a secret." (It is indeed the
case, in Christmas-tree references from the 1820s and 1830s, both in stories set in America and in reports from Germany, that Christmas trees are
invariably set up in a room that is normally off-limits to the children—the
library, the parlor, or, as here, the drawing room.[66])

In real life, obviously, the surprise factor would be effective only once
or twice; after that, the children would surely catch on. But even after the
surprise was gone, the ritual would retain a lingering utility: It would continue to keep virtually total control of the gift exchange in the hands of
the parents—control of the time and place, and of the knowledge of how
many gifts there would be and what they were. Frequently, permission for
the children to enter the till-then secret room is signified by the ringing
of a bell (in one instance, the children cannot enter until the third time
the bell is rung!).

In this 1836 story, we might say, the Christmas-tree ritual was explicitly represented as a tactic by which the parents might seize total control of the gift exchange. The main part of the tale consists of a series of
disappointments for its little "anti-heroine"—moments at which her expected presents do not appear. The first of these moments is especially
striking. It is when the children "catch" their parents "by calling out
'Christmas gift'—knowing that, according to the old custom, if they could
say it before their parents, they were entitled to a present."[67] (This is a ritual we will encounter again in Chapter 7, where it will be performed by
slaves in the antebellum South.) But now the old ritual leads to nothing.
It is only at the very end of the day, after several more such disappointments (and when the children have ceased to expect anything at all) that
the carefully orchestrated surprise of the Christmas tree is sprung.

The difference between the ritual of crying out "Christmas gift" and that of waiting for the "Christmas tree" is the difference between children playing the role of active agents in the gift exchange and their assuming the passive role of silent, grateful recipients. The Christmas-tree ritual, as it was introduced to American reading public, was designed to render children completely passive participants in the process. (Just so, as we will see in the next chapter, were new rituals of Christmas charity designed to make poor people themselves passive recipients of largesse.)

The Christmas-tree ritual had another lingering effect. That effect was a hidden one—hidden, I suspect, even among those who had adopted the ritual. It was to manipulate children's behavior, perhaps even their feelings, in a new way. At the end of the story we have just examined, "The Christmas Tree," there is a kind of explanatory epilogue in which the father, Mr. Selwyn, places his new ritual in historical context. When he himself was a child, Mr. Selwyn tells his children,

> "no little girl or boy ever went to bed on Christmas Eve without hanging up a stocking, which they expected would be filled with gifts by the good Christkingle. They were always up bright and early the next morning, to see what was given to them. The good children were always sure of having their stockings filled with cakes, sugar plums, and little presents by the Christkingle, but the naughty ones would find a rod thrust in theirs by the old Bellsnickel. . . . [The Christkingle was regarded] as a kind of fairy, or good genius—such as you read of in fairy tales—who rewarded good children and the Bellsnickel was an evil genius, who punished the bad ones."[68]

A generation earlier, in other words, it would have been easy to deal with a girl like little Mary Selwyn; if her parents were trying to teach her a lesson, she would have received her just desserts from the Belsnickle. But Mr. and Mrs. Selwyn are just as interested in their daughter's inner life as they are in her actual behavior. They want her to learn how to control even her selfish expectations. (Mr. Selwyn tells her at the very end that " 'you ought to submit with cheerfulness to your situation' "—to "submit" rather than to nag; and to do so "with cheerfulness.") They want her to be truly, spontaneously grateful. Not only is young Mary to make no demands for presents, she is not even supposed to harbor any *desire* to receive them.

As a practical matter, of course, that was impossible. What was possible was only concealment. Stories like "The Christmas Tree," if

they were actually put into practice, secretly encouraged children to behave hypocritically—to pretend they didn't know or care what their parents were really planning. Ultimately, the effect of such stories was to
encourage children to deny (even to themselves) their own selfish feelings, or else to feel guilty about having them. Children were being encouraged to feign, first to their parents and then to themselves, both
selfless indifference and spontaneous joy; to act as if they enjoyed their
presents only because they were expressions of love—because they were
"affection's gift."

SOME PERFECT CHILDREN

Beginning in about 1840, yet another kind of Christmas story began to appear. This kind of story was about children who were already perfect in the
Romantic, Pestalozzian sense, children who did not need to be taught a
lesson about selflessness because they were utterly unselfish by nature.[69]
At the very least, these children were willing, even eager, to sacrifice their
own Christmas gifts to make other children (or even grown-ups) happy.
On occasion they were willing, even eager, to sacrifice their very lives. Per-
haps the best-known of these stories is Louisa May Alcott's classic novel
Little Women (1868). This book opens with an extended Christmas se-
quence in which the four young title characters voluntarily give their
Christmas presents to an impoverished neighboring family.[70] Louisa May
Alcott herself was the daughter of Bronson Alcott, the radical Pestaloz-
zian Transcendentalist—and a man who had raised his children in the
Pestalozzian fashion.

   Little Women was of course a tremendous best-seller, but by the time
it was published in 1868 these issues (along with the Christmas tree itself)
had thoroughly permeated middle-class American culture. But as it happens, another associate of Bronson Alcott's had addressed a wide audience
on similar matters a full generation earlier. This was Margaret Fuller, the
first great female American intellectual figure. Back in 1835, Fuller had assisted Alcott in running his radical Temple School, and it was she who actually wrote the controversial 1836 book, *Conversations with Children, On
the Gospels,* that had caused so many conservative Unitarians (including
Harriet Martineau) to take offense. Fuller had also been among the very
first American intellectuals to devote serious study to German language
and philosophy.[71]

   In 1844 Margaret Fuller was living in New York and trying to support herself by writing for Horace Greeley's successful new newspaper, the *New York Tribune*. It was she who authored the Christmas editorial that appeared in the *Tribune* on December 25, 1844, an editorial read by thousands of people. Fuller wrote:

> Christmas would seem to be the day peculiarly sacred to children, and something of this feeling shows itself among us, though rather of German influence, than of native growth. The evergreen tree is often reared for the children on Christmas evening, and its branches cluster with little tokens that may, at least, give them a sense that the world is rich, and that there are some in it who care to bless them. It is a charming sight to see their glittering eyes, and well worth much trouble in preparing the Christmas tree. . . .
>
> We borrow the Christmas tree from Germany. Might we but borrow with it that feeling which pervades all their stories about the influence of the Christ child, and has, I doubt not—for the spirit of literature is always, though refined, the essence of popular life—pervaded the conduct of children there.[72]

Here Fuller retold two German Christmas legends. The first was about "St. Hermann Joseph," a lovely child who one day offered an apple to a church sculpture of the Virgin and child—and the sculpted young Jesus "put forth its hand and took the apple." From that time forth, "little Hermann" took every gift he received and carried it "to the same place. He needed nothing for himself; but dedicated all his childish goods to the altar." The second legend was about "the holy Rupert," a young prince who gave away his possessions whenever he saw a suffering child. One cold day Prince Rupert gives away his coat, stops and falls asleep on the road home, and has a dream. (He dreams of a mild old man who bathes a group of children in a river and then places them "on a beautiful island, where they looked white and glorious as little angels." One of these children turns out to be little Jesus, who is wearing the coat that Rupert had given him.) Upon waking, Rupert takes ill from having stayed out in the cold without a coat. He dies, and at last he is able to join the band of little children he has helped.

Margaret Fuller acknowledged that these stories were legends—Catholic legends, at that—but she insisted that they were useful, good legends, and Protestants should not reject them. "The thought of Jesus, as a child, has great weight with children who have learned to think of him at all." That is, the child Jesus can become a model for modern children. "In earlier days, the little saints thought they imitated the Emanuel by giving apples and coats [i.e., like Hermann and Rupert]; but we know not why, in our age, that esteems itself so enlightened, they should not become also the givers of spiritual gifts. . . ." If children were taken seriously (and educated properly) at home, they could save the world. If they were not, the fault lay in the parents:

> The cause of education would be indefinitely furthered, if in addition to formal means, there were but this principle awakened in the hearts of the young[:] that what they have they must bestow. . . . Were all this right in the private sphere, the public [sphere] would soon right itself also, and the nations of Christendom might join in a celebration such as "Kings and Prophets waited for" and so many martyrs died to achieve, of Christ-Mass.

Margaret Fuller spent part of her own Christmas Day that year visiting the inmates of the city's asylum for deaf and dumb children. The experience, she reported three days later, was one of personal "edification and delight." The children at the asylum put on a theatrical performance for the visitors, a performance that demonstrated that they were capable of expressing intense and authentic emotion. Fuller wrote: "It was gratifying to see the faces of so many children of eternal silence radiate with intelligence, and evincing a knowledge and elevation of sentiment which it would seem impossible, thus benighted, to acquire."[73]

The performance put on by these deaf and dumb children represented one end of the spectrum of New York's Christmas season in 1844. Like an increasing number of New Yorkers, Horace Greeley found it considerably more satisfying than what was still going on—and would continue to go on—at the other end of that same spectrum. Writing a week later, another *Tribune* reporter commented on what the streets of the city were actually like on New Year's Day:

> The grog shops, we regretted to observe, overflowed throughout the day—so did some of their visitors toward evening. This was the worst feature of the anniversary, though the howling, and popping and banging through the preceding night were little better. What a profundity of emptiness there must be in that boy's head who deems gun-firing an appropriate observance of the solemn, majestic, noiseless march of Time.

This reporter had even seen one 18-year-old youth "loading and firing a fowling-piece through the streets at midday!" And he concluded with a sentence that expressed the behavioral concerns of one culture in terms of the generational assumptions of another: "The mother of that boy has much to answer for."[74]

CHAPTER 6

Tiny Tim and Other Charity Cases

HOME-LIFE IN GERMANY

*T*HE YEAR 1853 marked two important achievements in the life of young Charles Loring Brace. The first achievement was practical: Brace helped establish the Children's Aid Society, a New York charitable institution that would become, within his lifetime and due chiefly to his unceasing efforts, the most important charitable organization in the city and probably the entire United States. Brace's other achievement was literary: the publication of a book. That book, *Home-Life in Germany*, would soon be forgotten, overshadowed both by Brace's subsequent literary work and, more important, by his labors with the Children's Aid Society itself. But it is of interest here, if only because of the light it casts on Brace's subsequent charitable work with children, and also on his enduring interest in Christmas.

Home-Life in Germany was a travelogue of sorts, the account of an extended visit Brace had made to that country two years earlier, at the age of 25. During his visit Brace was struck by several important contrasts between Germany and his native United States. For example, Germans tended to be far less individualistic and self-reliant than Americans were. On the other hand, family life—the main subject of Brace's book—was far more important in Germany than it was in America.

The contrast between the home life of the two cultures came to a head at Christmas. Brace devoted an entire chapter of *Home-Life in Germany* to an account of the Christmas celebration in that country. Here, too, the graciousness of German culture contrasted with the emptiness Brace found in the United States:

> As I recall our hollow home-life in many parts of America—the self-ishness and coldness in families—the little hold HOME has on any one, and the tendency of children to get rid of it as early as possible, I am conscious how much after all we have to learn from these easy Germans.

Brace acknowledged that there was a certain "compensation" for this failing: In the United States "a boy is an independent, self-reliant man . . . , when he is [still] in leading-strings in Germany." But for the most part, that compensation was inadequate, because self-reliance alone was no asset at all—unless it was softened by unselfish geniality. Otherwise, it would only intensify the hollowness of American home life. And that was just what was happening in the United States, where the acquisitive spirit was destroying family values:

> Materialism—the passion for money-making and excitement, is eating up the heart of our people. We are not a happy people; our families are not happy. Men look haggard and anxious and weary. We want something more genial and social and unselfish amongst us . . .

What was needed was an antidote to raw materialism, and such an antidote was provided by the domestic Christmas. "Any family-festivals of this kind," Brace wrote—"anything which will make home pleasanter, which will bind children together, and make them conscious of a distinct family-life, is most strongly needed." For Brace (as for so many Americans), Christmas was now above all a domestic idyll, an opportunity to produce and foster family values as an antidote to materialism and selfishness. Once again, Germany offered an object lesson for Americans:

> There is something about this German Festival, which one would seldom see in *our* home enjoyments. People do not seem to be enjoying themselves, because it is a "duty to be cheerful." . . . They are cheerful, because they cannot help it, and because they all love one another. The expression of *trustfulness* through the children of these families . . . was very beautiful to see. They were all so happy, because they had been making one another happy.

Christmas in Germany was an occasion of unforced, spontaneous mutuality. Brace connected this domestic Christmas with authentic religious piety: "Good people are to recognize that there is a religion in Christmas feasts, as well as in prayer-meetings; that a father who has made his home gloomy, has done quite as great a wrong to his children, perhaps, as he who made it irreligious. We want these German habits— these birth-day and Christmas festivals—this genial family life . . ."[1] It is difficult to imagine a better definition of what modern historians have taken to calling the "religion of domesticity."

There was more. Brace reported that in Germany such close-knit, nurturing families were to be found much further down the social ladder than they were in America—indeed, down nearly to the bottom of the working class. Like so many Americans of this period, Brace saw Germany as the one place in the world where true family values had permeated almost the entire society. And the consequences were even apparent in public—for example, the German working class was far more polite and deferential than its American (or English) counterpart. Brace cited a vivid example. He had once "asked an English groom for directions in the streets of London, and was told in answer, 'How the h–ll should I know?' " An American laborer, he added, would be almost as rude. But in Germany things were different: "A German stands—says to you with a half bow, '*Be good enough* to take the second street,' etc., and touches his hat as he goes." (Brace added that such a response might "perhaps" be "a little too much" for a Yankee to take, but he added that it was still "a very pleasant thing.") Brace attributed that difference to a single point: the lessons in the natural "expression of any feeling" that almost all German children learned from their families; the kind of feelings that were "laughed at in childhood" by the parents of their American counterparts. (Brace added that in the United States such feelings were "pruned" away.)[2] In other words, Brace attributed working-class rudeness in the United States to a home life that was "cold, unsocial, disagreeable."

In a way, this was what most impressed Brace about the German Christmas itself: how far down the social ladder it reached. That was just how he introduced his chapter on the German Christmas. The Berlin lodging house at which Brace had been staying over the holidays was owned by a man who was "hopelessly in debt"; nonetheless, Brace watched this man "bringing home an armful of presents." Then there was the local shoemaker, whose family lived in the basement of Brace's lodging house; the family was so poor that the children often seemed to go hungry. But, sure enough, Brace spotted "through the low window, a green

Christmas tree, and the children are tying on the bits of candle." Brace summed up his point by asserting that in all of Berlin, "There are not a dozen families so poor, as not to have their [Christmas] tree."[3]

Brace did not need to add the obvious: Men who celebrated Christmas like the Berlin shoemaker who lived in the basement were the kind of men who would never talk back to their betters, who would never say, "How the h–ll should I know?" They were, on the contrary, precisely the kind of men who were likely to answer a stranger's question with a polite half bow and a deferential touch of the hat. And they would raise their children to do the same.

EBENEZER SCROOGE AND THE CRATCHITS

There is a very famous fictional family of the mid-nineteenth century— and a British family, at that—which resembles that of Brace's real-life shoemaker. It is the Cratchit family, the central household in Charles Dickens's classic 1843 novella *A Christmas Carol*. Too poor to provide adequate medical care for their children (the youngest of whom, Tiny Tim, is for that reason a cripple), the Cratchits are intensely genial, close-knit, and nurturing—everything that Bob Cratchit's employer, Ebenezer Scrooge, is not. For Dickens, as for Brace, the social warmth of the Cratchit family achieves its apotheosis at Christmas. Despite their poverty, the Cratchits have a merry time of it. And their merriment is a celebration of domesticity itself. What Brace wrote of German families at Christmas makes for an apt summary of the scene Dickens paints. The Cratchits' joy has nothing to do with a "duty to be cheerful." Rather, "they are cheerful, because they cannot help it, and because they all love one another." They are "happy, because they had been making one another happy."

There is another characteristic of what Brace considered to be "German" culture that applies to the Cratchits. They are polite and well-mannered to their superiors, even in the face of incessant provocation (in their case, provocation by Ebenezer Scrooge). It is impossible to imagine Bob Cratchit snarling to Scrooge, "How the h–ll should I know?" Even in private, at the family's Christmas dinner, Bob Cratchit refuses to say a mean word about his employer.

To be sure, the Cratchits are fictional creations. But as social types, even though they are surely exaggerated, they are not altogether unreal. To begin with, they are not really members of the British working class.

Every bit as much as Brace's shoemaker, they are integrated into the larger society. (The shoemaker was an independent artisan, and he lived in a respectable neighborhood, in the same boardinghouse as Brace himself.) The actual working classes of mid-nineteenth-century Britain (and America) were composed chiefly of industrial laborers—men and women who worked in textile mills or coal mines. But Ebenezer Scrooge was apparently not an industrial capitalist, but rather a merchant. (We learn almost nothing about the nature of Scrooge's line of work, except that he owns a warehouse.) Nor was Bob Cratchit an industrial laborer; he was a clerk. He worked not on an assembly line but in an office, an office of his own (however ill heated it may have been in the winter). Indeed, as far as we can tell, Cratchit was Scrooge's *only* employee, and a trusted one at that. In modern parlance, he was (albeit barely) a white-collar worker, more like a bank teller than a coal miner or a mill operative. However badly Cratchit was treated by Scrooge, he was not apt to be laid off in hard times, as many industrial workers would have been. And however badly Scrooge treated Cratchit, the two men maintained a close working relationship (Cratchit's office was located right next to Scrooge's). Again, this stands in sharp contrast to the conditions of most industrial workers, whose employers would not even have been able to identify them, by either name or face.

Cratchit is literate, too (indeed, that is one of the requirements of his job), and so is at least one of his sons. One reason for the literacy may be that Cratchit's wife and their children all stay at home; unlike their counterparts in most working-class families of the time, they do not labor for wages to help support the family. Cratchit exhibits none of the behavior that respectable people of the time associated with working-class culture: He does not drink to excess, he does not spend all his wages on payday; he is not (we must assume) sexually promiscuous. In modern parlance, he is the head of a stable, child-centered family. All this is not to deny that Bob Cratchit is an exploited worker, but only to observe that he is hardly a realistic symbol of the industrial proletariat. It would be more accurate to identify him (in nineteenth-century terms) as a man who is struggling to become part of the respectable—and respectful—petite bourgeoisie.

A Christmas Carol is often read today (and it was often read in the nineteenth century) as if it painted a vivid picture of alienated class relations in the period of the Industrial Revolution, and as if it evoked ways of bridging the vast gulf that had emerged between the top and bottom strata of society—through the kind of fellow feeling that Ebenezer Scrooge comes to experience after his conversion. But that is not the case.

The vast and depressing face of the Industrial Revolution scarcely appears in this book. The poor themselves never make any demands of Scrooge, and for that matter he never encounters them. (We never see him approached by a beggar, for example.) In fact, the only contact Scrooge has with the poor is in his vision—a dream, as it turns out, that unfolds in the safety of his own bed. And even in that dream, none of the poor ever curse or threaten him. The most horrible vision Scrooge has—a vision evoked by the Ghost of Christmas Future—is the indifference expressed by his business acquaintances when they learn of his death.[4]

In other books Dickens addressed other kinds of social relationships: the gap between bourgeois and proletarian in *Hard Times,* for example, or the inadequacy of institutionalized charity in *Oliver Twist.* What *A Christmas Carol* deals with, in a practical way, is something less vast but in its own way equally troubling. In *A Christmas Carol* Dickens addressed not the great social divisions among classes estranged from one another by wealth, distance, and occupation but the daily, intimate class differences among people who were much closer to one another on the social scale.

For if Bob Cratchit is not a member if the industrial working class, neither is Ebenezer Scrooge an upper-class industrial capitalist. This is true in a purely economic sense, since Scrooge seems to be a merchant and not an industrialist. And it is also true in a behavioral sense. In terms of his own lowly origins (he began as an apprentice to Old Fezziwig) and also his adult behavior, Scrooge, too, is essentially a member of the petite bourgeoisie, a self-made man who has spent his life striving hard (and at the cost of all human relationships, whether public or private) to attain a sense of security. He is a man who has not managed to grasp the point that such mighty striving is no longer required of him. No matter how wealthy he may be, Scrooge is not really a rich man; it might be more accurate to describe him as a poor man who has a lot of money.

That is, until the end of the book. Whatever else Scrooge's conversion represents, it also marks his realization that he has "made it," after all—that he can finally afford to ease up on himself and others. Considered sociologically, Scrooge's conversion may mark his entry into the easy culture of the upper-middle-class world, a world for which he has previously been eligible only in an economic sense, but which his temperament has heretofore barred him from joining. In the more contemporaneous language of Charles Loring Brace, Scrooge is finally ready to transform the emotionally hollow culture of sheer greed into a more fulfilling culture in which everyday activities and relationships are softened by family values.

From both perspectives, one of the signs of Scrooge's social rise is that he finally accepts his obligation to treat his clerk, Cratchit, in a more humane fashion.

That obligation, however, has its limits, even at Christmas. For when, at the very end of the book, Scrooge signifies to the Cratchits that he has changed, he does so by giving them a Christmas turkey, the largest bird he can find. But he has the turkey *sent* to the Cratchits; he does not deliver it in person—despite what several of the movie versions of *A Christmas Carol* may suggest. Presents, yes, but not "presence." Scrooge is the "founder of the feast," but he does not participate in the Cratchits' actual Christmas dinner. Instead, he chooses to take dinner with his own family—at the house of his nephew, Fred. The message was clear: It was enough to *provide* such known employees with a gift. (And while this is surely not the point of the book, it is of course evident that even the gift amounts to good business practice. For henceforth Scrooge will surely be able to count on Bob Cratchit's heightened loyalty and diligence: Cratchit will become an even better employee.)

In other words, *A Christmas Carol* addressed the relationship of the well-to-do not with the faceless poor but with the poor who were personally known and whose predicament might provoke pangs of conscience. It offered a perspective on how to deal with people who neither belonged to one's own family or social circle nor were members of the anonymous proletariat. This was a real problem in a society where Christmas rituals were becoming domesticated and class differences themselves were being reshaped. Scrooge was not a country squire; Cratchit was not his tenant or apprentice. Maybe, had either been the case, each would have known just what to do at Christmas (and, of course, there would have been no story). But the creation, in England and America, of vast armies of middle-class people and wage earners produced a new type of society in which the old rituals of inversion and misrule no longer made much sense.

Indeed, the relationship between the youthful Scrooge and his master, Old Fezziwig, had been a paternalist one, a relationship of patron and client. Scrooge was Fezziwig's apprentice, not his employee. Indeed, Fezziwig held an old-time Christmas, too, attended by an array of his dependents. But as Dickens himself well knew, that was in an earlier age, in a precapitalist culture. Cratchit could never have been Scrooge's apprentice. The economic system had changed, and with it the social relationships between patron and client. (In a still later age, employers might re-create Old Fezziwig's Christmas in the form of an office party—but the employees' families would not participate in that.) The fact that Scrooge did not share a meal with the Cratchits makes the point: The rituals were changing. What Dickens showed his readers was how to navigate the ritual waters of the Christmas season so as to avoid the dual shoals of the guilt that might stem from not giving at all across class lines and the messiness (not to say futility) that would result from giving to every beggar who walked the streets or knocked on one's door.

Still, and for all that, there is something elusive about *A Christmas Carol*. Its message has proven malleable, subject to different readings. During the century and a half since its publication in 1843, progressive liberals have claimed this book as a plea to ameliorate the evils of industrial capitalism. And free-enterprise conservatives have been equally able to claim it for their own. Thus the *New York Times* in 1893, in the depths of a very severe depression, used *A Christmas Carol* to make the point that private charitable resources were sufficient to relieve pressing want, and the commitment of the city's most wealthy citizens to do so was strong: "[A]t no time in the history of the city has private helpfulness come more eagerly or more prodigally to the reinforcement of good public deeds." Philanthropically minded employers had "plunged into the fray with all the noble ardor of all the benevolent philanthropists ever fabled by Charles Dickens," performing "prodigies of kindness" reminiscent of a "recreated and rejuvenated Scrooge." For the *Times*, the message was clear: "Who . . . shall dare to say hereafter that corporations have no souls . . . ?"[5]

That editorial was based on a plausible reading of *A Christmas Carol*. But it was equally plausible to read the book as an attack on capitalism. The elusiveness of *A Christmas Carol* may in part be what has allowed it to become an enduring literary classic—or, actually, more than a classic, for this book has entered a legendary realm beyond the category of literature itself. The name *Scrooge* has entered the language as a generic descriptive, and his story has become part of the common lore of the English-speaking world.

ON THE EVILS OF INDISCRIMINATE GIVING

A Christmas Carol does deal, briefly, with larger questions of wealth and poverty, first at the very beginning of the book and once again at the very end. Scrooge is approached at the start by a pair of men who visit his office to solicit a cash donation to help the destitute. These men represent an unnamed charitable agency, and their own social status is clear: They are "gentlemen" (meaning that they are of a class above that to which Scrooge himself belongs). Scrooge, of course, turns these gentlemen down, in the famous exchange in which he retorts that there are prisons and workhouses to house the destitute, and that he is paying taxes to support these. Then, at the end of the book, after his conversion, Scrooge sees these same two gentlemen on the street, and he approaches them and proceeds to offer the contribution he had earlier refused. (We never learn how *large* a contribution, since Scrooge whispers the sum in their ear. All we know is that the charitable gentlemen are delighted.)

In that sense, Scrooge's conversion also has to do with his new ability to make a distinction between the different kinds of Christmas obligations he owes to different kinds of people. To members of his family he owes face-to-face participation, and (as we have seen) to the known poor with whom he deals regularly, he must send a present. But his debt to the unknown poor, the faceless suffering poor of industrial society, can be paid at a greater distance, by offering a donation to a private charitable agency; and the agency itself will provide the poor with "meat and drink, and means of warmth." Scrooge's conversion entails his ability to create a new categorical distinction. If the reborn Scrooge were approached by a beggar on the street, or at his door, he could now respond with a clear conscience by saying, in effect, *I gave at the office.*

By the 1840s, Christmas giving was beginning to be polarized into just those two different activities. Gifts for one's own family and friends now took the form of "presents," while gifts that were given to the needy took the form of "charity." There were important differences between the two. The gifts given to family and friends consisted of luxury items, ordinarily purchased by the givers and presented directly to their recipients, either face-to-face or accompanied by a personal note. The gifts given to the faceless poor consisted mostly of necessities, which were ordinarily purchased and distributed not by the givers but by a charitable organization, which mediated between the other parties and eliminated the need for any direct contact between donor and recipient.

It had not always been that way. Before the era of the domestic and commercial Christmas in the nineteenth century, as we have seen, "presents" and "charity" were one and the same, and they were given to the same people—directly and face-to-face. Indeed, on a small scale such rituals persisted well into the nineteenth century (and beyond). For example, in 1837 the Lenox, Massachusetts, branch of the Sedgwick family held just such an event. It was centered, interestingly enough, around a Christmas tree—the first such tree that any member of the Sedgwick family had ever erected. Joining the children around this tree, in the parlor of Charles Sedgwick's house, was a group of the family's local dependents who had been "collected" (the word used by Susan Ridley Sedgwick, Charles' sister-in-law, who described the scene in a private letter to her husband). Among the dependents, Susan Sedgwick reported, were "several of Charles' poor pensioners, several blacks, and among others the deaf & dumb lad, whom you may remember to have applied for, to get him in at Hartford [i.e., a School for the Deaf and Dumb]." The lad "looked perfectly delighted," Susan Sedgwick noted, and she went on to report with pride that a little black girl named Josey (a crippled child, apparently) joined in dancing around the Christmas tree, "turning round & round, now assisted by one, & now by another of the children—all fear of amalgamation [i.e., race mixing] entirely forgotten." "It was really quite affecting to witness [Susan Sedgwick insisted] so much happiness, so diffused, and yet created from such simple materials. . . ."[6]

But that kind of ritual was becoming increasingly difficult to carry off. Lenox, Massachusetts, represented a vestigial pocket of rural paternalism—a self-conscious pocket, at that—and the Sedgwicks were both willing and able to play the role of gracious squires to their poor "pensioners." In the urban areas of the nation, especially, such gestures were much more difficult to bring off. The urban poor were now living in separate neighborhoods, and (except for domestics and menials) they had little occasion for personal contact with the well-to-do. And when such contacts did take place, especially at Christmas, they were likely to take an awkward or even hostile form, mixed perhaps with a bit of mockery, and the whole exchange lubricated with alcohol.

Still, the distinction between presents and charity was new, and it should not be surprising that it required a good deal of reinforcement. During the middle decades of the nineteenth century, the press, the economic elite, and even those who were most deeply concerned with helping the poor, all pressed the notion that organized charities provided the most appropriate means of assisting the poor.

Horace Greeley, for example, reminded his *New York Tribune* readers in 1843 that "enough was expended on this festival uselessly . . . which would, if rightfully appropriated, have set in operation the means of ultimately banishing Pauperism and its attendant miseries from the land."[7] *Rightfully appropriated* was the operative phrase here: Money should be offered to the poor through organized charities rather than through what was now being universally attacked with a dismissive phrase: "indiscriminate giving." Greeley was especially critical of what had become the dominant form of face-to-face charity—begging on the streets. One *Tribune* Christmas editorial opened with the blunt heading "DO NOT GIVE TO STREET BEGGARS," and went on to dismiss that practice in no uncertain terms: "Whenever you see one of these City pests approaching, button up both pockets. . . ."[8] Another editorial (this one from a depression year) explained that "the evil of street-begging" would inevitably increase as a result of the hardness of the times. "Impostors will abound more than ever," for example. But buttoning up one's pockets was psychologically difficult: "he who rejects a petition for the needs of a night's lodging or a meal may have his own warm rest disturbed by the reasonable apprehension that fearful exposure and distress have resulted from his prudence."[9]

On this occasion the *Tribune* handed out meal tickets instead of cash to beggars. But making contributions to organized charity offered a more effective solution. It would obviate the need for face-to-face encounters along with the danger of fraud, and it would be far more efficient. The *Tribune* pleaded with its readers to send their donations to one of the charity organizations, because "that way of helping the poor" might not be perfect, but "it is more effectual and humane than any other yet adopted."[10] Or, as the same paper put it in still another Christmas editorial: "Let us give not merely as cases of destitution may present themselves, but through the regularly organized channels for the dispensation of social charity wherewith our own and most other cities are blessed. . . ."[11]

If the middle-class press criticized "indiscriminate giving," it also generally attacked another alternative to private charities: governmental support for the poor through programs of public assistance or public works. Many workingmen themselves called for just such programs, especially during years of severe depression—the kind of devastating depression that regularly shook the new capitalist economy. When the times were hard, many employers simply laid their workers off—and there was no unemployment insurance to see them through. In one depression year, 1854, a large group of unemployed New York workers held a meeting on Christmas Day, forming themselves as the "Mechanics' and Workingmen's Aid Association." The assembled workers passed a resolution that demanded that tenants "shall not be turned out of their homes by avaricious landlords" and called for what amounted to a rent strike by appointing a "vigilant committee" to oversee the response. The city had made a special $10,000 appropriation for the poor, and the workers demanded that some of those funds be given directly to the association itself. One speaker denounced the municipal soup kitchens as "haughty and contemptuous" (and added that they served watery soup). Another speaker called for public-works programs instead of soup kitchens. A third demanded that the city itself subsidize up to 50 percent of rent payments for the unemployed.[12]

The newly established *New York Times* responded to the situation by acknowledging that "these were hard times" and expressing special sympathy for the fact that "men are poor this winter who were never poor before." (This was as much as to say that such men were more worthy of sympathy than those who had always been poor.) In passing, the *Times* even proposed paternalist gestures on the part of those employers who could afford it: "retaining their workmen, though they are not profitable." But the editorial reserved the bulk of its space to stress the superiority of giving through such established institutions as the churches and the newly formed Children's Aid Society. This was presented in the name of simple efficiency. Money contributed to such organizations "will 'find' where the misery is." Such institutions have well-established "channels" and employ "effectual and discriminating" techniques; they have at their disposal well-tooled "machinery" to make sure that each individual dollar "reaches to-morrow the very family that is famishing to-day for lack of it." Implicitly, the paper argued that any contribution not mediated by those organizations was nothing but a form of indiscriminate giving. "If a man has money, and does not know how he can make the most of it, let him step into the offices of any of those excellent institutions, in whose hands, if you place a dollar, you do what, individually, you could not make five dollars do."[13]

A decade later, the same newspaper actually argued that this kind of charity was little more than a continuation of the long-standing tradition of Christmas generosity on the part of the British gentry and nobility. In the previous century, the argument went, "[n]o hungry faces were allowed to be seen around the baron's hall, or the monk's open doors, or the citizen's gate." That tradition was being maintained into the present with hardly a hitch: "Modern times have continued this pleasant custom of benefaction. Yesterday, we doubt not, the faces of thousands of the poor were made happy with the good fare provided by the generosity of the charitable. . . . The bounty of others . . . heaped the tables of the outcast with good things." But in fact it was only to the work of charitable institutions that the paper was referring—to "the missions, the industrial schools, the lodging-houses for homeless boys and girls, [and] the almshouses and asylums and refuges." And the editorial concluded by giving its readers the now-standard advice: Those good-hearted individuals "who fear to do as much injury as good by their indiscriminate charities, should seek out the great public almoners, our benevolent societies, who have reduced charity almost to a science, and probably seldom err on the side of too much generosity."[14]

As matters grew worse during the following decades, and workers responded by attempting to unionize, the press became even more insistent that private benevolence was far superior to either indiscriminate giving or public assistance. At Christmas in 1893 several local unions were out on strike. But the *New York Times* responded with a warning that it acknowledged might seem "strange" to its readers: "Strange as it may sound, there is danger of overdoing the charitable relief business, or at least of misdoing it, if it is not put under concentrated, intelligent, and judicious direction."

> But there is need of great discretion in organizing and directing agencies for the relief of the poor in times like these. More than ever is it important that this work should be done intelligently and judiciously. Lavish and indiscriminate giving to applicants, however vouched for, will result in waste. . . . Worst of all, it will encourage and embolden beggary and attract worthless vagrants from all quarters.

The editorial decried the use of public moneys to ease the situation, insisting that "organized arrangements for distributing this superfluity among the needy through private benevolence are much better than efforts to use public authority and public funds for the relief of the poor or the unemployed."[15] What the editorial did not mention, though it would have been clear to any reader who also followed the labor columns of the same paper, was that not one of the established charitable organizations was willing to provide assistance to workers who were out on strike.[16]

CHARLES LORING BRACE, NEWSBOYS, AND THE CHILDREN'S AID SOCIETY

As late as the early 1850s, the major charitable institutions in cities like New York were of two sorts: either municipal agencies (such as the almshouse and the workhouse for adults, and the city nursery for children) or arms of the city's churches, which established "missions" to the urban poor (there were seventy-six of these missions operating in 1865). These institutions did not disappear, but during the 1850s they were supplemented by a new set of private philanthropic organizations dedicated exclusively to serving impoverished groups. At the same time, several church missions became quasi-autonomous operations. One of the first and most famous of these was the Five Points Mission, founded in 1852 by the Ladies' Home Missionary Society, a Methodist group, and located in one of the city's most blighted and dangerous areas (the Five Points was the site of a notorious gang war in 1857). Together with a similar agency, the Five Points House of Industry, founded in 1853, these missions offered charitable relief to neighborhood families and provided children with classes that taught them industrial or domestic skills.[17]

Increasingly, these organizations came to focus their energies on a single group within the neighborhood they served: *impoverished children*. And very soon, organizations began to emerge that were devoted exclusively to children. The most effective (and aggressive) of these agencies—and probably, within a decade or two, the single largest and best-known charitable organization in the United States—was the Children's Aid Society, established in 1853 under the guiding influence of the young reformer Charles Loring Brace.

Brace came to the C.A.S. from the Five Points Mission, where he had worked in 1852, during the year that followed his visit to Germany. It was the end point of an eight-year period that Brace spent in seeking a clear vocation for himself. Born in 1826 in Litchfield, Connecticut, of old New England stock (his father later became principal of the Hartford Female Seminary, where Catharine and Harriet Beecher served as teachers), Brace graduated from Yale in 1846 and returned there a year later to study theology. Ambitious to make his way in a more cosmopolitan setting, he also studied at the Union Theological Seminary in New York. But he began to harbor sympathies for abolitionists and other reformers (including the European radicals who were leading the revolutionary movements of 1848). Late in 1849 Brace visited New York's municipal facilities on Blackwells Island, where he preached to the poor in the almshouse and met with prisoners and ill prostitutes. It was like a conversion experience: "I never had my whole nature so stirred up within me," he reported, "as at what met my eyes in those hospital wards."[18]

Early the next year Brace embarked on the European visit that brought him to Berlin in November, ostensibly to continue his theological studies. (It was in Berlin, a month after his arrival, that he witnessed the German Christmas celebration he would later write about.) But his sympathy for the oppressed was very much alive, and while touring Hungary in the spring of 1851 he was actually imprisoned for a month on charges of aiding the Hungarian nationalist revolutionaries led by Lajos Kossuth. Brace returned to New York after being released (through the efforts of the U.S. minister) and wrote a book about his experiences. But now he had finally determined what he wished to do with his life: He would dedicate himself to working for the poor. In that way he would be able to combine his religious commitment and training with his progressive secular politics. In 1852 Brace began working for the recently founded Five Points Mission but left the next year in order to establish the Children's Aid Society, the institution with which he remained associated for the remaining thirty-three years of his life. As the executive secretary of the C.A.S., Brace was an early representative of an emerging social type in American history (and also a new group in the history of Christmas patronage)—the salaried managerial class.

As a matter of pragmatic principle, the Children's Aid Society devoted its work exclusively to young people. Brace had come to the firm conclusion that targeting adults was virtually useless—"like pouring water through a sieve," as he once put it. All too often, adults wasted charitable relief on alcohol or worse. Moreover, whatever assistance they received (and on this point Brace's ideas resemble that of many modern conservatives) only created a sense of dependency that further ensured their ongoing pauperization. Brace was persuaded that the only "hopeful field" was among "the young." If one worked exclusively with children, he believed, "crime might possibly be checked in its very beginnings, and the seed of future good character and order and virtue be widely sown."[19]

Brace carried this principle very far. He decided not only that adults could not be part of the solution to the problem of poverty but also that they constituted the immediate source of the problem. It was, ironically, the family life of New York's poor population that was destroying the character of its children. Brace had long been deeply aware, as *Home-Life in Germany* revealed, of the power of family life to mold the character of children, for better or for worse. (Indeed, he was so sensitive to the family's influence that, as we have seen, he even felt that middle-class American families were failing to offer the genial, nurturing environment necessary to develop healthy adults.) But the families of the poor were worse than inadequate—they were, as Brace put it, actual "poison" for their own children.

Brace argued that this was true of mothers as well as fathers. In making such an argument he was confronting the heart of the reigning domestic ideology—the belief that all mothers could be counted on, by their very natures, to nurture their children through thick and thin. Brace was prepared to attack this belief almost head-on. At Christmas, 1855, he published in several New York newspapers a plea for charity that consisted of several little "Scenes for Christmas." One of these scenes pictured a proud and respectable young mother who had been reduced to poverty by a combination of hard times and her husband's drinking. That was a familiar nineteenth-century scenario. But Brace went further. He argued that the young mother had lost her self-respect; she had even lost "the last thing a woman of her former [respectable] habits loses—the pride in neat appearance." (And he added: "If she could but see it, it is just such dowdiness which sends the husband to the dram-shop instead of home.") Brace concluded that it would be of little avail to offer assistance to this pathetic woman: "The husband will probably die a drunkard; [and] the young wife, who had left comfort and home for his poverty, will either kill herself or perish of a broken-heart." But then there were the children: "There is the hope. Who will aid us in doing something for them?"

Brace used such accounts to make a radical argument: It was not enough to *help* the children—they actually had to be separated, permanently so, from their parents. In another of his 1855 "Christmas Scenes"

Charles Loring Brace. This woodcut was taken from a picture made late in Brace's life. *(Courtesy of the Fine Arts Library, Harvard College Library)*

(this one titled "The Cold Home"), Brace contrasted a pair of "tidy, sweet children" with their chilly mother and her "cheerless" house. He had tried to persuade the mother to let the girls attend an industrial school (offering to provide them with clothing if they would do so), and he promised "that the boy should find a home if he would come to our office." Brace was adamant: "[T]hough for her pure young children too much could hardly be done, in such a woman [herself] there is hardly any confidence to be put." And he confidently generalized from this woman's case: "In nine cases out of ten, it is probable, some cursed vice has thus reduced her, and that, if her children be not separated from her, she will drag them down, too."[20]

So Brace devised a new scheme. It involved persuading parents to send their children to the Children's Aid Society (or persuading the children themselves to go there)—in order to ship them out of the city altogether, to new homes in the American West, in villages with stable families, ample opportunities for employment, and the kind of individualistic ethos that would offer the boys fertile soil to develop their competitive tendencies into socially productive channels. ("Manless land for landless men" was a slogan of the movement.) In its first four decades the "placing out" scheme—it would later be dubbed the "orphan train" program—managed to transport some 90,000 boys to new homes and lives in the West.[21] And it helped bring international renown to Charles Loring Brace.

In opting for this strategy, Brace had come to embrace the qualities of competitiveness and self-reliance that he sensed in many of New York's poor children, children who had been thrown on their own devices. He saw such behavior as a sign of potential ambition that, healthfully channeled, could transform bad habits into productive ones. Even in *Home-Life in Germany*, Brace had acknowledged that self-reliance was a virtue (in America "a boy is an independent, self-reliant man . . . , when he is [still] in leading-strings in Germany"). But in that book he had seen self-reliance only as a "compensation" (and a partial one, at that) for the absence of strong family ties between American children and their parents. Now, as secretary of the Children's Aid Society, Brace paid more attention to encouraging self-reliance than to fostering family ties. Knowing that many of New York's poor children could be enticed with relative ease to leave home, Brace put to practical use what he had previously lamented as the weakness of family ties among American youths. He reported in just those terms the mood among a group of boys leaving New York for the West in 1855: "All seemed as careless at leaving home forever, as if they were on . . . [an] excursion to Hoboken." Life in the labor-starved, Protestant-dominated West, he argued, would be likely to transform a "rough, thieving New York vagrant" into an "honest, hardworking West- ern pioneer."[22] According to the historian Paul Boyer, Brace did not sys- tematically track the later careers of the orphan-train riders: He "showed little interest in determining whether the boys he sent West actually be- came settled members of their communities; it was enough that they were 'being absorbed into that active, busy population.' "[23]

But it would be a mistake to think that this complex man had turned into a simple apologist for the spirit of free enterprise. Despite his endur- ing admiration for the independent human spirit, Charles Loring Brace never lost the deep distrust of nineteenth-century capitalism that in- formed *Home-Life in Germany.* At the very height of the Gilded Age, in 1882, he published a work of theology that attempted to trace the chang- ing role of Christianity in human history. In that book, *Gesta Christi,* Brace noted tentatively that the New Testament itself was permeated by a "certain tone" that was, "if not of 'communism,' at least in favor of greater distribution of wealth than would suit modern ideas." Jesus and the apos- tles "almost denounce the rich," he wrote, and "their sympathies are strongly with the working classes; they urge continually the diffusion of property, in whatever way would benefit the world." At another point in the same book Brace insisted that there was "in many of the aspirations and aims of communism, a certain marked sympathy or harmony with the ideals of Christianity." But he was also quick to add that "[n]othing, how- ever, in Christ's teachings tends towards any forcible interfering with rights of property, or encourages dependence on others." As that final clause suggests, Jesus might be a socialist, but Brace would not relinquish the idea that he was also a man of self-reliance! Here as clearly as any- where in his writings may be found a clue to the coherent philosophy that Brace never quite managed to articulate.[24]

BUT IT WAS not philosophy that earned Brace the respect of the phil- anthropic community, in any case. It was his practical organizational skills which did that, and his ability to deal effectively with poor children them- selves. Those interpersonal skills came increasingly to the fore over the years. From the beginning, the Children's Aid Society did not restrict it- self to sending children West, and by the 1860s it was becoming clear that the supply of street children in New York far exceeded the demand for their labor on the farm.[25] So the C.A.S. came increasingly to focus its efforts on the industrial schools and lodging houses it had established in the city. The first and most successful of these local establishments—the one that captured the attention of the public, and became Brace's personal pride and joy—was a lodging house designated specifically for a single subset of poor children: the city's newsboys.

We have encountered newsboys before, during the 1840s, shortly after they came into existence as a result of the development of an urban "penny press" (see Chapter 3). Often homeless, they eked out their subsistence by hawking afternoon newspapers and "extra" editions on the streets of the city. By the 1850s newsboys constituted a familiar and sometimes aggressive segment of the urban population, and they were notorious for their streetwise impertinence and for the racket they made at their beloved theater. Charles Loring Brace referred to them as "a fighting, gambling set." Consisting largely of immigrant Irish Catholics, the newsboys seem to have spoken in an argot of their own, and they were usually known only by nicknames—"Pickle Nose," "Fat Jack," Mickety," "Round Hearts," "No-Nothing Mike," "O'Neill the Great," "Wandering Jew," even (in one case) "Horace Greeley."[26]

The Newsboys' Lodging House that Brace set up in 1854 provided many of these boys with a stable household. By 1867 the Children's Aid Society was operating five such lodging houses in poor districts of New York, one of which was located at the corner of West Twenty-fourth Street and Eighth Avenue, just at the edge of the former Chelsea estate owned by Clement Clarke Moore![27] The newsboys became a source of special pleasure for Charles Loring Brace. Working with them became for him a secular version of the ministry to which he had originally intended to devote himself. From time to time Brace even delivered brief sermons to his charges, nonsectarian sermons that avoided any effort to lure the always-suspicious "newsies" away from their Catholic heritage. (He delivered one of these sermons at Christmas, emphasizing Jesus' humble birth and upbringing "among common laboring people" and the fact that his own chosen ministry was to "the great masses of mankind—the poor laboring people—just such as you are, boys." And in another sermon Brace called Jesus "the working-man's friend.")[28]

Guided by what was probably a combination of private admiration and pragmatic tactics, Brace dealt with these newsboys without sentimentality, without pretending that they embodied purity or selflessness. He came to relish what he saw as the independence, competitiveness, and signs of *ambition* that characterized the culture of newsboys, even the aggressive edge they displayed, and he worked to encourage those attributes.

Whatever else they were, newsboys were by definition not beggars—they *worked* for their own support. The most successful among them earned as much as $3 a day and sometimes even more.[29] (The aspiring young author Horatio Alger spent several months in residence at the original Newsboys' Lodging House, and he based several of his novels on that experience.)

Brace retained, at the same time, his earlier sense that the newsboys needed to grow up in an environment that was genial and cheerful, and he tried with considerable success to make every Newsboys' Lodging House into just such an environment. Brace was skillful in dealing with newsboys on their own terms, and he made sure he hired a flexible and well-trained staff. Indeed Brace, along with many others, admired the newsboys' independent spirit, their solidarity, and their internal code of honor. As one scholar has put it, "Newsboys inhabited a twilight realm somewhere between desperate poverty and democratic manhood."[30] Brace knew better than to patronize the newsies, and he even took pleasure in watching them ridicule any visiting speakers who did. The lodging houses were characterized, as Paul Boyer has put it, by "the prevailing high spirits, the street slang, and the boisterous shouts of tough little gamins totally unintimidated by the surroundings of a benevolent institution."[31] Such geniality satisfied Brace's own deep craving for the unforced social warmth he had first encountered in Germany at Christmastime.

So it may be no coincidence that the high point of the year at every Newsboys' Lodging House was the annual Christmas dinner. Those dinners became a regular institution during the last four decades of the nineteenth century and were reported with relish in the press. (Between 1870 or so and the early 1900s, the annual dinners at the original Lodging House were regularly arranged and paid for by a wealthy New York businessman named William Fliess. Other prominent New Yorkers often agreed to host dinners at the other lodging houses. Theodore Roosevelt did so, for example, every year from 1870 to 1873, and on at least one of those occasions the future president presented a $25 cash prize to a newsboy who had submitted the best essay in a writing competition.)[32]

Year after year, New Yorkers read about the gusto and speed with which the newsboys consumed the food placed before them. As one report put it, "Dyspeptics who cannot enjoy the eating of a good Christmas dinner ought to make it a point to go to the Newsboys' Lodging House . . . at 7 o'clock in the evening of Christmas Day and see the newsboys eat." Such accounts sometimes recorded exactly how much the boys consumed—in one year, when 450 boys were fed, it amounted to "670 pounds of turkey, 200 pounds of ham, 3 barrels of potatoes, 3 barrels of turnips, 200 loaves of bread, and 350 pies." The reporter calculated this with mock precision as coming to "one-twenty-fifth of their own weight."[33] (Only once, in 1888, have I found an acknowledgment that something more serious may also have been at stake for the boys: Their "stomachs [were] small with chronic hunger.") The Christmas dinners were often described in military terms, as in 1888, when the story was headed "NEWSBOYS WILL BE FED. They Battle with a Dinner and Win a Great Victory." Or in 1890: "THE NEWSBOYS' ANNUAL TRIUMPH OVER TURKEY AND PIE."

The press accounts took equal delight in reporting the newsboys' raucous behavior on such occasions—their expertise in "cutting such capers . . . as only street arabs know." But these high jinks seem never to have gotten out of hand, in part because of the skill with which the lodging-house staff arranged matters, including even the placement of the tables:

> [C]are is taken to have every seat at every table accessible [to adults], so that in case any newsboy becomes intoxicated by the lavish display of viands, and forgets how he should behave while at a banquet, he may be reached before he has filled the eyes of more than two of his neighbors with pie. The wisdom of this provision has been shown time and time again.[34]

All in all, such scenes can be seen as the inventive fulfillment, in a very different set of circumstances, of the very Christmas fantasy that Charles Loring Brace had first described in *Home-Life in Germany*—a scene of genuine, spontaneous cheer in which people did not "seem to be enjoying themselves, because it is a 'duty to be cheerful,' " but simply "because they cannot help it."

THE PATIENT POOR

The Children's Aid Society was a great success by nineteenth-century standards. By the end of the century, sister organizations had been established in Boston, Philadelphia, Baltimore, Washington, Cleveland, Chicago, St. Louis, and San Francisco.[35] And other charitable institutions, too, began to direct much of their attention to the children of the poor.

Pleas for giving charity to poor children reached their height during the Christmas season, and they seem to have made for an effective fund-raising technique.[36] The effectiveness was no accident. Almost certainly it stemmed from a powerful convergence of older and newer holiday traditions: those older traditions in which Christmas was the major occasion in the year for offering gifts to the poor and those more recent traditions in which Christmas was the major occasion for giving gifts to children. Impoverished children embodied simultaneously the core of both rituals. Little wonder, then, that those children became the object of such attention in mid-nineteenth-century American cities.

What people may actually have expected of those children was problematic. Charles Loring Brace was among the few who seem to have been able to accept the rough-edged behavior of the "street arabs" with something that approached unadulterated admiration. Others persisted in trying to see them in a more romantic light.

As it happens, newsboys themselves were a source of fascination for middle-class Americans in the decades after 1850. There seemed to be something almost exotic about them. It was as if people were intrigued by their own uncertainty about whether newsboys were lost Victorian children waiting to be redeemed or just young hoodlums in the making. A fair number of books about newsboys appeared in the 1850s and 1860s. One of these, *Ragged Dick* (1867), was written by Horatio Alger, who based the novel on his own observations in the original Newsboys' Lodging House.[37] The title character of this book is spunky and ambitious, but he is also polite.

In none of these books, however, is the confusion as clear as it is in Elizabeth Oakes Smith's novel *The Newsboy* (1854). Published in the same year that Brace opened the first Newsboys' Lodging House, this otherwise forgettable book offers an extraordinary example of authorial ambivalence. The hero of *The Newsboy* starts out as an uncouth homeless urchin who knows nothing about his parents. When he is asked who his mother is, he responds almost like little Topsy, the incorrigible slave girl in *Uncle Tom's Cabin*, a book that had been published only two years earlier. The newsboy replies, "Got none." ("Well, your Dad, then?" "Got none." "Whew! Who owns you?" "Nobody.")[38] And the young newsboy uses rough language, too. On one occasion he responds to the solicitous question of a stranger by yelling, " 'What in h–l is that to you?' " (This response is virtually identical to that which Charles Loring Brace had received from the English laborer he had similarly accosted on the street.)

But in the course of the novel, without any training or support, this boy turns out to be a saintly child. He refuses to try alcohol or tobacco

(" 'It's agin my nater,' " he explains); he disdains to complain about his condition; and he befriends and supports—emotionally as well as financially—a variety of other outcasts, even becoming a surrogate parent to an adult woman. At one point the author is actually able to refer to her childish hero as "a miracle of goodness," an instinctively perfect little boy.[39] And at the end of the book he proves his worth by voluntarily sacrificing any prospect of marrying the wealthy girl he loves. If this newsboy begins the novel as a male version of Stowe's Topsy, he ends it as a male version of another young character from *Uncle Tom's Cabin*—little Eva. Such a child hardly resembled the kind of real-life newsboy that Charles Loring Brace had to deal with.

It was with sentimental fantasies such as that of Elizabeth Oakes Smith that charitable agencies had to contend, but also to exploit, during the second half of the nineteenth century. And on no occasion did those

Two Images of Newsboys. The street urchin on the right appeared in the 1872 edition of Elizabath Oakes Smith's novel *The Newsboy*. The appealing little boy on the left was the subject of an 1857 picture by the New York painter James Henry Cafferty, titled "Newsboy Selling New York Herald." For all the contrast between them, the two pictures are essentially mirror images of each other. *(Both illustrations: Courtesy, Harvard College Library)*

fantasies become more pervasive than at Christmas. The original model for such fantasies was another fictional character, Dickens's Tiny Tim. This boy is a cripple, but spiritually he is a perfect model of humanity, a paragon of patient, cheerful selflessness. (He is even more forbearing than his father in the face of adversity, and with the added vulnerability of his lameness.) In fact, characters like Tiny Tim resemble nothing so much as the selfless German children we encountered in Chapter 5, the children idealized by Coleridge and Pestalozzi.

It was fictional children like Tiny Tim—needy children who were forbearing and grateful, and sometimes disabled as well—who would become the ordinary objects of charity in scores of stories and sketches written in the middle of the nineteenth century. *A Christmas Carol* was only the first of a host of stories published over the next several decades (and beyond) that evoked the gap between rich and poor, and used young children to imagine ways of bridging this gap through acts of direct personal generosity at Christmas. One such sketch, a nonfiction account published in 1844 (the year after *A Christmas Carol* appeared), sets the scene. Traveling on the ferry between New York and Brooklyn, the writer has encountered a small girl, palpably impoverished, and is struck by something unusual in the girl's demeanor, something that set her apart from "the whining, obtrusive beggars of this large city." Sitting quietly amid the other, more prosperous patrons of the ferry, this child signified "poverty that complains not." Her face conveyed "utter hopelessness," but also a striking "resignation." The writer was drawn to that, and other passengers were, too: "Children crushed to the earth with poverty and crime are common in large cities: they are painfully numerous. But it is seldom that such quiet, uncomplaining little sufferers are met there."[40]

Here was the basis of the familiar, almost stereotypical genre in which poor children stand huddled in the cold outside the home of a rich family, gazing patiently through the window at the latter's Christmas luxuries. As might be expected, these stories invariably deal with a Christmas encounter between someone rich and someone poor, an encounter in which the former is touched by both the plight and the patience of the latter (generally a child). The encounter is marked by a special Christmas gift that leaves both the giver and the recipient deeply touched. It is the old exchange of gifts for goodwill.

Again and again, it was the passivity, the uncomplaining resignation, of such fictional children in the face of pervasive, ambient opulence that rendered them fit objects of direct charity. It was because they asked for nothing that they proved themselves worthy of receiving something. In one such story a little girl clothed in a dress that is faded but "clean" is looking into the window of a toy shop on Christmas Eve. But when a prosperous woman standing next to her wonders out loud whether the girl " 'wanted something she couldn't get,' " the girl responds in "an unexpectant manner," saying only that the toys were " 'good to look at.' " The prosperous woman thereupon offers the poor little girl a gift of $5, and the girl proceeds to give the money to her mother. After the prosperous lady learns about the girl's selfless gesture, her *own* daughter, too, decides to pass along some of her surplus Christmas presents. At the end, the reader is assured that the poor little girl will "never forget" these gifts in times of future hardship.[41]

There is a deeper pattern to some of these stories, and it is a revealing one. It has to do with resolving the vexatious public issues of class division—issues that were essentially unresolvable within any version of the prevailing ideological language—by transforming them, under cover of fiction, into issues that *are* resolvable: private issues of family, morality, and forgiveness. I have not found a single nineteenth-century Christmas story that deals forthrightly with the dynamics of American class relations.

In the commonest version of this pattern, the poor children turn out, at the end, to be related to their benefactors by blood itself. Take, for example, a story published in *Godey's Lady's Book* in 1858, with the title "Christmas for Rich and Poor." This story was accompanied by a two-page illustration showing precisely the now-familiar stereotypical scene: the rich family inside on the left side, the poor children outside on the right. Any reader of this story would have been led to assume that the story dealt with class divisions. And indeed, as it happens, the two children *are* poor, and their mother is ill as well. They had been out earlier that evening (the story is set on Christmas Eve), attempting to buy a small present for their mother in a local shop, and there they had been approached by a wealthy older man who overheard their plight (and witnessed their selfless demeanor) and immediately invited them to visit his house later in the evening so that he could provide them with food to take to their sick mother. That they do (once inside the house they observe toys "scattered in careless profusion"). But as they stand conversing with the rich man's daughter, waiting for their promised basket of food, it transpires that they are actually the children of the rich man's *other* daughter, his favorite and most indulged daughter, a woman who had shamed the family fifteen years earlier by eloping (on Christmas Eve, at that) with a man whom her father had refused to let her marry. The wayward daughter's husband had soon proved unable to support her decently, and after his death she and her two children had fallen into abject poverty. All this while her wealthy father had refused to have anything to do with her. But now, on *this* Christmas Eve, he is eager to relent. The story ends with a scene of forgiveness and reconciliation.[42]

In other words, the division of social class that separated the "rich" from the "poor" of this story's title was more apparent than real. Not only did these poor children behave like well-trained members of respectable society—that is actually what they were. The real problem that the wealthy man in the story had to deal with was not that of social class but of family dynamics. The cathartic gesture he makes at the end is one in which he forgives his daughter, after fifteen years of exile, and takes her back into the family. Of course, he feels relieved and cleansed by this act, but his catharsis, and that of the story's readers, have little to do with the expectations raised by the story's title and its accompanying illustrations.[43]

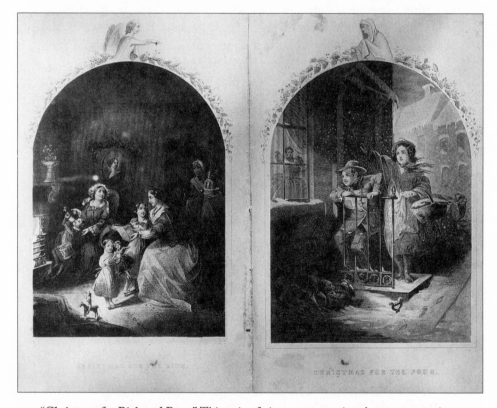

"Christmas for Rich and Poor." This pair of pictures were printed on two opposing pages of *Godey's Lady's Book* for December 1858. They provided the illustration for the story of the same title. *(Courtesy, American Antiquarian Society)*

THE JADED RICH

At the same time that Christmas stories appeared about poor children who were patient and grateful, other stories were appearing that portrayed the jaded responses of more prosperous children. By the 1850s, fictional accounts about such jaded rich children were becoming commonplace. An 1854 children's book written by Susan Warner, the author of the 1849 best-seller *The Wide, Wide World,* drove this point home. In this book, *Carl Krinken: His Christmas Stocking,* Warner indicated that the presents received by the children of the rich made them feel "*dis*content." Such well-off children were hard to please, Warner wrote; they generally "fretted because they had what they did, or because they hadn't what they didn't have." The Christmas stocking of a typical rich child was stuffed with "candy enough to make the child sick, and toys enough to make him unhappy because he didn't know which to play with first. . . ." Warner added sarcastically: "It was a woful [sic] thing if a top was painted the wrong color, or if the mane of a rocking-horse was too short, or if his bridle was black leather instead of red."[44] Several decades later, no less popular a writer than William Dean Howells would write a delightful story about a little girl who expresses a wish that Christmas could come every day—and who has her wish fulfilled in horrific fashion. After a few weeks, the girl and her friends become so sick of receiving "disgusting presents" that they begin to throw them out on the street unopened, and soon the police began to warn the children "to shovel their presents off the sidewalk, or they would arrest them." Before long, the overworked garbage collectors of the city are refusing to pick up any more Christmas trash! Eventually, of course, the little girl learns her lesson.[45]

On a more modest scale there was the story that Harriet Beecher Stowe had written in 1850, "Christmas; or, The Good Fairy." In that story (discussed in Chapter 4), Stowe indicated that Christmas shopping for one's own family and friends had become difficult, since such prosperous folk were "sick, and sated, and tired with having everything in the world given [them]" at Christmas. But Stowe's tale went on to propose a solution to this problem. Its plot hinged on just that point: It was easy enough, after all, to find people who had not been sated by Christmas presents, people who could be counted on to be intensely grateful for even the smallest trifle.

Those people, of course, were the poor. The language Harriet Beecher Stowe chose to describe them is quite suggestive. A poor person offered the prosperous shopper a "fresh, unsophisticated body to get presents for"; the poor as a class provided the rich with a supply of "unsophisticated subjects to practice on." And that is just what this story is about. Its prosperous main character becomes a "good fairy" for a poor family who lives in the neighborhood—and, indeed, the poor family does respond with all the gratitude anyone could wish.

Unsophisticated subjects to practice on. This may sound like strange language. But others were making much the same point. Take Louisa May Alcott, for example. The four young heroines of *Little Women,* in the opening chapters of that novel, do the very thing that Stowe proposed: They go off on Christmas morning (after receiving their own presents of the New Testament) and bring gifts to a poor family in the neighborhood. There is evidence that many Americans shared this concern. In the last two decades of the nineteenth century, there was something of a movement to form Christmas clubs for prosperous children, clubs that were designed to foster selfless behavior during the Christmas season by encouraging their members to hold Christmas parties for their less-privileged peers, and to give away some of their own old Christmas presents. The Children's Christmas Club of Portland, Maine, organized in 1882, pressed its members "to save [old] toys, books, and games, instead of carelessly destroying them," and to present these castoffs at a Christmas dinner held for the children of the local poor. A similar club was later formed in Washington, D.C., with the daughter of the U.S. postmaster general serving as its president, assisted by the daughter of the U.S. president himself, Chester Arthur.[46]

Such material suggests that some members of the American bourgeoisie were facing a real Christmas dilemma. Their own children had become jaded with presents. On the other hand, the actual poor—who were unlikely to be surfeited with gifts—were a sea of anonymous proletarian faces, and in any event they were as likely to respond to acts of token generosity with embarrassment or hostility as with the requisite display of hearty gratitude. Giving to the *children* of the needy would solve the dilemma neatly.

Typically, the children selected to participate in such events (as in the case of the Portland Children's Christmas Club) came from a pool that had been carefully screened by charitable organizations. These needy children made ideal recipients of face-to-face charity. They could be counted on to be both well behaved and truly grateful. They would respond neither with the jaded indifference of more privileged children nor with the guarded resentment their own parents might display. And they would *show* their gratitude, with touching smiles and exclamations. Face-to-face charity—the exchange of gifts for goodwill—could be made to work in mid-nineteenth-century America, after all. But the economic divide could be bridged only by going across generational lines. In short-hand language, class had to be mediated through age.

In any case, from mid-century on—and with what appears to have been increasing frequency into the 1890s—some well-to-do Americans devoted part of their Christmas days to visiting the children of the poor. These visits were ordinarily encouraged and arranged by the charitable agencies themselves. The first instance I have found of what would become the standard ritual took place in 1844, when Margaret Fuller chose to spend part of Christmas Day with the children in New York's Asylum for the Deaf and Dumb—and to report on her visit in the *New York Tribune* (this episode is recounted in Chapter 5). After 1850, New York's charitable agencies for children institutionalized this kind of event. They began to hold formal open houses that more prosperous residents of the city were invited to visit on Christmas Day, open houses that received lots of publicity (they also served as effective fund-raisers).

A favorite place to visit was the children's nursery on Randalls Island, the municipal establishment in the East River (it also contained the city hospital, insane asylum, and almshouse). On Christmas Day, 1851, the *New York Tribune* reported that "quite a large party of ladies and gentlemen" attended "a capital entertainment" given to the children at the municipal nursery and hospital. The following year, too, the *Tribune* reported that the children on Randalls Island were visited by "several dignitaries, including several merchants of the City," who brought "a supply of juvenile presents suitable to the season." On this occasion the children "marched in procession to meet them at the dock." And of course they "most gratefully accepted and heartily enjoyed" the dinner that followed.[47]

And so on in subsequent years (the Randalls Island open houses continued into the twentieth century). Of course, Randalls Island was physically cut off from the rest of the city. But charitable institutions located within the city, even in its less savory areas, also invited visitors on Christmas Day.[48] The most heavily publicized of these was in the Mission House located in the Five Points section, the most notorious slum area in the city (in the entire nation, for that matter). But the terms in which the *Tribune* reported the first such occasion, in 1853, are revealing. The report, headed "CHRISTMAS AT THE FIVE POINTS," indicated that the Mission

House (located on the site of a former brewery) was "open all day" and received many visitors. In fact,

> [t]he streets were thronged in that neighborhood with well-dressed ladies and gentlemen, and some of the richest carriages of the City; the effect of which was to make the topers [i.e., drunkards], male and female, shrink back into their dens, while the children saw and felt the effects of such visits to the House of Industry, which was crowded to excess all the afternoon, while several hundred Christmas presents were bestowed upon the scholars of that school. . . .[49]

This was an intriguing description. It assured its readers that the Five Points area was transformed on this occasion, its menace momentarily defused. The more unpleasant denizens of the neighborhood simply withdrew from sight when the respectable outsiders came to visit, and only the presence of children was felt.[50]

What impelled people to make such visits? Pangs of conscience certainly played a part, but there is surely more. (To ease one's conscience, it would have been enough to have made a substantial contribution, and stayed at home.) The visitors—and, just as important, the many others who merely read about them in the newspapers—seem to have needed to experience, in person or by report, the "gratefully accepted and heartily enjoyed" gifts, the "happy faces and joyful voices." Such a need may have addressed an unspoken fear that was shared by many Americans in just these decades—a fear that the urban social order was coming apart, that industrial capitalism was leading to social collapse. From that angle, visits to poor children offered a kind of symbolic reassurance that the social order still held together, after all. It was not only a merry Christmas that the happy faces demonstrated; it was the viability of industrial capitalism itself.

But I suspect that such a "political" motivation is not the whole answer. The grateful exclamations and smiles of the poor children may have fulfilled another need as well—a need to experience spontaneous affectionate gratitude *in itself*; to participate in social interactions that evoked a powerful emotional response that was difficult to achieve within middle-class family life. Charles Loring Brace had written about the absence of truly warm social relations among American families, the forced and "hollow" nature of domesticity. During the latter part of the century, other commentators made similar points. The very importance that domestic life had taken on in nineteenth-century American society had led many people to harbor a set of powerful expectations that real families found it difficult to fulfill. The middle-class family was becoming a victim of its own utopian fantasies.[51] Here, too, Christmas became a volatile flash point.

To glimpse something of what may have been at stake, let me cite a rare personal account of one of these Christmas visits. In 1875 the press reports about the annual Christmas pilgrimage to Randalls Island noted the presence among that year's visitors of a celebrity, Louisa May Alcott. (Alcott was now living in New York, eight years after the publication of *Little Women* had propelled her into literary stardom.) Alcott and her party visited first the municipal orphanage, then the children's hospital, and finally the home for retarded children. Alcott herself carried a large box of dolls and a bundle of candy. At every stop, one newspaper reported, "Miss Alcott . . . mingled with the little ones, giving to each a doll and some candy, accompanying each gift with some kind greeting." Alcott was deeply moved by the experience, and she wrote a lengthy private letter to her family describing it. Her letter is filled with graphic descriptions of the children's gratitude, intense and helpless—the sudden "cry of delight," the outstretched "groping hands," the sighs of "oh! oh!," the "cheer of rapture," the "silent bliss." (One little girl was "so overcome" by the present Alcott gave her that "she had an epileptic fit on the spot.") It was the first Christmas Alcott had spent "without [family] dinner or presents," but she liked it "better than parties": "I feel as if I'd had a splendid feast," she concluded, "seeing the poor babies wallow in turkey soup, and that every gift I put into their hands had come back to me in the dumb delight of their unchildlike faces trying to smile."[52]

It is easy to look back at this with distaste. From one angle, Alcott was exploiting the youthful recipients of her benevolence—using them as what I'm tempted to call "charity objects," almost an economic equivalent to the sexual representation of women in pornography. Alcott appears to have deeply craved the overwhelming gratitude displayed by the objects of her charity. In contrast to the aggressive begging of wassailers in pre-nineteenth-century Christmas rituals, these Gilded Age dependents took the role of passive, responsive instruments on whose emotional vulnerability Alcott seems to have "played."

But that isn't entirely fair. People like Louisa May Alcott had good reason to feel stifled by the constraints of domesticity, even as they were unable to liberate themselves from its assumptions. By the final decades of the nineteenth century, women were bearing the brunt of the tension (and the labor) that the Christmas season ordinarily entailed in prosperous households. The *Ladies' Home Journal* actually published an article in 1897 that acknowledged this as a cultural problem. Men in "thousands of homes" across America would be "truly thankful when this Christmas business is over," the article began (it was written by a man). Why so? "[B]y seeing their wives, mothers, sisters, or daughters reach Christmas day utterly tired out, [and] with the prospect of a siege of illness as soon as Christmas is over."[53]

These were women on whom the emotional work of Christmas had devolved, along with the bulk of the shopping and the cooking—women who felt themselves chiefly responsible for making sure that their husbands and their children (or, as in Alcott's case, their fathers) were satisfied with the holiday experience. The task was daunting, and even partial failure (or anxiety about the prospect of failure) meant that guilt would be added to fatigue. Little wonder that Christmas was so often followed by "a siege of illness" for middle-class women.

Such women wished for a little relaxation, surely. But they also welcomed any opportunity to see their efforts rewarded with the kind of intense response their own families were often unable to provide. They were seeking intense sensation along with social justice. Not long afterward, some of these women would manage to link those dual urges together by turning to such activities as social work (in places like Jane Addams's Hull House) or the radical Christian Social Gospel movement, which openly addressed the issue of bringing a capitalist social order into conformity with the teachings of Jesus (Charles Loring Brace can be considered a forerunner of this movement). Or, farther afield, these same women might have joined such emerging enterprises as the Colonial Revival and other forms of what the historian Jackson Lears has termed "antimodernism."[54]

In any event, the problem was not of their making. These women (and some men, too) were doing the best they knew how. The problem was not with their needs but with the dynamics of the society in which they lived. The problem was with a constricting domestic ideology that caused many people of means to harbor unsatisfied expectations of achieving personal fulfillment through family life alone. And the problem was also with an inequitable economic system that caused many of the same people—those, indeed, with the strongest ethical sense—to experience profound guilt, a guilt that, for good reason, could not be easily assuaged.

CHARITY AS SPECTATOR SPORT

By the final decade of the nineteenth century, well-to-do New Yorkers had begun to arrange new and larger kinds of Christmas visitations to the poor, and these gala events reeked—strongly—of exploitation. During the 1890s some New Yorkers began to treat charity, almost literally, as a kind of spectator sport, performed on a large scale in arenalike spaces before a paying audience. On Christmas Day, 1890, a midday dinner was served to 1,800 poor boys (many of them newsboys) at Lyric Hall, a theater at the corner of Sixth Avenue and Forty-second Street. A newspaper account made clear what was taking place: "Every floor was crowded with lookers-on, principally members of the Children's Aid Society and other charitable people." This meal was followed, that same evening, by the traditional dinners held at every Newsboys' Lodging House in the city. It was as if the newsboys were being asked to put on performances at different holiday venues—as if there were something erotically charged about watching hungry children eat.[55]

The next year a newly formed organization, the Christmas Society, held a massive gift distribution at the newly constructed Madison Square Garden, an event attended by some 10,000 needy children, many of whom were accompanied by their mothers. Gifts were attached to a series of ropes that, in turn, were attached by pulleys to the roof of the Garden. The organizers of this event planned to attract the children of wealthy families as spectators, but few attended (one headline read: "THOUSANDS OF LITTLE ONES MADE HAPPY IN MADISON SQUARE GARDEN—CHILDREN OF THE RICH STAY AWAY").[56]

Wealthy children were apparently not interested in watching hordes of their less-fortunate peers, but the parents of those wealthy children soon proved susceptible to the lure. It was, of all things, the Salvation Army that provided them with the opportunity. Beginning in 1898, this organization's army of Christian soldiers organized immense public dinners for impoverished New Yorkers, held at Madison Square Garden. These dinners were great public spectacles, expertly organized. As the hungry and homeless were fed at tables on the arena floor, under the glare of electric lights, more prosperous New Yorkers paid to be admitted to the Garden's boxes and galleries, where they observed the gorging. The event was reported as a front-page story in the *New York Times*, with a headline that announced, in block capitals, "THE RICH SAW THEM FEAST."

The press reported in detail how "nearly 20,000 men, women, and children gathered from the highways and byways of the city in one great surging throng," waiting patiently to be admitted to enter the arena. The crowd was kept waiting until after the spectators had been admitted—through a separate entrance:

> To the Madison Avenue entrance came the spectators of the extraordinary scene . . . , men in high hats, women in costly wraps . . . the great concourse of the prosperous and happy. . . . They were to furnish the lighter shade to the pleasure, with their air of contentment, and prosperity, and perchance sympathy. . . .
>
> At the other entrance to the Garden [on Fourth Avenue] gathered the pilgrims from the illimitable abodes of poverty and wretchedness.

The several thousand wealthy observers entered first, so that they could look on as the "hungry multitude" was admitted. "In the boxes and gallery of the great building," the story ran, "sat many thousands of well-fed and prosperous people, among them many women who had come in carriages and were gorgeously gowned and wore many diamonds, who looked on in happy sympathy . . . , who had come to see the spectacle of thousands being made happy." There were four large sections of tables on the arena floor, and it was there that the poor, sitting in the upper gallery till their turn was called, were fed 2,200 at a time. This was a charity event on an industrial scale, a kind of Gilded Age version of Bracebridge Hall in which the entertainment itself was produced on an assembly line. Even so, the food ran out before everyone could be served.

Before the meal, both rich and poor joined together in singing the hymn "Praise God from Whom All Blessings Flow." The hymn was sung in unison, "position and fortune forgotten for one brief moment." It was a moving occasion, the *Times* reporter wrote: "The pathos of it all was in the expression contained in the smiles of thanks." And the reporter concluded hopefully, suggesting that the very scale of the event foretold an imminent solution to the vexing problems of capitalism: "Neither any Continental city nor even London ever had to do anything approaching this in magnitude. It means the dawning of a new era, the bridging of the gulf between the rich and poor."[57]

Only a single report, in the *New York World,* suggested that what had happened was more a matter of voyeurism than of class reconciliation:

Some seemed to look upon this feeding of the ravens as a spectacle, and whispered and pointed at poorly clad men and women who ate ravenously, or smiled when a piece of turkey was surreptitiously slipped into a capacious pocket.[58]

There was still another strange twist. The Salvation Army hit upon a novel fashion for raising funds to pay for these events: They hired unemployed men to play the part of street-corner Santa Claus, soliciting passersby for contributions as they did their Christmas shopping. (This technique is still employed by the Salvation Army.) Given the long history of the transformation of Christmas in the nineteenth century, there was irony as well as ingenuity in this tactic, for what it did was to re-create the structure, though not the substance, of a much older ritual in which the poor were informally sanctioned to approach the rich during the Christmas season and beg for gifts. Even the fact that the needy men who acted as street-corner Santas were begging *in disguise* was deeply rooted in the mumming tradition. (After all, Belsnickles had done much the same thing in Pennsylvania towns at least as late as the 1870s.) But of course what the Salvation Army Santas were doing was profoundly different from older forms of Christmas wassailing and mumming: Their public begging was sanctioned only because they were not soliciting for themselves. They did not get to keep the money but had to turn it over to the organization for which they worked. They were in fact the paid employees of a charitable organization. (It is not clear whether they were paid a flat rate or a percentage of what they raised.) Perhaps these Santas were also permitted to attend the Madison Square Garden dinners they themselves had helped to make possible. But even if they were, it would only be because they had been given a ticket of admission by their employers. In that sense, the entire Santa Claus ritual was nothing less than a microcosm of the workings of nineteenth-century capitalism itself.

REVENGE OF THE NEWSBOYS: THE RETURN OF YOUTH MISRULE

There is a final twist to this story, a twist that reveals still another microcosm. In 1902 the Salvation Army's charity dinner was moved from Madison Square Garden to another arena, the Grand Central Palace. Once again, 20,000 people were fed. But this time the event failed to go exactly as planned. The problem resulted from the fact that approximately 1,000 of the banqueters were young people, most of them newsboys, and they were seated separately in sections of their own at the two ends of the hall. These arrangements proved to be a mistake. (Charles Loring Brace would have known better, but he had been dead for a dozen years.) The youths took advantage of the opportunity to engage in activities other than eating:

> They made so much noise that for a time it was thought they would break up the religious meeting that followed. They hurled pies and every other thing they could lay their hands on at one another, and even at those who waited on them.

The story in the *Tribune* reported what happened in deadpan language and considerable detail:

> General Daniel E. Sickles and his daughter, Miss Mary Sickles, who were among the invited guests, attracted considerable attention. They spent most of the time entertaining the boys. Miss Sickles carried a Blenheim spaniel [a fancy breed] in her arms. She called it Bulwer [a fancy name]. When the boys set their eyes on Bulwer they began hurling mince pie and turkey at him. Miss Sickles was taken by surprise, and let Bulwer slip from her arms to the floor. Bulwer ran over to where General Sickles was seated. The boys set up a great shout and hurled knives, forks and spoons at him. Then they began cheering and shouting to General Sickles to make a speech. He laughed and said he was not able to do so.

Finally, order disintegrated completely:

> There was an apparent shortage of mince pie for a time, and the youngsters thought that they were being overlooked. They began hurling bread and potatoes at those who waited on them, and said that they did not want turkey, but wanted more pie. Miss Sickles went into the kitchen and came out a minute later with her arms laden with pieces of pie. "Three cheers for Mama!" shouted the urchins, and they made a rush to take the pie from her. Miss Sickles pleaded with them to keep quiet and be patient, but they would have none of her advice. One boy, whom another called "Pinkie," upset one of the plates on which were piled a number of pieces of pie, and there was a wild scramble to see who could get the most. Miss Sickles put the other plate of pie on the table and fled in dismay.[59]

The organizers learned their lesson. The next year a somewhat smaller group of young people were invited (again, most of them newsboys), and this time the organizers had taken a precaution: The boys "were arranged in a corner of the hall all by themselves, where they could give vent to their boyish caprices without disturbing the more sedate." The tactic seems to have worked. The youths "occasionally let out a deafening war whoop just to break the monotony and let other folk know they were there"—but apparently that was all.[60] Two years later, in 1905, 600 newsboys attended, and as many as 10 policemen were assigned to control them. Even so, a substantial number were ejected from the hall during the course of the meal.[61]

WITH SUCH TRADITIONS of misrule emerging in the very midst of this kind of "spectatorial" event, an event devised by (and in large measure *for*) the well-to-do who came to observe the fruits of their charity, we have come full circle. Newsboys, as we know, had long been prone to such behavior at Christmas. As poor and youthful males, they came from the single sociodemographic group that had been most closely associated with Christmas misrule from at least as early as the sixteenth century.

A newspaper report of one of the Christmas dinners, held in 1895 at a Newsboys' Lodging House, made it clear that the newsboys' rowdy behavior was not mere random chaos but the expression of an elaborate and venerable ritual. The reporter explained it in this way: "There are many queer and quaint customs among the newsboys which are strictly kept on Christmas, and which lend originality to their doings at their dinners." For one thing, they would never deign to dress up on such occasions: "All the newsboys come in their everyday clothes. Any one who would have ventured to present himself in his best suit would have been regarded by the [other] lads as aspiring 'ter shine in de upper crust.'" And they insisted on eating their Christmas dinners in a particular sequence, beginning with dessert:

> They always begin to eat a dinner by disposing of the pies, the puddings and other dessert dishes first. Each lad gets away with several large-sized pies and seldom tastes of pudding if there are any pies in sight. Then comes the turkey and the cranberry sauce.[62]

The newsboys had a reason, then, to disrupt the 1902 Salvation Army dinner: The food was not being served in the proper sequence, and there were not enough pies. As the report of that chaotic event pointed out, "They began hurling bread and potatoes at those who waited on them, and said that they did not want turkey, but wanted more pie." (The newsboys' reversal of the standard dinner sequence was itself a kind of misrule—inverting the normal order of things. The pie-throwing itself was probably part of the ritual.)[63]

But there was probably a more important reason as well for the newsboys' behavior. For if Christmas charity had become a spectator sport for the well-to-do, that meant it had become a form of what E. P. Thompson, referring to eighteenth-century England, has termed political "theater." (In this case, it was theater in the most literal sense, complete with an arena equipped with a stage floor and galleries, as well as a separate entrance for the paying audience.) The well-to-do New York spectators expected the poor to "perform" for them, as it were, by eating their Christmas meal with manifest gusto and gratitude.

But from this perspective it is also fair to say that the spectators were putting on a performance of their own, by dressing up in their "gorgeous gowns" and flashiest jewelry. There was an earlier precedent for that, too. E. P. Thompson has also proposed that eighteenth-century gentry "theater" provoked a kind of responsive "counter-theater" on the part of the plebeians themselves, a dramatic assertion of their own identity, thrown mockingly back in the face of the gentry. And so with the newsboys in latter-day New York. The taunts and the pie-throwing, like the refusal to dress up, are understandable enough. These boys *were* hungry, after all, and the banquet they were being given was almost certainly the best food they would get all year. Yet it was surely demeaning to the newsboys that their own pleasure was also a spectacle to be observed by the rich. As early as 1876, a story about the annual dinner implicitly conveyed this point, even though the reporter ascribes the boys' reaction to being watched to mere self-consciousness: "To appreciate the enjoyment of these boys properly one will have to see them when they sit down to hide away the ribs of beef," the story began, only to continue with the acknowledgment that, unfortunately, "it will not do to be seen when seeing; for your newsboy, brave and sometimes impertinent as he sometimes is upon the street, is as sensitive, when he has his knees under the table as if he had been brought up in a hot-house, and was the most sensitive plant that grows."[64]

Ostensibly, then, the newsboys' display of misrule was a matter of mere juvenile high jinks. But surely it was also a form of counter-theater, aimed at those who were observing them. (As the 1903 *New York Times* reporter put it, they "let out a deafening war whoop just . . . to let other folk know they were there.") This counter-theater served as a gesture that was meant to restore some of the dignity the newsboys had lost by being forced to make their own hunger a matter of public display. Among other things, it announced that they weren't so thoroughly dependent on their mince pies, or their patrons, that they couldn't afford to engage in a dramatic gesture of wasting the former by throwing them at the latter. In the process, the newsboys managed to make the most important point of all. They might be known as "Pinkie," or "Pickle Nose," or "No-Nothing Mike"—but whatever they were called, it would not be *Tiny Tim.*

CHAPTER 7

Wassailing Across the Color Line: Christmas in the Antebellum South

INTRODUCTION

CHRISTMAS 1867 arrived in the midst of a depression. But that year the *New York Times* interrupted its standard admonition about remembering the plight of the city's poor in order to offer a plea on behalf of a still worthier object of seasonal charity. There was already enough "ostentatious benevolence" directed at the urban poor in New York and other Northern cities, the paper admonished—"cities which, despite depression, are yet wealthy and happy." So the arrival of Christmas might better serve to remind Americans of a forgotten portion of American society that was destitute indeed. It was the South—the defeated South. In that benighted region "a merry Christmas will not be known anywhere." The newspaper painted a sorry scene: "Despair, or something like it, reigns in the mansions, and destitution is supreme in the hovels. Grim poverty makes its presence felt everywhere. Those who were once rich find themselves menaced by want, and those who, though always poor, were always provided for, now find themselves hungry and helpless."

The Civil War had ended less than two years earlier, and a short-lived effort to force the "Radical Reconstruction" of the South was barely under way. But the *New York Times* seized this occasion to make a plea for sectional reconciliation between the vanquished South and the victorious

North. More precisely, the plea was for reconciliation between the respectable white populations of the two regions. When the *Times* spoke of
the South's "poor" who lived in "hovels," it was referring to ex-slaves. That
was why it made the point that in the past the poor had "always been provided for." Slavery itself had ensured the physical well-being of those in
bondage; the system had generated a "bond of sympathy" that "held these
classes together." But emancipation had severed that bond. The result was
racial tension that could, if it were not defused, easily exceed in severity
any class conflict that existed in the Northern states.

In other words, it was not the *poverty* of the South's black population that chiefly unsettled the New York newspaper writer. What really
bothered him was the potential consequences of that poverty—consequences that might even involve racial violence. Southern whites were
filled with "vague apprehension" about what might happen; for their part,
the region's black population was making demands—"demands that yield
not to reason." Those unreasonable demands were for social and economic justice. And the effect was a dark uncertainty: "Neither side knows
what is coming. The blacks will not accept freedom as a substitute for
food, and the whites are fearful of the excesses to which famine-stricken
ignorance not seldom yields."

It was Christmas that underlined this grim situation. Not only had
Christmas been a time of charity and generosity on the part of white people in the slave South, it had also been a season of special joy for the slaves
themselves—a time when the "bond of sympathy" between the races was
most evident. The picture of harmonious Christmases under slavery offered an instructive contrast to the present state of things:

> Slavery then put on its holiday garb. There was feasting and merry-
> making everywhere [in the slave community]. . . . The bondsmen for
> the time forgot their bondage, and for a week gave themselves up to
> the rollicking enjoyment in which Sambo distances all competitors.[1]

It may seem insensitive for a Northern newspaper to argue that former slaveholders in the South required more sympathy than did unemployed workers in the North. And even that insensitivity might seem to
pale in the face of the paper's cynical use of Christmas as a way of pointing out the social benefits of slavery to black people. Still, this Northern
newspaper was not alone in noting that the Christmas season was a time
of special resonance in the slave South. For decades, Southerners them-

selves had been doing the same thing, and they would continue to do so for several decades more. And what makes the point even more striking is that it was made by black as well as white Southerners.

Many African-Americans wrote about their experience of Christmas under slavery, and it is difficult to avoid sensing the importance they attached to this holiday in clarifying what they had to say about slavery itself. Three of the best-known individuals who had been raised as slaves chose to focus an entire chapter of their autobiographies on a discussion of Christmas. Writing from very different positions on the ideological spectrum, both Frederick Douglass and Booker T. Washington described Christmas under slavery as an occasion on which slaveholders systematically degraded African-Americans by encouraging them to get drunk. And Harriet Jacobs, in her fictionalized autobiography, *Incidents in the Life of a Slave Girl*, poignantly described a Christmas she spent as a fugitive hiding in the crawl space of a house in Edenton, North Carolina, trying to evade an owner who desired to make her his concubine.

The fact that slaves themselves took their Christmas experiences so seriously suggests that we might, too. Indeed, by exploring the meaning of this holiday in a slave society, we can deepen our understanding of what happened when a familiar set of rituals were practiced under conditions of *extreme* inequality. For these rituals do turn out to be familiar, though they emerged from the very different world of early-modern Europe. The examination of Christmas rituals in a slave society therefore provides an intriguing lens through which we can view similar rituals in the peasant cultures of European society. It allows us to see more clearly how Christmas rituals there, too, could serve as underpinning for enormous inequalities of power and wealth. It brings us, in a sense, full circle from the place where we began.

A WHITE CHRISTMAS:
HOLIDAY SEASON IN THE BIG HOUSE

When we think of Christmas in the Old South we commonly think of elegant dinners and romantic plantation balls. Just as Washington Irving's evocative stories about Christmas on the fictional English estate at Bracebridge Hall helped define the image of a traditional Christmas for generations of Americans, so, too, did scores of postbellum Southerners write nostalgically of what Christmas had once been like in old Dixie. Several Southern writers actually used Irving's sketches as their models. One even attempted to convey the flavor of a typical Christmas dinner in colonial Virginia by quoting *verbatim* a passage from Irving's picture of Christmas dinner at Bracebridge Hall![2]

The romantic associations of Christmas in old Dixie are misleading not only because they usually ignore the experience of the slaves but also because they misrepresent the experience of white people. Like the inhabitants of early-modern Europe, or of any agricultural society in a nontropical climate, planters in the antebellum American South took late December as their major season of heavy eating, boisterous drinking, and letting off steam. The harvest was complete, there was relatively little work to be done, and plenty to eat and drink. Once again, the parallels to Washington Irving are telling. Irving's account of Christmas at Bracebridge Hall, like the myth of Christmas in old Dixie, retained the drinking; but the drunkenness was gone. The elaborate paternalist rituals of the gift exchange remained, but the aggressive stepping out of ordinary behavioral bounds and social roles had been forgotten. Wassailing was preserved, but it had been transformed from a rowdy begging ritual into jolly songs of goodwill.

But Christmas meant carnival in the antebellum South. As early as 1823 a rural white Southerner attacked the Christmas season for being a "general scene of dissipation and idleness." Some folk spent the time making "rough jokes." "Apprentice boys and little negroes" fired guns and crackers. And everyone—"parents, children, servants, old, young, white, black, and yellow"—drank hard. "And if you inquire what it is all for, no earthly reason is assigned . . . , except this, 'Why man! It is Christmas.' "[3]

At the time, everybody commented on how much Southern whites drank during the Christmas season. Northern visitors (especially those of a temperance bent) were particularly offended by it. One of them claimed that "[s]udden calls for the doctor to attend cases of delirium tremens . . . were numerous during Christmas." But Southerners reported it themselves, in diaries, letters, and newspapers. It is clear that people—women among them—commonly began drinking at breakfast. Amanda Edmonds of western Virginia did so year after year in the late 1850s and 1860s. In 1861 the first thing she did in the morning was to have "a joyful eggnog drink—I really got tight. The first signs of Christmas that I've seen." Nor was the drinking restricted to adults, as one Northerner reported: "The good cheer of the occasion descended almost to dissipation, and I, unaccustomed to the conviviality that prevailed, looked on with apprehension, when egg-nog, punch, and toddy were freely served to the children."[4]

The drinking was still going on in Norfolk, Virginia, in the 1870s, where the local newspaper regularly commented on the number of arrests made for disorderly conduct on December 25. Part of the reason was that alcohol (and food) was being served gratis, in an unmistakable example of the "open house" long expected of British landlords and tavern keepers at Christmas. Even the local newspaper was offended: "The various bar-rooms and restaurants in the city treated their customers to egg-nog, apple toddy, lunch, &c."

The alcohol did its usual work, releasing the inner spring of ordinary behavioral constraint. "During the entire day crowds of men and boys paraded the streets—the former drinking at every bar they saw, and the latter firing crackers and torpedoes and blowing those inevitable horns."[5] Noise-making was another essential ingredient of the Southern white Christmas, especially the firing of guns (and firecrackers, their symbolic representations). As early as 1773 one visitor recorded in his diary that "I was waked this morning by Guns fired all around the House." Two generations later, the practice was still so common that the young Robert E. Lee was able to allude to it when asking a recently married woman friend a rather personal question about her wedding night: "Did you go off well like a torpedo cracker on Christmas morning?"[6]

The noise-making and the drinking were part of a larger picture, in which normal behavior was forgotten and normal social relationships were turned on their heads. Young women like Amanda Edmonds were permitted to step outside their gender roles and get drunk first thing in the morning; and young men were permitted to step outside their age roles and act as if they dominated space ordinarily allotted to their elders. This is how one Southerner described the scene in 1868:

> It was the custom, and still is, in the more isolated communities, for a crowd of young men to band together, and with guns and every sort of instrument of music, or of noise, go "Christmasing" among their neighbors. It was great sport to frighten off the fiercest dogs with their racket. If the proprietor heard them coming and got the first shot it was their treat [i.e., they had to give him a gift]; but they generally stole up quite noiselessly, and opened fire and called out, "Treat! treat!" as they marched around his dwelling with their discordant music. This was called "serenading and shooting up."[7]

The writer may not have realized this, but less than a century earlier the British would have given it another name: They would have called it wassailing.

William Nevison Blow, whose family had been the major landown-
ers in an isolated county of antebellum Virginia, remembered from his
boyhood the way Christmas transformed virtually every social relationship. The holiday would begin on Christmas Eve, with the preparation
and consumption of eggnog. Then, at midnight, the boy would hear the
sudden eruption of gunfire from every direction, and the responsive howling of many dogs. Soon "the [entire] County is awake and Christmas has
come." Christmas Day itself would begin with early-morning eggnog and
culminate in a semidrunken fox hunt. This was no ordinary fox hunt but
a promiscuous episode of misrule that attracted men and boys from the
entire county—rich and poor, white and black: "the word Christmas is a
talisman that levels all barriers."

The fox was all but irrelevant to this hunt. The hunters, perhaps 100
in all, along with their 200-odd dogs, constituted a collective mob of noisy
revelers, "yelping, howling, shouting, singing and laughing." By midafternoon the exhausted participants would conclude the hunt and begin the
first of an extended series of Christmas dinners that would go on for two
full weeks. Each day was structured like the first—a hunt followed by a
dinner, each accompanied by alcohol. But with every passing day the lev-
eling process was taken even further. On the second day of Christmas,
some of the fox hunters, instead of returning to their homes, would spend
the night at the house where they had taken their dinner. Then, the next
morning, that group would leave together "to continue the hunt, dine,
sleep and dance with another member of the hunt and move on, so that at
the end of a week they have visited half a dozen neighbors and find themselves twenty miles from home." What resulted was a generalized open
house that obliterated the boundaries of individual families and reconsti-
tuted the entire county as a single vast household.[8]

As in the North, such practices came under scrutiny, though less
sharply. By the 1840s, and probably earlier, the Southern-plantation gentry had begun to reform their Christmas customs—to replace open houses
with more exclusive parties for invited guests. But even among the gentry
this change was slow and imperfect. Susan Dabney Smedes, the daughter
of a Mississippi planter, remembered that her family's plantation house
"was crowded with guests, young people and older ones too," and that "no
one in the neighborhood invited company for Christmas Day, as, for
years, everybody was expected at Burleigh [plantation] on that day." But
it is not wholly clear whom Smedes meant by the word "everybody," since
she quickly added that her father held a second party as well, this one intended specifically for the lower orders: "On one of the nights during the

holidays it was his custom to invite his former overseers and other *plain neighbors* to an eggnog-party [emphasis added]."

In fact, Mr. Dabney used the preparation of the eggnog as a ritualized display of paternalist condescension: "In the concoction of this beverage he took a hand himself, and the freedom and ease of the company, as they saw the master of the house beating his half of the eggs in the great China bowl, made it a pleasant scene [even] for those who cared nothing for the eggnog."[9] Here was a quintessential ritual of Christmas social inversion, where the "master of the house" graciously makes a symbolic gesture of deference to his dependents: by inviting them into his house; by publicly helping to prepare the food he serves them; and by offering them a dish that was lavish, rich, and special. (Besides getting people drunk, eggnog was a luxury item, a blend of special ingredients—whiskey, eggs, sugar, and fresh cream.) We shall encounter another instance of the highly formalized preparation of eggnog, and for the same ritual purpose—although the recipients of that ritual will not be white.

CHRISTMAS IN THE QUARTERS: GESTURES OF PATERNALISM

The resemblance between Christmas in the antebellum South and Christmas in early-modern Europe is clear enough. Present in both cases is the same carnival atmosphere, the intense (and extended) season of public revelry, the lifting of ordinary behavioral constraints, the stepping out of ordinary roles in the social hierarchy, the face-to-face giving of presents by the high-in-status to their poorer dependents. But there is one striking difference between Christmas in these two societies: In the antebellum South, the axis along which all these holiday rituals were practiced was, above all, that of *race*.

Liberty

For the great majority of slaves, Christmas was marked by the same sanctioned relaxation of normal behavioral constraints that we have already encountered among whites. As the *New York Times* would point out in 1867, Christmas was the one time of year when slaves were released from the obligation to work, usually for several days. They became, in a sense, free—free from labor, free to do whatever they wished, free even to travel off their masters' property. One Northerner, living on a plantation as a tutor to the owners' children, reported that "[t]hroughout the state of South Carolina, Christmas is a holiday, together with 2 of the succeeding days . . . especially for the negroes. On these days the chains of slavery . . . are loosed. A smile is seen on every countenance."[10]

The three days of holiday this man noted were, if anything, at the low end of the normal range, which probably ranged from three days to a full week. But a number of slaveholders went outside this range. Some gave only Christmas Day itself as a holiday;[11] a very few allowed no holiday at all.[12] At the other extreme, in one part of Missouri (a border state) it was customary to permit more than five weeks of freedom—from Christmas Day until February 1. A slave from this area later recalled: "During Christmas time and de whole month of January, it was de rulin' to give de slaves a holiday in our part of de country. A whole month, to come and go as much as we pleased and go for miles as far as we wanted to, but we had better be back by de first of February."[13]

Of course, the very expectation of holiday leisure could easily be manipulated by slaveholders for their own purposes. The historian Eugene Genovese points out that slaveholders used the promise of Christmas as an incentive to help get the plantation cleaned up after the harvest had been gathered. And there was always the threat of withholding holiday privileges if the slaves displeased their master. But this was done very rarely. Genovese writes: "Throughout the South . . . the slaves claimed those arrangements sanctioned by local custom and generally got their way."[14]*

---

* On the other hand, Charles Ball, a freed black who had for many years been a slave in South Carolina, suggested in 1831 that masters had the upper hand, and that slaves had lost their traditional privileges as a result of the introduction of large-scale cotton production in the early nineteenth century. Ball observed that in South Carolina, Christmas "comes in the very midst of cotton picking. The richest and best part of the crop has been secured . . . but large quantities of cotton still remain in the field, and every pound that can be saved from the winds, or the plough of the next spring, is a gain of its value, to the owner of the estate. For these reasons, which are very powerful on the side of the master, there is [ca. 1830] but little Christmas on a large cotton plantation. In lieu of the week of holiday, which formerly prevailed even in Carolina, before cotton was cultivated as a crop, the master now gives the people a dinner of meat, on Christmas-day, and distributes among them their annual allowance of winter clothes. . . ." Ball remembered exactly how and when the change had come about: "As Christmas of the year 1805 approached, we were all big with hope of obtaining three or four days, at least, if not a week of holliday [sic]; but when the day at length arrived, we were sorely disappointed, for on Christmas eve, when we had come from the field with out cotton, the overseer fell into a furious passion, and swore at us all for our laziness, and many other bad qualities. He then told us that he had intended to give us three days, if we had worked well, but that we had been so idle, and had left so much cotton yet to be picked in the field, that he found it impossible to give us more than one day; but that he would go to the house, and endeavor to procure a meat dinner for us, and a dram in the morning. . . . We went to work as usual the next morning, and continued our labor through the week, as if Christmas had been stricken from the calendar." Charles Ball, *Slavery in the United States: A Narrative of the Life and Adventures of Charles Ball, A Black Man* (Lewiston, Pa., 1836), 206–208.

Frederick Douglass, who had been raised as a slave, offered an explanation of why planters sanctioned this custom. He argued that planters were forced to offer Christmas holidays in order to prevent insurrection, and that the practice actually served white self-interest by providing a safety valve (his own term) to contain black discontent. Douglass wrote:

> From what I know of the effect of these holidays upon the slave, I believe them to be among the most effective means in the hands of the slaveholder in keeping down the spirit of insurrection. Were the slaveholders at once to abandon this practice, I have not the slightest doubt it would lead to an immediate insurrection among the slaves. These holidays serve as conductors, or safety-valves, to carry off the rebellious spirit of enslaved humanity.[15]

Douglass was making a large claim for the importance of Christmas in slave society. Whatever the truth of his contention that without such a holiday the South would be gripped by a series of strikes and revolts, Douglass's argument was based on a broadly shared assumption: Christmas was something that mattered a great deal in the slave community.

Misrule

Slaves made many uses of their "liberty." They might merely rest from work or sleep in.[16] They might travel, visiting family and friends on nearby plantations.[17] They might spend the time attending religious revival meetings. Or they might use the time to take advantage of a rare moment of economic autonomy, making wares that they could sell in the market or selling whatever goods they had managed to produce or grow during the previous year. (This latter privilege was based on an informal tradition that any fruit of a slave's labor at Christmas belonged to the slave himself—once again, an inversion of ordinary rules.)

But perhaps the activity that was most frequently reported and remembered involved revelry: eating, drinking, dancing, making noise, and making love. Solomon Northup, a free black who was kidnapped into slavery in Louisiana, later wrote of Christmas as "the times of feasting, and frolicking, and fiddling—the carnival season with the children of bondage . . . the only days when they are allowed a little restricted liberty, and heartily indeed do they enjoy it." A white Southerner used the same term, calling Christmas "the time of the blacks' high carnival"; while another white man described the period as "times of cramming, truly awful. . . . [T]hey stuffed and drank, and sang and danced." The wife of ex-U.S. president John Tyler wrote in 1845 that the family's slaves "have from now a four days' holiday and have given themselves up completely to *their* kind of happiness—drinking, with nothing on earth to do." An anti-slavery Northerner was less accepting of the situation and used his disapproval to point a finger: "Ah! white man! [at Christmas] the 'nigger' gets as drunk as you! Rum is an ultra-democrat—it levels down!" (What this man failed to recognize was that from the perspective of the white Southerner, such leveling-down was one of the ritual *purposes* of the drinking. And what he did not point out was that on most plantations slaves were forbidden to drink at any other time of the year.)[18]

It seems clear that the constant drinking and dancing—it often lasted through the night—led to intensified sexual activity. This matter was rarely addressed directly in the descriptive accounts, but it is suggested both by the surviving texts of slave Christmas songs and by the entries in plantation record books that indicate the phenomenon of "grouped" slave marriages during the Christmas season. Young John Pierpont of Boston confided to his diary that "[n]o restraint is imposed upon their inclinations, no lash calls their attention from the enjoyment of all those delights which the most unrestrained freedom proffers."[19]

More than one visitor explicitly described the slave Christmas as a modern version of the old Roman Saturnalia. John Pierpont noted that it "might more than compare with the bacchanal feasts and amusements of antiquity." A reporter publicly wrote that Christmas was "the great gala season of the negro. It may be likened to the saturnalia of the Romans." (Then, not wishing to undercut his favorable picture of the slave system by going too far for middle-class tastes, he added that unlike the original Saturnalia, the slaves' Christmas was "modified by decency and decorum.") Another writer, too, termed the occasion a "grand Saturnalia," and suggested something of what this amounted to in language whose euphemisms were not intended to conceal the author's meaning: "From three to four days *and* nights are given as holiday, during which every indulgence and license consistent with any subordination and safety are allowed. . . . [A]ll society seems resolved into chaos. . . ."[20] Christmas in the quarters, it seems, was indeed a season of misrule.

Not all slaveholders tolerated such behavior. Some felt that it was unchristian; others considered it a threat to good order.[21] But the great majority seem to have gone along, if only because they still accepted the notion that Christmas was a ritual occasion when normal behavior was *supposed* to change, and when even the "low"—in fact, the "low" especially—were expected to live well. Of course, as anthropologists are well aware, even *that* notion was based on the understanding that such ritualized inversions of ordinary behavior also served to affirm and reinforce the primacy of ordinary behavior at all other times. In the case of Southern slavery, "ordinary behavior" meant constant sobriety and hard work. Some white Southerners openly argued that allowing their slaves the liberty to engage in seasonal excess was actually a means of maintaining good order and productivity. One Alabamian, writing in 1852, argued: "Some will say that this plan will not do to make money, but I know of no man who realizes more to the hand than I."[22]

It was Frederick Douglass who voiced the most powerful argument that owners allowed slaves to drink and lose their self-control at Christmas as a means of preserving white hegemony—indeed, that owners actively encouraged such revelry. Douglass acknowledged that the majority of slaves spent the Christmas holidays "drinking whiskey," and he added that this, as well as other forms of excess, was just what their masters wanted:

> Their object seems to be, to disgust their slaves with freedom, by plunging them into the lowest depths of dissipation. For instance, the slaveholders not only like to see the slave drink of his own accord, but will adopt various plans to make him drunk. . . . Thus, when the slave asks for virtuous freedom, the cunning slaveholder, knowing his ignorance, cheats him with a dose of vicious dissipation, artfully labeled with the name of liberty. The most of us used to drink it down, and the result was just what might be supposed: many of us were led to think that there was little to choose between liberty and slavery. We felt, and very properly, too, that we had almost as well be slaves to man as to rum. So, when the holidays ended, we staggered up from the filth of our wallowing, took a long breath, and marched to the field,—feeling, upon the whole, rather glad to go, from what our master had deceived us into a belief was freedom, back into the arms of slavery.[23]*

---

* Francis Fedric, an escaped slave, claimed that his master actually forced his slaves to get drunk, and that he explicitly told them he did so in order to force them to internalize their enslavement: "About Christmas, my master would give four or five days' holiday to his slaves; during which time, he supplied them plentifully with new whiskey, which kept them in a continual state of beastly intoxication. He often absolutely forced them to drink more, when they had told him they had had enough. He would call them together, and say, 'Now, you slaves, don't you see what bad use you have been making of your liberty? Don't you think you had better have a master, to look after you, to make you work, and keep you from such a brutal state, which is a disgrace to you, and would ultimately be an injury to the community at large?' Some of the slaves, in that whining, cringing manner, which is one of the

Frederick Douglass was by no means alone in believing that Christmas excess was demeaning to the slaves. But most of the African-Americans who shared his distaste chose to express their response in pious Christian terms. On plantation after plantation, religious revivals (run by Baptists or Methodists) vied with festive revels as the activities of choice among the slaves. Allen Parker, a former slave from North Carolina, recalled: "In some other cabin, perhaps on the same plantation, while the young people were dancing, the old ones would be holding a prayer 'meetin',' notice having been sent out as in the case of the dance. . . ." Susan Dabney Smedes recalled a wholesale religious conversion that completely put an end to dancing on her grandfather's Mississippi plantation. She fondly recalled those Christmases when, all day and all night too, she would hear "the sound of the fiddles and banjos, and the steady rhythm of their dancing feet":

> But a time came when all this [slave revelry] was to cease. The whole plantation joined the Baptist church. Henceforth not a musical note nor the joyful motion of a negro's foot was ever again heard on the plantation. "I done buss' my fiddle an' my banjo, an' done fling 'em 'way," the most music-loving fellow on the place said to the preacher, when asked for his religious experience.[24]

Some planters shrewdly feared that such evangelical reform could pose a threat to their authority, and they took steps to counteract it. James Hammond of South Carolina reminded his slaves that "[c]hurch members are privileged to dance on all holyday occasions; and the class-leader or deacon who may report them shall be reprimanded or punished at the discretion of the master." The autobiography of ex-slave Jacob Stroyer suggests that some masters went even further: "A great many of the strict members of the church who did not dance [at Christmas] would be forced to do it to please their masters." (And, he adds poignantly: "No one can describe the intense emotion in the negro's soul on those occasions when they were trying to please their masters and mistresses.")[25]

Not surprisingly, the religious meetings attended by slaves bore a certain resemblance to the very revels they were meant to replace. Like the Christmas dances, the Christmas revival meetings often lasted all night;

baneful effects of slavery, would reply, 'Yees, Massa; if we go on in dis way, no good at all.' Thus, by an artfully-contrived plan, the slaves themselves are made to put the seal upon their own servitude." (Francis Fedric, *Slave Life in Virginia and Kentucky; or, Fifty Years of Slavery in the Southern States of America. By Francis Fedric, an Escaped Slave* (London, 1863), 28.

like the dances, too, they were characterized by ecstatic feelings that were partly generated by rhythmic singing and the stamping of feet.[26] It was for this reason that when New England reformers, attempting to assist liberated slaves during and after the Civil War, encouraged the freedmen to hold religious services at Christmas, these reformers were sometimes shocked by the result. One such person, spending Christmas, 1862, with Colonel T. W. Higginson's black regiment at the newly liberated Port Royal, South Carolina, was startled at the soldiers' behavior: "They had no 'taps' Christmas Eve or night, and the [enlisted] men kept their 'shout' up all night." As late as 1878, another New England abolitionist who had founded a school for freedmen in Lottsburgh, Virginia, was utterly dismayed by what happened at a Christmas service she had carefully set up for them:

> The religion of these coloured people is very demoralising. It has no connection with moral principle. They have just had a "three days' meeting" in the old stolen schoolhouse, and made night hideous with their horrible singing and prayers, and dancing in a wild, savage way. The noise and shuffling and scraping can be heard in every direction, and our house, though not very near, seems almost shaken by their dancing.[27]

Gifts

Christmas misrule entailed even more than leisure and "liberty." It also meant a symbolic turning of the tables between masters and slaves. Christmas was the one occasion of the year at which plantation owners formally offered special presents to their human chattel—the high deferring to the low. It was a rare planter who did not give something to his slaves at Christmas. At a minimum, the gifts were small—the kind of things we might dismiss today as trinkets but which the slaves had good reason to value: sugar, tobacco, or hats; along with ribbons, bandannas, and other decorative items for the women. Some slaveholders distributed money. An especially lavish (and ostentatious) example of this practice was reported by Richard Jones, a former slave from South Carolina, whose account also reminds us of how demeaning such ritualized generosity could be:

> Marse allus carried a roll of money as big as my arm. He would come up to de Quarter on Christmas, July 4th and Thanksgiving, and get

up on a stump and call all the chilluns out. Den he would throw money to 'em. De chilluns got dimes, nickels, quarters, half-dollars and dollars. At Christmas he would throw ten-dollar bills. De parents would take de five and ten dollar bills in change, but Marse made dem let de chilluns keep de small change. I ain't never seed so much money since my marster been gone.[28]

Often, slave owners provided much of the food and drink that made the slaves' festive parties possible. Alcohol was standard at these frolics, often as much as the slaves could consume during the course of the holiday. William Allston's agent in Charleston wrote in 1815: "I send also two Demi Johns of Whiskey for the Negroes at Christmas. . . ." (Remember that alcohol in any amount was forbidden to slaves except on this occasion.) Gifts of food, often fine food, usually accompanied the liquor. Former slaves remembered with pleasure, even many years later, the special food they had received at Christmas. "Oh, what a time us Niggers did have on Christmas Day!" recalled Georgia Baker during her old age in the 1930s: "Marse Lordnorth and Marse Alec give us everything you could name to eat: cake of all kinds, fresh meat, lightbread, turkeys, chickens, ducks, geese and all sorts of wild game. There was always plenty of pecans, apples and dried peaches too at Christmas." Solomon Northup, a free black who was kidnapped into slavery in Louisiana and later wrote an account of his misfortunes, was willing to wax nostalgic over the wonderful food with which he and his fellow slaves had been "furnished" on Christmas: In addition to biscuits, fruit preserves, and all kinds of pies, Northup remembered that "chickens, ducks, turkeys, pigs, and not infrequently the entire body of a wild ox, are roasted." For one wealthy South Carolina planter a single ox was not enough: "On the morning of Christmas, Col. Alston gave orders that as many beeves might be butchered as to supply all with meat, which as a general thing is not allowed them. No less than 21 bullocks fell sacrifices to the festivity."[29]

What these accounts make plain is that what many planters did for their slaves at Christmas was exactly what landed gentlemen in Europe had long been expected to do for their dependents on this occasion: offer them the *best* food, food from the private stock, the same food that would ordinarily be shared only with family and invited guests. An 1857 article on "Christmas in the South" that appeared in *Frank Leslie's Illustrated Newspaper* was certainly exaggerating the picture, but not inventing it, when it reported that the slaves consumed the kinds of dishes "that would create a sensation at a palatial residence wedding party":

On these occasions the culinary resources of the "great house" are brought into requisition, and "young mistress" spends many hours in the kitchen superintending the production of rich cakes and other delicacies which now garnish the plentiful board of festive plantation life.[30]

One former slave later recalled that "On Christmas de marster would give us chicken and barrels o' apples and oranges." (But he went on to put the matter in cooler perspective: " 'Course, every marster weren't as free handed as our'n was. . . . I'se heard dat a heap o' cullud people never had nothin' good t'eat.") Still, slaves eagerly awaited their Christmas gifts. One later recalled his feelings of intense anticipation in terms that almost had the ring of "A Visit from St. Nicholas":

> That night their slumbers were filled with dreams and visions of new suits, new shoes, new caps and new dresses. These things were not given out until Christmas morning. And while this glad day was perhaps only a month off, yet the month seemed longer, the days seemed longer and the nights seemed longer than at any other season of the year. The anxiety, the longing and the solicitude for the dawn of Christmas morning is indescribable.[31]

Of course, the intensity of that longing also suggests what the slaves' diet was like the rest of the year. One slave made it plain that the meat he and his fellows received on Christmas constituted their entire annual allotment: "they never had meat except at Christmas, when each hand on the place received about three pounds of pork." Another told an interviewer that he had " 'not tasted meat since last Christmas.' "[32]

And the expectation of special gifts (like the expectation of holiday time itself) raised hopes that could be used for purposes of social control, by the threat of withholding some or all the gifts if the planter's rules were broken. The historian Kenneth Stampp notes that "the value and quantity of the presents often depended upon their conduct during the past year." And planters themselves openly confirmed the point when they listed the rules they used to regulate the lives of their slaves. One noted that if he discovered any of his slaves drinking alcohol during the year, the standard punishment he imposed was "a whipping and a forfeiture of . . . five dollars next Christmas." Another planter punished *all* his slaves at Christmas for petty thefts that had been committed during the previous year: "if a depredation is committed, *no matter by whom*, my negroes are [collectively] responsible for it, and double its value is deducted from the Christmas present." This planter's standard gift for his slaves consisted of corn, so he was able to boast that "a few barrels of corn are made the means of saving my property to perhaps ten times the amount the whole year; and I am also spared the painful necessity of frequent chastisements."[33]

That dismissive comment about "a few barrels of corn" suggests another, equally cynical use of Christmas gifts—when planters used the ritual of Christmas gift-giving to provide their slaves with necessities (winter clothing, for example). The historian Norrece Jones has pointed this out, adding that "[p]lanters could thus arrange to appear loving and magnanimous before 'their people'—even when furnishing basic necessities."[34]

But even when the presents were more special than that (and they usually were), some whites knew very well that this generosity also worked to protect their own interests. Here, again, the dynamics of Christmas in the slave South help to illuminate those in Europe, where, too, the landed gentry expected to get something in return for their generosity: the goodwill of their dependents. (Remember the verses of the old English wassail songs, wishing "master" and "mistress" good health and fortune in the coming year.) E. P. Thompson has shown that landed gentlemen could always try to use a generous handout at Christmas as a way of making up for "a year's accumulation of small injustices." In the slave South, one white overseer showed how clearly he understood the meaning of the Christmas gift exchange when he wrote to the planter who employed him: "I killed twenty-eight head of beef for the people's Christmas dinner. I can do more with them in this way than if all the hides of the cattle were made into lashes."[35]

Gestures of Deference

If anyone had cared to accuse Southern slaveholders of resorting to such a cynical strategy, most of them would certainly have rejected the charge. They would have insisted that their actions were wholly sincere, and that their gifts were intended as expressions of goodwill, a demonstration that they considered slaves to be members of their household rather than mere pieces of property. And to prove their paternalist sincerity, they could have pointed out that there was more to their generosity than the gifts themselves, and that the actual distribution of the gifts involved a significant set of gestures dictated by the special nature of the Christmas season— gestures of symbolic deference in which they momentarily became the servants of their own slaves. Ultimately, and in hindsight, the matter of

Slave Space and Free Space. On this North Carolina plantation (photographed in the twentieth century), the picket fence next to the Big House marked a racial boundary beyond which field hands were ordinarily forbidden to go. Records show, however, that on Christmas Day the slaves were permitted to cross that boundary and to shake hands with the whites—a gesture that signified equality. *(Courtesy, North Carolina Division of Archives and History)*

"sincerity" makes little difference. But the gestures are worth examining nonetheless.

On many plantations slaves were asked to approach the Big House to receive their gifts in person from their master and his family (along with the family's best wishes). Former slaves vividly remembered their childhood experiences. "Them Christmas Days was something else!" one slave recalled. "If I could call back one of them Christmas Days now, when I went up to the [big] house and brung back my checkered apron full! Lord, I was so happy! Great big round, peppermint balls! Big bunches of raisins, we put aprons full on the bed and then went back to the house to get another apron full." Another reported: "Marse Alec would call the grown folks to the big house early in the morning and pass around a big pitcher full of whiskey, then he would put a little whiskey in that same pitcher and fill it with sweetened water and give that to us chillun."[36] On a few plantations the slaves were even permitted to enter the Big House. One Northern visitor to the Tidewater reported that "they take the kitchen for a ball room and dance all night and sing all day." William Nevison Blow remembered that "the negroes form a procession leading to the dining room door to greet the 'old Marster and Missus' and 'little Marster and little Missus' and receive their presents, and the men a dram, for which each returned a toast." Susan Dabney Smedes remembered that "the negroes in their holiday clothes were enjoying themselves in their own houses and in the 'great house' too." And a former slave reported that on her plantation "on Christmas Day big dinners were given for all the slaves and a few ate from the family's table after they [the whites] had finished their dinner."[37]

More often, it was the other way around: Masters and their families visited the slave quarters to attend the slaves' own party there. But wherever these scenes took place, in the quarters or at the Big House, some planters and their families used the occasion to make elaborate gestures of deference to their slaves. Frequently they themselves joined in the festivities.[38] Just as often, they either prepared the party meal themselves or personally superintended its preparation. Occasionally a master even made the ostentatious gesture of serving the slaves part of the meal himself. One North Carolina slaveholder centered his version of the ritual around the preparation and distribution of eggnog: After the drink was "pronounced right," it was ceremoniously placed out on the piazza (on a beautiful mahogany table that came from the Big House). At this point the slaves assembled and were ritually handed one glass apiece:

> My grandfather knew every one of his negroes, big and little, by name; and his greeting was always personal to each. They came up in couples, according to age and dignity, and the unvarying formula was: "Sarvant, Master; merry Christmas to you, an' all de fambly, sir!" "Thank you, Jack; merry Christmas to you and yours!"[39]

If the white men of the planter's household sometimes prepared the alcohol for their slaves' frolic, it was the white *women* of the household who helped to prepare the *food*. According to one report, the " 'young mistress' spends many hours in the kitchen superintending the production of rich cakes and other delicacies which now garnish the plentiful board of festive plantation life." More conspicuously, white women sometimes personally served the slaves the food at their dinner. One plantation diary contains the following succinct entry for December 25, 1858: "Spent the day waiting on the negroes, and making them as comfortable as possible."[40]

Whites were aware of the symbolic significance of these gestures of deference. They often referred to the unprecedented degree of "familiarity" between masters and slaves on this occasion. One Tennessee slave owner claimed that at Christmas his "people" were "as happy as Lords." Another man wrote: "Here all authority and all distinction of colour ceases; black and white, overseer and book-keeper, mingle together in the dance." Another planter stressed how different Christmas was from the only other holiday he permitted his sixty slaves—the Fourth of July: "The one in July is celebrated with a dinner and whiskey. The Christmas

"Winter Holydays in the Southern States." This woodcut illustrated a pro-slavery story that appeared in the December 1854 issue of *Frank Leslie's Illustrated Newspaper.* The accompanying text offered this description of the activities shown in the picture: "[T]he [white] ladies of the family interest themselves in the amusements and entertainments of the negroes, giving superintendence to the making of pastry, the adornment of the tables, and whatever else will add to the refinement of the festivity. On such occasions, the 'stately mistress' and her 'aristocratic daughters' may be seen assisting, by every act of kindness, and displaying in the most charming way the family feeling and patriarchal character of our Southern institutions; while the negroes, on their part, never feel that they are duly and affectionately remembered unless the white family, or most of its members, are present, to witness and participate in their enjoyments." *(Courtesy, American Antiquarian Society)*

holiday is a very different thing. It lasts from four to six days, and during this *jubilee* it is difficult to say who is master. The servants are allowed the largest liberty."[41]

It is difficult to say who is master. Of course, it was not difficult at all. But what is interesting is that these words were published in an article on the "Management of Servants," not a propaganda piece but a set of rules intended solely as "in-house" advice, so to speak, for the use of the writer's fellow slaveholders. Believing that such occasions of ritual inversion actually took place is not by any means tantamount to succumbing to nostalgia or pro-slavery ideology. Neither does acknowledging that this was the case mean that the slave system was benign or even fundamentally paternalist. What it *does* mean is that many slaveholders wished to *believe* that it was paternalist and benign, and that they were willing to act out their wish on this one, symbolically charged occasion—an occasion that lasted for only a few days each year.

In other words, it was far easier to act out a ritual that produced a symbolic representation of a paternalist society than it was to produce the actual society. And acting out the ritual brought real returns, not just material advantages (in the form of a more pliant workforce) but psychological benefits. By permitting a season of misrule, and performing the requisite gestures of deference, slaveholders were able to affirm that they had fulfilled their personal obligations within a paternalist order. In turn, this permitted them to affirm the paternalist humaneness of the slave system itself, in the face of external attacks (and, sometimes, of their own inner doubts). All this was a big payoff, and at relatively small cost. Consider this extraordinary passage, from a private letter written by a Louisiana slaveholder in 1836:

> We have had a "right merrie" Christmas; and I do not know where I have seen such an expression of content and happiness, as my negroes exhibited during the festival. Some of them seem to have their countenances perfectly set to an expression of good humor, and all of them meet me today with a smile and a "happy new year to you, master." I am much more reconciled to my condition as a slaveowner, when I see how cheerful and happy my fellow creatures can be in a state of servitude, how much I have it in my power to minister to their happiness, and when I reflect that most of the evils of slavery neither result inevitably from it, nor as a consequence, nor are invited by the interest of the master, which is always in accordance with the welfare of his subjects.[42]

Or this striking statement, presented to the 1824 North Carolina state legislature by Dr. James Norcom of Edenton, North Carolina:

> During the Season of Christmas our Slaves ... have been in the habit of enjoying a State of comparative freedom. .... These festivities are not only tolerated by the whites, but are virtually created by them; for without the aid voluntarily contributed by their masters, their servants would be destitute of the means of making or enjoying them. At such a season, instead of driving these wretched creatures, with cold and unfeeling sensibility from our doors, the heart of charity dilates toward them, & the angel of humanity whispers in our ears that they are entitled to a part of those blessings which their labor has procured us. . . . [43]

I cite Dr. Norcom's statement for an additional reason: One of his *own* slaves was none other than the aforementioned Harriet Jacobs, whose autobiography would later describe the Christmas she spent hiding in the crawl space of an Edenton house. And it was from Norcom himself that Jacobs was hiding—*he* was the man who had tried to force her into sexual slavery. It is not pleasant to think that people like James Norcom were

Dr. James Norcom. This resident of Edenton, N.C., plays two roles in our story: He was the impassioned defender of the right of slaves to perform the John Canoe ritual (see pages 287–8), and he was the owner of Harriet Jacobs, a woman he pursued relentlessly in an effort to force her to become his mistress. *(Courtesy, North Carolina Division of Archives and History)*

"sincere" in their paternalist commitment to the "freedom" that slaves enjoyed during the Christmas season. But accepting such a possibility sheds
some light on how real slaveholders were able to accept the slave system.

And it also serves to illuminate the larger meaning of Christmas. For
it is worth wondering whether this was not the same role that Christmas
has played in other societies as well, nonslave societies from early-modern
Europe to present-day America. A key reason for the enduring popularity of this holiday may well be that it has provided a profoundly ritualized
means of helping people to come to terms with their own complicity in a
larger system that they realize must breed injustice. That may be as true
for a member of the seventeenth-century English landed gentry as it is for
a Southern planter. Or, for that matter, for a modern plutocrat who makes
generous Christmas donations to a deserving cause.

CHRISTMAS IN THE QUARTERS: SLAVES AS ACTIVE AGENTS

In most of the cross-race rituals I have just described, the slaves themselves appear to be little more than the passive objects of their owners'
largesse. But there is more to it than that. What is intended by the patrons
is not always what is taken by the clients. And it should not be surprising
that slaves attempted to play a more active role in those rituals, to turn
symbolic privileges into real ones—to "appropriate" them, in modern parlance. Two distinguished scholars who have examined similar forms of
popular revelry and carnival misrule in early-modern Europe—Natalie
Zemon Davis and E. P. Thompson—have shown how European peasants
and apprentices appropriated similar rituals, in a process that involved
tacit "negotiations" carried on in the context of an unequal set of power
relationships. There are indications that the very same thing happened on
the slave plantation.

"Christmas Gift!" and Other Games

The form taken by the slaves' "appropriation" usually involved the dynamic of the gift exchange itself, the exchange of gifts for goodwill. There
is a spectrum of ways in which such a ritual can be sealed—from the
meekest expressions of thanks and goodwill upon the receipt of a gift
(*"Sarvant, Master; merry Christmas to you, an' all de fambly, sir!"*) to the
most aggressive combination of demands and threats, in which goodwill

is contingent upon one's demands being met *("Come, butler, draw us a bowl of the best / . . . / But if you draw us a bowl of the small, / Then down will come butler, bowl, and all.")* While slaves in the antebellum South were not in a position to operate at the most aggressive end of that spectrum, they were sometimes able to approach it.

In the most inoffensive form, slaves (house slaves, at least) might simply enter a room in the Big House on Christmas morning, wish the their master's family a "Merry Christmas," and wait, becomingly, for their gift. As early as 1773, a Northerner temporarily employed in Virginia recorded such a practice (making it sound—and the parallel is surely no coincidence—much like a bellhop who has just shown some guests to their hotel room):

> Nelson the [slave] Boy who makes my fire, blacks my shoes, does errands &c. was early in my Room, drest only in his shirt and Breeches! He made me a vast fire, blacked my Shoes, set my Room in order, and wish'd me a joyful Christmas, for which I gave him half a Bit [i.e., 5½ shillings]. Soon after he left the Room, and before I was Drest, the Fellow who makes the Fire in our School Room, drest very neatly in green, but almost drunk, entered my chamber with three or four profound Bows, & made me the same salutation; I gave him a Bit, and dismissed him as soon as possible. —Soon after[,] my Cloths and Linen were sent in with a message for a Christmas Box, as they call it; I sent the poor slave a Bit, & my thanks. —I was obliged for want of small change, to put off for some days the Barber who shaves and dresses me.[44]

Slaves commonly made gestures that were more overtly aggressive, if still ostensibly friendly. Often this involved startling the master's family by making noise in front of the Big House, generally at the crack of dawn. Typically, they did so by shouting "Merry Christmas!" The goodwill latent in that phrase could always be subverted by the manner in which it was expressed. Indeed, this seems to have been a ritually sanctioned way for slaves to get away with rousing white people from a night's sleep. One white visitor reported in *Harper's Monthly:*

> Just as the light appears they form themselves into a procession, and preceded by a fiddle and a variety of rude instruments, above all of which is to be heard boisterous singing and laughing, they march round the house, crying out at intervals, "Wake up! wake up! Christmas has come!"[45]

But the commonest form of this ritual was the game of "Christmas gift!" This was essentially a variant of the wake-up call. A former slave described one version of the game: "The cock crowing for sunrise is scarcely over when the servants steal into the Big House on tiptoe so they can catch everybody there with a shouted 'Christmas gift!' before the kitchen fire is even started or the water put on to boil for the early morning coffee." In response, each member of the white family who is thus "captured" must hand over a gift to the slave who has "caught" him or her. Susan Dabney Smedes describes the game with similar affection:

> On Christmas mornings the servants delighted in catching the family [i.e., the owner's family] with "Christmas giff! Christmas giff!" betimes in the morning. They would spring out of unexpected corners and from behind doors on the young masters and mistresses. At such times [she adds in explanation] there was an affectionate throwing off of the reserve and decorum of every-day life.[46]

The recollections of a onetime Georgia field hand named James Bolton suggest that the custom was not always limited to house servants: "We runned up to the big house early Christmas morning and holler out, 'Morning, Christmas Gif!' Then they gave us plenty of Santy Claus, and we would go back to our cabins to have fun till New Year's Day."[47]

Unlike the practice of simply waiting for gifts to be distributed on Christmas Day, the game of "Christmas gift!" offered the slaves a symbolic moment in which they themselves actively turned the racial hierarchy upside down—an opportunity to step outside their servile roles, to shout at their owners and make a direct demand for gifts. Within the extraordinary limits imposed by the system of chattel slavery, this must have seemed a powerful, if brief, gesture of autonomy.[48]

What gives the ritual even more interest is its malleability. Within the black community, for example, it became something of a game between the generations rather than the races, with children using it to beg from their elders. And the game also moved from the black to the white community, from the slave quarters to the Big House, as white children imitated black children, waking their own parents on Christmas morning by shouting the words "Christmas gift!"

By the 1830s "Christmas gift!" had become a common intergenerational ritual between white children and grown-ups even outside the South. We have already encountered it in Philadelphia, in Mrs. G.'s story "The Christmas Tree" (see Chapter 5). In the South, Thomas Nelson Page recalled it as a chief pleasure of Christmas in antebellum Virginia. Amanda Edmonds, who lived in Virginia, participated in the practice regularly over a ten-year period, and recorded it in her diary (we have met her before, in connection with getting drunk on Christmas morning). In her 1863 entry, for example, Edmonds wrote: " 'Christmas Gift' rings louder this morning than for several years. I catch everyone and set the most complete and successful trap for my friend, Mr. Triplett; after his saying last night, he knew I could not catch him for he had a trap for me."[49]

Amanda Edmonds was no child at this point; in 1863 she was 24 years old. But—and this is the key—she was still single, and for that reason she continued to occupy the role of a "young person."[50] For the sole determinant of who could appropriately go "begging" at Christmas seems to have been that of dependent status. (For a more detailed discussion of this subject, see Chapter 3.) "Christmas gift!" was, after all, a "domesticated" version of that rowdier, more public custom—which was itself a variant of the old wassail ritual—in which roving bands of youths startled householders at night with gunshots and shouted demands for food and drink. That may be why it proved to be so malleable.

SLAVES SOMETIMES WENT beyond even this ritual in stepping out of character. Planter's daughter Susan Dabney Smedes phrased this in idealized terms: At Christmas "there was an affectionate throwing off of the reserve and decorum of every-day life." To demonstrate her point, Smedes herself offered the following anecdote: "One of the ladies of the house had heard *an unfamiliar and astonishingly loud laugh* under her window, and had ventured to put an inquiring head out [emphasis added]." What the woman saw didn't quite make sense. It was "one of the quietest and most low-voiced of the maidservants." The quiet maidservant, realizing that her mistress wished to know what was going on, replied to her tacit question "in a voice as loud as a sea-captain's." The words she used only confirmed the point already made by the unfamiliar sound of her voice. They were: *"Hi! ain't dis Chris'mus?"*[51]

"Putting on Airs"

Christmas also offered slaves an opportunity to openly imitate—even mimic—white behavior. Stories abound that tell of slaves "dressing up" at Christmas. For the most part this was a surely a matter of looking their best at a time when they did not have to dress for work (and when they had often just received gifts of finery). In 1853 one planter noted that as Christmas approached his slaves were all "brushing up [and] putting on their best rigging." Whites were characteristically amused by the sight of their slaves dressing like genteel white folk. But it could also become a parody of white manners. To grasp what may actually have been happening, we need to penetrate the invariably patronizing tone in which white reporters described these situations. Rebecca Cameron recalled a family slave known as Uncle Robin, who at Christmas "dressed in my great-grandfather's regimentals, and looking, of course, supremely absurd."[52] We don't know what was going on in Uncle Robin's mind, of course. But putting on the master's clothing was surely a gesture that carried profound symbolic implications. One example will make the point. In the course of the Nat Turner rebellion, several black men who had just murdered their owners employed the first moments of their freedom to perform this very ritual gesture—they dressed themselves in the clothing of their dead masters, whose bodies were even then lying in the same room.

We can get a hint of what "putting on airs" sometimes meant to slaves by looking at the way they sometimes behaved under those circumstances, imitating the manners as well as the dress of genteel white people. A Northern visitor, listening "to the Christmas revelry that sounded from the negro quarters," summed up her reaction by writing, simply, that "it seemed almost a burlesque of the performances inside the mansion."[53]

The "burlesque" was surely a complex gesture, a mixture of high spirits, mockery, and envy. One patronizing account of Christmas on the plantation, written by a white man in 1854, describes the "assumed refinement" of slaves during the "holiday festivities":

> In these imitations of "white folks," some "sable [black] wild flower," that it was supposed had never looked into a parlor, will put on airs that would be quite impressive amidst ton [i.e., high society] at Saratoga or Newport; while a "field nigger" will hit off some of the peculiarities of master, or of an eccentric visitor, that are instantly recognized, but had never been noticed before.[54]

We might well ask, Who is really getting the last laugh here? And what was really going on in *this* story, told by Bessie Henry, a white woman from Salem, Massachusetts, in an 1832 letter to her sister back home (Henry was teaching school on a Tidewater plantation near Richmond). After saying the usual things about how slaves behaved at Christmas ("they take the kitchen for a ball room and dance all night and sing

"High Life" at Christmas. A white Southerner's later recollection of the Christmas dance performed by her family's slaves. The couple in front have dressed in high style and are imitating—or parodying?—the elegant and coy gestures of the white gentry. A report in one antebellum magazine described the slaves' "high life" at Christmas in this way: "They now drop their plantation names of Tom, Bill, Dick, and Caesar, Moll, Kate, and Nancy, and use, in addressing one another, the prefix of Mister, Mistress, or Miss, as the case may be; and the highest compliment that can be paid them is to be called by the surnames of their masters." Interestingly, the very same reversals are described in a 1759 British play, *High Life Below Stairs,* that was often performed at Christmas in England and America well into the nineteenth century. *(Courtesy, American Antiquarian Society)*

all day"), Henry concluded her report by recounting a scene she had just witnessed: "Yesterday I saw one of them pick up an old leaf of a book and fold it up very carefully. I asked him what he was going to do with it. [He replied,] 'Oh Missus, I jest goin' in there [referring presumably to the slave quarters] to hold it up and make tence [i.e., pretense] read and [hear] all the niggers say 'See, he like white folks, he read.' "[55]

Bessie Henry reported this story without trying to explain it. The man she wrote about did not do this in order to be observed by white people; Henry came upon him as he was taking the sheet of printed paper into the slave quarters. When he was discovered, the slave said simply that he was going to pretend to read. There may have been envy or even ambition in his purpose, but surely there was parody in it (even, perhaps, if this slave really *did* know how to read). The mimicking of white manners was something whose meaning the whites failed to grasp—just as they failed to grasp the meaning of black spirituals. Both involved what might now be termed "signifying"—a gesture that was intended to appear "cute" to white observers but was laden with an irony that only fellow slaves were able to appreciate.

"John Canoe": Wassailing Across the Color Line

Finally, in some places the veil of irony was dropped altogether and replaced by ritual encounters that bordered on direct confrontation. Those encounters make up the single most intriguing and aggressive Christmas ritual practiced by American slaves.

"Christmas is coming," wrote the editor of the *Wilmington* (North Carolina) *Daily Journal* on December 23, 1851, and he proceeded to warn his readers to expect "the little and big niggers begging for quarters."[56] What the editor was referring to was a ritual known by the name "John Canoe" (or "John Kooner"). This ritual was practiced only in a single region of the South, the coastal area of North Carolina, from Edenton (near the Virginia line) in the north to Wilmington in the south. (A similar ritual, with the same name, was practiced—and still is—on the islands of the British West Indies, especially Jamaica.)

The John Canoe ritual was described at length by a number of contemporary observers, and it has subsequently been analyzed at some length by modern folklorists. Essentially, it involved a band of black men—generally young—who dressed themselves in ornate and often bizarre costumes. Each band was led by a man who was variously dressed in animal horns, elaborate rags, female disguise, whiteface (and wearing a gentleman's wig!), or simply his "Sunday-go-to-meeting suit." Accompanied by music, the band marched along the roads from plantation to plantation, town to town, accosting whites along the way and sometimes even entering their houses. In the process the men performed elaborate and (to white observers) grotesque dances that were probably of African origin. And in return for this performance they always demanded money (the leader generally carried "a small bowl or tin cup" for this purpose), though whiskey was an acceptable substitute. One of the best accounts of a John

Canoe ritual was written by a Northern woman—an abolitionist, in fact—who was shocked and embarrassed by what she took to be a degrading display of unabashed begging. Her account was published in 1837 in William Lloyd Garrison's abolitionist magazine *The Liberator:*

> I was passing to church on this morning [December 25], with a party of ladies in an open carry-all, when we perceived a rabble advancing. The sound of bells, clashing of tin plates, and blowing of stage horns, were all heard, accompanying a loud screaming voice to these words, sung in the peculiar negro accent:—"We bees Jonny Cooner; good masser, missus, chink, chink, and we drink to Jonny Cooner, Cooner." The gesture to these words was the extending and passing round a hat for the collection of pence.
>
> John Cooner was represented by a slave in a mask, with a tall, hideous figure, twice the length of a natural man, with patches of

John Canoe in Whiteface. Also from Jamaica, this eighteenth-century picture shows John Canoe performing a mocking parody of white fashion: He has donned whiteface and is wearing a gentleman's wig and fancy gloves. (The houseboat on his head was part of the John Canoe ritual in Jamaica, though not in North Carolina.) *(Courtesy, American Antiquarian Society)*

John Canoe Band. This picture comes from Jamaica, but it suggests something of the aggressiveness of the John Canoe marchers. *(Courtesy, American Antiquarian Society)*

every shade and color hanging from him, and bells attached to him to gingle [sic] at all his grotesque motions. . . .

Such uncouth gestures, shrieking, dancing, and fighting of boys, who were ragged and without hat or shoes, were enough to frighten our horses as they passed. We were filled with pity and disgust, and felt it a relief, when our little black driver turned down a bye-way, for very shame at the sight. There are grades amongst the slaves, as in all other classes of society; and those who rank highest, will not join in this species of beggary and frolic combined. . . . My heart sickened when I thought to myself, "Is this the happiness of slaves at Christmas?"[57]

But Southern slave owners generally did not take offense. In 1824, Dr. James Norcom of Edenton, the future "owner" of Harriet Jacobs, personally defended the custom against the charge that it led to disorder:

Although trifling evils sometimes result from these extraordinary indulgences, they continue to be tolerated and practiced. It is so to be regretted that drunkenness is too common on these occasions; but this also is habitually overlooked and never punished, unless it becomes outrageous or grossly offensive.[58]

Writing to his daughter thirteen years later, Norcom even suggested that the John Canoe bands provided the only manifestations of Christmas cheer: "Had it not been for the John Koonahs that paraded through the town in several successive gangs[,] Christmas day would have pass'd without the least manifestation of mirth cheerful joy or hilarity."[59]

As it happens, Harriet Jacobs, too, left a positive account of the John Canoe ritual (conceivably of the same 1837 bands that Dr. Norcom described so affectionately). Like her owner, Jacobs remembered the John Canoe bands as the single "greatest attraction" of Christmas (although, like the Northern woman who found the ritual so degrading, Jacobs wrote that the slaves who performed it were "generally of the lower class"—mostly field hands, she noted). Jacobs, too, provided a detailed description of John Canoe:

> Two athletic men, in calico wrappers, have a net thrown over them, covered with all manner of bright-colored stripes. Cows' tails are fastened to their backs, and their heads are decorated with horns. A box, covered with sheepskin, is called the gumbo box. A dozen beat on this, while others strike triangles and jawbones, to which bands of dancers keep time.

And she stressed the elaborate preparations made by the participants:

> For a month previous they are composing songs, which are sung on this occasion. These companies, of a hundred each, turn out early in the morning, and are allowed to go around till twelve o'clock, begging for contributions. Not a door is left unvisited where there is the least chance of obtaining a penny or a glass of rum. They do not drink while they are out, but carry the rum home in jugs, to have a carousal [there]. These Christmas donations frequently amount to twenty or thirty dollars.[60]

I would love to see the texts of the songs that the John Canoe bands spent a month preparing. But we do have something that's every bit as good, thanks to Harriet Jacobs. In her account of the John Canoe bands,

Jacobs notes that "[i]t is seldom that any white man or child refuses to give them a trifle." But she adds that "[i]f he does [refuse], they regale his ears with the following song"—and here she records words to a song that ridicules the ungenerous individual by making him out to be a poor man (that is, poor rather than *stingy*). The strategy is brilliant, as is its tactical execution (especially the sarcastic refrain *so dey say*):

> Poor massa, so dey say;
> Down in de heel, so dey say;
> Got no money, so dey say;
> Not one shillin, so dey say;
> God A'mighty bress you, so dey say.[61]

In fact, a twentieth-century folklorist has retrieved another such verse, and it is identical in its tactic of employing ridicule to shame the object of its attention:

> Run, Jinnie, run! I'm gwine away,
> Gwine away, to come no mo'.
> Dis am de po' house,
> Glory habbilulum! [i.e., hallelujah][62]

Such tactics may even cast some light on an ostensibly very different begging song, one from the British wassail tradition. It is the familiar song that concludes with the lines: "If you haven't got a penny, a ha'penny will do; / If you haven't got a ha'penny, then God bless you!" In the context of the John Canoe songs, it is possible that this final "blessing" was intended to convey similar sarcasm—that it was, in effect, a curse.

Anthropologists have argued inconclusively about the origin of the John Canoe ritual. The general nature of the debate is whether John Canoe was an African ritual or an English (or American) one.[63] I would argue that it was both, and that what is striking is how many elements were shared by African and English traditions. One contemporary observer casually referred to the band as "mummers." The John Canoe ritual may well have been African in origin, but it surely found its mark in antebellum America, where Christmas begging was still commonplace, and specifically in the South, where the wassail tradition itself was still being practiced by those roving bands of young white males who startled prosperous householders with nocturnal gunfire and entered their houses demanding food, drink, and money. At the very least, there was a convergence of African and European traditions, and the John Canoers understood that convergence and exploited it. Its origins and "exotic" content

Winslow Homer, *Dressing for the Carnival* **(1877).** American artist Winslow Homer painted this oil canvas in southern Virginia at the very end of Reconstruction. An immensely respectful and dignified representation, it shows John Canoe being dressed by his wife and another woman as the children watch in fascination. Behind the group stands a picket fence—presumably there for the same purpose as the picket fence in the illustration on page 274, to divide black space from white space. (Homer made this painting in the summer—thus the leafing trees—but records suggest that it was a Christmas ritual that the black family was reenacting for the artist.) (*All rights reserved, The Metropolitan Museum of Art, Lazarus Fund, 1922.* [22.220])

aside, what makes the John Canoe ritual so fascinating is the degree to which its structure and its content were almost wholly comprehensible to the white people who were its immediate objects.

Take, for example, the "ridicule song" that was recorded by Harriet Jacobs. In writing about this very song, one folklorist argues that "the parallel with African songs of derision is evident."[64] But so is the parallel with the wassail songs of English begging bands, or at least the part of those songs that contained a threat ("Down will come butler, bowl, and all"). To be sure, instead of the threat of physical damage characteristic of the wassail songs, the John Canoe songs resorted to *ridicule*. But it is easy to see why. The ridiculing strategy could be (as this folklorist implies) an expression of ongoing African traditions, but it could also indicate that the John Canoers knew that they were not in a position to threaten their white patrons with physical harm. Ridicule was as far as they could go. In any event, it is easy to see how songs of ridicule would have been not merely understood but even brilliantly effective in white Southern society, where generosity was a sign of gentility (and the lack of it a sign of vulgarity). The overt message of such a song was not that its object was stingy but that he was poor. And such an announcement, even if it was meant sarcastically, amounted to a direct charge of low social status. In any case, the very *prospect* of being subjected to ridicule was an implicit threat, a threat that could have been just as effective as the threat to do damage. In that sense, the song of ridicule *was* a threat song. The song (like the entire John Canoe ritual) constituted behavior that must have marked the very limit of what was acceptable among slaves.

Waiting for the Jubilee: The "Christmas Riots" of 1865

John Canoe marked the limits of what was permissible, but not of what was possible. On occasion slaves used Christmas to take control of their lives in ways that were far from symbolic. For example, the season offered them unique opportunities to escape slavery altogether by running away, taking advantage of the common Christmas privilege of traveling freely (and along roads that might now be crowded with unfamiliar black faces).[65] Christmas also presented a tempting occasion for more aggressive forms of resistance. Sanctioned disorders could always overstep the bounds and edge into violence, riot, or even revolt. A striking number of actual or rumored slave revolts were planned for the Christmas season—nearly one-third the known total, according to one historian. Accounts of Christmas insurrections were especially rampant in 1856, when they were reported in almost every slave state.[66]

But the most serious rumors of planned insurrections at Christmas—rumors that amounted, in the end, to very little—came just *after* the slaves were finally emancipated, with the end of the Civil War, in December 1865. That is the point at which the memory of the traditional rituals of the Southern Christmas converged with a moment of serious political crisis in the lives of both black and white Southerners.

Some political history, then. If ever there was a time when the hopes of African-Americans were at fever pitch, it was in 1865. Those hopes had been raised by a set of executive orders and congressional acts, passed during the war itself, and for essentially military purposes. The Union army

of General William Tecumseh Sherman had marched irresistibly through
Georgia late in 1864, finally taking Savannah in late December. (Sherman
telegraphed President Lincoln a famous message offering him Savannah
as a "Christmas present.") Sherman's march had created a refugee army of
slaves, tens of thousands of newly liberated people who were now impoverished and homeless, and who turned for assistance to the Northern
troops. To deal with this army of refugees, General Sherman issued, in
January 1865, a proclamation that would have important consequences:
Special Field Order No. 15. This proclamation set aside for the freedmen
any lands (in the area of his recent march) that had been confiscated by
the Union army or abandoned by their white owners. These lands, to be
divided into forty-acre lots, included some of the best real estate in Georgia and South Carolina.

Two months later, in March, the United States Congress established
a new federal agency, the Freedmen's Bureau, designed to deal more systematically with the slaves' difficult but imminent transition to freedom.
The Freedmen's Bureau adopted Sherman's policy and extended it to the
entire Confederacy. In late July, the head of the Freedmen's Bureau, General Oliver O. Howard, issued to his staff "Circular No. 13" (a circular was
a memorandum intended to circulate to all agents of an organization).
The circular contained a set of procedures that would divide abandoned
or confiscated Southern plantations into forty-acre lots and distribute
them to black families. Each of these families would receive a written cer-
tificate of possession. (The policy became associated with the catch phrase
"forty acres and a mule.")

But in the summer of 1865, with the war over, Lincoln dead, and Andrew Johnson in the White House, federal priorities in Washington underwent a significant change. President Johnson decided that the most
important task facing the United States was not that of dealing with the
freed slaves but rather that of reestablishing the loyalty of white Southerners. To accomplish this it was necessary to "restore" abandoned lands
to their former owners. The President now instructed General Howard to
reverse his policy and to withdraw Circular No. 13. The Freedmen's Bureau was ordered to persuade the former slaves to abandon their hopes for
land—and instead to sign labor contracts for the coming year with their
former masters.

Both blacks and whites knew this was a crucial issue. Each side knew
that the key to the future lay not just in legal freedom from slavery but also
in the linked questions of land and labor. Whoever was able to own the

one would also be able to control the other. Without working on land that belonged to them (or that they could later purchase), the freedmen and their families would be at the mercy of their former owners. And both sides knew that plantation owners would never voluntarily sell their land to blacks. Without land reform, the freedmen could never control their own labor. They would be working under conditions that were almost identical to those imposed under slavery.

The situation was profoundly muddled during the fall of 1865. Most agents of the Freedmen's Bureau—though not all—were then dutifully engaged in trying to extinguish the very hopes they had earlier helped to spread.[67] In reality the cause of land reform was lost. But many freedmen could not bring themselves to believe that they were being betrayed by the very people who had just liberated them.

At this time of mixed and confusing messages, large numbers of Southern blacks came to pin their lingering hopes on the coming Christmas season. Word passed through the African-American community, often spread by Union soldiers, that when Christmas arrived the government would provide them with land and the other necessities of economic independence. An ex-slaveholder from Greensboro, Alabama, wrote to his daughter that the Union troops who were stationed near his plantation had assured his former slaves "that our lands were to be divided among them at Christmas," and he added in frustration that they had already ceased doing any work: "Almost all are living along thoughtless of the future [and paying no attention to] what they will do after Christmas, when all will be turned adrift."[68]

It should not be surprising that the freedmen chose to hold such high hopes for the Christmas season, since for African-Americans Christmas had long been associated with a symbolic inversion of the social hierarchy—with grand gestures of paternalist generosity by the white patrons who had always governed their lives.[69] In 1865 those white patrons happened to be the government of the United States. To intensify black hopes still further, the Thirteenth Amendment to the U.S. Constitution (abolishing slavery) was due to take effect on December 18, one week to the day before Christmas.

By mid-November of 1865, Southern newspapers were publishing stories about these Christmas dreams. One story insisted that blacks throughout the South continued to believe "that about Christmas they were to have lands partitioned among them; and their imaginations have been heated with the expectation of becoming landholders, and living as their old masters used to do without personal labor." Another story (titled "The Negroes at Christmas Time") reported that blacks throughout the South entertained expectations of "being furnished, about Christmas, by the Government, with the necessities of 'housekeeping' . . . waiting in a life of ease and idleness, for the jubilee. . . ." And a newspaper in Mississippi reported that "wildly credulous and wildly hopeful men are . . . awaiting the millennium of the 25th of December, who expect a big division of land and plunder on that day."[70]

Without personal labor . . . a life of ease and idleness . . . awaiting the millennium . . . waiting for the jubilee. For white Southerners these were also code words. What they meant was that many blacks had not returned to work for their old masters at war's end (in fact, the crops of the 1865 season had largely gone unharvested), and that they were refusing to sign degrading labor contracts with their former masters for the coming season. Alabama landowner Henry Watson reported that "Not a solitary negro in the country has made a contract for next year. The soldiers told them not to make them, that if they did they would be branded and become slaves again!"[71] Their refusal posed a serious threat to the regional economy and especially to the well-being of the planter class.

It also indicated that the freedmen might be politically organized. Whites tended to interpret the hopes of the freedmen as aggressive and threatening, a sign that they were ready to turn to violence. And whites, like blacks, looked to the Christmas season as the time when matters would finally come to a head. Interpretations varied as to precisely how, and for what reason, violence would break out. Some whites thought it would happen spontaneously.[72] An Atlanta newspaper warned that the holiday might start out as a "frolic," but that it would soon turn into something considerably more menacing. Emboldened by alcohol and encouraged by "bad white men," the blacks could be easily "persuaded to . . . commit outrage and violence." A planter from South Carolina told a visiting reporter that "some families will be murdered and some property destroyed," and he concluded ominously, "*It will begin the work of extermination.*"[73]

The fears of the one race commingled in a volatile fashion with the hopes of the other. As December approached, an increasing number of Southern whites became convinced that the freedmen were actively plotting an organized insurrection. All across the South, "apprehensions" of such an insurrection during the Christmas holidays were reported (and spread) by newspapers. In mid-November a Louisiana newspaper reported that "there is an increasing dread of what may turn up in the future. The negroes are, by some means, procuring arms, and are daily becoming more insolent." Toward the end of the month the *Cincinnati Daily Enquirer* headlined a story "A NEGRO CONSPIRACY DISCOVERED IN MISSISSIPPI" and explained that "a conspiracy had been organized among the blacks, extending from the Mississippi River to South Carolina, and that an insurrection was contemplated about Christmas."[74] Such stories were printed and reprinted by newspapers throughout the South. Some of the rumors were quite detailed. A letter printed in the *New Orleans True Delta* cited a "reliable" report that blacks would collectively revolt "on the night before Christmas" and "wreak their vengeance" on whites whose names had already been chosen. The victims were to be identified to their attackers "by signs and marks placed on each house and place of business"— these marks would consist of coded numbers, as well as the letters *X* and *O* "set in chalk marks."[75]

I T W A S largely to the Freedmen's Bureau that there fell the task of persuading the freedmen that Christmas would not be ushering in the "jubilee," that further disruption of the Southern economy would harm them as well as whites, that the signing of labor contracts was now their best available recourse—and that insurrection would be futile. Under orders from President Johnson himself, the head of the Freedmen's Bureau, General O. O. Howard, spent the late fall touring the South in order to communicate these points. On November 12, General Howard sent a policy statement to his staff:

> It is constantly reported to the Commissioner and his agents that the free[d]men have been deceived as to the intentions of the Government. It is said that lands will be taken from the present holders and be divided among them on next Christmas or New Year's. This impression, wherever it exists, is wrong. All officers and agents of the Bureau are hereby directed to take every possible means to remove so erroneous and injurious an impression. They will further endeavor to overcome other false reports that have been industriously spread abroad, with a purpose to unsettle labor and give rise to disorder and suffering. Every proper means will be taken to secure fair written agreements or contracts for the coming year, and the freedmen instructed that it is for their best interests to look to the property-holders for employment. . . .[76]

On another occasion, General Howard warned the freedmen directly that there would be "no division of lands, that nothing is going to happen at Christmas, that . . . [you] must go to work [and] make contracts for next year. . . . [I]nsurrection will lead to nothing but [your] destruction." Most agents of the Bureau dutifully (if reluctantly) passed along the word that the freedmen's Christmas hopes were nothing but a pipe dream—or, as a Memphis newspaper put it, "a la mode Santa Claus." Colonel William E. Strong, the bureau's inspector general, addressed a group of Texas freedmen in plain language:

> I have been sent here from Washington, to make a speech to the colored people. I have little to say, and that is in plain words. Winter is coming on—go back to your former masters, work, be obedient, and show that you are worthy of freedom. You expect the Government to divide your late master's lands out to you, and about the first of January you will get buggies and carriages; but you are mistaken. You will not get a cent. It all belongs to the former owners, and you will not get anything unless you work for it. It is true that rations have been given to some of you, but you will not get any more. You have had good masters, I know. I have been through here long enough to find out for myself.[77]

But white Southerners were skeptical about whether such a cautionary message would be heeded by the black community. What was needed, one newspaper argued (in a sarcastic reference to the abolitionist leanings and the New England background of many Freedmen's Bureau officials) was straight talk from "imposing" men "who were born at least one thousand miles distant from Cape Cod." Of course, the planters themselves reiterated the message to their ex-slaves. But the slaves would not heed their warnings, either. As one Mississippi newspaper conceded, "It amounts to nothing for former masters and mistresses to read these orders to negroes. . . . They do not believe anything we can tell them."[78]

Some whites consciously manipulated the fear of an insurrection as a way of convincing state and federal authorities to allow Southern whites to rearm themselves—and to disarm (and harass) the freedmen. An Alabama official used just such an argument in a letter to the governor of that state: "I am anxious to organize the local company. It is feared the negroes will be troublesome about Christmas unless there is some organization that can keep them in subjection."[79]

But many whites were truly fearful. The mistress of one plantation near Columbia, South Carolina, later recalled how she was terrified by the nocturnal singing that came from what until recently had been her slave cabins—singing that evoked "expectations of a horde pouring into our houses to cut our throats and dance like fiends over our remains."[80]

It is possible that some African-Americans were indeed harboring thoughts (if not making plans) of a Christmas revolt. But those plans could hardly have amounted to a coordinated conspiracy. What is far more likely is an explanation that places both white fears and black hopes in the context of the intense expectations that normally surrounded Christmas on the slave plantations. For if Christmas was a time when slaves expected gestures of paternalist largesse, it was also a time when they were used to "acting up." (In that sense, the Atlanta paper may have been shrewd in suggesting that the Christmas insurrection might begin as a "frolic.")

What was happening in late 1865 was that a serious, contested set of political and economic issues—issues involving the radical redistribution of property and the radical realignment of power—chanced to converge with a holiday season whose ordinary rituals had always pointed, however symbolically, to just such a redistribution of property and just such a realignment of power. On both sides of the color line there was a shared mythos about Christmas that made the holiday loom with ominous weight in the watershed year of white defeat and black emancipation.

THERE WAS no insurrection. Confrontations, yes—even, in a number of cities, violent riots. The most serious of these was in Alexandria, Virginia, where two people were killed. But it soon transpired that the Alexandria riot was actually initiated by whites, and that both victims were black. By December 28 or 29, it was clear that the danger had subsided. "The *ides* of Christmas are past," one Southern paper proclaimed, "without any insurrection of the colored population of the late slave holding states. There is no probability of any combination of freedmen for hostile purposes; neither are they likely to combine, at present, for political or industrial objects." Another paper simply reported that "some cases of collision between blacks and whites occurred on Christmas, but there was no organized demonstration on the part of the former."[81]

It was now possible to reinterpret the events of December 25, to put them back into the old, familiar antebellum categories. Newspapers reassured their readers that such "collisions" as did occur were "isolated" events, and that they were not even political in nature but merely a function of old-fashioned Christmas rowdiness—occasioned by alcohol, not ideology. The Virginia correspondent of a Washington newspaper reported with relief that "a few brawls in Norfolk and Portsmouth were the result of whiskey, and had no political significance whatever." "Too much whiskey," claimed one paper; "much bad whiskey," added another; "some colored men, very much under the influence of bad whiskey," chimed in a third.[82] And the newspapers now reported arrests for drunkenness and disorderly conduct by placing their notices in the police log, not the political columns. The racial identity of the offenders now hardly mattered. On December 27, the *Richmond Daily Whig* reported that "Christmas was celebrated in this city with unprecedented hilarity."

> It was more a street than a home celebration. "King Alcohol" asserted his sway and held possession of the town from Christmas eve until yesterday morning. Liquor and fire-crackers had everything their own way. A disposition was manifested to make up for lost time. This was the first real old fashioned Christmas frolic that has been enjoyed in the South for four years. The pent up dissipations and festivities of four Christmas days were crowded into this one day. . . .[83]

By December 29, the *New Orleans Picayune* even chose to use humor as a way of marginalizing the racial content of the violence that had indeed erupted in that city on Christmas Day. Under the heading "EVERY ONE OUGHT TO BE ELOQUENT IN HIS OWN DEFENSE," the paper reported that one white man, arrested on Christmas for rowdy behavior, testified in his defense: " 'Your honor, I am charged with being a disturber of the peace. It is a mistake, your honor. I have kept more than a hundred niggers off the streets these Christmas times. May it please your honor, I have a bad cold.' " The man's case was dismissed.[84]

THE CRISIS had passed, and it was now possible for white Southerners to return to the underlying problem—the collective refusal of the freedmen to work for their old masters. That would take care of itself, the New Orleans *Daily Picayune* explained, as the freedmen came to understand that their "true friends" were the Southern planter class and not the Northern demagogues who had falsely promised them land. When that truth at last dawned upon them—as it inevitably would—"they will learn where to learn their own true interest and duty."

The same editorial went on to explain bluntly just what that would mean:

> As the season passes by, without bringing them the possessions they coveted, and the license to be idle, which they expected with them, and they learn that they must look for support to themselves—for the government will decline to help those who do not help themselves—the relations of labor to capital will begin to be freed from one of the most perplexing of the elements that have kept them unsettled; and to adjust themselves upon the natural basis of the mutual dependence of planter and freedmen on justice to each other for their mutual prosperity.[85]

In other words, the freedmen would soon be forced back into virtual slavery. A newspaper in Richmond even resorted to a nostalgic evocation of the old interracial Christmas rituals, along with a rueful acknowledgment that the planters were unable to perform the role of patrons in the gift exchange. Not only would the freedmen fail to receive their masters' land, but they might even have to do without the "usual presents" they customarily received on this occasion. But that was an aberration, indicating only that the planters were temporarily impoverished and not that race relations had changed:

> Heretofore every one of these four millions of beings expected and received a Christmas present, and partook of the master's good cheer. Now, alas, that former master is penniless, and he who depended upon his bounty is a homeless wanderer. The warm blanket, the cheerful fire, the substantial fare, the affectionate greetings, and the gifts they have been accustomed to receive at the hands of old and young will, we fear, be sadly missed.

The Richmond editor summed up the prospect by referring to the eclipse of an old tradition: "The familiar salutation of 'Christmas gift, master,' will not be heard." But the real object of this nostalgia was the master's loss, not the disappointment of his former slaves. That point came across clearly enough in the editor's concluding shot, an expression of hope that in another year or so things would be back to normal for the freedmen—"that their future condition may be better than their condition is at present, and that the next Christmas may dawn upon a thrifty, contented and well regulated negro peasantry."[86]

Even now, with the Civil War lost and the black population legally free, the capital city of the Confederacy continued to link rituals of Christmas misrule with the maintenance of the antebellum racial hierarchy. A "contented and well regulated negro peasantry" was, after all, just what was needed to sustain a prosperous class of white planters. The cry of "Christmas gift!" would be music to their ears.

The Ghosts of Christmas Past

CHRISTMAS IN TUSKEGEE

*I*T WAS the cry of "Christmas gift!" that awakened Booker T. Washington one night in 1880, that first winter in Tuskegee, Alabama. But the cry was not music to his ears. Washington and his wife first realized that the holiday season had arrived when, past midnight on Christmas Eve, local black children began "rapping at our doors, asking for 'Chris'mus gifts! Chris'mus gifts!'" The visits continued almost without pause until dawn: "Between the hours of two o'clock and five o'clock in the morning I presume we must have had a half-hundred such calls."[1]

Those calls were merely a foretaste of the holiday week to come—a week that, as Washington put it, "gave us an opportunity to get a farther insight into the real life of the people." And Booker T. Washington did not like what he learned:

> We found that for a whole week the coloured people in and around Tuskegee dropped work the day before Christmas, and that it was difficult to get any one to perform any service from the time they stopped work until after the New Year. Persons who at other times did not use strong drink thought it quite the proper thing to indulge in it freely during the Christmas week. There was a widespread hilarity, and a free use of guns, pistols, and gunpowder generally.

Then there were the frolics, held every night of Christmas week in one of the cabins that once had served as slave quarters on the local plantation. Washington described the frolics as "a kind of rough dance, where there was likely to be a good deal of whiskey used, and where there might be some shooting or cutting with razors." Perhaps redundantly, he added, "The sacredness of the season seemed to have been almost wholly lost sight of."

> In one cabin I noticed that all that the five children had to remind them of the coming of Christ was a single bunch of firecrackers, which they had divided among them. . . . In still another family I found nothing but a new jug of whiskey, which the husband and wife were making free use of, notwithstanding the fact that the husband was one of the local ministers. . . . In other homes some member of the family had bought a new pistol. In the majority of cases there was nothing to be seen in the cabin to remind one of the coming of the Saviour, except that the people had ceased work in the fields and were lounging about their homes.

The "lounging about" may have bothered Washington more than anything else. He even encountered an old local black preacher "who tried to convince me, from the experience Adam had in the Garden of Eden, that God had cursed all labor, and that, therefore, it was a sin for any man to work." Washington recognized the irony of the situation: The old preacher was "supremely happy" during Christmas week, "because he was living, as he expressed it, through one week that was free from sin."

Familiar material. Nor was Booker T. Washington the first African-American to criticize it. In slavery days, many black people, from pious Baptists and Methodists to secular radicals like Frederick Douglass, had decried the carnival aspects of the slave Christmas, arguing that it demeaned those who engaged in it.

Washington, too, understood that these practices were the lingering residue of slavery. But he managed to conclude the story he told on a happier note. In fact, Washington used his account of that first Christmas in Tuskegee to introduce a chapter devoted to the profound change he was able to produce in the character and habits of poor young black men who attended the famous college he established there. Washington went on to show the contrast between what he experienced in 1880 and the kind of Christmas celebration that he introduced to his students at Tuskegee. The transformation of Christmas was a paradigm of the larger changes he had set out to accomplish.

In the school we made a special effort to teach our students the meaning of Christmas, and to give them lessons in its proper observance. In this we have been successful to a degree that makes me feel safe in saying that the season now has a new meaning, not only through all that immediate region, but, in a measure, wherever our graduates have gone.

At the present time one of the most satisfactory features of the Christmas and Thanksgiving seasons at Tuskegee is the unselfish and beautiful way our graduates and students spend their time in ministering to the comfort and happiness of others, especially the unfortunate.

Booker T. Washington may have been exaggerating a little, but his success as an educator and administrator leaves little room to doubt the fundamental reality of his claim. A Tuskegee education meant both a change of behavior and an interior change of spirit, a reformation that Washington hoped would allow his students to integrate into mainstream American society. As Washington understood when he wrote his 1901 autobiography, *Up from Slavery,* Christmas provided an apt and powerful symbol of that very reformation.

And it provides us with an interesting reminder, a reminder that such a reform could and did originate within the African-American community itself. It is easy to think of the suppression of the carnival Christmas only as something that was imposed from outside. But this wasn't the case. The suppression also came from within. Booker T. Washington's students came to Tuskegee, in the depressing post-Reconstruction years that witnessed the emergence of Jim Crow, as members of a demeaned and betrayed group of Americans. They had little to risk, and a world to gain, by learning the skills and the values associated with respectable white society, including an appreciation of a "new meaning" for Christmas. In hindsight, there is something poignant about their efforts; we now know that even educated African-Americans were unable to achieve the respect and security that Booker T. Washington staked his career on providing, and to us what they lost in the process of reforming themselves may be more valuable than what they gained. But we should not doubt that for Washington and his students, learning a new meaning for Christmas seemed a form of empowerment. Suppression from outside was the most dramatic vehicle by which the old Christmas traditions came to an end. But it was not the only one.

JOHN CANOE AND THE WREN BOYS

John Canoe, too, eventually disappeared from the American mainland. It was still going strong in North Carolina as late as the 1880s, but by the turn of the twentieth century the old ritual had pretty much disappeared. Its ultimate suppression closely mirrors what we have just seen. According to interviews with elderly black residents of Wilmington, North Carolina, taken by a folklorist around 1940, the decline of the ritual was the result of new pressures both from whites and from within the black community.

What seems to have played the decisive role in suppressing the John Canoe bands was the emergence of a new political culture among the white people of Wilmington, a reformist culture that was unwilling to tolerate public drunkenness and the rowdy behavior that accompanied it. One black resident later recalled: " 'De policemen usta run the kooners because dey would get drunk and kick up a lot of fuss.' " Another's analysis was more elaborate:

> Kooner was ragin' here 'bout 1882 but hit done died out 'bout 1900. De reason hit died out was dat different city mayors came in to hold office and dey stopped all dat. Each Christmas hit got less and less and finally the city officers stopped dem from marching down de main street.

A key event may have been a serious riot that occurred during the 1898 John Canoe parade. In any event, one woman reported simply that " 'de whites finally run all de kooners away.' "

But the folklorist who conducted these interviews also reported that John Canoe began to be opposed by black ministers who felt that the custom "tended to degrade the Negroes in the eyes of the white people of the community," together with members of the emergent black middle class, who "began to look upon the exhibition as one that lowered their status in the eyes of the whites. They disliked to see 'their folks making a fool of themselves.' " And apparently some of the John Canoers themselves began to feel the same way. One old unreconstructed Wilmington black man reported that the "kooner folk got dicty [i.e., *snobbish, high-class*]. Then dey gave up ruffian's ways. Dey got educated." Booker T. Washington might have phrased it differently, but he would have been delighted with the result.[2]

All in all, then, the John Canoe ceremony fell victim to a combination of external suppression and internal reform. In its essentials, that was just what became of similar forms of Christmas revelry within white communities throughout Western culture. And it provides a model for exploring the transformation of Christmas in the white working-class culture of the nineteenth century as well.

Consider the Irish. In the 1840s Ireland constituted the major source of immigration to America, and that land was the major source of new membership in the American industrial working class. In those very years, as it happens, there was a major battle within the Irish community over the use of alcohol—even when it was used as part of the Christmas festivities.

Irish Christmas rituals in the early nineteenth century will be familiar to readers of this book, as they are reminiscent of both the English practices described in Chapter 1 and the slave practices described in Chapter 7. Even when the Irish rituals were religious, they retained the rowdy old carnival note—alcohol, sex, and aggressive begging. Take the midnight Mass on Christmas Eve, for example. This event (it was held outdoors, illuminated by great bonfires) was usually preceded and followed by what a nineteenth-century Irish writer termed "jovial orgies," perambulating groups who engaged in heavy drinking that often led to illicit sexual couplings.[3] By the 1830s, the church itself had largely abolished the midnight Mass.

Other Irish Christmas rituals lacked even the veneer of religion. In one urban version of the English wassail, during the weeks before Christmas, several hours before daybreak each night, a group of serenaders would stop at the houses of all the prosperous residents, calling out the hour of the morning and declaring the state of the weather (this ritual was known as "Calling the Waits"). The serenaders waited until Christmas Day to go around to every door, collecting "the expected remuneration." In one instance, in Kilkenny, the lead performer was accompanied each year by a dozen youths in blackface (a "retinue of young negroes," as they were termed in the original account), who stopped at the house of "every respectable family in the city"; there they would drink a holiday toast and be given a half crown in return. (According to this account, the members of the group often became so drunk that they had to be carried back to their own houses.)[4]

The best-known wassail ritual in rural Ireland involved groups of youths known as the Wren Boys. Dressed up in rags, ribbons and bits of colored paper (reminiscent of the John Canoers), the Wren Boys would march noisily through their village—stopping, of course, to sing in front of rich people's houses. (One of their songs is virtually identical to the "Gloustershire Wassail," quoted in Chapter 1. After asking for beer, this group of Wren Boys proceeded to pronounce the familiar mix of promise and threat: "And if you dhraw it ov the best, / I hope in heaven yer sowl will rest; / But if you dhraw it ov the small, / It won't agree wid'de wran boys at all.")[5]

But here, too, there was a change, a change initiated and spread from within. Beginning in the late 1830s, Ireland was swept by its own indigenous temperance movement, led by a Roman Catholic priest who was locally born and bred, Father Theobald Mathew (1790–1856). Father Mathew demanded total abstinence (or teetotalism), and he called on people to sign a written pledge that they would give up all forms of alcohol, in any amount. His movement swept through the Irish countryside like the religious revival it actually was, resonating deeply in both rural and urban areas. By 1842 an astonishing five million people had signed the temperance pledge.[6]

Much like Booker T. Washington's more systematic program of personal reform at Tuskegee, the Irish temperance movement took hold because it held out the promise of restoring dignity and self-respect to a conquered and oppressed people. In fact, Father Mathew's movement was deeply intertwined with the political movement for Irish independence from England. And Father Mathew himself promised his potential followers that sobriety would be a means of achieving social advancement for themselves and their children.[7]

Needless to say, Father Mathew's temperance crusade had an effect on the old Christmas rituals. For this there exists a wonderful account, in the form of a diary kept by a wealthy English gentlewoman, Elizabeth Smith, who, together with her husband, managed a large estate in the Irish countryside in the years around 1840. The husband seems to have played the part of country squire to his dependents (she called them his "pensioners"), offering them gifts and forgiving their debts at Christmastime.[8] Elizabeth Smith did not object to the begging, and her diary shows that she was quite happy to play her own part in the ritual. What troubled her was that many of these dependents had chosen to give up drinking! On Christmas morning, 1840, she made a mistake that haunted her throughout the day: "I forgot teetotalism when I mixed the puddings," she wrote, "and not one of the outside men would taste them." Mrs. Smith expressed grudging (and condescending) pleasure with the reformation— that "these unruly people have such self-command where they think it a sin to yield to temptation." But she was also disappointed that the old ways were changing. "What a pity," she mused, referring to her over-sight—or was it to her tenants' new-found sobriety?

In any case, early the following morning the Smiths were awakened by a group of Wren Boys shouting "a regular reveilee—the Wren—under our windows." The Wren boys, too, were keeping sober, and once again Mrs. Smith took note of the dampening effects: "This morning there were no young women of the party as there used to be. Maybe they don't find it merry enough now that whiskey a'n't in fashion."[9]

It's a fascinating reversal. Here in rural Ireland, we can witness a mid-nineteenth-century instance of exactly what both Frederick Doug-lass and Booker T. Washington claimed was true of the American South—a representative of the ruling classes who wished to see the Christmas drinking continue, and her dependents, who decided to stop it themselves.

From the mid-1840s on, just after Father Mathew's movement reached its peak, Irish people began to emigrate in massive numbers to the United States. Many of these immigrants had been affected by the move-ment, and others joined it after they arrived in America. Father Mathew himself spent two and a half years (from 1849 to 1851) touring the United States, spreading the total-abstinence pledge chiefly among his newly ar-rived countrymen. (This was the very time the American temperance movement was hitting a crest of its own, one that would inspire a wave of prohibitionist legislation in several American states. All six New England states, for example, passed temperance laws between 1851 and 1855). Even-tually, Irish-American newspapers that supported the cause of indepen-dence from England also began to print Clement Clarke Moore's "Visit from St. Nicholas" on Christmas Day.[10]

A LEGAL HOLIDAY

This puts in place the final large element in the process by which a carni-val Christmas was replaced by a domestic one. Victory in the battle for Christmas in America resulted from a convergence of interests that melded a variety of groups and classes. In the first place, as we have seen, the domestic reform of Christmas was an enterprise of patricians, fearful for their authority. (In New York, the reform was part of a larger project that was a response to the democratization and commercialization of the city—a strategic shift from the use of *politics* to that of *culture* as a way of retaining control of urban life.) That domestic reform, examined in Chapters 2 and 3, led to (and was part of) the development of a commercial Christmas trade (examined in Chapter 4). As such a trade developed, merchants needed the streets to be free of drunks and rowdies in order to secure them for Christmas shoppers. And shoppers themselves needed to feel secure in the streets.

But finally, especially in the 1840s and afterward, the development that I have just traced occurred—a reform from within the working classes themselves. With at least some working-class support for a domestic Christmas added to the existing (and growing) enthusiasm of the middle classes and the remnants of the old elite, something new began to happen. Christmas Day became officially recognized as a legal holiday in the United States. It was the individual states, one by one, that passed the necessary legislation. The movement swept the nation during the two decades that began in the mid-1840s. By 1865, twenty-seven out of thirty-six states (along with four territories) had set December 25 apart as a day when certain kinds of ordinary business could not legally be transacted.

There was an intriguing pattern to this legalization process, a pattern that can be detected by focusing on those states that were relatively late in granting legal recognition to Christmas Day. Of the twenty-four states that joined the United States no later than 1820 (the "first generation" of states, as we might think of them), by 1865 all but five had made December 25 a legal holiday. What is striking about the list is that four of the five states that had *not* done so were *slave states*—the two Carolinas, Mississippi, and Missouri. (Two other slave states, Texas and Florida—both admitted to the Union in 1845—waited until 1879 and 1881, respectively, to legalize Christmas.) The slave South seems to have been the laggard in this matter. Not New England, surely—all six states in that supposedly Puritan region of the country had recognized Christmas between 1845 and 1861 (Connecticut being the first to do so, and New Hampshire the last).[11]

To be sure, the pattern was not universal. The first three states to legalize Christmas all permitted slavery, while the final member of the "first generation" to do so—Indiana, in 1875—was a free state. And the Civil War itself may have had something to do with the South's relative recalcitrance (though the war did not stop Northern states from proceeding on this score). In any case, the meaning of the pattern is not fully evident, but there is one possible explanation. It has to do with how much pressure there was in any given state for a formal, legislatively mandated release from work at Christmas. Such pressure was strongest in New England, the most heavily industrialized part of the United States, but less so in the slave South, an agricultural region that was still governed (as we have seen) by a seasonal rhythm that may have made it unnecessary to dictate a holiday by force of law.

This hypothesis is partly borne out by looking at the Christmas legislation in a single, highly industrialized state—Massachusetts.[12] Christmas achieved legal recognition in Massachusetts in a pair of laws, passed in 1855 and 1856, respectively, during two turbulent sessions of a reform-minded legislature that was under the majority control of an insurgent "third party," the American Party—better known as the "Know-Nothings." The Know-Nothings are best remembered today for a single plank in their platform, a nativist hostility to the immigrants who were flocking to New England. But just as important, the Know-Nothings were a party that represented native-born urban workers (who actually held almost 25 percent of the total seats in 1855). The legislation passed by the Massachusetts Know-Nothing legislatures included measures to suppress gambling, prostitution, and—especially—the use of alcohol (the penalty for selling a single glass of liquor was six months' imprisonment). It also included a set of antislavery laws, as well as laws related to industrial welfare and safety in the workplace. The Know-Nothings almost succeeded in passing a bill that would have ensured factory workers a maximum ten-hour day. A recent study of the Massachusetts Know-Nothing legislature concludes that most of its legislation "specifically addressed the needs of an industrial society."[13]

The pro-labor sympathies of the 1855–56 Massachusetts legislature are suggested by the terms of the pair of laws that recognized Christmas Day. The 1855 law simply barred the collection of commercial paper on Christmas (as well as July 4), with the intention of putting a stop to large-scale commercial transactions. The 1856 law went further. It established Christmas and July 4, along with Washington's Birthday (previously unrecognized), as holidays for state workers, closing down "all public offices" on those days. (The expectation was that closing state offices would have a domino effect, leading to the closing of other businesses as well.) The import of this gesture is underlined by a further provision of the law, one that established a Monday holiday when any of the three dates fell on the Sabbath. Such a provision ensured that state workers would always receive a separate day off on these three annual occasions. In other words, Washington's Birthday was not afforded legal recognition simply for "patriotic" reasons, nor was Christmas afforded that recognition simply out of "religious" considerations.

The point is underscored when we examine the actual legislative debate that took place over the 1856 holiday bill. While the inclusion of Christmas as a possible Monday holiday served only to extend the law of 1855, the addition of Washington's Birthday to the bill provided a lightning rod for opposition to the entire bill, opposition that came chiefly from rural areas of Massachusetts. One rural representative argued that the legislature "should not take it upon itself to interrupt the business of the community." In reply, a representative from Boston declared that "[h]e favored the bill because he would have the number of holidays increased for the benefit of the working classes." And a representative from a nearby industrial town supported that position and added: "From January to January, there was one ceaseless strife and care; men were going down to early graves, just for want of a sufficient number of days of recreation."[14]

For many workers, the "want" of leisure time may have been particularly acute during the Christmas season. The acceleration of a commercial holiday trade during the 1820s, 1830s and 1840s meant that for an increasing number of Americans, December was now a season of increased work, not leisure. That was especially true of the workers who actually produced the holiday goods. On the one hand, such a development helped to ensure ongoing income during a part of the hitherto slow winter season. But on the other, it meant that the workers who produced goods for the holiday trade were losing the leisure that would have enabled them to take the Christmas season as a time of intense relaxation. In other words, a generation earlier, when the very rhythms of an agricultural society dictated a season of leisure, there had been no need for "legal" recognition of Christmas as a holiday. Little wonder, then, that the development of a holiday trade should have generated working-class support for at least a single day of leisure in which laborers, too—women as well as men—might consume a share of the holiday goods instead of producing it.

In short, by mid-century a variety of interests had converged to agree on the point that Christmas deserved civic recognition. This point brought together laborers and capitalists, producers and consumers, clients and patrons. By the 1860s, in all but a handful of states, there seems to have been no significant opposition to making December 25 a legal holiday. Before long, there was virtual unanimity on that score, and it has continued to the present. Today it is impossible to imagine the date as a purely private, voluntary event. Indeed, Christmas has become the most important single civic celebration in the American calendar year.

PURIM AND THE BLUES: REMAINS OF THE DAY

But odd residual pockets of resistance to a domestic Christmas remain even to this day, as vestiges of carnival behavior. Think of the office parties commonly held just before Christmas—occasions marked by otherwise-unthinkable gestures of familiarity between supervisors and their (often secretarial) support staff; the whole lubricated by a supply of free alcohol. More obvious still, think of New Year's Eve, the one day in the holiday season when rowdy public behavior is almost universally expected and even sanctioned. In the early nineteenth century, of course, "Christmas" and "New Year's" were often barely distinguished from each other (we have seen that Christmas trees were commonly set up on New Year's Eve, and several early printings of "The Night Before Christmas" were actually retitled "The Night Before New Year"). But by the latter part of the century, as Christmas Day secured its role as a time for children and presents, it was to New Year's Eve that most of the vestiges of carnival behavior fell.[15]

In recent years, though, we have been seeing a movement to "reform" New Year's Eve itself. The movement has resulted in the introduction of so-called First Night celebrations held in many American cities beginning in about 1980. Supported by downtown businesses, First Night events have been allowed to retain the public aura of the older holiday, but—and in this they are reminiscent of the nineteenth-century battle for Christmas—they are essentially efforts to suppress the use of alcohol. It is no coincidence that the First Night phenomenon has emerged from something that is very much like a late-twentieth-century temperance movement.

THERE ARE other pockets of carnival Christmas that are less obvious but even more interesting. Take the African-American community, for example. Even many Southern blacks who were pious and ordinarily sober insisted on drinking and frolicking at Christmastime. The folk singer Huddie Ledbetter, for example (better known as "Leadbelly"), recalled from his childhood around the turn of the century that even though his family attended church on Christmas Eve (the Ledbetters were fiercely committed Southern Baptists), after that they would drink hard liquor and dance all night for a full week.[16]

African-American Christmas music is still largely associated with such carnival behavior—at least in *the blues,* that quintessential African-American genre. I have found scarcely a single example of a conventional "children's" Christmas in blues music, but there are at least a score of Christmas blues about romance. "I begin to whoopee when it is almost Christmas time," one such blues begins. "If I don't get it by Christmas," another one ends, "I'll have a New Year's blues." And a third simply imagines that the day after Christmas is really St. Valentine's Day. Remember that Christmas in the slave South *was* a time of carnival for most slaves.[17]

Several Christmas blues simply associate the holiday with reunion with a woman—as in a very famous song, "Hellhound on My Trail," recorded in 1937 by the legendary musician Robert Johnson about a man on the run. The second verse of this driven piece offers the singer a moment of respite, a respite that he associates with Christmas, and a reunion with his absent lady friend. That verse begins as the singer expresses the flitting fantasy that if it were only Christmas, "Oh, wouldn't we have a time, baby?" It's romance he's thinking of here, not opening presents. This might be a vestige of slave culture, when Christmas provided a time of reunion for couples who lived on different plantations. In fact, in one blues song, Christmas stands first for leisure-time itself, as the singer rejoices that he doesn't have any work to do, so that "every day is Christmas." (Which means he will be free to join his girlfriend and spend all his time making love to her.) In another song, the singer laments that he is all alone at Christmas, and compares himself to "a rooster looking for a setting hen."[18]

It is characteristic of the blues to be filled with such wordplay, and especially with vivid double entendres. One Christmas blues consists entirely of an extended pun in which the singer searches for his Christmas present in his girlfriend's "dresser drawer." Or the wordplay might involve sly mockery of other elements of the middle-class domestic Christmas, especially Santa Claus himself. The singer may simply inform his lady friend that "Santa Claus will be to see you, this very Christmas night." Or he may be a "backdoor Santa," a surreptitious Lothario who makes his "rounds about the break of day." Or he may assure his woman that he is not too old to perform his expected role: "I'm gonna be your Santa Claus even if my whiskers is white." Other Christmas blues are based on a rich metaphoric brew involving stockings or Christmas trees. In one of these the singer, without bothering to explain himself, urges his woman to take her stocking and "hang it up on the head of the bed." In several other blues renditions, the singer proceeds to reverse the stocking's *sex* when he asks his girlfriend to "let me hang my stocking right on your Christmas tree."[19]

The possibilities of variation in the wordplay based on these stock phrases seem to be almost as limitless as those contained within the strict formal confines of blues music itself. In addition, all of these Christmas blues are in part *directed at* the conventional domestic Christmas ritual, a ritual they manage to transform into a kind of joyous sacrilege. (The "backdoor Santa," for example, gives presents to any children he encounters on his rounds, but only to keep them quiet while he is otherwise engaged with their mother—"Ho! ho! ho! ho!") Such gestures are a form of cultural theater, and the mocking commentary they offer is exactly what Mikhail Bakhtin, writing of the sixteenth-century European world of Rabelais, has placed at the heart of carnival sensibility.[20]

THE BLUES TRADITION, of course, represents only one aspect of the African-American Christmas. At the other end of the spectrum is the African-American holiday known as Kwanzaa. Based loosely on an African harvest celebration, this Christmas-season ritual has been gaining in popularity in recent years, especially among middle-class American blacks who wish to reclaim their African heritage. Domestic in its nature, Kwanzaa is a good instance of an "invented tradition," one that serves as an alternative to the mainstream Christmas holiday (but which also mirrors it in its essentially domestic features).

In this, Kwanzaa is similar to the old colonial holiday of *Thanksgiving*, which the Puritans introduced as a more acceptable alternative to Christmas. Thanksgiving was intended to offer New Englanders an opportunity for seasonal feasting after the conclusion of the harvest, an occasion that was not tainted by the pagan origin of Christmas or by its carnival associations. (In the late eighteenth century, when Christmas had begun to reenter the New England calendar, regional governors sometimes responded by ordering that Thanksgiving be held as close to Christmas as possible—in one year as late as December 20.)[21]

And in this respect both Thanksgiving and Kwanzaa are similar to the Jewish-American holiday of Chanukah. As innumerable commentators have pointed out, until recent times Chanukah was a distinctly minor holiday in the Jewish calendar. Even in its earlier history, though, it seems to have shifted its meaning to fit new circumstances. To begin with, it was simply a celebration of a military victory in the second century BC, the improbable victory of the Maccabees over their Syrian Greek occupiers, together with the rededication of the profaned Temple that followed. But nowhere in the original accounts was there any reference to the oil that miraculously continued to burn for eight days (the period of time required for such a ritual rededication). Only around the beginning of the Christian era, at a time when many Jews were becoming assimilated into Hellenic culture, did Chanukah become a "miracle of lights." Such a major reinterpretation achieved two ends: It played down the element of Jewish military might at a time when assimilated Hebrews would not have wished to appear warlike, and it imitated the Greek solstice celebration, which similarly entailed the burning of lamps (and would itself later be metamorphosed into the ritual of Yule logs and Christmas lights).[22]

There is only one element in the observance of Chanukah that mirrors any aspect of the carnival tradition: the element of gambling. Gambling was forbidden in medieval Jewish culture, but an exception was made during the eight days of Chanukah.[23] That custom survives today in the form of the little spinning top used by children and known as a dreidel. Dreidels can come to rest on any of four sides, each of which bears a special mark—rather like dice. The connection with dice is a real one: Dreidels were designed as gambling instruments.

But it is not Chanukah that we must look to for the closest Jewish version of the old Christmas. For that, we must turn to another Jewish holiday: the early spring festival known as Purim. This holiday marks the liberation of the Jewish people from still another ancient oppressor. Like the carnival Christmas, it is celebrated with the same radical inversion of social hierarchy and the same sanctioned transgression of behavioral boundaries. This point has in large measure been conveniently forgotten by assimilated Jews, but it is well remembered by the most traditional portion of the modern Jewish community. (Back in 1687, though, the Reverend Increase Mather of Boston was able to note that "the Days of Purim" were not intended as a "religious festival" but as what he termed a "political holiday," and Mather went on to observe that "Jews do not look upon these Days as Holy; they spend them in feasting, and in telling merry Stories.")[24]

Merry, indeed. Mather was correct, but he could easily have gone further than that. Purim is a latter-day Jewish Feast of Fools. Even today, in a modern parallel to the "Boy Bishop" ritual of medieval Europe, yeshiva students take on the role of rabbis. Sacred biblical texts are mocked, recited in nonsensical juxtaposition. Children are expected to interrupt the retelling of the Purim story with jeers and noisemakers. Outdoors, the holiday is a time of parade and masquerade, and of almsgiving, too.[25] The streets of Jerusalem and Brooklyn are thick with street theater on these occasions. There is even a rabbinic injunction to get completely drunk at Purim—literally, to drink so much that one can no longer tell the difference between the two central characters in the Purim legend, the hero, Mordecai, and the archvillain, Haman, a Persian who had unsuccessfully ordered the annihilation of the Jews. Metaphorically speaking, that means to get so drunk that one cannot distinguish good from evil. It is hard to imagine a more profoundly carnivallike gesture.

INVENTING REAL TRADITION

Here, then, and in some improbable places, are remnants of a carnival holiday tradition. But a word of caution is in order: We should pause before thinking of these as remnants of the "real" holiday tradition. We should not assume that Kwanzaa is less authentic than the blues or that Chanukah is less authentic than Purim or that Thanksgiving is less authentic than New Year's Eve. One set of all these celebrations may be "respectable" and (in the United States, at least) relatively recent, while the other may be rowdy and relatively older—but neither has a monopoly on authenticity.

To be sure, this book has argued that the "respectable" set of holidays—and particularly the familiar Christmas—represent something of an "invented tradition." This is no longer such a novel idea. One recent collection of essays, published in England under the title *Unwrapping Christmas,* actually opens with a blunt claim: "A consensus appears to be emerging around the interpretation of the contemporary Anglo-American Christmas which would place this festival firmly within the more general category of phenomenon termed 'the invention of tradition.' "[26] But while "the invention of tradition" offers a very useful historical tool, like all tools it is subject to abuse. The easiest and most tempting way to abuse the idea of invented traditions may be to believe that if a tradition is "invented," it is somehow tainted, not really authentic.

There are several reasons why such a belief is false. But the most important of them is that it is based on a profoundly questionable assumption—that before there were "invented" traditions there were "real" ones that were *not* invented. It is difficult, though, to imagine such a thing as a tradition that was not invented—and reinvented, and invented yet again. That is surely as true of the carnival Christmas as it is of Christmas as domestic idyll. As I noted in Chapter 1, the carnival Christmas varied widely from place to place and from time to time, and it is fruitless to define some primal unchanging tradition even in a small region of, say, England or Ireland. The wassail songs surely changed from one year to the next, depending in any given year on variables as unstable as the quality of the harvest or the ephemeral mood of the relationship between patrons and their clients.

To return to a point made in Chapter 1, it is useful to think of traditions not as static entities but as dynamic forces that are constantly being negotiated and renegotiated. Inversion rituals, for example, expressed the fault lines in the society of early modern Europe, the great inequalities of wealth and power that both separated the classes and bound them together. The very appeal that peasants and tenants sometimes made to "customary rights" (to old traditions, in other words) was on occasion used as a political gesture, to help preserve certain Christmas benefits (the best beer, for example, or an extra day of leisure) that could always come under challenge—in a year of poor harvest, or with the less-forthcoming son of a generous landlord. The appeal to age-old custom, then as later, was more political strategy than simple statement of fact: *We are entitled to it now, because we have always had it* might well mean little more than *You let us do it last year, and we want it again now.* It is in just this way that traditions have always been fashioned.

Yet this is difficult to accept. Today we may yearn for a past that has no past. We require *some* traditions to be unchanging, to exist outside of time—and if these cannot be our own traditions, then at least let them be the older ones that they displaced. If Santa Claus and Christmas trees turn out to be creations of the past two centuries, at least *carnival* itself must be rooted in deep cultural soil, as transcendent as the seasonal cycle itself.

But we must try to recognize such temptations for what they are. Our own culture has made us acutely aware of inauthenticities that pervade our own lives—in advertising, business, and politics. And that awareness presses us to seek out the practices of other, different societies, including those of our own past—distant places and times that carry the promise of being more "in touch" than our own with "what really matters." Invariably, these alien societies carry an implicit promise: They have remained untainted by the forces of commodity culture. Thus we are easily fascinated by "primitive" peoples whom we can make out to have had minimal contact with Western society. We tour the Third World, or untouched pockets of our own society, and we do not choose to suspect that the natives already know all about us and just what we expect them to be like (or to recognize that it is our own culture that is selling them to us as just another commodity). We read about times gone by and we do not wish to think those were just as complex, and as morally ambiguous, as our own times. But of course they were. Someone expressed this idea with great elegance by pointing out that "nobody has ever lived in the past."

One way to help clarify that point is to look for living expressions of carnival here in the present—not in hidden corners of our society but right where we encounter it in our ordinary lives. Are we really prepared to romanticize carnival behavior when it disturbs our own sense of civility or our personal privacy? It is one thing to lament the suppression of wassail, the Wren Boys, or John Canoe, but it may be quite another to feel comfortable with the aggressive begging that has returned to our cities and towns or with the deliberately offensive speech and manners of middle-class young people who are busy probing and transgressing the limits of acceptable behavior. The blues may be an expression of modern carnival, but so is the sound of young men—whether black or white—driving slowly down city streets with boom boxes blaring from open car windows. And for those of us who happen to reside in academic communities, so is the sound of postexamination festivities at the nearby fraternity house.

It is intriguing to force ourselves to think of such *Animal House* celebrations as modern carnival, or even as a latter-day form of street theater, youthful mockery directed in part at the workaday adult world whose privileges and burdens present-day young people are uncertain whether to envy or fear. And it is useful to force ourselves to think of those young people—at least the ones who attend high school or college—as the modern equivalent of peasants and apprentices, the "children and servants" who once "went abroad nights" in late December. There is something more than a purely symbolic connection linking the two groups. Students, more than any other members of middle-class society, live by a task-oriented seasonal rhythm marked, just toward the end of the calendar year, by a period of intense labor (not bringing in the harvest but studying for final exams); and that in turn is followed, just at Christmas, by an extended period of strenuous release and aggressive leisure. But to recognize that connection with the past does not make the *Animal House* scenario more endearing.

So it will not do to think there is a usable line, whether historical or aesthetic, dividing invented traditions from real ones. But neither does this mean that we cannot and need not make judgments. If this book has argued, on the one hand, that traditions are constantly changing and that the domestic Christmas idyll is surprisingly new, it has also argued that most of the problems we face at Christmas today—the greedy materialism, the jaded consumerism, the deliberate manipulation not only of goods but also of private desires and personal relationships into purchasable commodities—are surprisingly old. They date, in fact, to the emergence of the domestic Christmas itself. And they were being publicly debated, and lamented, as early as the 1830s.

This, too, is difficult to accept. It is natural to believe that the issues we face today are new ones—issues of unprecedented complexity the likes of which have never been encountered. The problems we associate with Christmas, in particular—the loss of authenticity, the decline of pure domestic felicity into an exhausting and often frustrating round of shopping for the perfect gifts—are the very problems we most easily associate with the facts of modern economic life, with advanced technologies of production and marketing. Even people who fervently believe in market capitalism sometimes blame it for cheapening Christmas. But what this book has suggested is that there never was a time when Christmas existed as an unsullied domestic idyll, immune to the taint of commercialism. It has argued that the domestic Christmas was the commercial Christmas—commercial from its earliest stages, commercial at its very core. Indeed, the domestic Christmas was itself a force in the spread of consumer capitalism.

That may be the case because domesticity and capitalism themselves, "family values" and accumulative, competitive ones, have been deeply interlinked from the very beginning, even when they have appeared to represent alternative modes of feeling (or seemed to be in conflict with each other). For there is that other kind of "Christmas blues," the middle-class blues that bespeak our disappointment in the family itself for its failure to provide the yearned-for intimacy that is its especial role and trust at Christmas. But to fulfill that role, to satisfy that yearning, how much finally depends—at both ends of the gift exchange—on the selection of just the right presents! As purchasers, how often do we end by using money as a substitute for what we fear is insufficient thoughtfulness and sensitivity?—by deciding, at the end of a lengthy shopping excursion, to buy expensive presents for our loved ones simply because we cannot think of that one simple gift that would be modest in price but perfectly intimate in effect.

It is just this circumstance that may help to explain why, in the second quarter of the nineteenth century, such rituals as Santa Claus and the Christmas tree (or stockings or gift wrapping) took such rapid and profound hold on the imagination of those who created a new domestic

Christmas. Perhaps the very speed and intensity with which those essentially new rituals were claimed as timeless traditions shows how powerful was the need to keep the relationship between family life and a commercial economy hidden from view—to protect children (and adults, too) from understanding something troublesome about the world they were making. In our own time, a century and a half later, that protection may be an indulgence we can no longer afford.

Notes

Chapter 1

1. James H. Barnett, *The American Christmas: A Study in National Culture* (New York: Macmillan, 1954), 19-20; Edward Everett Hale, "Christmas in Boston," *The New England Magazine* n.s., I (1889), 356-357; Francis X. Weiser, *The Christmas Book* (New York: Harcourt, Brace, 1952), 48-49. See also Hale's autobiography, *A New England Boyhood* (New York, 1893), 117. The idea that Christmas was universally rejected by the Puritans, and that it was not practiced in New England until the nineteenth century, has been casually accepted in virtually all the relevant scholarship. This is even true of the best article on the subject: Ivor Debenham Spencer, "Christmas, the Upstart," in *New England Quarterly* 8 (1935), 356-383. See also Katherine van Etten Lyford, "The Victory of the Christmas Keepers," *Yankee* (Dec. 1964), 76-77, 102-105; and Katherine Lambert Richards, *How Christmas Came to the Sunday-Schools: The Observance of Christmas in the Protestant Church Schools of the United States* (New York: Dodd, Mead & Co., 1934). A recent and notable exception is Richard P. Gildrie, *The Profane, the Civil, and the Godly: The Reformation of Manners in Orthodox New England, 1679-1749* (University Park: Pennsylvania State University Press, 1994).

2. Increase Mather, *A Testimony against Several Prophane and Superstitious Customs, Now Practiced by Some in New-England* (London, 1687), 35.

3. An Anglican minister in northern England, writing as early as 1725, acknowledged the pagan origins of these practices. Yule logs and candles, for example, were for pagans "an Emblem of the Sun, and the lengthening of Days," and they originated in an effort "to Illuminate the House, and turn the Night into Day." But he speculated that it became associated with the Nativity for Christian reasons—"a Symbol of that Light which was that Night born into the World." He argues that light has been associated with many things, and that one of these is that it has become "an emblem . . . of our Lord Jesus Christ." Henry Bourne, *Antiquitates Vulgares* (Newcastle, 1725), 127, 128, 130, 134. The best account of the non-Christian origins of Christmas rituals remains Clement A. Miles, *Christmas in Ritual and Tradition, Christian and Pagan* (London, 1912; reissued as *Christmas Customs and Traditions: Their History and Significance* (New York: Dover Publications, 1976), 159-360 passim.

4. Miles, *Christmas Customs and Traditions*, 173-174. According to the Reverend Henry Bourne, many in England and Scotland continued the season as late as Candlemas (Feb. 2). Bourne, *Antiquitates Vulgares*, 156.

5. See, for example, John Ashton, *A Right Merrie Christmasse: The Story of Christ-Tide* (London and New York, 1894), 6-8, 45, 246-250. The situation was similar in colonial America; see Barnett, *The American Christmas*, 9, 11.

6. I. Mather, *Testimony*, 25. For perspectives on the world of carnival, see Peter Burke, *Popular Culture in Early Modern Europe* (New York: Harper and Row, 1978), 199-203; Mikhail Bakhtin, *Rabelais and His World* (Cambridge: MIT Press, 1968); and Peter Stallybrass and Allon White, *The Politics and Poetics of Transgression* (London: Methuen, 1986), 171-190.

7. Ashton, *Right Merrie Christmasse*, 125-126.

8. I. Mather, *Testimony*, 36; Cotton Mather, *Grace Defended: A Censure on the Ungodliness, By Which the Glorious Grace of God, Is Too Commonly Abused* (Boston, 1712), 20. Increase Mather cited earlier authorities to confirm his point: " '[T]he Feast of Christ's nativity is attended with such profaneness, as that it deserves the name of Saturn's Mass, or of Bacchus his Mass, or if you will, the Devil's Mass, rather than to have the holy name of Christ put upon it.' " William Perkins argued that "the Feast of Christ's Nativity (commonly so called) is not spent in praising God, but in Revelling, Dicing, Carding, Masking, Mumming, and in all licentious Liberty for the most part, as though it were some Heathenish Feast of Ceres or Bacchus." (I. Mather, *Testimony*, 36.) For the Puritan war on Christmas in England, see Chris Durston, "Lords of Misrule: The Puritan War on Christmas, 1642-60," *History Today* 35 (Dec. 1985), 7-14; and David Underdown, *Revel, Riot, and Rebellion: Popular Politics and Culture in England, 1603-1660* (1985), 256-268. See also Gavin Weightman and Steve Humphries, *Christmas Past* (London: Sidgwick & Jackson, 1987), 38-53.

9. Bourne, *Antiquitates Vulgares*, x ("scandal"), 153-154, 156 (40 days of Christmas drinking), 147-149 (mumming), 139-141 (caroling).

10. For various inversion rituals, see John Brand, *Observations on the Popular Antiquities of Great Britain* (rev. by Sir Henry Ellis, 3 vols., London, 1849), I, 7-28, 415-531 passim; Ashton, *Right Merrie Christmasse*, passim; W. Carew Hazlitt, *Faiths and Folklore of the British Isles, A Descriptive and Historical Dictionary* (2 vols., 1905), I, 68-71, 119-125; II, 392-393, 437-438, 619-620.

11. I. Mather, *Testimony*, 35.

12. François Maximilien Misson, *Travels in England*, quoted in Hazlitt, *Faiths and Folklore*, 120-121, and in Brand, *Popular Antiquities*, I, 495. Misson added: "In the taverns the landlord gives [i.e., gives away, for free] part of what is eaten and drank in his house that and the next two days: for instance, they reckon [charge] you for the wine, and tell you there is nothing to pay for bread, nor for your slice of Westphalia [ham]." See also a 1570 account in Barnabe Googe, "The Popish Kingdom," quoted in Brand, *Popular Antiquities*, I, 13.

13. Robert Herrick, *Hesperides* (London, 1648); quoted in Brand, *Popular Antiquities*, I, 71-471; also Ashton, *Right Merrie Christmasse*, 75.

14. To add a touch of sexual banter, the song opens with a demand that the "prettiest maid" [i.e., maiden] in the house "roll back the pin . . . [and] let us all in." One version of the "Gloucestershire Wassail" is in Brand, *Popular Antiquities*, I, 7-8. A recorded version of this song, performed in the appropriate spirit, can be found on the album *The Second Nowell: A Pageant of Mid-Winter Carols*, vol. 2 (John Roberts, Tony Barrand et al.), Front Hall Records.

15. Ashton, *Right Merrie Christmasse*, 225 ("invited into the house"). For the Scottish version of wassailing, called Hagmena (or Hogomany), see Ashton, *Right Merrie Christmasse*, 217.

16. See Burke, *Popular Culture in Early Modern Europe*, 199–203; Natalie Zemon Davis, "The Reasons of Misrule: Youth Groups and Charivaris in Sixteenth-Century France," in Natalie Zemon Davis, *Society and Culture in Early Modern France* (Stanford: Stanford University Press, 1975), 97–123.

17. *Money*, Dec. 1991, 82.

18. Ashton, *Right Merrie Christmasse*, 34–35.

19. John Taylor, *The Complaint of Christmas*, quoted in Durston, "Lords of Misrule," 11.

20. Ashton, *Right Merrie Christmasse*, 27 (1644 law), 34–37 (popular resistance to the suppression).

21. David D. Hall, *Worlds of Wonder, Days of Judgement: Popular Religious Belief in Early New England* (New York: Knopf, 1989), 10.

22. William Bradford, *Of Plymouth Plantation, 1620–1647* (New York: Knopf, 1952), 97.

23. For examples of occasional instances of the emergence of popular customs (including a citation to the first instance of Christmas disorder to be examined below), see Hall, *Worlds of Wonder*, 210–211.

24. For a fine account of Marblehead maritime culture, including a subsequent conflict over the celebration of Christmas, see Christine Leigh Heyrman, *Commerce and Culture: The Maritime Communities of Colonial Massachusetts, 1690–1750* (New York, W. W. Norton: 1984), 216–302.

25. *Records and Files of the Quarterly Courts of Essex County* (8 vols., Salem, 1911–1921), II, 433. Hoar's age is from ibid., IX, 208. William Hoar's occupation as a fisherman is ibid., VI, 401.

26. The Hoar clan's activities are reported ibid., VII, 43–55, 81, 181–183. For a modern account, see Barbara Ritter Dailey, " 'Where Thieves Break Through and Steal': John Hale Versus Dorcas Hoar, 1672–1692," in *Historical Collections of the Essex Institute*, vol. 128 (1992), 255–269.

27. *Essex Quarterly Courts*, VII, 331–332. For a follow-up to this episode, see ibid., VII, 424.

28. Braybrooke, a weaver, was taxed in the lowest 15 percent of Salem Village rate payers in 1681, and in 1700 he was renting a small parcel of land from a local landowner, Thomas Putnam, Jr. Fuller was the son of a bricklayer; in 1690 he was taxed in the lowest quartile. Flint was the younger son of a sturdy farmer, and would later inherit the less desirable portion of his parents' estate; he did not flourish. And Foster was assessed the minimum for the 1683 county rate. (Data are from *Essex Institute Historical Collections* 51 [1915], 190–191; ibid. 53 [1917], 336; Paul S. Boyer and Stephen Nissenbaum, eds., *Salem-Village Witchcraft: A Documentary Record of Local Conflict in Colonial New England* [Boston: Northeastern University Press, 1993], 321–322, 353–355; *Essex Quarterly Courts*, VII, 424; Sidney Perley, *The History of Salem, Massachusetts* [3 vols., Salem, 1924], III, 422.)

29. Boyer and Nissenbaum, *Salem-Village Witchcraft*, 262 (anti-Parris petition) and 350 (list of villagers withholding taxes).

30. Samuel Sewall, *The Diary of Samuel Sewall, 1674–1729.* (2 vols., New York: Farrar, Straus & Giroux, 1973), I, 90 (Dec. 25 and 28, 1685); I, 128 (Dec. 25, 1686).

31. John Tully, "Tully 1687. An Almanac" (Boston, 1687); John Tully, "Tully 1688. An Almanac . . . *Imprimatur* Edw. Randolph, Secr." (Boston, 1688).

32. Ibid., 15–22. Selections from these prognostications are reprinted in Harrison T. Meserole, ed., *Seventeenth-Century American Poetry* (Stuart Editions, N.Y.: New York University Press, 1968), 512–515. The copy of this almanac I have used (from the "Early American Imprints" series on microfilm) was purchased and used by Samuel Sewall him-

self. Other copies lack the "Prognostications," which may have been copied from an English almanac. There is a good discussion of early New England almanacs, and Tully's in particular, in Hall, *Worlds of Wonder*, 54–61. See also Bernard Capp, *English Almanacs, 1500–1800: Astrology and the Popular Press* (Ithaca: Cornell University Press, 1979).

33. Mather wrote: "The impious and mischievous men, against whom the Inspired Writer is now engaged [in the sermon's text, are guilty of the following:] First The Ungodly Men stand charged with Filthiness. They were, that I may use the most agreeable Term, which the French Translation leads me to, A very *Dissolute* Generation. I take notice, by the way, that the Greek term, here used for, *Lasciviousness*, or *Wantonness*, is derived from the name of the town *Selga;* a Place infamous for such dissolute Practices." He concluded this series of euphemisms by admitting, "I am lothe here to explain my self too particularly." C. Mather, *Grace Defended*, 2.

34. Cotton Mather, *Advice from the Watch-Tower; in a testimony against evil custumes. A brief essay to . . . offer a . . . catalogue of evil customes growing upon us* (Boston, 1713), 31–40.

35. Ibid., 34–35.

36. See John Demos, "Families in Colonial Bristol, Rhode Island: An Exercise in Historical Demography," in *William and Mary Quarterly*, Third Series, 25 (1968), 56–57. The seasonal rhythm of conceptions is from a paper delivered by Kenneth Lockridge at SUNY, Stony Brook, in 1969. For a fine account of premarital sex and marriage at the end of the eighteenth century, see Laurel Thatcher Ulrich, *A Midwife's Tale: The Life of Martha Ballard, Based on Her Diary, 1785–1812* (New York: Knopf, 1990), 134–161. The laments of such ministers as Cotton Mather have conventionally been interpreted as mere "jeremiads," an irrational response to the decline of Puritanism. But recent scholarship supports my own sense that these were part of a reasonable response to the reemergence of popular culture in New England. The best recent study is Gildrie, *The Profane, the Civil, and the Godly*. This is the only work which shows that Christmas itself was making a comeback at the turn of the eighteenth century.

37. William Brattle, "An Ephemeris . . . for . . . 1682 (Cambridge, 1682). The verse actually concluded with a couplet that ridiculed those who believed its message.

38. Titan Leeds, "The American Almanac for . . . 1714" (Boston 1714). This was a Boston reprint of a Philadelphia imprint.

39. Samuel Clough, "The New-England Almanack" (Boston, 1702); Nathaniel Whittemore, "An Almanac" (Boston, 1719).

40. Nathanael Ames, "An Astronomical Almanac for . . . 1749" (Boston, [1748]); George Wheten, "An Almanac for . . . 1754" (Boston, [1753]).

41. Nathaniel Whittemore, "Almanac" (Boston, 1719). It is interesting that this admonition does not challenge the legitimacy of the ritual. By warning householders not to let their dependents "run *too much* abroad at Nights," it seems only to be admonishing them not to stay out *all night*, or *every night*.

42. Nathanael Ames, "An Almanac for . . . 1746" (Boston, 1746).

43. Historians once believed that "Yankee Doodle" was the work of British soldiers who were satirizing New England rustic manners, but it now seems likely that its words were a local American product—a kind of sophisticated rural self-parody. Evidence also suggests that the earliest of these verses date not from the era of the American Revolution but from a full generation earlier—from the early 1740s. The preeminent argument for the American origins of the verse is J. A. Leo Lemay, "The American Origins of 'Yankee Doodle,' " *William and Mary Quarterly*, 33 (1976), 435–464. Lemay dates at least some of the verses to the 1740s (even though they were not actually published until the late 1760s and 1770s and later), using references to events that took place in King George's War, especially the capture of Louisburg (on Cape Breton) in 1745 (ibid. 443–447).

44. This verse—and several others cited below—comes from a version of "Yankee Doodle" called "The Lexington March," published in London, probably in 1775 (the only copy is owned by the Huntington Library). For evidence that these verses were of American composition, see Lemay, "Yankee Doodle," 436–438.

45. For election day: "Lection time is now at hand, / We're going to Uncle Chace's, / There'l be some a drinking round / And some lapping lasses." (*Yankee Song* Broadside, Essex Institute; quoted in Lemay, "Yankee Doodle," 450. For cornhusking: "Yankee Song" (owned by Essex Institute), quoted ibid., 448. For a late-eighteenth-century rural New England diary that records the association of cornhuskings with "abandoned drinking and sexual liaisons," see Ulrich, *Midwife's Tale*, 146–147.

46. This verse is from "The Lexington March" (Huntington Library copy). "Mother Chase's" corresponds to "Uncle Chace's" in the election verse quoted in the previous note. The verse quoted above continues with the following: "Punkin Pye is very good / And so is Apple Lantern; / Had you been whipp'd as oft as I, / You'd not have been so wanton."

47. Mather relegated to a footnote in the published text of this sermon (probably an indication that it was not part of the sermon as he originally delivered it in church) his demonstration that Jesus could not have been born in December.

48. Mather, *Grace Defended*, 19.

49. As early as 1706, Daniel Leeds warned in an almanac published in New York that "More health is gotten by observing diet / Than pleasure found in vain excess and Riot." (Lines at Dec. 26–29; in Daniel Leeds, *Leeds, 1706. The American Almanack* [New York, 1706].) Twenty years later, in a Philadelphia almanac, his son Titan Leeds attacked both gambling and "surfeiting." (Titan Leeds, *The American Almanack for . . . 1726* [Philadelphia, (1705)].)

50. Other New England almanacs, while not sounding the dietary urgency of Nathanael Ames, typically combined notes of moderation with those of mirth, as when the "Bickerstaffe" almanac for 1777 assured its readers that "to keep your stomach warm / A moderate glass can do no harm." ([Ezra Gleason, *Bickerstaffe's Boston Almanack, for . . . 1777* [Boston, 1777].)

51. As Eric Foner has pointed out, Franklin urged men like himself "to remember that 'time is money,' and condemned [the old] practice of observing the traditional pre-industrial 'holiday' of 'Saint Monday' and spending the day at the alehouse." (Eric Foner, *Tom Paine and Revolutionary America* (New York: Oxford University Press, 1977), 35). Another self-made New Englander who urged temperance in his almanacs is Roger Sherman of Connecticut.

52. Robert R. McCausland and Cynthia MacAlman McCausland, eds., *The Diary of Martha Ballard 1785–1812* (Camden, Maine: Picton Press, 1992), 742 (1807); 828 (1810); 852 (1811).

53. Ibid., 565. "Ephraim" and "Cyrus" were Martha Ballard's still-unmarried sons; Patty Town was a grown-up granddaughter who was spending a few months at her grandmother's in order to help with the housework (see entries from Oct. 15, 1801, to Feb. 8, 1802, ibid., 559–569 passim). Cyrus Ballard remained a bachelor all his life.

54. Ibid., 320. For Dolly and Sally Cox, see Ulrich, *A Midwife's Tale*, 144–145, 220–221. Only a few months later Barnabas Lambard would marry Martha Ballard's daughter Dollie.

55. Ballard, *Diary*, 320 (Daniel Bolton); 217 (Mrs. Lithgow); 596 ("pumkin and apple pies" and clothes-mending); 624 ("puding and roast").

56. Ibid., 217 (1791); 770 (1808); 771 ("childn here").

57. Ibid., 714. A goose was clearly a special gift, and a seasonal one at that. According to the index to the published diary, there is only one record of a goose in the entire

document; but the index is inadequate, failing to note either this New Year's goose or a Thanksgiving goose mentioned on page 621.

58. Ibid., 743. For further examples, see entries for Dec. 24, 1808, Dec. 30, 1810, and Dec. 22, 1811.

59. Ibid., 770.

60. Ibid., 396. This is the first example I have found in the history of New England of a commercial Christmas present. But see Chapter 4, p. 133.

61. Milton wrote this poem as a young man, in 1629, but he remained sufficiently proud of it to place it first in a later collection of his poetry.

62. Increase Mather, manuscript diary, Dec. 19, 1664 (in Mather Family Papers, American Antiquarian Society, Diary Typescript: Box 3, Folder 1, 48–49). I have inferred the subject of Mather's sermon from circumstantial evidence. Much of his reading the previous week (as recorded in his diary) had dealt historically and critically with Christmas. It included Rudolf Hospinian, *De Festiorum* (Tiguri, 1592), William Prynne, *Histrio-Mastix* (London, 1633), and two references I have not been able to trace: Stuckins' [?] *De Antiq.* and Caudrey, *De Christmass* (the reading is recorded in the entries for Dec. 12–14, 1664). This episode is alluded to in Michael G. Hall, *The Last American Puritan: The Life of Increase Mather, 1639–1723* (Middletown, Conn.: Wesleyan University Press, 1988), 66.

63. J.B. [Joseph Browne], "An Almanac . . . for . . . 1669" (Cambridge, 1669); J.D. [John Danforth], "An Almanac . . . for . . . 1679" (Cambridge, 1679).

64. Edward Holyoke, "An Almanac . . . for . . . 1713" (Boston, 1713: "Licensed by His Excellency the Governour"); Titan Leeds, "The American Almanac for . . . 1714" (Boston, 1714); Increase Gatchell, "The Young American Ephemera for . . . 1715" (Boston, 1715). The James Franklin almanacs are: Poor Robin, "The Rhode Island Almanac for . . . 1728 (Newport, 1728) and "The Rhode Island Almanac for . . . 1729" (Newport, 1729). In his Boston newspaper, the *New England Courant,* Franklin had featured a front-page poem in defense of Christmas in the issue of Dec. 17–24, 1722.

65. Nathanael Ames, "An Almanac for . . . 1760" (Boston, 1759). The ads are in the *Boston Post-Boy,* Dec. 3, 1759 and the *Boston News-Letter,* Dec. 6, 1759.

66. Roger Sherman, *An Astronomical Diary . . . for . . . 1758* (New Haven, 1758), 1.

67. Purcell set many of Tate's poems to music, including what may be his greatest vocal solo, "The Blessed Virgin's Expostulation." Nicholas Brady wrote the libretto to Purcell's 1692 "Ode for St. Cecilia's Day."

68. Nicholas Brady and Nahum Tate, *A New Version of the Psalms of David, Fitted to the Tunes Used in the Churches* (Boston, 1720). The printing history of this collection can be traced most easily through Clifford K. Shipton and James E. Mooney, *National Index of American Imprints Through 1800: The Short-Title Evans* (2 vols., Worcester: American Antiquarian Society, 1969). On Dec. 24, 1722, James Franklin printed two other Christmas hymns in his Boston newspaper, the *New England Courant.*

69. Isaac Watts, *Hymns and Spiritual Songs* (Boston, 1720). One of these Nativity hymns was placed third in this lengthy collection (It opens: "Behold, the grace appears, / The promise is fulfilled; / Mary the wond'rous virgin bears, / And Jesus the child." It also reports that the "promis'd infant" is "born to day"). The second hymn, from *Horae Lyricae* [Lyric Poems] (Boston, 1748), begins: "Shepards rejoice, lift up your eyes."

70. Joseph T. Buckingham, *Personal Memoirs and Recollections of Editorial Life* (2 vols., Boston, 1852), I, 19; quoted in Hall, *Worlds of Wonder,* 37. The folklorist Peter Benes has estimated that by 1780 almost half of the New England churches were singing the Watts version; another 25 percent were using Tate and Brady; and most of the remaining churches were singing from the old Bay Psalm Book. (Peter Benes, "Psalmody in Coastal Massachusetts and the Connecticut River Valley," in *The Bay and the River, 1600–1900 (Annual proceedings of the Dublin Seminar for New England Folklife,* vol. 6 [Boston: Boston

University, 1982], 117–131; esp. 125.) Like the Anglicans Brady and Tate, the great English hymnist and religious poet Isaac Watts (1674–1748), though a steadfast Congregationalist, designed his verses to evoke powerful emotions rather than to offer plain and strictly faithful translations of the original biblical texts.

71. William Knapp, "An Hymn on the Nativity," in Thomas Walter, *The Grounds and Rules of Musick Explained* (Boston, [1760]). The other songs were William Tans'ur, "An Anthem for Christmas Day," in [Daniel Bayley,] *The Royal Melody Complete* (Boston, 1761); "An Hymn for Christmas Day," in Daniel Bayley, *A New and Complete Introduction to the Grounds and Rules of Musick* (Newburyport, Mass., 1764); William Knapp, "An Anthem for Christmas Day"; anon., "A Christmas Hymn"; and Joseph Stephenson, "O Zion that Bringest," all in Joseph Flagg, ed., *Sixteen Anthems* (Boston, 1766); Stephenson, "An Anthem, Out of the Second Chapter of Luke"; Stephenson, "Hark, Hark"; "Boston, A New Hymn for Christmas Day"; "Great Milton" ("Joy to the World"); and Stephenson, "An Anthem Out of the Fortieth Chapter of Isaiah" ("O Zion that bringst glad tidings"), all in Daniel Bayley and A. Williams *The American Harmony* (2 parts, Boston, 1769).

72. In chronological order of publication, these were: "An Hymn for Christmas or Charlston [sic]" and "Boston, for Christmas," both published in *The New-England Psalm-Singer* (1770); "Boston" (same music as "Boston, for Christmas," but with a different text), "Judea," and "Bethlehem" (all in *The Singing-Master's Assistant*) [1778]; "Emmanuel for Christmas" (in *The Psalm-Singer's Amusement* [1781]); "Shiloh, for Christmas" (in *The Suffolk Harmony* [1786]); and "An Anthem for Christmas" (in *The Continental Harmony* [1794]). In addition, Billings may have been asked in 1782 to compose an elaborate Christmas hymn (also on a Watts text, but for soloist, chorus and organ) for Trinity Episcopal Church in Boston. (See David P. McKay and Richard Crawford, *William Billings of Boston: Eighteenth-Century Composer* [Princeton: Princeton University Press, 1975], 132–133. A discussion of Billings's Christmas songs can be found ibid., 141–146.)

73. Isaiah Thomas, *Worcester Collection of Sacred Harmony* (Worcester, 1786), 188–194; Daniel Read, "A Christmas Anthem," *The Columbian Harmonist No. III* (New Haven, 1785), 9–13. Technically, the "Hallelujah Chorus" is not a Christmas song, and *Messiah* itself was not written or initially performed as a Christmas oratorio. In 1795, Thomas would publish, as a separate imprint, a "Christmas Anthem," with music by Isaac Lane— to a text by Isaac Watts. (See Isaac Lane, "Christmas Anthem" [Worcester, 1785]).

74. F. B. Dexter, ed., *The Literary Diary of Ezra Stiles* (3 vols., New York, 1901), II, 103).

75. Ibid., II, 315.

76. The Yale community seems to have been a center of Christmas activity in the 1780s. In 1786 the Yale College Chapel was the site of a performance of a large-scale Christmas cantata, "An Ode for Christmas," composed specially for the occasion and subsequently published in a New Haven musical magazine. This "Ode" was sung by three separate four-part choirs (each representing one of the shepherds) and an additional three-part choir (in the role of the angel Gabriel). The published version of this elaborate piece indicated that it had received "universal applause." *American Musical Magazine* (New Haven, 1787), vol. 1, 27–30; microfilm in American Periodicals Series I: Reel 6.

77. Francis G. Walett, ed., *The Diary of Ebenezer Parkman 1703–1782: First Part, 1719–1755* (Worcester, Mass.: American Antiquarian Society, 1974), 160 (1747), 195 (1755).

78. Manuscript diary of David Hall, in pre-Revolutionary Massachusetts Diaries, Massachusetts Historical Society: Microfilm 5:1. (Entries are missing for many of the years in the 1750s.) Hall composed extended Christmas meditations in 1763, 1768, and 1769. He is not to be confused with the historian David D. Hall.

79. John Birge manuscript Daybook (Pocumtuck Valley Memorial Association Library), p. 62. This document was unearthed by Carrie Giard, an undergraduate student at the University of Massachusetts, Amherst. (Birge's final comment—"I cannot see why it was much better than Burglary"—implies that other people did *not* think of such Christ-

mas intrusions as burglary, and supports the idea that this kind of seasonal misrule operated just at the boundaries of acceptable behavior.)

80. [Joseph Green,] "Entertainment for a Winter's Evening: Being a Full and True Account of a very strange and wonderful Sight seen in Boston on the twenty-seventh of December at Noon-Day" (Boston, 1750), 5–6 ("diverting Christmas tale"; " 'tis love . . . house of God"), 11 ("eating"). For another modern account of this event, see Steven Bullock's *Revolutionary Brotherhood: Freemasonry and the Transformation of the American Order, 1730–1840* (Chapel Hill: University of North Carolina Press, 1996). The Masons celebrated the name day of *two* saints named John; the other was St. John the Baptist, whose name day happened to fall on June 24. In effect, the Masons were celebrating both the winter and the summer solstice. Capt. Francis Goelet recorded three visits to the Freemasons' Boston lodge, at Stone's Tavern, all in October 1750. See *New England Historical and Genealogical Register*, 24 (1870), 53.

81. E. P. Thompson, "Patrician Society, Plebeian Culture," in *Journal of Social History*, vol. 7 (1974), 382–405.

82. Green, "Entertainment," 12.

83. "The News-Boy's Christmas and New Year's Verses" (Broadside, Boston, 1770). The *Massachusetts Gazette and Boston Post-Boy* for Dec. 23, 1771, printed a devotional poem, "An Hymn on Christmas Day."

84. W. W. Newell, "Christmas Maskings in Boston," in *Journal of American Folk-Lore* 9 (1896), 178.

85. H. E. Scudder, ed., *Recollections of Samuel Breck, with Passages from His Note-Books (1771–1862)* (Philadelphia, 1877), 37. Breck was raised as an upper-class Bostonian. From 1780 to 1792 (when he moved to Philadelphia), his family lived in a "remarkably fine" house at the corner of Winter and Common (now Tremont) Streets, with an acre of land. The house was sold for $8,000 in 1792. (Ibid., 37–38.) This was presumably where Breck saw the Anticks.

86. *The [Boston] Mercury*, Dec. 20, 1793. According to the Oxford English Dictionary, the word *antic* originally meant "a grotesque gesture, posture, or trick." It was commonly used to refer to "a grotesque pageant or theatrical representation . . . ; hence, a grotesque or motley company."

87. *The [Boston] Mercury*, Dec. 24, 1793, and the *Columbian Centinel* [Boston], Dec. 25, 1793; *The Diary of William Bentley, pastor of the East Church, Salem* (4 vols., Salem: The Essex Institute, 19-5-14), II, 78. The Anticks were not the only perpetrators of Christmas violence in Boston in 1793. On Christmas Eve *another* mob disrupted religious services in the local Roman Catholic church. (*Columbian Centinel* [Boston], Dec. 25, 1793.)

88. *Massachusetts Centinel*, Dec. 23 and 26, 1789; see also Russell E. Miller, *The Larger Hope: The First Century of the Universalist Church in America, 1770–1870* (Boston: Unitarian Universalist Association, 1979), 321.

89. Earl Morse Wilbur, *A History of Unitarianism* (2 vols., Cambridge: Harvard University Press:, 1945–52), vol. 1, 400–414. The one marginal exception to the Unitarian front was the Old South Church, which "remained nominally orthodox by the narrowest margin, [although] its minister, Dr. Eckley, denied the supreme divinity of Christ" (ibid., 400).

90. *Boston Daily Advertiser*, Dec. 24, 1817. See also *Independent Chronicle*, Dec. 24, 1817, and *Boston Gazette*, Dec. 25, 1817 and Dec. 29, 1817 (a confirmation that all of this actually happened).

91. Quoted in Caroline Sloat, "Before There Was Christmas," *Old Sturbridge Visitor* 24 (1984), 10.

92. See *Boston Intelligencer*, Dec. 12, 19, and 26, 1818; *Boston Gazette*, Dec. 21 and 24, 1818; *Boston Daily Advertiser*, Dec. 22, 1818; *The Idiot*, Dec. 24, 1818; *New England Galaxy and Masonic Magazine*, Dec. 18 and 25, 1818.

93. *Boston Daily Advertiser,* Dec. 22, 1818; *New England Galaxy,* Dec. 25, 1818 (this letter is signed "South End").

94. Notice in *Massachusetts Spy* [Worcester], Dec. 22, 1818. Bancroft had the sermon published as "The Doctrine of Immortality: A Christmas Sermon" (Worcester, 1819). Aaron Bancroft was an open Unitarian who had been preaching Christmas sermons each year since 1816. See "The Diary of Isaiah Thomas 1805–1828," in *Transactions and Collections of the American Antiquarian Society* IX (1909), 337 (1816), 368 (1817), 412–413 (1818). The 1659 Massachusetts law was printed in the *Boston Intelligencer and Evening Gazette,* Jan. 2, 1819. For data on the open churches, see *Boston Gazette,* Dec. 24, 1818. The previous year a collection of Christmas hymn texts was printed in Boston (it may have been part of the same movement): G. Carseer, *Hymns for the Nativity of Our Saviour* (Boston, 1817).

95. *Boston Recorder,* Dec. 19, 1818. The previous year the approval of this paper had been implicit: ibid., Dec. 30, 1817.

96. *Boston Gazette,* Dec. 23, 1819; *Farmer's Cabinet* (Amherst, N.H.), Dec. 25, 1819 (the previous Christmas the same paper had reported favorably on the Boston business closings, and two local religious societies actually held devotional meetings in Amherst). See also *New-England Galaxy,* Dec. 24, 1819; *Boston Intelligencer,* Dec. 25, 1819; *Independent Chronicle,* Dec. 22 and 25, 1819.

97. *New England Galaxy,* Jan. 2, 1824.

98. "On Public Festivals," *Missionary Herald at Home and Abroad* [*The Panoplist and Missionary Herald*] (Boston), vol. 16 (Feb., 1820), 57–59; *Boston Statesman,* Dec. 27, 1828.

Chapter 2

1. The episode is recorded by Pintard in a letter written in stages between Dec. 8, 1820, and January 4, 1821 (the passage I have used was written on January 1): *Letters from John Pintard to his Daughter 1816–1833* (4 vols., New York: New-York Historical Society, 1940): vol. 1, 359. I have modernized Pintard's spelling and punctuation. The revelers who disturbed Pintard's sleep would have constituted a callithumpian band consisting of young working-class men; by the 1820s, these bands had become a menace in the eyes of more prosperous New Yorkers. See Paul A. Gilje, *The Road to Mobocracy: Popular Disorder in New York City, 1763–1834* (Chapel Hill: University of North Carolina Press, 1989), 254–255.

2. *The Hudson [N.Y.] Weekly Gazette,* Jan. 4, 1787. This item was brought to my attention by Robert Arner.

3. E. P. Thompson, "Patrician Society, Plebeian Culture," in *Journal of Social History,* vol. 7 (1974), 382–405 (see esp. 390–394). The resurgence of paganism in England during this period has often been noted; Thompson's splendid article places it in a richly subtle context.

4. E. P. Thompson deals with the English version of the charivari in two articles: "'Rough Music': Le Charivari anglais," *Annales* (1972); and "Rough Music," in E. P. Thompson, *Customs in Common: Studies in Traditional Popular Culture* (New York: The New Press, 1993), 467–533.

5. Such employers collectively resisted the ongoing tendency of their workers to treat the month of December as a period of leisure and festivity. An instance of English worker resistance to celebrating Christmas on a single day is reported in J. M. Golby and A. W. Purdue, *The Making of the Modern Christmas* (Athens, Ga.: University of Georgia Press, 1986), 76. This book offers a very good overview of the history of Christmas in England.

6. For England, see J. M. Golby, "A History of Christmas" (1981), quoted in Daniel Miller, "A Theory of Christmas," in Daniel Miller, ed., *Unwrapping Christmas* (Oxford: Clarendon Press, 1993), 3. Golby has traced references to Christmas in the *Times* of London from 1790 to 1836.

7. For the transformation of New York, see Gilje, *The Road to Mobocracy;* Christine Stansell, *City of Women: Sex and Class in New York, 1789–1860* (New York: Knopf, 1986); Elizabeth Blackmar, *Manhattan for Rent, 1785–1850* (Ithaca, N.Y.: Cornell University Press, 1989); Sean Wilentz, *Chants Democratic: New York City and the Rise of the American Working Class, 1788–1850* (New York: Oxford University Press, 1984); and Raymond A. Mohl, *Poverty in New York, 1783–1825* (New York: Oxford University Press, 1971). The recorded population of New York City increased from 33,131 in 1790 to 202,589 in 1825.

8. Gilje, *The Road to Mobocracy,* 239 (also 135–213). The best brief account of the transformation of early-nineteenth-century New York is Stansell, *City of Women,* 4–10.

9. Blackmar, *Manhattan for Rent,* 170–172. According to Blackmar, the poor "used the streets as a common landscape" that provided an opportunity for unregulated, spontaneous encounters with others, encounters that made it possible for them "to gain or supplement subsistence by peddling fruits, oysters, hardware, used clothing, or sexual favors" (or by scavenging, gambling, shoplifting or fencing stolen goods). "No less than foraging on rural common land, the 'liberty' of the streets supported the city's poorest residents." See also 41–42.

10. See, for example, letter of Dec. 17, 1828, in Pintard, *Letters,* III, 51–52.

11. Oct. 28, 1818, in Pintard, *Letters,* I, 151. For the Society for the Prevention of Pauperism, see Stansell, *City of Women,* 30–36 (also 18, 71, 164), and Mohl, *Poverty in New York,* ch. 5. The S.P.P.'s purposes included the discouragement and "prevention of mendicity and street begging"; the group argued that existing relief policies only served to encourage laziness and dependence on charity (Mohl, *Poverty in New York,* 245). Pintard himself wrote that the S.P.P. was intended to stem the growth of "the present system of relieving the poor," by providing "not . . . alms but labor, so that there shall be no pretext for idleness," and "to expel the drones from society." (Pintard, *Letters,* I, 151.)

12. Dec. 16, 1828, ibid., III, 51–52.

13. This item was actually printed as a broadside: "The following piece, which was desired to be inserted in the New-York Journal of this Day, Dec. 24, 1772, but omitted for want of room, will be inserted next Week."

14. Gilje, *The Road to Mobocracy,* 130–133, 253–260. See also Susan G. Davis, " 'Making Night Hideous': Christmas Revelry and Public Order in Nineteenth-Century Philadelphia," *American Quarterly,* 34, No. 2 (Summer 1982), 185–199; esp. 186–192. This is the best study of the battle for Christmas in a nineteenth-century city. See also Susan G. Davis, *Parades and Power: Street Theatre in Nineteenth-Century Philadelphia* (Philadelphia: Temple University Press, 1986), 38–39, 76–78, 103–109, 158–159.

15. Ibid., 255. The mayor was Philip Hone. In 1837 Hone recorded in his diary a New Year's Day scene at the house of a subsequent mayor: "[T]he rabble . . . use his house as a Five Points tavern. . . . [T]he scene . . . defies description . . . the tables were taken by storm, the bottles [of wine and punch] emptied in a moment. Confusion, noise, and quarreling ensued, until the Mayor, with the assistance of his police, cleared the house and locked the doors. . . . Every scamp . . . considers himself authorized to use him and his house and his furniture at his pleasure; to wear his hat in his presence, to smoke and spit upon his carpet, to devour his beef and turkey, and wipe his greasy fingers upon the curtains, to get drunk with his liquor. . . ." Hone suggests that similar scenes had happened before. Allan Nevins, ed., *The Diary of Philip Hone, 1828–1851* (2 vols., New York, 1927), I, 235–236).

16. Quoted in Gilje, *The Road to Mobocracy,* 254.

17. *New York Advertiser,* Jan. 4, 1828; Gilje, *The Road to Mobocracy,* 257–259; Luc Sante, *Low Life: Lures and Snares of New York* (New York: Farrar, Straus & Giroux, 1991), 341–342.

18. Davis, *Parades and Power,* 108; Gilje, *The Road to Mobocracy,* 260.

19. May 27, 1823, in Pintard, *Letters,* II, 137–138.

20. Charles Jones, "Knickerbocker Santa Claus," *New-York Historical Society Quarterly* 38 (1954), 356–383 (see 367–371).

21. Ibid., 370–371.

22. For example, see Dec. 18, 1827, in Pintard, *Letters,* II, 382.

23. Dec. 16, 1827, in Pintard, *Letters,* II, 382.

24. Dec. 16, 1827, ibid., II, 382; Jan. 2, 1828, ibid., III, I.

25. For the St. Nicholas Day banquets, see Pintard, *Letters,* I, 38 (1816); I, 156 (1818). For New Year's Day, see ibid., I, 44 (1817); I, 161 (1819); I, 358–359 (1821); II, 117 (1822); II, 320, 324 (1827); III, 1 (1828); III, 117 (1830). In 1832 Pintard anonymously published in the *New York Mirror* (Dec. 29, 1832, 207) an essay lamenting the decline of New Year's open houses among the New York elite and attributing it to the nouveaux riches. (This anonymous essay was brought to my attention by Elizabeth Blackmar.) Pintard's authorship is indicated ibid., IV, 114–115, 117.

26. Eric J. Hobsbawm and Terence Ranger, eds., *The Invention of Tradition* (Cambridge: Cambridge University Press, 1983). Anthropologists have dubbed this phenomenon, rather meanly and a little unfairly, *fakelore* (as distinct from more authentic *folklore*).

27. J. M. Golby and A. W. Purdue, *The Making of the Modern Christmas* (Athens, Ga: University of Georgia Press, 1986), 43.

28. "Keeping Christmas," *Mirror of Literature, Amusement, and Instruction* 10 (1825), 514–518. (This magazine, published in Boston, reprinted British material.) Another essay on the same topic simply argued that the old rural Christmas was a complete bore! "A Country Christmas," ibid. 5 (1823), 168–172.

29. For Christmas as a day of prayer, see Pintard, *Letters,* I, 356 (1820); II, 114 (1821); II, 210 (1825). For "St. Claas": ibid., II, 384 (1827); III, 53–540 (1828); III, 115 (1829); III, 206 (1830); III, 305 (1831); IV, 116 (1832).

30. While Pintard's basic Santa Claus ritual remained essentially the same after he first devised it, Pintard did continue to tinker with the details. In 1827–29, the family's presents were placed in stockings hung by the chimney, but in 1830 they were placed on a table. The presents themselves changed, too: candies and fruit at first; toys were added in 1828 (a drum), and in 1832 the toys were replaced with books (because toys "cost much and are soon broken").

31. There were allusions to St. Nicholas' Day in 1773 and 1774, but Jones explains these in reference to the American Revolution (i.e., as a patriotic alternative to St. George's Day), and not as precursors of the St. Nicholas cult that would develop a generation later. Jones, "Knickerbocker Santa Claus," 362–364.

32. Ibid., 376. In another study Jones even suggests that the Dutch themselves took up the St. Nicholas cult from America—in the twentieth century, and largely for the sake of the tourist trade: Charles W. Jones, *St. Nicholas of Myra, Bari, and Manhattan: Biography of a Legend* (Chicago: University of Chicago Press, 1978), 307–308.

33. Washington Irving, *A History of New York* (2d ed., 2 vols., New York, 1812), vol. I, 247 (Book 4, ch. 5).

34. Jan. 15, 1822, in Pintard, *Letters,* II, 121–122.

35. Irving, *History of New York* (1812 ed.), vol. I, 116 (Book 4, chs. 5–6); "with characteristic slowness. . . ." appears only in the first edition (N.Y., 1809), vol. I, 116 (Book 2, ch. 5); Irving deleted the passage in the 1812 edition. For a somewhat later (and highly self-conscious) expression of this same Knickerbocker enterprise, see James K. Paulding, *The Book of Saint Nicholas, translated from the Original Dutch* (New York, 1836), a "biography" of the saint, dedicated to the St. Nicholas Society of New York, and with a preface dated "Nieuw Amsterdam, 1827." See also Peter H. Myers, *The Young Patroon; or, Christmas in 1690. A Tale of New-York* (New York, 1849).

36. Sean Wilentz terms Moore a "level-headed Episcopalian conservative." (See *Chants Democratic,* 79.) The only book-length study of Moore, short and hagiographic, is Samuel W. Patterson, *The Poet of Christmas Eve: A Life of Clement Clarke Moore, 1779–1863* (New York: Morehouse-Gorham Co., 1956). For Moore's ancestral background (and the Tory sympathies of his family), see 22–29, 31–36, 48–51. His wife—they married in 1813—was a member of the Cortland family (64–66). For information on Moore's slaves, see 5, 48. The political tracts Moore published include *Observations upon Certain Passages in Mr. Jefferson's Notes on Virginia* (New York, 1804), a critique of Jefferson's irreligion; and *A Sketch of Our Political Condition* (New York, 1813), condemning the Jefferson and Madison administrations (and the War of 1812) for their destruction of rural life! A shorter biographical sketch is Arthur N. Hosking, "The Life of Clement Clarke Moore," appended to the 1934 reprint of a facsimile edition of Moore's "A Visit from St. Nicholas" (New York, 1934).

37. Moore's professorship initially paid a token $750, a figure that eventually increased to $2,000. See Patterson, *The Poet of Christmas Eve,* 77–79.

38. Hosking, "Life of Moore," 23.

39. April 8, 1830, in Pintard, *Letters,* III, 137. For Moore's wealth, see Charles Lockwood, *Manhattan Moves Uptown: An Illustrated History* (Boston: Houghton Mifflin, 1976), 205; Patterson, *Poet of Christmas Eve,* 106–110.

40. Isaac N. Phelps Stokes, *The Iconography of Manhattan Island, 1498–1909* (6 vols., New York, 1915–28), vol. 5, 1602. Moore writes of eminent domain in *A Plain Statement, Addressed to the Proprietors of Real Estate in the City and County of New-York* (New York, 1818), 13–18. A few years later, the city made plans to fill in an area under the Hudson River, in the process moving the river away from Moore's estate. (Phelps Stokes, *Iconography,* vol. 5, 1603). By the 1830s some of that land was occupied by the Manhattan Gas-light Works, a company that was installing street lights in that area of the city, and digging a network of underground pipes in order to do so. (See *New York As It Is* [New York, 1837], 14.)

41. *Longworth's City Directory* (New York, 1821), 315.

42. Nov. 3, 1832, in Pintard, *Letters,* IV, 106. By the end of the 1820s, the area that had come to be known as Chelsea Square was home to a substantial population, much of it poor and/or immigrant. By the 1830s Moore was watching Irishmen on St. Patrick's Day marching along the periphery of his property—down Twenty-third Street, then turning south on Eighth Avenue. See Patterson, *Poet of Christmas Eve,* 92–93. Like most of the men who owned great uptown estates, Clement Clarke Moore erected fences around his property.

43. Hosking, "Life of Moore," 28–31.

44. Moore, *Plain Statement,* 6, 12, 39, 62. Elizabeth Blackmar shrewdly suggests that Moore's complaint was based on his understanding that New York's urban development actually functioned as a public-works program to provide jobs for the poor and the unemployed—a program Moore opposed (Blackmar, *Manhattan for Rent,* 162–163). Cartmen, whom Moore singled out for criticism, had developed a reputation for especially rude and surly behavior by 1820, breaking speed limits and running down pedestrians—much like the modern taxi drivers who partly replaced them. See Graham Hodges, *New York City Cartmen, 1667–1850* (New York: New York University Press, 1986), 116–117, 127. Hodges indicates that many wealthy New Yorkers chose to move out of downtown New York after being awakened regularly by the sound of "hundreds of cartmen racing their vehicles at dawn" (p. 121). In the late 1820s Moore was actually planning to move out of Chelsea to a still-rural area of Manhattan several miles to the north; he changed his mind only when his wife died in 1830. In 1839 Moore purchased an estate up the Hudson River at Sing Sing, and in 1850 he rented a house in Newport, Rhode Island, where he spent his remaining summers. Patterson, *The Poet of Christmas Eve,* 93–94, 149–150.

45. Irving, *A History of New York,* vol. 1, 120 (Book 2, ch. 7); see also 454, 639, 655.

46. *The Children's Friend* (New York, 1821).

47. Irving, *A History of New York* (1812 ed.), vol. 1, 253 (Book 4, ch. 6: "ease, tranquillity"; vol. 1, 246 (Book 4, ch. 5: "meddlesome and fractious"); vol. 1, 254 (Book 4, ch. 6: "long pipes . . . short pipes"). Irving introduced the story of the "pipe plot" only in the 1812 edition.

48. Lauren J. Cook, "Snow White Little Instruments of Comfort: Clay Pipes and Class Consciousness at the Boott Mills Boarding Houses," a paper delivered at a meeting of the New England Historical Association, Lowell, Massachusetts, April 21, 1989. There was a practical reason for workers' use of short pipes: they made it possible to smoke while working. But what may have begun as a practical necessity became, by the nineteenth century, a political gesture. By the same token, smoking a long pipe became an *assertion* as well as a sign of genteel leisure (as, for example, the long pipes in Washington Irving's "Rip Van Winkle").

49. "Southwark Watchman's Address for Christmas Day, Dec. 25, 1829" (Philadelphia, 1829), Broadside collection, American Antiquarian Society. Coincidentally, even the meter (of the odd lines, at least) is identical to that of "A Visit from St. Nicholas."

50. Among some British Jews today, I have been told, the gesture still thrives, signifying *stumm!*, or "hush."

51. *New York Sun*, Sept. 21, 1897.

52. Patterson, *Poet of Christmas Eve*, 99–101.

53. Blackmar, *Manhattan for Rent*, 195–196. See also Lockwood, *Manhattan Moves Uptown*, 205. John Pintard made the same point in 1832; see letter of Nov. 3, 1832, in Pintard, *Letters*, IV, 106.

54. Blackmar, *Manhattan for Rent*, passim.

Chapter 3

1. *New-York American* [for the country], Jan. 4, 1822.

2. *New-York Weekly Commercial Advertiser*, Jan. 3, 1823. Stone added that such a change would also provide the "young ladies" who hosted the visits with "an opportunity for a contest of skill in making coffee."

3. "Sainte Claus," in *New-York Evening Post*, Dec. 26, 1820 (this poem was reprinted from the *Northern Whig*).

4. "Ode to Saint Claas, Written on a New Year's Eve," *New York Advertiser*, Jan. 4, 1828 and *New-York American*, Jan. 4, 1828.

5. For another example of Santa as Lord of Misrule, see Francis H. Davidge, "Christmas Is Coming," in T. S. Arthur, ed., *The Brilliant* (New York, 1850), 22–26. This sketch was apparently written by a Southerner, and it was in the South that Santa Claus continued for decades to be described as a "trickster." See, for example, Joel Chandler Harris, "Something About 'Sandy Claus' ": ch. 7, *On the Plantation: A Story of a Georgia Boy's Adventures During the War* (New York, 1892), 104–121, in which a pair of slaves describe Santa Claus as a kind of Brer Rabbit figure.

6. *New-York Advertiser*, Jan. 4, 1828. This was the same callithumpian parade described in Chapter 2 (pp. 54–55).

7. *New-York American*, Dec. 28, 1827.

8. Ibid., Dec. 30, 1828. A year later the same newspaper came out in favor of excluding alcohol from the New Year's visitation ritual (ibid., see letter appearing Jan. 1, 1830).

9. Eliza C. Follen, "Life of Charles Follen," *The Works of Charles Follen* (5 vols., Boston, 1842), I, 562.

10. *New York Morning Herald,* Dec. 25, 1839. The theater at which "Santiclaus" appeared was the Broadway Circus, perhaps the only New York theater that was still attracting a "mixed"-class audience at this time. See also *New York Tattler,* Dec. 27, 1839. These items were brought to my attention by Dale Cockrell.

11. *New York Daily Herald,* Dec. 23, 1839.

12. Dec. 26, 1848, in Allan Nevins and Milton Halsey Thomas, eds., *Diary of George Templeton Strong* (4 vols., New York: Macmillan, 1952), I, 338–339.

13. *New-York Tribune,* Dec. 23, 1850. The paper went on to suggest that these gangs had the tacit support of politicians (presumably from Tammany Hall).

14. *New-York Tribune,* Jan. 3, 1852. For a survey of riots in nineteenth-century New York, see Luc Sante, *Low Life: Lures and Snares of New York* (New York: Farrar, Straus & Giroux, 1991), 339–356, a chapter bearing the apt title "Carnival."

15. *New-York Tribune,* Jan. 3, 1852.

16. See also the *New-York American* for Dec. 26 and 30, 1840, juxtaposing riot reports (in one column) with an upbeat editorial (in another) about Christmas shopping and "the merry days [of] childhood and youth."

17. Samuel Taylor Coleridge, "Christmas at Ratzeburg," in *The Friend* (Burlington, Vermont, 1831), 322. Coleridge continues: "About seven or eight years old the children are let into the secret, and it is curious how faithfully they keep it!" Readers who studied the piano as children may recall "Knecht Ruprecht" as the title of a mock-scary piece from Robert Schumann's "Album for the Young." In Alsace, a similar figure was named Hanstrap.

18. *Pennsylvania Gazette,* Dec. 29, 1827; quoted in Alfred Shoemaker, *Christmas in Pennsylvania: A Folk-Cultural Study* (Kutztown: Penn. Folklore Society, 1959), 74.

19. Ibid., 74–75.

20. See, for example, P. E. Gibbons, "The Pennsylvania Dutch," *Atlantic Monthly,* Oct. 1869, 484; quoted ibid., 76.

21. Diary of James L. Morris (from Montgomery, Penn.); quoted ibid., 74.

22. *Pottstown Lafayette Aurora,* Dec. 21, 1826; quoted ibid., 73–74.

23. Morris diary entry, Dec. 24, 1844, quoted ibid., 74; *Norristown Herald and Free Press,* Dec. 31, 1851; *Lancaster Daily Evening Express,* Dec. 26, 1873; *Carlisle Herald,* Jan. 2, 1873; all quoted Shoemaker, *Christmas in Pennsylvania,* 77.

24. *Reading Berks and Schuylkill Journal,* Dec. 27, 1851; *Norristown Olive Branch,* Dec. 31, 1853; *Easton Daily Express,* Dec. 27, 1858 (all quoted Shoemaker, *Christmas in Pennsylvania,* 76).

25. *Pottstown Ledger,* Dec. 26, 1873; quoted ibid., 77.

26. Susan G. Davis, " 'Making Night Hideous': Christmas Revelry and Public Order in Nineteenth-Century Philadelphia," *American Quarterly* 34 (1982), 185–199 (quotation from 190–191).

27. *Philadelphia Daily Chronicle,* Dec. 26, 1833; quoted Shoemaker, *Christmas in Pennsylvania,* 86; partly quoted in Susan G. Davis, *Parades and Power: Street Theater in Nineteenth-Century Philadelphia* (Philadelphia: Temple University Press, 1986), 81.

28. *Philadelphia Public Ledger,* Dec. 27, 1839.

29. Davis, " 'Making Night Hideous,' " 191.

30. *Philadelphia Public Ledger,* Dec. 25, 1839.

31. Ibid., Dec. 27, 1848. On Dec. 30, 1856, Philadelphia patrician Sidney Fisher noted in his diary that he had "[h]ad trouble with our servants—cook and waiter got drunk this afternoon & I was obliged to have the police to take them away." Nicholas B. Wain-

wright, *A Philadelphia Perspective: The Diary of Sidney George Fisher Covering the Years 1834–1871* (Philadelphia: Historical Society of Pennsylvania, 1967), 264.

32. *Philadelphia Public Ledger,* Dec. 25, 1844. Or take Sidney Fisher: On Christmas Day, 1840, that patrician "ate pretty well & drank claret, champagne & Madeira [at dinner], again at supper drank Burgundy, Madeira & whiskey punch, besides 4 cigars at home." Diary entry, Dec. 26, 1840, in Wainwright, *A Philadelphia Perspective,* 108.

33. For the open shops, see, for example, the 1841 column of Christmas Day amusements: "[W]e briefly note below where are kept and may be obtained the good things prepared for the times, the large use of which is part of the performances of the day." Although "businesses" were reported closed, that term apparently referred to large-scale financial and manufacturing enterprises.

34. *Nile's National Register,* Jan. 1, 1842, 288 (this item was brought to my attention by Carol Sherif). See also *Philadelphia Public Ledger,* Dec. 27, 1843, and Dec. 25 and 27, 1844. These promenades may have been a source of Edgar Allan Poe's story "The Man of the Crowd," a dark tale about a man who gets swept up in a vast crowd while promenading through the streets of a large city. The story (set in London, which Poe had never seen) was published in 1840, after the first Christmas Poe spent in Philadelphia.

35. *Philadelphia Public Ledger,* Dec. 27, 1841 ("struggling and jostling"); Dec. 26, 1842 ("the whole city").

36. Ibid., Dec. 27, 1843 ("more drunken men and boys"); Dec. 25 and 27, 1844. Philadelphia was not the only city in which regular public rituals were burlesqued. In New York, the military companies that marched out of the city each Christmas Day on the way to target-shooting were burlesqued by similar bands of "fantasticals."

37. *Philadelphia Public Ledger,* Dec. 27, 1845; Dec. 25, 1846.

38. In 1801 *Poulson's American Daily Advertiser* carried a watchman's address asking for money (Dec. 25, 1801). But in 1802 the same newspaper published a warning, under the heading "Christmas Reflections," urging religious piety instead of revelry and excess—at least on Christmas Day itself: "Pause—ye giddy and ye gay. . . . Forego, for *one* day at least, the resplendent and fascinating charms of dissipation." (Ibid., Dec. 25, 1802.)

39. The four almanacs: "Citizens & Farmers' Almanack for . . . 1825" (Philadelphia, [1824]); "Grigg's Almanack, for . . . 1825" (Philadelphia, [1824]); "New Brunswick Almanack, for 1825" (Philadelphia, [1824]); and "The United States National Almanac" (Philadelphia, 1825). The newspapers: *Saturday Evening Post,* Dec. 23, 1826; *National Gazette,* Dec. 24, 1827 (Moore poem); *Poulson's,* Dec. 26, 1827 (Bracebridge Hall). The "Bracebridge Hall" extract was a passage defining Christmas as "the season for gathering together of family connections. . . ."

40. *Poulson's,* Dec. 24, 1828; *National Gazette,* Dec. 26, 1828; *Poulson's,* Dec. 26, 1829 (Santa Claus ritual)); *National Gazette,* Dec. 24, 1830.

41. Nathaniel Whittemore (Boston, 1719), lines opposite Dec. 18–21; Henry Dwight Sedgwick to Theodore Sedgwick, manuscript letter, Dec. 24, 1805, in Sedgwick Family Papers V (Massachusetts Historical Society), Box 2.13; *Boston Daily Advertiser,* Dec. 22, 1818; John Pintard to his daughter, Dec. 16, 1827, in *Letters from John Pintard,* vol. 2, 382; *New-York Tribune,* Jan. 2, 1854. For comparison, here is the text of a wassail sung by young people in England: "We are not daily beggars / That beg from door to door, / But we are neighbors' children, / Whom you have seen before. . . . / We have got a little purse / Made of stretching leather skin, / We want a little of your money / To line it well within." (Quoted Ashton, *Right Merrie Christmasse,* 111–112.)

42. See, for instance, John R. Gillis, *Youth and History: Tradition and Change in European Age Relations, 1770–Present* (New York: Academic Press, 1974); for an American version, see John Demos, *A Little Commonwealth: Family Life in Plymouth Colony* (New York: Oxford University Press, 1970). Phillipe Aries, *Centuries of Childhood: A Social History of*

Family Life (New York: Knopf, 1962), shows brilliantly how this began to change in the seventeenth century among the European aristocracy and nobility.

43. The ritual had reached America by the middle of the eighteenth century. A little broadside printed in 1765 or 1766 (probably in Boston) contains the following short verse, written by a blacksmith's apprentice: "This is unto all GENTLEMEN who shoes [sic]] here, / I wish you a merry Christmas, a happy New Year: / For shoeing your Horses, and trimming their Locks, / Please to remember my New-Years Box." (This is catalogued as Bristol #B2818; S-M41768; Ford #137. Ford says it was "probably" printed in New England because it was found together with other New England material.) For the history of Christmas boxes, see Ashton, *A Right Merrie Christmasse,* 202–204 (Samuel Pepys and Jonathan Swift); see also J. A. R. Pimlott, *The Englishman's Christmas: A Social History* (Sussex, England: Harvester Press, 1978), 72–73.

44. *Nurse Truelove's Christmas Box* (Worcester, Mass., 1786 [and several times thereafter]); Emily E. F. Skeel, *Mason Locke Weems, His Work and Ways* (3 vols., New York, 1929), III, 29. An advertisement headed "Christmas Box" appeared in the *New-York Evening Post,* Dec. 24, 1802.

45. Both volumes were originally printed in Boston in 1747. The former was reprinted six more times by 1804; a last edition appeared in 1824.

46. *A Present to Children* (New London, 1783); *Present for Misses* (Worcester: I. Thomas, 1794); *A Present for a Little Boy* (Philadelphia, 1802); *A Present for a Little Girl* (Philadelphia, 1804).

47. "How am I pleas'd with painted toys? / I feed the foolish fire: / Trifles and fashions cover my eyes / And cheat my warm desire. / On jointed babes [i.e., dolls] I fix my hope. / In my fond arms carest; / I dress the mimic-puppets up, / And hug them to my breast." (*A Present to Children* [New London, Conn., 1783], 9.)

48. *Boston Daily Advertiser,* Dec. 22, 1818. This letter is also discussed in Chapter 1.

49. Rex Cathcart, "Festive Capers? Barring-Out the Schoolmaster," *History Today* 38 (Dec. 1988), 49–53. Cathcart suggests that barring-out may have begun as a substitute for the earlier inversion ritual known as the "Boy-Bishop," which was suppressed at about the same time. See also Keith Thomas, *Rule and Misrule in the Schools of Early Modern England* (Reading, England: University of Reading Press, 1976). For barring-out in England, see Maria Edgeworth, "The Barring Out" (Philadelphia, 1804); Brand, *Popular English Antiquities,* I, 441–434; and Ona and Peter Opie, *The Lore and Language of Children* (Oxford, England, 1959).

50. "The Further Affidavit of James Blair . . . ," in William S. Perry, ed., *Historical Collections Relating to the American Colonial Church* (2 vols., Hartford, 1870), I, 137–138. Virginia was also the site of an apparently more peaceful barring-out much later in the same century. A Northern visitor noted in his diary on Dec. 18, 1773, that "Mr Goodlet was barr'd out of his School last Monday by his Scholars, for the Christmas Holidays, which are to continue til twelfth-day. . . ." (Hunter Dickinson Farish, ed., *The Journal and Letters of Philip Vickers Fithian* [Williamsburg, Va., 1943], entry for Dec. 18, 1773, 34.)

51. *Philadelphia Democratic Press,* Dec. 18, 1810; quoted Shoemaker, *Christmas in Pennsylvania,* 24. Another Pennsylvanian, writing later in the century, recalled the custom from his childhood in the 1850s: "The windows were nailed fast, one and all; the benches were dragged from all parts of the room and piled against the door,—a long row extending to the stove, as a prop. . . . For one brief hour the scholars were master,—the tables turned, as it were, and riot ran high and wild." (Charles H. Miller, *Lykens Twenty Years Ago* (Lykens, Pa., 1876), 13; quoted ibid., 27.)

52. Horace Greeley, *Recollections of a Busy Life* (New York, 1868), 43–44. For an Indiana example from the 1830s, reported in vivid detail, see *A Home in the Woods: Oliver Johnson's Reminiscences of Early Marion County, as Related by Howard Johnson* (Blooming-

ton: Indiana University Press, [1951]), 56–64. (This item was brought to my attention by Burton Bledstein.)

53. For background on school culture in New England, see Robert A. Gross, *An Age of Revolution* (forthcoming, Hill & Wang), ch. 3. Barring-out presumably died off later in the century, as Christmas vacations became an official part of the school calendar rather than something negotiated ad hoc by the schoolboys themselves (and as the teaching profession itself became professionalized—and feminized). Even in colleges, a similar custom may have been practiced, although by the nineteenth century it more generally took the form of students simply leaving the campus at Christmastime, sometimes with the encouragement of the faculty. (See *Diary of George Templeton Strong*, Dec. 22–23, 1835, I, 8–9.) But students at Yale were engaging in an annual Christmas Eve "Callithumpian anniversary" during the 1830s and 1840s: Late at night, "painted and masked, wearing all sorts of hideous and fantastic dresses; some having drums, some tin kettles, some horns," they would march through New Haven, "carrying devastation and ruin wherever they go, levelling fences, breaking windows, destroying the unfortunate barrels of whiskey, which may happen to be exposed. . . ." (An extended account of this ritual appeared in the *New York Herald*, Dec. 30, 1837.) After the 1847 callithumpian parade, one Yale student was actually indicted for attempted murder (*Hampshire Gazette* [Northampton, Mass.], Dec. 28, 1847, and Feb. 8, 1848).

54. See Seba Smith, "Yankee Christmas," in *'Way Down East; or, Portraitures of Yankee Life* (New York, 1854), 29–52; previously printed in the *New York [Weekly] Herald*, Dec. 24, 1842. See also "Doesticks' Description of the Christmas Party at His Friend Medary's," in *Frank Leslie's Illustrated Newspaper*, Jan. 2, 1858, 75.

55. Eliza Leslie, "Snow-Balling; or, The Christmas Dollar," in *The Violet* (Philadelphia, 1839 [c. 1838]), 36–52.

56. *New York American*, Dec. 26, 1840. An exemplary study of Philadelphia's "mechanics" during these years is Bruce Laurie, *Working People of Philadelphia, 1800–1850* (Philadelphia: Temple University Press, 1980).

57. "Christmas Eve," in *Christmas Blossoms, and New Year's Wreath for 1850* (Philadelphia, 1850), 38–39.

58. *Christmas Holidays; or, A Visit at Home* (Philadelphia [American Sunday School Union], [1827]), 19–20.

59. Lydia Maria Child, *The Girl's Own Book* (Boston, 1833), iv.

60. This is not the only such example. The American Antiquarian Society's copy of Robin Carver, *The Book of Sports* (Boston, 1834) is inscribed on its flyleaf with the date "Jan. 1st, 1835."

61. *New-York Daily Advertiser*, Dec. 26. 1817; *New-York Daily Advertiser*, Dec. 24, 1824). See also an ad in the *New England Palladium*, 1822–23, for "instructive games on cloth, with te-totems." A *te-totum* was a top.

62. *Cincinnati Daily Gazette*, Dec. 23, 1844.

63. Ibid., Dec. 23, 1845.

64. *Liberty Hall and Cincinnati Gazette*, Dec. 24, 1821; *New England Galaxy*, Dec. 26, 1823.

65. Quotations from Claire McGlinchee, *The First Decade of the Boston Museum* (Boston: Bruce Humphries, Inc., 1940), 132. See also A. E. Wilson, *Christmas Pantomime, the Story of an English Institution* (London, 1934; reprinted as *King Panto; the Story of Pantomime* [New York: E. P. Dutton, 1935]); R. J. Broadbent, *A History of Pantomime* (London, 1901). McGlinchee writes that "[t]his type of entertainment was superseded by the Christmas show, a queer medley of burlesque, musical comedy, fairy play, and revue. The term 'pantomime' was kept, even though dialogue had been introduced."

66. For a good description of theater as a "male club" (and the mid-nineteenth-century effort to transform it into "respectable" family fare), see Richard Butsch, "Bowery B'hoys and Matinee Ladies: The Re-Gendering of Nineteenth-Century American Theater Audiences," *American Quarterly* 46 (1994), 374–405.

67. *New York Weekly Herald,* Dec. 30, 1837; *New York [Daily] Herald,* Dec. 26, 1844.

68. Ibid. The tickets had probably been purchased for the newsboys by their employers, as a Christmas present. See *Brother Jonathan,* Holiday Extras dated Jan. 1, 1843, and Dec. 25–Jan. 1, 1844 (which reported that they had gone to the Chatham Theater).

69. The best account of the newsboys' love of theater is in an 1852 novel by Elizabeth Oakes Smith, *The Newsboy* (New York, 1854), 25–33, from which I have taken some of my description. See also *Tom Brice, the News-boy* (New York, 1862), 4–5; and Charles Loring Brace, *The Dangerous Classes of New York, and Twenty Years' Work Among Them* (New York, 1872), 345–346.

70. *Philadelphia Public Ledger,* Dec. 25, 1844.

71. For this quotation and those in the following paragraph, see ibid., Dec. 27, 1843.

72. Ibid., Dec. 25, 1845.

73. Ibid., Dec. 24, 1845.

74. *Kriss Kringle's Book* (Philadelphia, 1845), 6. The title of the book is—deliberately—malleable. The cloth cover reads "Kriss Kringle's Book," and that title is repeated at the very end of the preface. But the title page itself reads "St. Nicholas's Book," and that is the way the book is referred to at *another* point in the preface. When the book was reprinted in 1846 the title page read "The Christmas Book," while a third printing, in 1852, read "Kriss Kringle's Book."

75. *Kriss Kringle's Christmas Tree: A Holliday* [sic] *Present for Boys and Girls* (Philadelphia, 1845), 77 ("sword or drum"); *Kriss Kringle's Raree Show, for Good Boys and Girls* (Philadelphia, 1845).

76. *Oxford English Dictionary* (definition of *raree show*).

77. *Kriss Kringle's Raree Show,* 5.

78. The socially disruptive, subversive potential of books (especially fiction and romance) was well recognized in the early nineteenth century (critics employed virtually all the same arguments that are used today against children's watching television). Novels were even written to warn their readers about the dangers of reading other novels! In one novella, published in 1824 and set during the Christmas vacation from school, the parents keep their collection of books in a locked bookcase, and a series of mishaps is set off when the mother is obliged to entrust the key to her oldest daughter. ([Lucy Lyttleton Cameron,] *The Sister's Friend; or, Christmas Holidays Spent at Home* [Boston, 1824]).

Chapter 4

1. John Birge manuscript Daybook (Pocumtuck Valley Memorial Association Library), p. 89. This reference was discovered by Carrie Giard, an undergraduate student at the University of Massachusetts. Carrie also discovered that two years later, in 1771, another Deerfield shopkeeper paid one of his clients 10½ shillings "cash at Christmas" in return for "four days [i.e., of labor] at Christmas." (We can only speculate as to why this man desired to have cash at Christmas.) John Russell manuscript Account Book (Pocumtuck Valley Memorial Association Library), pp. 153–154.

2. Harriet Beecher Stowe, "Christmas; or, The Good Fairy," in *National Era* 4 (Dec. 26, 1850). This was the same magazine in which Stowe was shortly to begin serial publication of her novel *Uncle Tom's Cabin.* The story was later reprinted in *The Mayflower, and Miscellaneous Writings* (Boston, 1855); it did not appear in the original (1842) edition of that volume. For scholarly works that date the commercialization of Christmas to the turn

of the twentieth century, see William B. Waits, *The Modern Christmas in America: A Cultural History of Gift Giving* (New York: New York University Press, 1993); and, implicitly, William Leach, *Land of Desire: Merchants, Power, and the Rise of a New American Culture* (New York: Pantheon, 1993); as well as James H. Barnett, *The American Christmas: A Study in National Culture* (New York: Macmillan, 1954), 79–101. This interpretation is part of a larger analysis that places the emergence of modern American consumer culture in the decades 1880–1920. See, for example, Simon J. Bronner, ed., *Consuming Visions: Accumulation and Display of Goods in America, 1880–1920* (New York: W.W. Norton & Co., 1989); Richard Wightman Fox and T. J. Jackson Lears, eds., *The Culture of Consumption: Critical Essays in American History, 1880–1980* (New York: Pantheon, 1983). For a recent reevaluation (and one that deals with the "carnivalesque" as well), see Jackson Lears, *Fables of Abundance: A Cultural History of Advertising in America* (New York: Basic Books, 1994), chs. 1–5. But another historiographical strain dates the origins of the consumer revolution far earlier, even to the middle of the eighteenth century; see page 340, note 16.

3. *Salem Gazette,* Dec. 18, 1806; *New-York Evening Post,* Dec. 26, 1808. Philadelphia's first ad for Christmas presents came in 1812. If we include ads for "New Year's Presents"—or "Holiday Presents"—this dating needs to be moved back a decade or two earlier. Salem came in in 1804, two years before the ad that named Christmas. (It was placed on Dec. 21, 1804—four days before Christmas—by the same bookseller. Headed simply "Elegant Presents for Children," it was followed on January 1 by a similar ad headed "Elegant New Year's Presents for Children." It is as if this bookseller was testing the cultural waters before actually daring to name Christmas.) But Salem was not the first American community to advertise New Year's gifts. The first community to do so was another New England town, Worcester, Massachusetts, in 1783 (more about Worcester a little later). New York followed in 1789; Philadelphia, in 1796; Boston, in 1801. *Salem Gazette,* Dec. 21, 1804, and Jan. 1, 1805. Other New England examples: Amherst, New Hampshire, in 1811; Portsmouth, New Hampshire, in 1816.

4. "Christmas and New Year's Presents," in *New England Galaxy and Masonic Magazine,* Dec. 26, 1823. By 1825 the same periodical was able to claim that Christmas was a season "which custom from time immemorial has pointed out as a proper one for giving and receiving remembrances, and tokens of affection" (ibid., Dec. 23, 1825).

5. E.N.T., "Christmas and New Year's Presents," *Christian Register,* Dec. 20, 1834. In Worcester, Massachusetts, one man noted in his diary on Christmas Eve: "[G]eneral preparation for Christmas: the children must have presents and the parents, uncles, and aunts are all getting them." (Levi Lincoln Newton Diaries, 1837–1843, in manuscript collection, American Antiquarian Society.)

6. *Farmer's Cabinet* (Amherst, N.H.), Jan. 2, 1835. The story urged children to buy books rather than candy for the holidays.

7. The same pattern is true of ads labeled "New Year's" or "holiday" gifts. Worcester, Massachusetts (1783): "New Year's Gifts [all of them books] for Children"; New York (1789): books "for young gentlemen and ladies"; Boston (1801): "Books for Young Persons"; Portsmouth, New Hampshire (1816) "Juvenile books, suitable for To-morrow [New Year's Day]."

8. In contrast, I have found only a single advertisement that advertised presents for servants. During the 1822 Christmas season, one Boston bookstore, after advertising a great variety of books and games for children of various ages, added that it also had "a large collection of Narratives, Popular Stories, &c., very cheap and neat editions, suitable for presents to Domestics and others." (*New England Palladium,* Jan. 3, 1823.) The 1820s may have been the last decade in which such an ad could reasonably appear; after that, servants would not have been considered real members of the household. (Conversely, the early 1820s were also virtually the *first* time such an ad could have appeared; only a decade or two earlier, *nobody* would have received a commercial Christmas present.) In January 1820, a prosperous New York woman recorded spending "2.6" [2s. 6d.?] for "N[ew] Year presents

to servants." The following December the same woman made a similar entry: "New Year presents to servants[:] 1.56." [Jane Minot Sedgwick?], Accounts and Commonplace Book, 1817–59, in Miscellaneous Sedgwick Papers (Massachusetts Historical Society), vol. 16.

9. *New-York Herald,* Dec. 23, 1839; *New-York American,* Dec. 27, 1841; see also *New-York Tribune,* Jan. 3, 1844.

10. In 1844, the first Christmas ads in the *New-York Tribune* appeared as early as December 12.

11. [Philadelphia] *National Gazette,* Dec. 24, 1841.

12. *Philadelphia Public Ledger,* Dec. 25, 1841.

13. The idea probably originated in New York, where one paper reported in 1838 that "[f]our or five mammoth cakes have been made in this city to be cut up on New Year's Eve. That at Ameli's, 395 Broadway, is the largest ever made in this city. It weighs about 3300 pounds, and is worth $1500" (*New York Weekly Herald,* Dec. 22, 1838). But even as early as 1819, a New York baker advertised a "mammoth cake . . . weighing 300 pounds" (*New York Evening Post,* Dec. 28, 1819).

14. The quotation is from Eliza Leslie, "Snow-Balling; or, The Christmas Dollar," in *The Violet* (Philadelphia, 1839 [c. 1838]), 36–52.

15. *New York Daily Herald,* Dec. 23, 1839.

16. Cary Carson, Ronald Hoffman, and Peter J. Albert, eds., *Of Consuming Interests: The Style of Life in the Eighteenth Century* (Charlottesville: University Press of Virginia, 1994).

17. Emily E. F. Skeel, *Mason Locke Weems, His Work and Ways* (3 vols., New York, 1929), III, 29. This advertisement originally appeared in the *Georgia Journal* (Milledgeville), Nov. 18, 1810.

18. *Worcester Spy,* Dec. 25, 1783; Dec. 23, 1784.

19. In some years, at least, Isaiah Thomas published more books during the holiday season than at other times of the year. In 1794, for example, between March and late November he placed a total of anywhere from one to four book ads in any given issue (the paper was published weekly). But on November 26 he placed five such ads, a number that went up to six on December 10, and then to nine on both December 17 and 24, before falling back to seven on December 31, then to four on January 7 and 14, and to a single one on January 21. It would appear that in some years Thomas printed his books on a seasonal cycle, a cycle that peaked during the Christmas season. There were other children's books that we can assume were published for the Christmas trade, since the word *Christmas* was part of their title (and they had no other Christmas-related content). See, for example, "Peter Pinchpenny," *The Hobby Horse; or, Christmas Companion* (Boston, 1804).

20. Copies of these two Munro and Francis catalogs are held by the American Antiquarian Society.

21. For the decentralized nature of the American book trade, see two books by William Charvat: *Literary Publishing in America, 1790–1850* (Amherst: University of Massachusetts Press, 1993); and *The Profession of Authorship in America, 1800–1870: The Papers of William Charvat* (Columbus: Ohio State University Press, 1968), ch. 1.

22. *New York Herald,* Dec. 23, 1839. Bennett's $3 minimum suggests the financial level below which Gift Books did not penetrate.

23. *The New-York Book of Poetry* (New York, 1837).

24. David Kaser (ed.), *The Cost Book of Carey & Lea, 1825–1838* (Philadelphia: University of Pennsylvania Press, 1963), 68–108, 280–284. This paragraph is based on the work of UMass graduate student Richard Gassan—who also devised the idea of calculating these figures.

25. *The Annualette: A Christmas and New Year's Gift for Children* (Boston, 1840), preface. There was a similar verse in the same Gift Book for 1841.

26. *The Pearl* (Philadelphia, 1837), 186. The publishers of *The Pearl* may well have pressured their authors to insert such advertising copy into their work. In another children's Gift Book, *Christmas Blossoms* for 1850, a Santa-like figure named Uncle Thomas embeds the same point in a passage explaining the advantages of mass production and mass marketing:

> What a wonderful thing printing is! It seems hard to understand how the world could have got along so long and so well without it. . . . Even after printing was invented, it was, for a long time, so costly that books were often bound with strong iron rings fastened to the leather, and were fixed to the walls of the library or the sides of the book-cases, by means of iron chains, for fear they should be stolen. How happy, then, Uncle Thomas should be that he can now print his Christmas Blossoms, and send them over the country so cheaply that everybody can easily get to see them. He can now talk to six millions of little boys and girls, and shake hands with them on paper all at once (pp. 19–20).

27. *St. Nicholas' Book, for All Good Boys and Girls* (Philadelphia, 1842), 6.

28. John Davis to Elizabeth Bancroft Davis, Dec. 26, 1826, in John Davis Papers, American Antiquarian Society.

29. Reprinted in *Albany Journal,* Dec. 16, 1846.

30. *New York Herald,* Dec. 23, 1839.

31. *The Brilliant: A Gift Book for 1850* (New York, 1850). This was edited by T. S. Arthur, best remembered today as the author of the temperance novel *Ten Nights in a Bar-Room.*

32. *Philadelphia Public Ledger,* Dec. 24, 1844.

33. In a Boston bookshop in 1823, King Solomon "might there find his own proverbs illustrated, and made familiar to the eye of childhood, by means of the graphic art; and the [wonders] of Egypt and the realm of his favorite queen of Sheba, displayed in miniature, to furnish up an evening of entertainment for the nursery." ("CHRISTMAS AND NEW YEAR S PRESENTS," in *New England Galaxy and Masonic Magazine,* Dec. 26, 1823.)

34. *New Hampshire Gazette* [Portsmouth], Dec. 22, 1818; "The Diary of Isaiah Thomas 1805–1828," in *Transactions and Collections of the American Antiquarian Society* X (1909), 171. Bibles had long been commercial products, but never before to this degree.

35. *Albany Journal,* Dec. 16, 1846 (reprinted from the *New York Tribune*).

36. Peter J. Wosh, *Spreading the Word: The Bible Business in Nineteenth-Century America* (Ithaca, N.Y.: Cornell University Press, 1994), 19–21. Wosh adds that the Harpers "established the Bible as an article of mass consumption, an attractive centerpiece for the proper Victorian bookshelf. The medium rather than the message assumed center stage as mere possession of the volume conferred cultural status on, and testified to the good taste of, the purchaser" (ibid., 20). See also R. Laurence Moore, *Selling God: American Religion in the Marketplace of Culture* (New York: Oxford University Press, 1994), 17–18, 34–35. An excellent reference source is Margaret T. Hills, *The English Bible in America: A Bibliography of Editions of the Bible and the New Testament Published in America 1777–1957* (New York: American Bible Society, 1961).

37. The dates of these inscriptions also confirm that these personal Bibles, like Gift Books, were seen as appropriate presents to be given during the Christmas season (or, in one of these cases, at Thanksgiving).

38. Louisa May Alcott, *Little Women; or, Meg, Jo, Beth and Amy* (Boston, 1869), Ch. 2.

39. See Richard H. Brodhead, *Cultures of Letters: Scenes of Reading and Writing in Nineteenth-Century America* (Chicago: University of Chicago Press, 1993), 95–96.

40. Susan Warner, *The Wide, Wide World* (New York, 1851), ch. 3, 30–31 (this scene is also briefly described in Moore, *Selling God,* 34). Later in the novel, in a scene set at Christmas, the feeling of helplessness became especially acute. Ellen and her friends are discussing Christmas presents they are about to make out of satin cloth and morocco leather they have received. They agree to choose which pieces each of them will take. "But this business of choosing was found to be very long and very difficult. . . ." One girl says: "I declare it's too vexatious! Here I've got this beautiful piece of blue satin, and can't do any thing with it; it just matches that blue morocco—it's a perfect match—I could have made a splendid thing of it, and I have got some cord and tassels that would just do—I declare it's too bad." She is told by another girl: "Well, choose, Margaret." But Margaret replies: "I don't know what to choose—that's the thing. What can one do with red and purple morocco and blue satin? I might as well give up" (ibid., 292–293). For another example, see Anna Warner, *Mr. Rutherford's Children. Second Volume* (New York, 1855), 91–96. (Anna Warner was Susan Warner's sister and her sometime collaborator.)

41. The Sedgwick family maintained its cohesion and distinction well into the present century; one of its more recent members, Edie Sedgwick, achieved notoriety—and an early death from drugs—as a movie starlet in Andy Warhol's "stable." See Jean Stein, *Edie, An American Biography* (New York: Knopf, 1982).

42. Pamela Sedgwick to Theodore Sedgwick, Dec. 18, 1792 (Sedgwick Family Papers, Collection III, Box 1.13) and Dec. 25, 1794 (ibid., Box 1.18); see Henry Van Schaack to Theodore Sedgwick, Dec. 25, 1788 (Sedgwick Family Papers I, Box 1.12—"Merry Christmas"). Theodore Sedgwick himself returned such salutations for the first time only on Jan. 1, 1795, in a pair of letters, one to his wife and the other to Ephraim Williams (Sedgwick Family Papers V, Box 1.14). Note: The Sedgwick Family Papers are catalogued in five separate collections at the Massachusetts Historical Society, labeled I-V, respectively. Henceforth these will be referred to as "Sedgwick I" [etc.]. The papers of Catharine M. Sedgwick are catalogued separately.)

43. Henry Van Schaack to Theodore Sedgwick, Jan. 2, 1784 (Sedgwick I, Box 1.5). Van Schaack jokingly added that his wife had "eloped," so there would be no women present. Eight years earlier, when Sedgwick and Van Schaack were both serving in the War for Independence, Sedgwick sent his friend a copy of a soldier's drinking song in mid-December; the song concluded: "Its not right for a soldier to grumble I know / But there is one grudge that I lawfully owe / those Damnable Sutters[?] how slighly [i.e., slyly] they'll come / and charge us one Dollar for a Quart of rum. / Sweet Connecticut if I shall see you one [once] more / for the price of one Quart I could have three or four. / I would Drink & be Merry my Toast it shall be / Success to the Lads that shall gain Liberty" (Sedgwick I, Box 1.1).

44. Theodore Sedgwick to Ephraim Williams, Jan. 9, 1795 (Sedgwick III, Box 2.1); Henry Van Schaack to Theodore Sedgwick, Dec. 25, 1799 (Sedgwick I, Box 4.4). Van Schaack said the wine was "excellent" and asked Sedgwick to get more. "As long as I can drink such wine you and others may consume Madeira and Claret and Cherry [Sherry] and Lisbon. . . ." Van Schaack's brother Peter had also received a gift of wine from Sedgwick (ibid.).

45. The phrase comes from his letter to Pamela Dwight of Jan. 1, 1795 (Sedgwick V, Box 1.14).

46. Pamela Sedgwick to Theodore Sedgwick, Jan. 1, 1798 (Sedgwick III, Box 2.10). On New Year's Eve, 1799 / 1800, Theodore Sedgwick, Jr., wrote to his father: "I should [prefer to] live in a Town, at this season" (Sedgwick III, Box 2.16). And in 1808 Catharine M. Sedgwick wrote to her sister Frances Watson on Dec. 25 that she felt "secluded and alone" in Stockbridge (Sedgwick IV, Box 2.12).

47. Catharine Sedgwick to Frances S. Watson, Dec. 28, 1807–Jan. 1, 1808, Catharine M. Sedgwick Papers I (Massachusetts Historical Society), Box 1.1. (Note: Catharine M. Sedgwick's papers are catalogued in three separate collections at the Massachusetts Historical Society. Henceforth these will be referred to as "CMS I" [etc.], and Catharine M. Sedgwick's name will be abbreviated "CMS.")

48. Henry Dwight Sedgwick to Theodore Sedgwick, Dec. 24, 1805 (Sedgwick V, Box 2.13).

49. Theodore Sedgwick to Henry Dwight Sedgwick, Jan. 2, 1806 (Sedgwick III, Box 3.7).

50. Eliza S. Pomeroy to Henry D. Sedgwick (Sedgwick V, Box 5.1). A letter from Theodore Sedgwick to Henry D. Sedgwick, written the next day, Jan. 2, 1812 (ibid.), makes no reference to this "feast."

51. For Christmas: CMS to Robert Sedgwick, Dec. 23–24, 1817 (Sedgwick IV, Box 3.9); Charles Sedgwick to CMS, Dec. 25, 1820 (Sedgwick IV, Box 3.23); for New Year: Jane Sedgwick to Louisa Minot [part of a letter from Henry D. Sedgwick to William Minot], Dec. 29, 1820 (Sedgwick IV, Box 3.23).

52. Ibid. ("mince pies"). It was actually New Year's rituals in New York that were unknown in Boston, as Henry D. Sedgwick pointed out in a letter to his Boston fiancée: "Tomorrow is the commencement of a new year consecrated here to a species of brisk hilarity and hurried sociability of which you have scarcely an idea in Boston. After Church, which is out at ***1/2*** past 12 & before dinner at 3 you are expected to call on all your friends everywhere to get a glass of wine & a cookie (small cake). You cannot stay at one place more than 3 minutes." [Henry D. Sedgwick] to [Jane] Minot (from N.Y.C.), Dec. 28–31, 1816; quoted passage is dated December 31 (Sedgwick V, Box 8.9). The next day Henry D. Sedgwick described the scene: "On New Year's day Robert began his visits at a quarter past twelve. I accompanied him. It is considered indispensable to visit all your friends at that season. . . . We finished our rounds or rather ex[h]austed our time at a quarter past 3 having made more than 30 visits in every part of the city. There were still several omissions which he very much regretted." [Henry D. Sedgwick] to [Jane] Minot, Jan. 1, 1817 (Sedgwick V, Box 9.1).

53. This was not because of a dearth of young people in the family. From 1795 to 1820 there were twenty Sedgwick children born to the third generation (i.e., Theodore Sedgwick's grandchildren).

54. "Vous savez notre cher pere que nous vous aimons et que nous n'avons rien a vous donner si nous avions ete dans la ville certainement nous vous avarions donne quelque chose. A l'un qui est toujours indulgent et toujours genereaux a tout le monde et surtout a ses enfans a [sic] billet est presente par Theodore Sedgwick et M. Sedgwick." Maria and Theodore Sedgwick III to their father, Theodore Sedgwick, Jr., Jan. 1, 1824 (Sedgwick II, Box 6.17). Theodore III was 12, and his sister was 10 years old. Of course, the letter itself was the real present, displaying, as it did, the children's command of a foreign language.

55. See, for example, Elizabeth Sedgwick to Robert Sedgwick, Oct., 1835: "The fact is the whole responsibility of affairs falls upon her shoulders, and even hers are not broad enough to bear it" (Sedgwick V, Box 17.14). This was one of the rare acknowledgments of the way Catharine Sedgwick was handed responsibility by her relatives. As for her love of children, Catharine Sedgwick wrote of one little boy, the son of two of her close friends: "He had better come to his Aunt Catharine who has nothing to do but to make time pass agreeably to children from two to ten years old." CMS to Eliza Cabot Follen, April 1, 1833 (CMS I, Box 8.8). Catharine Sedgwick didn't much like the commercial part of Christmas, but it was she who ended up doing much of the family's shopping, because other family members trusted her judgment (and as an unmarried woman, she was expected to have the time).

56. CMS to Katherine Sedgwick, Dec. 28, 1825 (CMS I, Box 1.9). This passage was a postscript to a letter otherwise addressed to young Katherine's father, Charles Sedgwick (Catharine's youngest brother). Catharine Sedgwick herself had sent this same niece a present of books.

57. What is just as striking (but not apparent from the above description) is that the woman who sent the present, "Aunt Speakman" (Jane Sedgwick's aunt on her mother's side) was a Bostonian. One of the lingering ambiguities of the Christmas season (it would not be resolved for another generation) was when to open presents—on December 25 or January 1? Ultimately, it was all the same thing, inasmuch as the date was less important than the sheer fact of the gifts (indeed, as we shall see, the first Christmas trees in the Sedgwick family would be set out on New Year's Day). But it is striking nonetheless that New York was the city that held out for New Year's, while December 25 was more customary in Boston.

58. Elizabeth B. Sedgwick (Mrs. Charles) to CMS, Dec. 31, 1827 (Sedgwick IV, Box 5.3: misfiled because misdated 1828—"Episcopal style"); Susan Sedgwick to Jane M. Sedgwick, Jan. 5, 1828 (Sedgwick V, Box 14.1—"the most entire satisfaction").

59. Susan R. Sedgwick to Theodore Sedgwick, Jr., Jan. 6, 1828 (Sedgwick II, 7.8).

60. Elizabeth E. Sedgwick to her father, William Ellery, Jan. 12, 1828 (Sedgwick V, Box 14.1).

61. Elizabeth E. Sedgwick to William Ellery, Jan. 3, 1829 (Sedgwick V, Box 14.7).

62. Jane Sedgwick to her brother William Minot, Jan. 1, 1830 (Sedgwick V, Box 15.1).

63. Katherine Sedgwick [Minot] to CMS (from Lenox), Jan. 1, 1830 [a postscript to a letter otherwise written by Charles Sedgwick (Sedgwick IV, Box 5.7).

64. Elizabeth Ellery Sedgwick to her father William Ellery, Jan. 5, 1830 (Sedgwick V, Box 15.1).

65. Elizabeth E. Sedgwick to her father, Wiliam Ellery, Jan. 9, 1831 (Sedgwick V, Box 15.11).

66. "Lizzy Sedgwick" to Katherine Sedgwick, Jan. 2, 1831 (Sedgwick IV, Box 5.7). Three years later, Catharine Sedgwick teased Lizzie on the morning of New Year's Day: "Lizzie woke with the first ray of light—jumped into my bed & I quizzed [i.e., teased] Sue & her unmerci[full]y with a descrip[tio]n of the Tables [of presents] awaiting them—boxes of pills, doses of castor-oil, crust of bread, mug of water, &c." CMS to Kate Sedgwick, Dec. 29, 1834–[Jan. 2, 1835] (CMS I, Box 1.17).

67. Charles Sedgwick to CMS, Dec. 24, 1832 (Sedgwick IV, Box 5.12). See also the letter Theodore Sedgwick received in 1824 from his two children, apologizing for not having bought a present for him.

68. Charles Sedgwick to his daughter Katherine Sedgwick [included in a letter from his wife], Jan. 1, 1834 (Sedgwick IV, Box 5.17).

69. Elizabeth Sedgwick (Mrs. Charles) to her daughter Kate Sedgwick, Jan. 7, 1836 (Sedgwick IV, Box 6.5). The missing presents turned up the following evening. For other examples, see Susan R. Sedgwick to her son Theodore Sedgwick III, Dec. 16, 1830 (Sedgwick II, Box 7.14), and Theodore Sedgwick, Jr., to Theodore Sedgwick III, Dec. 17, 1832 (Sedgwick II, Box 7.19).

70. CMS to Kate Sedgwick, Dec. 17, 1832 (CMS II, Box 1.9).

71. Jane Sedgwick to CMS, Jan. [prob. 4], 1834 (CMS III, Box 4.1).

72. Elizabeth D. Sedgwick (Mrs. Charles) to Kate Sedgwick, Jan. 1, 1834 (Sedgwick IV, Box 5.17).

73. Kate Sedgwick to CMS, Jan. 1, 1830 [postscript to a letter from Charles Sedgwick (Sedgwick IV, Box 5.7).

74. Elizabeth D. Sedgwick to her daughter Katherine Sedgwick, Jan. 1, 1834 (Sedgwick IV, Box 5.17).

75. CMS to Kate Sedgwick, Jan. 7, 1833 (CMS I, Box 1.15). Or again, CMS to Katherine Sedgwick, Dec. 29, 1834[–Jan. 2, 1835]: "Your Aunt & E. rec'd handsome wax flowers from the Rod[ha]ms & mingling a few fresh geranium leaves with them they passed with these artifi[cia]l New Yorkers for as natural as mine. Do you believe they'd know a live lion from a dead dog?" (CMS I, Box 1.17.)

76. Susan Sedgwick to Theodore Sedgwick, Jr., Dec. 30, 1835 (Sedgwick II, Box 8.5).

77. CMS to Kate Sedgwick, Dec. 17, 1832 (CMS II, Box 1.9).

78. CMS to her sister Frances Watson, Dec. 23, 1831 (Sedgwick IV, Box 5.9).

79. CMS to Kate Sedgwick, Jan. 7, 1833 (CMS I, Box 1.15).

80. Jane Sedgwick to CMS, Dec. 22–24, 1833 (CMS III, Box 3.14).

81. All the above from CMS to Kate Sedgwick, Dec. 31, 1830 (CMS I, Box 1.13).

82. "Major Longbow's Description of Jos. Bonfanti's Fancy Store," American Antiquarian Society. This verse was printed sometime between 1824 and 1837, probably during the mid-1820s. Bonfanti published another Christmas verse-advertisement during the 1824 Christmas season, sixteen verses describing the shop's most alluring gifts—but without any reference to Santa Claus (this appeared in the *New York Advertiser,* Jan. 1, 1825).

83. *Daily Cincinnati Gazette,* Dec. 24–18, 1844. This same newspaper printed the following editorial notice on Dec. 24: "SANTA CLAUS. This renowned friend of good boys and girls held a grand levee at LOUDERBECK's yesterday, and was waited upon by hundreds of the little people of the Queen City. Hearing of what was going on, we called around just about sun-down, but were rather late. The old gentleman, with his arms full of Christmas presents, was on the eve of retiring for the night. Seeing us however, he paused a moment, although he had one leg down the chimney, and allowed us to scan his features. He is very certainly a benevolent old gentleman, and altogether as comical in appearance as any one we have ever seen. He holds another levee today, and such of our little friends as did not visit him yesterday, should not fail to make him a call" (*Cincinnati Daily Gazette,* Dec. 24, 1844). The same picture turned up in an 1851 jeweler's advertisement in Bangor, Maine. (1851 Bangor City Directory.)

84. [Philadelphia] *North American,* Dec. 25, 1841, quoted in Alfred Shoemaker, *Christmas in Pennsylvania, A Folk-Cultural Study* (Kutztown: Penn. Folklore Society, 1959), 46; *Philadelphia Public Ledger,* Dec. 27, 1841.

85. *Daily Cincinnati Gazette,* Dec. 23 and 24, 1844. The earliest reference I have found to a living impersonation of Santa Claus dates from 1833, when a student at the General Theological Seminary in New York (Clement Clarke Moore's institution, located in Chelsea) attended a church Christmas fair in Morristown, New Jersey, and reported that "[i]t was held . . . under the auspices of a figure called St. Nicholas who was robed in fur, and dressed according to the description of Prof. Moore in his poem." Manuscript diary of Francis Prioleau Lee, Dec. 31, 1833, in the archives of the General Theological Seminary. (Sandra D. Hayslette brought this item to my attention while she was an undergraduate student at the College of William and Mary.) It is possible that this St. Nicholas was a constructed figure and not a real person.

86. For a stimulating discussion of this paradox, see Karen Hultunen, *Confidence Men and Painted Women: A Study of Middle-Class Culture in America, 1830–1870* (New Haven: Yale University Press, 1982). In the capitalist order, personal relationships were based on competition, limited only by law and contract, while in the domestic order those relationships were founded on affection and loyalty. In retrospect, it is clear enough that capitalism and domesticity went hand in hand with each other. But at the time, people sometimes experienced the two as being in mutual tension, a tension that was resolved by assigning the two to operate in what were sometimes termed "separate spheres." Domes-

tic values took precedence within the home and family; capitalist values held sway in most of the world outside, the world of business and politics.

87. *New York Tribune,* Dec. 25, 1855. Horace Greeley himself had editorially resisted Christmas consumerism throughout the 1840s. For a while he ran annual editorials attacking lavish spending as socially harmful.

Chapter 5

1. The first expression of this new concern I have found is a story by Eliza Leslie, the author of "Snow-Balling." It is "The Souvenir," in *The Pearl* for 1830 (Philadelphia), 106–123, a story about a little girl who gives away the Gift Book she has received as a Christmas present.

2. The scene is recorded in Harriet Martineau, *Retrospect of Western Travel* (2 vols., London and New York, 1838), I, 178–179; and in Eliza C. Follen, "Life of Charles Follen," *The Works of Charles Follen* (5 vols., Boston, 1842), I, 386–387. Harriet Martineau thought this was the Follens' first Christmas tree, but Eliza Follen's account indicates that it was probably their fourth.

3. Follen's two exiles are described in George W. Spindler, *The Life of Karl Follen: A Study in German-American Cultural Relations* (Chicago: University of Chicago Press, 1917), 76–84; see also Follen, *Works,* I, 3–158.

4. Ibid., I, 149 (reading *Redwood*); 150 (1825 visit); 152 (Stockbridge visit); 163 (Sedgwick introduces Cabot to Follen). The Follens' little boy was particularly fond of Catharine Sedgwick (he called her "Aunt Catharine"), and she returned his affection.

5. Ibid., I, 303 (new house). The Harvard position paid only $500 per annum. One of the three men who contributed the money was Eliza Follen's father. See Douglas Stange, "The Making of an Abolitionist Martyr: Harvard Professor Charles Theodore Christian Follen (1796–1840)," in *Harvard Library Bulletin,* vol. 24 (1976), 17–24.

6. Follen, *Works,* I, 379.

7. Ibid., I, 342–346. Douglas Stange argues that the termination was unrelated to Follen's abolitionist activities, and that Harvard had never planned in the first place to offer Follen a permanent job; he attributes the anti-Harvard interpretation to radical Garrisonian propaganda—the desire to create abolitionist martyrs (ibid., 19–20, 23). I disagree: Stange's argument is based on a literal interpretation of a letter written by Harvard president Josiah Quincy, a letter that was almost certainly designed to protect Harvard's interests by ascribing to purely administrative causes what was actually a thoroughly political decision. Compare the following letter from William Minot to Jane Sedgwick, April 14, 1836: "The Follens . . . are full of prejudices & have communicated . . . very erroneous notions of the condition of Harvard College as to discipline & instruction. They are disappointed in their places & impute the failure to others instead of themselves. The Dr. [Follen] is a learned & very laborious man of good talents, an excellent teacher of the German language, but deficient in the qualifications of an interesting & useful public lecturer, and he & his wife are dissatisfied because the College would not give him the professorship of moral philosophy which has been vacant ever since the death of Mr. Fiske[?], for which he is by no means fit. They have both thrown themselves into the melee of this abolition controversy[,] & by their indiscreet zeal have annoyed their friends & as I think injured the cause of emancipation" (Sedgwick Family Papers V [Massachusetts Historical Society], Box 18.2).

8. Follen, *Works,* I, 360–361; Catharine Sedgwick to Jane Sedgwick, Mar. 29, 1835, in Catharine Sedgwick Papers III (Massachusetts Historical Society), Box 4.3; see also Catharine Sedgwick to Eliza Cabot Follen, July 28, 1835, in CMS I, Box 8.8.

9. Follen, *Works,* I, 360–368 (quotation from 362).

10. For analyzing and dating Follen's loss of this position, see Catharine Sedgwick to Eliza Cabot Follen and Catharine Sedgwick to Jane Sedgwick, both dated December 19, 1835 [though not postmarked until January 3, 1836] (CMS Papers I, Box 8.8). See also Follen, *Works*, I, 374–378.

11. Follen, *Works*, I, 387–403; Martineau, *Retrospect*, II, 165–168. Follen seems to have developed this style early in life: In response to being taunted by his father and brothers, he devised a facade of "perfect self-control" to hide his feelings (Follen, *Works*, I, 7–8.)

12. R. K. Webb, *Harriet Martineau: A Radical Victorian* (London: Heineman, 1960), 43–133.

13. Catharine Sedgwick to Jane Sedgwick, May 3, 1835 (CMS III, Box 4.3).

14. See CMS to Eliza L. Follen, July 28, 1835 (CMS I, Box 8.8).; Ellery Sedgwick to Elizabeth Sedgwick, July 31, 1835 (Sedgwick Family Papers V [Massachusetts Historical Society], Box 17.11). In September, Martineau visited Newport, where she met Elizabeth Ellery Sedgwick (who reported conversing with her through Martineau's notorious hearing aid—she was hard-of-hearing—which Mrs. Sedgwick called the "dreaded trumpet." Elizabeth Ellery Sedgwick to Robert Sedgwick, Sept. 10, 1835 (Sedgwick V, Box 17.13).

15. Harriet Martineau, *Retrospectives of Western Travel* (2 vols., London and New York, 1838), II, 164. Twenty years later, Martineau wrote: "I felt that I could never be happy again if I refused what was asked of me: but to comply was probably to shut against me every door in the United States but those of the Abolitionists. I should no more see persons and things as they ordinarily were: I should have no more comfort or pleasure in my travels; and my very life would be . . . endangered by an avowal of the kind desired" (Harriet Martineau, *Autobiography* [3 vols., London, 1877], II, 30).

16. Martineau, *Autobiography*, II, 32–42; Martineau to Fanny Wedgwood, Jan. 17, 1840, in Elizabeth Sanders Arbuckle, ed., *Harriet Martineau's Leo Fanny Wedgwood* (Stanford, Cal.: Stanford University Press, 1983), 30 ("nearest friend").

17. Martineau, *Retrospect*, II, 173–176.

18. Follen to Harriet Martineau, Nov. 30, 1835, *Works*, vol. 1, 381–383 ("if the world separate itself"); Follen to Martineau, undated (but late December), ibid., 385 ("our Holy Triple Alliance").

19. Martineau's publisher, Saunders and Otley, could hardly have been willing to print a book that was so personally revealing—and so politically controversial (for the terms of her book contract, see Webb, *Martineau*, 156). Whenever she wrote about Charles Follen's role in the abolitionist movement (as she did in reporting his stoical performance before the Massachusetts legislative committee in early 1836, an event she witnessed), Martineau kept her own relationship with him completely out of her account. Conversely, whenever she wrote of that personal relationship (as she did in recounting the western trip she took with the Follens in the late spring of 1836, or—to return to the subject of *this* book—the evening of the famous Christmas tree), she disguised Follen's identity by referring to him simply as "Dr. F.," an apolitical figure who, in this guise, invariably played a secondary role to his young son, "my little friend Charley." The use of "little Charley" was an effective literary device. The boy also served as a rhetorical substitute for his father, and made it possible for Martineau to convey in utterly nonpolitical ways her close relationship with Charles Follen (who appeared in the wholly domestic role of Charley's father).

20. Richard H. Brodhead, *Cultures of Letters: Scenes of Reading and Writing in Nineteenth-Century America* (Chicago: University of Chicago Press, 1993), 13–47.

21. Lawrence J. Friedman, *Gregarious Saints: Self and Community in American Abolitionism, 1830–1870* (Cambridge: Cambridge University Press, 1982), actually uses as an epigraph the Follen letter I have quoted above.

22. *Liberator*, Dec. 21, 1833 (juvenile choir concert); William Lloyd Garrison to his mother, Dec. 24, 1836, in Walter M. Merril and Louis Ruchames, eds., *The Letters of*

William Lloyd Garrison (6 vols., Cambridge: Harvard, 1971-81), II, 194 ("young fanatic"). The annual Antislavery Fairs can be followed over the years in the *Liberator*. For an African-American participant in many of these fairs, see Ray Allen Billington, ed., *The Journal of Charlotte Forten, A Free Negro in the Slavery Era* (New York: Norton, 1981), 66, 78, 87, 133, 125-126. See also Debra Gold Hansen, *Strained Sisterhood: Gender and Class in the Boston Anti-Slavery Society* (Amherst: University of Massachusetts, 1993), 123-139; and Deborah van Broekhoven, "Spheres and Webs: The Organization of Antislavery Fairs, 1835-1860," paper delivered to the American Historical Association, December, 1988.

23. *Liberator*, Dec. 20, 1834.

24. Catharine M. Sedgwick, "New Year's Day," in *The Token and Atlantic Souvenir: A Christmas and New Year's Present* (ed. S. G. Goodrich; Boston, 1836 [c. 1835]), 11-31 (quotation from 14-15).

25. Elizabeth E. Sedgwick to William Ellery, Jan. 13, 1834 (Sedgwick V, Box 17.1). On January 1, 1829, bad weather kept the number of visitors down to about thirty. But next year the weather was "absolutely perfect," and from noon until 4 p.m. she received "a constant succession of guests." Poor health prevented Mrs. Sedgwick from receiving visitors the next two years, but in 1834 she was back in form.

26. Catharine Sedgwick to Kate Sedgwick, Dec. 29, 1834[-Jan. 2, 1835] (CMS I, Box 1.17).

27. Sedgwick, "New Year's Day," 26-28.

28. Ibid., 28.

29. Ibid., 18-20. The Christmas tree functioned as a literary device that seemed to take the presents hung upon it out of the realm of the commercial marketplace. It is no accident that Sedgwick described those presents, hanging on the branches of the tree, as St. Nicholas's "fruit"—as if they were the *natural* growth of the tree itself (ibid., 17). (It was common for writers to describe the hanging presents with that metaphor, and it may have been why presents were often hung from the tree at this time, and not placed under it in the modern fashion.)

30. The anticommercial promise of Christmas trees may well have been related to the social position of people like Catharine Sedgwick, who was a member of a prominent gentry family from rural Massachusetts, the kind of patrician who easily associated the fashionable world of New York with an upstart bourgeoisie. A story like "New Year's Day" was, on the face of it, an attack on the fashionable world written from "above" (Sedgwick makes plain that Lizzy Percival comes from an older and more distinguished family than do any of her visitors). But by associating the Christmas tree itself with Lizzy's German maidservant, Sedgwick managed to ally herself imaginatively with the world "below"—a world equally detached from bourgeois American culture.

31. Quoted in Alfred Shoemaker, *Christmas in Pennsylvania: A Folk-Cultural Study* (Kutztown: Penn. Folklore Society, 1959), 52. In 1824, two years later, a humorous notice in a York (Penn.) newspaper suggests that Christmas trees could still be put to the service of a different Christmas tradition: carnival and courtship. That year a local young men's club (the Society of Bachelors) announced that—in return for receiving a "Cart load of Gingercakes" from any "Old Maids" who would pay them a visit on "second Christmas eve"— they would set up a "*Krischtkintle Baum.*" ("It's decorations shall be superb, superfine, superfrostical, schnockagastical, double refined, mill' twill'd made of Dog's Wool, Swingling Tow, and Posnum [sic] fur; which cannot fail to gratify taste"—ibid., p. 52.) The rhetoric here suggests that the occasion was to be a young people's carnival. As for the picture (see page 196) by John Lewis Krimmel (1776-1821): Milo M. Naeve, *John Lewis Krimmel: An Artist in Federal America* (Newark: University of Delaware Press, 1987), dates this picture to 1819-20; while Anneliese Harding, *John Lewis Krimmel: Genre Artist of the Early Republic* (Winterthur, Del.: Winterthur Publications, 1994), 45, gives the date as 1812-13.

32. Memoirs of Baroness Oberkirch, quoted in Alexander Tille, "German Christmas and the Christmas-Tree," in *Folk-Lore: A Quarterly Review of Myth, Tradition, Institution, and Custom* (London), III (1892), 166–182. This and the following paragraphs are based on the above article, along with the following: Kurt Mantel, *Geschichte des Weinachtsbaumes* (Hanover: M. u. H. Schaper, 1975), 5–32 and passim; Alexander Tille, *Die Geschichte der Deutschen Weinacht* (Leipzig, 1893), 256–278; Alexander Tille, *Yule and Christmas: Their Place in the German Year* (London, 1899), 103–106, 170–176, 214–218; and Ingeborg Weber-Kellerman, *Das Weinachtfest: Eine Kultur- und Sozialgeschichte der Weinachtszeit* (Lucerne and Frankfort: Christmas. J. Bucher, 1978), 104–131. See also Phillip V. Snyder, *The Christmas Tree Book* (New York, 1976), 14. I have used these sources to arrive at the above interpretation, but the interpretation itself is my own.

33. George Bancroft to his parents, Aaron and Lucretia Bancroft, Dec. 30, 1820, in Bancroft Papers, American Antiquarian Society.

34. "Christmas Eve; or, The Conversion. From the German," *Atheneum*, VII (May–June, 1820). This story had appeared earlier that year in a French magazine, *La Belle Assemblée* (Jan. 1820). For a much later story (which placed the origin of the Christmas tree even earlier), see Henry Van Dyke, *The First Christmas Tree* (New York, 1897, illustrated by Howard Pyle), set in the German forests in A.D. 722.

35. For Coleridge's gentry associations in Ratzeburg, see Oswald Doughty, *Perturbed Spirit: The Life and Personality of Samuel Taylor Coleridge* (East Brunswick, N.J., 1981), 150–152. Coleridge himself, in a 1798 letter, referred to his society as "Gentry and Nobility." His description of the house in which he observed the Christmas tree refers to two parlors. (Coleridge was rather offended by the sexual looseness he witnessed in Ratzeburg.)

36. Samuel Taylor Coleridge, "Christmas Within Doors, in the North of Germany," *The Friend* (Burlington, Vt., 1831), 321–322.

37. Ibid., 322. This scene took place "in the great parlour" of his host's house. The ritual contained some of the old elements of Christmas as judgment day: Just before the presents are actually distributed, "the mother says privately to each of her daughters, and the father to his sons, that which he has observed most praise-worthy and that which was most faulty in their conduct." It is interesting that the parents tell the children their faults "privately"; this has the ring of a new practice (like the Christmas tree itself).

38. Catharine Sedgwick diary, Jan. 19, 1836, in CMS I, Box 11. The Burlington edition of *The Friend* was reprinted in 1831.

39. *Christian Register*, III (Apr. 24, 1824), 152. I suspect that I have not completely tracked down the printing history of Coleridge's little report, or the history of the way it reappeared in American sources, sometimes without attribution.

40. Lydia M. Child, *The Little Girl's Own Book* (Boston, 1831), 286–287. (The title was registered for copyright on December 25, 1830, and the preface wished the children who read it "a merry Christmas and a happy New-Year" (ibid., iv). The book was reprinted several times, into the 1850s.

41. J. K. Smith, *Juvenile Lessons; or, The Child's First Reading Book* (Keene, N.H., 1832), 70–71. (This last statement of this lesson reveals that Coleridge himself, and not Lydia Maria Child, was almost surely the source.) Circumstantial evidence suggests that J. K. Smith, too, was a progressive Unitarian. Smith's book went through three editions, all published in Keene, between 1832 and 1842.

42. *Youth's Companion*, XIV (Dec. 25, 1840), 129. This magazine was edited by Nathaniel Willis, the father of two writers who were very popular in their day, N. P. Willis and Fanny Fern. The children in this "story" go on to propose (again following Coleridge's report) that on Christmas Day their parents give them notes " 'telling them what faults they have overcome during the year, and what they have still left to overcome.' " (" 'I should like that,' " one of the children says.)

43. Philip J. Greven, *The Protestant Temperament: Patterns of Child-rearing, Religious Experience, and the Self in Early America* (New York: Knopf, 1977), 206. Greven adds that such parents (whom he calls "moderates," as distinct from "evangelicals") "were preoccupied with self-established and self-maintained boundaries over their passions and appetites" (p. 206). Theodore Parker, "Phases of Domestic Life," quoted ibid., 168. For an overview of attitudes toward child rearing in nineteenth-century America, see Bernard Wishy, *The Child and the Republic: The Dawn of Modern American Child Nurture* (Philadelphia: University of Pennsylvania Press, 1968); and for a splendid and provocative recent analysis of the corporal-punishment debate, see Brodhead, *Cultures of Letters*, 13–47. An influential nineteenth-century book on this subject is Horace Bushnell, *Views of Christian Nurture* (Hartford, 1847).

44. Mrs. [Elizabeth] Sedgwick, "The Game at Jackstraws and The Christmas Box," in *The Pearl; or, Affection's Gift* (Philadelphia, 1834), 17–52.

45. Ibid., 31, 36, 46.

46. Ibid., 32, 46–47. This same number of *The Pearl* contained a prefatory poem about holiday gifts, signed "A.D.W." and dated from Stockbridge (the author was almost certainly a friend of the Stockbridge Sedgwicks). This poem concludes with two stanzas advertising *The Pearl* itself: "And here is one,—look, Ellen dear,— / That I from all would choose; / Its very name 't is sweet to hear; / 'Affection's Gift' who'd lose ["Affection's Gift" was the subtitle of *The Pearl*]." "True, true, dear Sarah, I am sure / We need not look for [presents] more, / While here we have, so chaste and pure, / 'The Pearl' for thirty-four" (ibid., 10).

47. Elizabeth E. Sedgwick to Robert Sedgwick, Aug. 22, 1835 (Sedgwick V, Box 17.12).

48. Ralph Waldo Emerson, "Nature," in *Nature, Addresses and Lectures* (*The Complete Works of Ralph Waldo Emerson*, 12 vols., Boston, 1903–4), I, 8–9.

49. Ralph Waldo Emerson, "Historic Notes of Life and Letters in New England," ibid., vol. 10, 325. I am indebted to Conrad Wright for this reference.

50. Quoted in E. Biber, *Henry Pestalozzi, and His Plan of Education* (London, 1833), 447–448.

51. "S." [Susan Sedgwick], " 'Record of a School: Exemplifying the general principles of spiritual culture," *The Knickerbocker*, 8 (Feb. 1836), 113–130. Mrs. Sedgwick called Alcott an "enthusiast" and an "ultra." Richard Brodhead makes a compelling linkage between radical educational theory and the abolitionists' horror of the use of the lash on slave plantations. See Brodhead, *Cultures of Letters*, 13–14, 35–42.

52. For this episode, see Follen, *Works*, I, 360–378 passim; and specifically, 362 ("individual talent and taste"), 375 ("legitimate and innocent desires"). Follen maintained, as Elizabeth Palmer Peabody later reported, "that the child should be handled not with reference to his future, but to his present perfection; that the father of the man is the perfect *child* in the balance of childish beauty, and not the child prematurely developed into a man; that education which does the latter both destroys the child and dwarfs the man." This is quoted in Spindler, *Charles Follen*, 107–109 (the quotation is from Elizabeth Palmer Peabody's 1880 volume *Reminiscences of W. E. Channing*, 250–257). For further evidence of Follen's adherence Pestalozzian principles: In 1826 he tried to procure some "fables" by Pestalozzi (*Works*, I, 161). And in 1828 he attempted to revise William Russel's Pestalozzian "Teacher's Manual," a work evidently still in manuscript (ibid., 240).

53. Diary entry, Dec. 26, 1827, in Follen, *Works*, I, 222.

54. Elizabeth E. Sedgwick to Ellery Sedgwick, Aug. 4, 1835 (Sedgwick V, Box 17.9—this letter is addressed to "My dear precious son"); Elizabeth E. Sedgwick to Robert Sedgwick, undated but postmarked Sept. 1, 1835 (Sedgwick V, Box 17.12); Robert Sedgwick to Ellery Sedgwick, Jan. 3, 1836 (Sedgwick V, Box 18.1).

55. E. Biber, *Life and Trials of Henry Pestalozzi* (Philadelphia, 1833), 38–43. (The quotation marks appear in the original.) The translator continued: "Christmas-eve is abroad as here [i.e., in England and America], the time when children receive gifts of every kind from their parents, godfathers, &c.; but instead of 'Christmas boxes,' they are. The preparation of the 'Christmas tree' is a family mystery, and if the child asks from whence all the goodly things come, the answer is, 'The Christchild brought them.'"

56. Ibid., 43.

57. Pestalozzi actually made the same connection. Somewhat like John Pintard (and many others of their generation), Pestalozzi waxed lyrical about the paternalist social relations that had characterized Christmas in the old days—meaning, in Pestalozzi's case, the early days of Christianity itself. On Christmas Eve, Pestalozzi wrote, the high and the low together—patrons and clients—gathered in a spirit of harmonious reciprocity. On such occasions, the patrons expressed their spiritual [piety] by offering "earthly gifts" to their clients. "Thus stood the mother among her children, the master among his workmen, the landlord among his tenants. Thus assembled the congregation before its pastor; thus the rich entered the cottage of the poor . . ." (ibid., 38). But that was in the old days. In modern times, Pestalozzi implied, neither side in this exchange, whether workmen and masters, tenants and landlords, even congregations and pastors, had kept their part of the arrangement. But with children, Pestalozzi insisted, the old relations could and did still continue to function in their original harmony, and in the enactment of these relations with the young the intense spirituality of the old days could be re-created. (To an extent, Pestalozzi was simply playing on the symbolism of the Magi bringing gifts to the Christ child, with the assembled children taking the role of the Christ child. But for Pestalozzi the connection between children and the Christ child was real as well as symbolic—and it was here that his words crossed the line from symbolic social inversion into something much more radical.)

58. Ibid., 43.

59. Ibid., 39.

60. Ibid., 43.

61. Mrs. G. "The Christmas Tree," in *The Pearl; or, Affection's Gift: A Christmas and New Year's Present for 1837* (Philadelphia, 1837 [c. 1836]), 179–189.

62. Ibid., 179.

63. Ibid., 180.

64. Ibid., 180, 183.

65. Ibid., 183–185.

66. This point constitutes further evidence that Christmas trees were used by prosperous families, families who could afford to live in houses that contained enough rooms to do this job—and who were up-to-date enough for these rooms to be "specialized" to the extent that at least one of them was off-limits to the children.

67. Ibid., 180. The same custom is implied in Catharine Sedgwick's 1836 story "New Year's Day." There the children "waked [Lizzy Percival, the heroine] at dawn with . . . cries of 'Happy New Year'"; and the servants "besieged her door with their earnest taps and their heart-felt good wishes, and each received a gift and a kind word to grace it." (Sedgwick, "New Year's Day," 17.)

68. Mrs. G., "The Christmas Tree," ibid., 186.

69. For example: [Christophe von Schmid,] *The Christmas Eve: A Tale from the German* (Boston, 1842, etc.; apparently translated by Elizabeth Palmer Peabody); Theodore Parker, *Two Christmas Celebrations* (Boston, 1859); Lydia Maria Child, "The Christ-Child and the Poor Children," in her *Flowers for Children* (Boston, 1861), 9–48; L. D. Nicholas, "Willy Ely's Christmas Tree," *Our Young Folks* 2 (1866), 737–740; Louisa May Alcott, "Tilly's Christmas," in her *Aunt Jo's Scrap-Bag* (Boston, 1872), 122–133.

70. Louisa May Alcott, *Little Women; or, Meg, Jo, Beth and Amy* (Boston, 1869), ch. 3.

71. The best book about Fuller is Charles Capper's analytic biography *Margaret Fuller, An American Romantic Life: The Private Years* (New York: Oxford University Press, 1992), the first of two projected volumes, taking Fuller's career only up to 1841.

72. *New York Tribune*, Dec. 25, 1844. I ascertained the authorship of this essay from Charles Capper. For another "German" legend, printed in an American newspaper in the mid-1830s—complete with suffering child, a vision of the infant Jesus, and a Christmas tree—see "The Forlorn Child's Christmas Eve, a translation from the German of Ruckert," in the *Philadelphia Public Ledger*, Dec. 24, 1836.

73. *New York Tribune*, Dec. 28, 1844.

74. Ibid., Jan. 3, 1845.

Chapter 6

1. Charles Loring Brace, *Home-Life in Germany* (New York, 1853), 225.

2. Ibid., 122–124.

3. Ibid., 221–222. Brace was staying at a lodging-house near the Lindenstrasse (ibid., 121).

4. *A Christmas Carol* never even shows us the poor, even though the book opens by evoking a general vision of a society riven by vast economic and social divisions. But the book provides hardly a glimpse of poverty, and none at all of discontent. The Ghost of Christmas Past takes us back into the time of Scrooge's childhood, a time portrayed as if it antedates capitalism altogether. The Ghost of Christmas Present takes Scrooge on a tour of England, but the only workers he chooses to show us are miners (a happy family, singing Christmas songs) and, even more briefly, a group of sailors at sea. Real poverty does make one appearance on this tour—but only in the form of a pair of allegorical figures labeled "Want" and "Ignorance." And these figures, who do not move or speak, take the innocent form of a pair of young *children*. In any case, even this brief excursion into the industrial hinterlands of "Christmas Present" is fictionally framed on either side by two lengthy and richly detailed stops at which we witness Christmas dinner with the families of a pair of characters who are already familiar to us: The first is at the house of Scrooge's merry nephew Fred; the second is at the Cratchits'. Because these two scenes are portrayed so vividly, they end up satisfying us emotionally. But both Fred's Christmas dinner and (as we have seen) the Cratchits' are bourgeois events—even though the Cratchits' dinner has all the pathos (without any of the accompanying resentment) of a proletarian meal.

5. *New York Times*, Dec. 25, 1893. See also ibid., Dec. 25, 1876: "Should the weather prove fine there seems to be no reason why everybody, including all the possible Bob Cratchits and Tiny Tims in the great Metropolis, should not to-day have the happiest of 'Merry Christmases.' The times are hard, it is said, but the charitable institutions are all bountifully supplied with substantial food, and with an abundance of toys and fruit and candy for the children. . . . In the markets the dealers say that never before were there so many purchases by employers who desired to reward faithful employees, and to make their gifts in the shape of poultry."

6. Susan Sedgwick to Theodore Sedgwick II, Jan. 2, 1838, in Sedgwick Family Papers II (Massachusetts Historical Society), Box 8.15. Sedgwick assured her husband that "It would have just suited you—sufficiently republican, yet in excellent taste." She went on to note that "We came away at half past 8, & reached home in time to get seasonably soust[?!]"

7. *New York Tribune*, Jan. 3, 1844. See also ibid., Dec. 24, 1845: "Who can devote even one day to hilarity and social enjoyment until he shall have at least devoted as much of his worldly substance as that day's enjoyment will cost him to the relief of the misery so imminent and appalling."

8. Ibid., Dec. 30, 1853.

9. Ibid., Dec. 22, 1854.

10. Ibid.

11. Ibid., Jan. 1, 1848. Greeley went on to insist on the need to attack poverty as a systemic problem.

12. *New York Times,* Dec. 26 and 27, 1855.

13. "How to Help the Poor," *New York Times,* Dec. 25, 1854.

14. Ibid., Dec. 26, 1866. See also ibid., Dec. 25, 1868 ("The evils of individual, which is, as a general rule, indiscriminate, charity, are almost equal to its benefits; and the truly charitable will wisely give what they can to the organized societies") and Dec. 23, 1871 ("A dollar given to an institution like this [the Children's Aid Society] is sure to be more fruitful than twenty bestowed in undiscriminating alms").

15. Ibid., Dec. 25, 1893.

16. For the cloakmakers, see ibid., Dec. 26, 1894.

17. For the Five Points, see Paul Boyer, *Urban Masses and Moral Order in America, 1820–1920* (Cambridge: Harvard University Press, 1978), 68–69, 81. For the missions: Marilyn Irvin Holt, *The Orphan Trains: Placing Out in America* (Lincoln, Neb.: University of Nebraska Press, 1992), 98–102. See also Peter C. Holloran, *Boston's Wayward Children: Social Services for Homeless Children, 1830–1930* (Boston: Northeastern University Press, 1994); and Luc Sante, *Low Life: Lures and Snares of New York* (New York: Farrar, Straus & Giroux, 1991), esp. pp. 305–312.

18. [Emma Brace,] *The Life of Charles Loring Brace, Chiefly Told in His Own Letters* (London, 1894), 75–76.

19. Charles Loring Brace, *Short Sermons to Newsboys* (New York, 1866), 13. For Brace, see Boyer, *Urban Masses,* 97–107; Holt, *The Orphan Trains,* 41–79, 120–155. See also Christine Stansell, *City of Women: Sex and Class in New York, 1789–1860* (New York: Knopf, 1986); Thomas Bender, *Toward an Urban Vision: Ideas and Institutions in Nineteenth-Century America* (Lexington, Ky.: University of Kentucky Press, 1975).

20. *New York Times,* Dec. 25, 1855. A recent examination of New York's orphan children is Bruce Bellingham, "Waifs and Strays: Child Abandonment, Foster Care, and Families in Mid-Nineteenth-Century New York," in Peter Mandler, ed., *The Uses of Charity: The Poor on Relief in the Nineteenth-Century Metropolis* (Philadelphia: University of Pennsylvania Press, 1990), 123–160.

21. Boyer, *Urban Masses,* 98. For a history of the movement, see Holt, *The Orphan Trains,* passim.

22. Boyer, *Urban Masses,* 99 ("excursion to Hoboken" quotation); Brace, *The Dangerous Classes of New York, and Twenty Years' Work Among Them* (New York, 1872), 114.

23. Boyer, *Urban Masses,* 100.

24. Charles Loring Brace, *Gesta Christi; or, A History of Humane Progress Under Christianity* (New York, 1882), 95, 414.

25. Bender, *Towards an Urban Vision,* 147–149.

26. Brace, *Sermons to Newsboys,* 38. The most sympathetic and perceptive modern treatment of newsboy culture is David Nasaw, *Children of the City: At Work and at Play* (New York: Oxford University Press, 1985), esp. pp. 62–87 and 149–166. Nasaw's study deals with the period 1900–20, when newsboy culture had changed (for example, most early-twentieth-century newsboys lived with their own families).

27. *New York Times,* Dec. 26, 1867.

28. Brace, *Sermons to Newsboys,* 108, 112, 117.

29. Ibid., 26.

30. Kevin Gilbert, "Friends or Dependents: Christmas Charity Dinners and Changing Images of the Poor in New York City, 1897–1915" (unpublished seminar paper, University of Massachusetts at Amherst, 1993). On the newsboys' code of honor, see Brace, *Dangerous Classes*, 98–99.

31. Boyer, *Urban Masses*, 98.

32. *New York Times*, Dec. 26, 1871; Dec. 26, 1872; and Dec. 26, 1873. Roosevelt was present once again in 1884 (ibid., Dec. 26, 1884).

33. *New York Times*, Dec. 26, 1890. "This compilation does not make any allowance for the turkey bones, but, on the other hand, the weight of the newsboys before beginning the repast is placed rather high."

34. Ibid.

35. Boyer, *Urban Masses*, 98.

36. Brace, *Dangerous Classes*, 395.

37. Horatio Alger, Jr., *Ragged Dick; or, Street Life in New York* (Boston, 1868). Most of the other books about newsboys were anonymously authored. These include *John Ellard, The Newsboy* (Philadelphia, 1860), a nonfiction account of the "Newsboys' Aid Society," founded in Philadelphia in 1858; *Tom Brice, the News-boy* (New York, 1862); *Willie Wilson, the Newsboy* (New York, 1865), a moralistic tale of a good boy; *Luke Darrell, the Chicago Newsboy* (Chicago, 1866); and [Thomas March Clark,] *John Whopper the Newsboy* (Boston, 1871), a fantasy adventure story of a newsboy's trip to China.

38. Elizabeth Oakes Smith, *The Newsboy* (New York, 1854; reprinted 1870), 17–18. Robert says later, " 'I never had any father; I was sea-born.' " (156).

39. Ibid., 17 ("agin my natur"), 374 ("miracle of goodness").

40. E.H.C., "The Sufferer," *Child's Friend*, Apr., 1844, 19–22.

41. Louise Chandler Moulton, "Just a Little Bit of Christmas," *Youth's Companion*, Dec. 21, 1865, 200. For other examples of poor children who do not ask for anything, see "Nelly's Christmas Gift," ibid., Dec. 20, 1877, 434–435 (in this story the little heroine is black); and also the two stories to be discussed below.

42. Annie Fraust, "Christmas for Rich and Poor," *Godey's Lady's Book* 57 (Dec. 1858), 513–516. See also Frank Lee Benedict, "The Orphan's New-Year's Eve," *Peterson's Magazine* 31 (Jan. 1864), 27–34, in which an impoverished orphan turns out to be the illegitimate daughter of the rich heroine's closest friend.

43. This story is also about the conflict between older notions of family structure, which gave fathers veto power over their children's marriage partners, and emerging notions which accorded children free choice. From still another angle, the daughter's "elopement"—and her subsequent banishment from the family—can be read as a symbolic way of touching on the issue of premarital sex and illegitimacy. Ironically, from this angle such stories do deal with social class, after all—in the form of the risk of downward mobility posed by sexual misconduct. (For a discussion of this question in a male context, see the story of young Robert Hamlin in Eliza Leslie's story "Snow-Balling," discussed in Chapter 3.)

44. Susan Warner, *Carl Krinken: His Christmas Stocking* (New York, 1854), 14, 22. This point follows out the implication of scenes about consumerism from *The Wide, Wide World* (discussed in Chapter 4).

45. William Dean Howells, "Christmas Every Day," in *Christmas Every Day and Other Stories Told for Children* (New York, 1893), 3–22.

46. Edmund Alton, "The Children's Christmas Club of Washington City," *St. Nicholas* 15 (1887), 146–149.

47. *New York Tribune,* Dec. 26, 1851; ibid., Dec. 29, 1852. For 1853, see ibid., Dec. 27, 1853.

48. The *Tribune* of Dec. 26, 1853, published an extensive list of the charitable agencies that had held open house the previous day—twenty in all.

49. Ibid., Dec. 27, 1853. For a similar story about a Boston institution, see "Christmas Eve at the Orphan Asylum," *Child's Friend* (Jan., 1856), 77–79.

50. There were three other reports of charity visitations in that same number of the *Tribune.* All three took place at institutions for children: Randalls Island, the New York Juvenile Asylum (the children there were served a dinner "which they enjoyed in a manner that would have made many a street vagrant envious"), and the Girls' Industrial School.

51. See Richard Sennett, *Families Against the City: Middle-Class Homes of Industrial Chicago, 1872–1890* (Cambridge: Harvard University Press, 1970).

52. *New York Times,* Dec. 26, 1875; *New York Tribune,* Dec. 27, 1875; Louisa May Alcott to the Alcott family, Dec. 25, 1875, in Joel Myerson and Daniel Shealy, eds., *The Selected Letters of Louisa May Alcott* (Boston: Little, Brown, 1987), 210–213. That same year Alcott published a novel in which several children experience a perfect, present-filled Christmas: " 'Now, I believe I've got every thing in the world that I want,' " one of them says. (Louisa May Alcott, *Eight Cousins; or, The Aunt-Hill* [Boston, 1875], 226–227.)

53. Edward W. Bok, "Complicating Christmas," *Ladies' Home Journal,* Dec. 1897. For women's work at Christmas, see Leslie Bella, *The Christmas Imperative: Leisure, Family and Women's Work* (Halifax, N.S.: Fernwood Pub., 1992).

54. Jackson Lears, *No Place of Grace: Antimodernism and the Transformation of American Culture, 1880–1920* (New York: Pantheon, 1981); Christopher Lasch, *The New Radicalism in America, 1889–1963: The Intellectual as a Social Type* (New York: Knopf, 1965). For an example of the Social Gospel applied to Christmas, see George Hodges, "What the Christmas Spirit Saith unto the Churches," *New England Magazine,* Dec. 1896, 469–476.

55. *New York Times,* Dec. 26, 1890.

56. Ibid., Dec. 26, 1891. The event was repeated only once, the following year. It is evident that this event was resented by the established charitable agencies, who saw it as drawing attention (and contributions) away from their own work. A representative of the Christmas Society told a reporter the following year, "The organized charities of the city say we have been the means of depriving them of subscriptions [i.e., contributions]." Rental of Madison Square Garden alone cost $800 (ibid., Dec. 27, 1892).

57. Ibid., Dec. 26, 1899. See also the 1901 report: "From the boxes many prominent people looked down upon the 3,000 Christmas diners, the majority of whom remained until the end of the entertainment." The article concluded with a list of prominent New Yorkers who "purchased boxes" for this event (*New York Times,* Dec. 26, 1901).

58. *New York World,* Dec. 26, 1899; quoted in Gilbert, "Friends or Dependents," 9.

59. *New York Tribune,* Dec. 26, 1902.

60. *New York Times,* Dec. 26, 1903. New York's mayor, Seth Low, was in attendance on this occasion.

61. Ibid., Dec. 26, 1905.

62. *New York Tribune,* Dec. 26, 1895. The article continues: "After eating three plates of turkey and as many dishes of sauce the soup is called for, and when they have got outside of one or two bowls they stuff their pockets with candy, apples, nuts, bananas and other good things and hasten to the gymnasium, where they exercise vigorously for an hour. . . . All these customs were kept strictly at the dinner last night." For other newsboys' dinners given by Fliess, see ibid., Dec. 26, 1895; *New York Times,* Dec. 26, 1899 (with descriptions of pie-throwing in previous years); *New York Times,* Dec. 26, 1901 (a dinner given

by Frank Tilford, who was quoted as saying: "Who is there that could watch these little fellows enjoying themselves without feeling happy?" Nevertheless, "twelve policemen were present to maintain order." *New York Tribune,* Dec. 26, 1908 (a history of the newsboys' Christmas dinners).

63. There may have been an additional reason for the newsboys' preferences: They were rejecting the "bourgeois" practice of separating sweet dishes from the rest of the food as a distinct course termed "dessert."

64. *New York Times,* Dec. 25, 1876.

Chapter 7

1. "Christmas at the South," *New York Times,* Dec. 25, 1867. Over subsequent decades, Southerners themselves evoked similar recollections of Christmas as part of the psychological arsenal they employed to plead with Northern whites for reconciliation along class and racial lines (which, they implicitly argued, ought to transcend the earlier opposition along regional lines). See, for example, three fictional works by Thomas Nelson Page: *A Captured Santa Claus* (New York; first published in 1891); "Polly: A Christmas Recollection," in *In Ole Virginia; or, Marse Chan and Other Stories* (New York, 1887), 187–230; and "The Christmas Peace," in *Bred in the Bone* (New York, 1904), 183–234. See also Joel Chandler Harris, "A Child of Christmas: A Christmas Tale of North and South," in *The Making of a Statesman and Other Stories* (New York, 1902), 71–151.

2. John Esten Cooke, "Christmas Time in Old Virginia," *Magazine of American History with Notes and Queries* 10 (1883), 443–459; the "Bracebridge Hall" passage is on p. 451. Another account, published in 1897 by Thomas Nelson Page, included, just as Irving had done, an extended description of the anticipation of the guests who were being driven in carriages to spend Christmas in their old family mansion. (The illustration for this section—it is captioned "At last the 'big gate' is reached"—was surely intended to evoke the highly popular illustration that Randolph Caledecott prepared for the 1875 edition of *Bracebridge Hall.*) It is no coincidence that Page, who helped invent the idea of the old Southern Christmas, was also largely responsible for inventing the myth of Old Dixie.

3. "Abolition of Christmas," *Evangelical and Literary Magazine* (Richmond) 6 (Dec. 1823), 636–639.

4. Charles G. Parsons, *An Inside View of Slavery: A Tour Among the Planters* (Boston, 1855; reprinted, Savannah, 1974), 27 (delirium tremens); Nancy Chappelear Baird, ed., *Journals of Amanda Virginia Edmonds, Lass of the Mosby Confederacy, 1859–1867* (Stephens City, Va., 1984), 9–10 (1857), 64 (1861); Mary A. Livermore, *The Story of My Life* (Hartford, 1897), 210 (drinking children). See also Baird, *Edmonds,* 243 (1866): " 'Christmas Gift' is uttered by all tongues this morning, then nog, breakfast, and almost tight!"

5. Norfolk *Public Ledger,* Dec. 26, 2876. Norfolk was a port town with a naval yard and many saloons; it experienced a race riot in 1866. See George C. Rable, *But There Was No Peace: The Role of Violence in the Politics of Reconstruction* (Athens, Ga.: University of Georgia Press, 1984), 31.

6. *Journals and Letters of Philip Vickers Fithian 1772–1774* (Williamsburg, Va., 1945), 52. The Robert E. Lee letter is quoted by James M. MacPherson, *New York Review of Books* 42 (Dec. 21, 1995), 15. For evidence that Christmas misrule was common in parts of the South at least as early as the late seventeenth century, see Michel Sobel's provocative book, *The World They Made Together: Black and White Values in Eighteenth-Century Virginia* (Princeton: Princeton Univ. Press, 1987), 37, 67, and 263n13.

7. M. M. Folsom, "Christmas at Brockton Plantation," *Southern Bivuoac* n.s. 1 (1886), 483–489; quoted passage is on p. 486.

8. William Nevison Blow, manuscript Memoir, Archives of the College of William and Mary. This item was brought to my attention by Patrick Breen.

9. Susan Dabney Smedes, *Memorials of a Southern Planter* (3rd ed., Baltimore, 1888), 160–161.

10. Quoted in Abe C. Ravitz, "John Pierpont and the Slaves' Christmas," *Phylon* 21 (1960), 384–385; also quoted in Eugene D. Genovese, *Roll, Jordan, Roll: The World the Slaves Made* (New York: Pantheon, 1974), 578. The one general exception to the pattern of free time involves house slaves, whose labor (unlike that of field hands) was needed at Christmas.

11. See also the testimony of Henry Cheatam, who attributed the policy to a mean overseer: "[D]ere weren't no celebratin', 'ceptin' at hog killin'. Dat was de biggest dat of de year." Quoted in Norman R. Yetman, ed., *Life Under the "Peculiar Institution": Selections from the Slave Narrative Collection* (New York: Holt, Rinehart and Winston, 1970), 56. A few planters—they seem to have clustered in the "new" States from Alabama to Texas—allowed no holiday at all. An ex-slave from Alabama remembered once having to build a lime kiln at Christmas (ibid., 147). An ex-slave from Oklahoma recalled that her owner "didn't [even] tell us anything about Christmas . . . , and all we done was work" (ibid., 329). The same informant also argued: "The way he made the Negroes work so hard. Old Master must have been trying to get rich" (ibid., 326). A planter's wife in Texas justified this policy by telling her slaves that "Niggers was made to work for white folks." But the powerful hold of the holiday even within this family is demonstrated by the fact that on at least one occasion another white woman living in the household secretly baked two Christmas cakes for the slaves (ibid., 70).

12. For example, Mingo White recalled: "On Christmas we didn't have to do no work, no more'n feed the stock and do de li'l work round de house. When we got through with dat we had de rest of de day to run round wherever we wanted to go. 'Course, we had to get permission from de master" (ibid., 314). See also Tatler, "Management of Negroes," in *Southern Cultivator* 8 (1850), 162–164: "Believing that the strolling about of negroes for a week at a time during what are called Christmas Holidays is productive of much evil, the writer has set his face against the custom. Christmas is observed as a Sacred Festival. On that day as good a dinner as the plantation will afford is served for the negroes, and they all sit down to a common table, but the next day go to work. From considerations both of morality and needful rest and recreation to the negro, I much prefer giving a week in July, when the crop is laid by, to giving three days at Christmas." Quoted in James O. Breeden, ed., *Advice Among Masters: The Ideal in Slave Management in the Old South* (Westport, Conn.: Greenwood Press, 1980), 258.

13. Yetman, *Selections*, 281. There was at least one ritual, practiced in the "low country" of Maryland, Virginia, and North Carolina, that allowed slaves to exert at least symbolic control over the length of the holidays: They were to last as long as the "Yule log" continued to burn in one piece. Slaves would choose the largest possible tree, chop it down a year in advance, soak it in water for the entire year, and light it early on Christmas Day in the hall of the Big House, where it would be the "back-log." The holidays would be over when the Yule log finally burned into two pieces—a process that could take a full week. This ritual was recalled by Booker T. Washington in "Christmas Days in Old Virginia" (1907), in Louis R. Harlan, ed., *The Booker T. Washington Papers* (14 vols., Urbana: University of Illinois Press, 1972–89), I, 394–397 (Yule log is on p. 397). See also John Williamson Palmer, "Old Maryland Homes and Ways," *Century* 49 (1894), 260; and Rebecca Cameron, "Christmas on an Old Plantation," in *The Ladies' Home Journal* (Dec. 1891), 5–8. This ritual was apparently devised by literary-minded Anglophile planters; it derived from an English custom in which tenants and servants were permitted to eat at the patron's table as long as the Yule log burned.

14. Genovese, *Roll, Jordan, Roll*, 574–575. I have not encountered a single case in which slaves were unambiguously deprived of their customary right to freedom from labor at Christmas. The two cases most nearly approaching this both seem to refer to the deprivation of other privileges. In 1854, James Henry Hammond denied slaves Christmas

celebrations at his plantation, on account of a poor (wasted) harvest. He wrote in his record book on Dec. 25, 1854: "No festivities, crops being lost—negroes not having done their duty." (Norrece T. Jones, Jr., *Born a Child of Freedom Yet a Slave: Mechanisms of Control and Strategies of Resistance in Antebellum South Carolina* [Hanover, N.H.: University Press of New England, 1990], 199.) In 1858 or 1859, on Robert Allston's South Carolina rice plantation, two slaves "were made to run the gauntlet for taking a hog out of the pen. The whole plantation being shared out of Xmas until they found out the crimnal [sic]." (J. H. Easterby, ed., *The South Carolina Rice Plantation as Revealed in the Papers of Robert F. W. Allston* (Chicago: University of Chicago Press, 1945), 34.

15. Frederick Douglass, *Narrative of the Life of Frederick Douglass, An American Slave* (Boston, 1845), 74–75. This is the first version of Douglass's autobiography; his description of Christmas is different in subsequent versions.

16. For example, one slave owner "followed the common practice of paying his slaves if they chose to work during the holidays when they would otherwise be free. [In 1853 he] paid several slaves fifty cents a day for splitting rails, hauling cotton and corn, and operating the plantation cotton gin." Orville W. Taylor, *Negro Slavery in Arkansas* (Durham, N.C.: University of North Carolina Press, 1958), 207.

17. Jones, *Child of Freedom,* 70–71.

18. Solomon Northup, *Twelve Years a Slave* (Auburn & Buffalo, 1854), 214; Irwin Russell, "Christmas-Night in the Quarters," in *Poems by Irwin Russell* (New York, 1888), 1 ("high carnival"); the Reverend Bayard R. Hall, D.D., *Frank Freeman's Barber Shop; A Tale* (New York, 1852), 103–104 ("Ah! white man"), 109–111 ("times of cramming"). See also Genovese, *Roll, Jordan, Roll,* 574. For one former slave's recollections, see John W. Blassingame, ed., *Slave Testimony: Two Centuries of Letters, Speeches, Interviews, and Autobiographies* (Baton Rouge: Louisiana State University Press, 1977), 652–653.

19. Genovese, *Roll, Jordan, Roll,* 578 (John Pierpont). See also Allen Parker, *Recollections of Slavery Times* (Worcester, Mass., 1895), 67. Several historians report that slave marriages were sometimes "grouped" at Christmas. See Blake Touchstone, "Planters and Slave Religion in the Deep South," in John B. Boles, ed., *Masters & Slaves in the House of the Lord: Race and Religion in the American South 1740–1870* (Lexington, Ky., 1988), 124; and Ulrich B. Philips, *American Negro Slavery* (New York: Appleton, 1918), 213. This claim is backed by the accounts of ex-slaves (e.g., Northup, *Twelve Years a Slave,* 221–222) as well as by plantation records. One plantation diary from 1859–60 records seven slave marriages at a single Christmas (Easterby, *Allston,* 453–454).

20. Ravitz, "Pierpont," 384–385; Thomas Bangs Thorpe, "Cotton and Its Cultivation," *Harper's New Monthly Magazine* 8 (1854), 447–463 (449: "saturnalia of the Romans"); Hall, *Frank Freeman,* 102–103 ("grand saturnalia"). For a concise account of slave revelry, see Albert J. Raboteau, *Slave Religion: The "Invisible Institution" in the Antebellum South* (New York: Oxford University Press, 1978), 224.

21. For example, a Florida newspaper argued in 1857 that it was foolish to believe that the "idle, lounging, roving, drunken, and otherwise mischievous [Christmas] week fits the Negro in the least degree for the discharge of his duties." (Kenneth M. Stampp, *The Peculiar Institution: Slavery in the AnteBellum South* (New York: Knopf, 1956), 170.

22. Quoted by Stampp, *Peculiar Institution,* 170, from *De Bow's Review* 13 (1852), 193–194.

23. Douglass, *Narrative,* 75–76. I would agree with Eugene Genovese in taking issue with Douglass's claim: "Douglass was right in thinking that the holidays . . . undermined the revolutionary impulse of the slaves, but he was wrong, I believe, in thinking that the cause lay in the slaves' being trapped in triviality and self-degradation." Rather, Genovese suggests that the counterrevolutionary effect of such "big times" was that they developed in slaves a patriarchal sense of "community with their white folks" (Genovese, *Roll, Jordan, Roll,* 580). On *this* issue I disagree with Genovese, and I would add another

point: Douglass was very much a man of bourgeois principles—for him, the loss of self-control through drinking and sexual excess signified a loss of self-respect. Finally, Douglass's rhetoric was bound to appeal to the temperance-minded audience that constituted a substantial part of his intended Northern readership.

24. Parker, *Recollections,* 67–68; Smedes, *Southern Planter,* 161–162. Alexander Barclay wrote in 1828 about slave life in Jamaica: "Such dances were formerly common, or I should rather say universal, at Christmas; but of late years have gone much out, owing to an idea impressed on the minds of the negroes, principally I believe by the missionaries, that the season ought rather to be devoted to religious exercises. It is now considered more becoming to attend the places of worship, or to have private religious parties among themselves; and in passing through a negro village on a Christmas night, it is more common to hear psalm-singing, than the sound of merriment. Alexander Barclay, *A Practical View of the Present State of Slavery in the West Indies* (3rd ed., London, 1828), 10–11.

25. Phillips, *Slavery,* 315; Jacob Stroyer, *My Life in the South* (Salem, Mass., 1879), 35.

26. Parker, *Recollections,* 67–68; see also Phillips, *Slavery,* 316–318. The music at these revivals was limited to the human voice (and other parts of the body); musical instruments were prohibited for religious reasons.

27. Report by Harriet Ware, Dec. 26, 1862; quoted in Elizabeth Ware Pearson, ed. *Letters from Port Royal, Written at the Time of the Civil War* (Boston, 1906), 124; Sallie Holley, *A Life for Liberty: Anti-Slavery and Other Letters* (New York, 1899), 229–230.

28. Yetman, *Selections,* 193 (also quoted in Jones, *Child of Freedom,* 70). See also Charles L. Perdue, Jr., Thomas E. Barden, and Robert K. Philips, eds., *Weevils in the Wheat: Interviews with Virginia Ex-Slaves* [Charlottesvile: University Press of Virginia, 1976], 229. Stampp, *Peculiar Institution,* 166, offers good examples from the 1850s. The gifts on one plantation were unusual enough to become a subject of humorous comment: "Every woman got a handkerchief to tie up her hair. Every girl got a ribbon, every boy a ballow [i.e., Barlow] knife, and every man a shin plaster. De neighbors call de place, de Shin Plaster, Barlow, Bandana place" (Yetman, *Selections,* 59).

29. Charles Kershaw [a factor] to Charlotte Ann Allston, Charleston, Nov. 29, 1815, in Easterby, *Allston,* 359. Allston himself, writing in the 1830s, noted: "the plantation stock to furnish . . . a beef for Christmas" (ibid., 257). Ravitz, "Pierpont," 384–385); Ronald Killion and Charles Waller, eds., *Slavery Time When I Was Chillun Down on Marster's Plantation: Interviews with Georgia Slaves* (Savannah: Library of Georgia, 1973), 11 (Georgia Baker); Northup, *Twelve Years a Slave,* 215–216. See also Sarah Virgil: "On Fourth of July and Christmas, Marster would give us the biggest kind of to-do. We always had more to eat than you ever saw on them days" (Killion and Waller, *Slavery Time,* 141.) Slaves often provided their own food and drink, from stock they had raised, made, or sold on their own during the year; sometimes they simply stole the master's food. See, for example, Harriet A. Jacobs, *Incidents in the Life of a Slave Girl* (ed. by Lydia Maria Child; Boston, 1861 [Cambridge, 1987 reprint; ed. Jean Fagan Yellin]), 180–181. Compare a Christmas song recorded by Joel Chandler Harris in 1858: "Ho my Riley! dey eat en dey cram, / En bimeby [by-and-by] ole Miss'll be sendin' out de dram."

30. Thomas Bangs Thorpe, "Christmas in the South," *Frank Leslie's Illustrated Newspaper* 5 (Dec. 26, 1857), 62.

31. Yetman, *Selections,* 73 ("barrels o' apples"); Jones, *Child of Freedom,* 70, quoted from the Reverend Irving Lowery, *Life on the Old Plantation* (Columbia, S.C., 1911), 13, 37, 67.

32. This slave was speaking in the month of June, so he had not eaten meat for almost half a year. His remark was made to Charles Ball, and reported in Ball, *Slavery,* 79–80. Norrece T. Jones, who has measured Christmas meat in the context of "ordinary" slave diet on one South Carolina plantation, writes that over a period of nine months, "workers received meat from their master during four weeks only" (Jones, *Child of Freedom,* 49).

33. Stampp, *Peculiar Institution,* 166; anonymous Mississippi planter, "Management of Negroes upon Southern Estates," *De Bow's Review* 10 (1851), 621–627; quoted in Breeden, *Advice Among Masters,* 253–254 ("whipping and forfeiture"); Jesse H. Turner, "Management of Negroes," in *South-Western Farmer* 1 (1842), 114–115 ("no matter by whom"); quoted ibid, 257–258.

34. Jones, *Child of Freedom,* 70. See also Ball, *Slavery in the United States,* 206–207.

35. Genovese, *Roll, Jordan, Roll,* 579; E. P. Thompson, "Patrician Society, Plebeian Culture," in *Journal of Social History,* vol. 7 (1974), 382–405 (see esp. 390–394); quoted in U. B. Phillips, "Plantations with Slave Labor and Free," *American Historical Review* 30 (1925), 742.

36. Cicely Cawthon, in Killion and Waller, *Slavery Time,* 40 ("something else!"); Georgia Baker, ibid, 11–12 ("Marse Alec"). See also Martha Colquitt, in Yetman, *Selections,* 62: "On Christmas mornin' all of us would come up to de yard back of de Big House and Marse Billie and de overseer handed out presents for all."

37. Smedes, *Southern Planter,* 161; Bessie M. Henry, "A Yankee Schoolmistress Discovers Virginia," *Essex Institute Historical Collections* 101 (1965), 121–132; "take the kitchen" quotation is on p. 129; Blow, "Memoir"; Mariah Calloway, in Killion and Waller, *Slavery Time,* 142 ("ate from the family's table"). One planter gave his slaves their gifts in the family kitchen. (Palmer, "Maryland Homes and Ways," 260). A Jamaican planter reported in the 1820s that "[i]n the evening they assemble in their master's or manager's house, and as a matter of course, take possession of the largest room, bringing with them a fiddle and tambourines" (Barclay, *Practical View,* 10).

38. For masters who visited the slave quarters, see Northup, *Twelve Years a Slave,* 215: "White people in great numbers assemble [there] to witness the gastronomical enjoyments." Another ex-slave later recalled that "[w]hile they danced and sang the master and his family sat and looked on" (quoted in Killion and Waller, *Slavery Times,* 116). For an extreme version of masters joining in their slaves' festivities, see Helen Tunnicliff Catterall, *Judicial Cases Concerning American Slavery and the Negro* (2 vols., Washington, D.C., 1926–37), vol. 2 (1929), 140–141. A misleading summary of this fascinating case can be found in Guion Griffis Johnson, *Ante-Bellum North Carolina: A Social History* (Chapel Hill: University of North Carolina Press, 1937): Johnson misinterprets the story as a matter of the owner's merely inviting the slaves home to perform for the "amusement" of his own family. See below, note 42.

39. Cameron, "Christmas on an Old Plantation," 5–8.

40. Thorpe, "Christmas"; Stampp, *Peculiar Institution,* 169. Thomas Nelson Page later recalled how his own family decorated the table for their slaves' Christmas dinner with "their own white hands"! Thomas Nelson Page, *Social Life in Old Virginia Before the War* (New York, 1897), 102.

41. Stampp, *Peculiar Institution,* 169 ("happy as Lords"; quoted from John Houston Bills ms. diary, Dec. 30, 1843); Barclay, *Practical View,* 10 ("all authority"); Foby, "Management of Servants," in *Southern Cultivator* 11 (Aug. 1853), 226–228 ("difficult to say who is master": quoted in Breeden, *Advice Among Masters,* 309; partially quoted in Genovese, 579). See also James Benson Sellers, *Slavery in Alabama* (University, Ala.: University of Alabama Press, 1950), 124.

42. John N. Evans to John W. Burrus, Jan. 1, 1836; quoted in Genovese, *Roll, Jordan, Roll,* 579–580. See also the following slave owner's diary entry from December 25, 1852: "I have endeavored . . . to make my Negroes joyous and happy, and am glad to see them enjoying themselves with such a contented hearty good will" (quoted in Stampp, *Peculiar Institution,* 169). One North Carolina planter was brought to court in 1847 for allowing members of his own family (including his young daughters) to dance with the slaves he had invited into the Big House on Christmas night. The judge in the case acquitted this man of the charges, and in his decision wrote of the defendant's behavior that "there was

nothing contrary to morals or law in all that . . . unless it be that one feel aggrieved, that these poor people should for a short space be happy at finding the authority of the master give place to his benignity. . . . It is very possible, that the children of the family might in Christmas times, without the least impropriety, countenance the festivities of the old servants of the family by witnessing, and even mingling in them." *North Carolina v. Boyce,* in Catterall, *Cases Concerning Slavery,* II, 140–141. See above, note 38.

43. Quoted in Johnson, *Ante-Bellum North Carolina,* 552–553, from ms. in N.C. Legislative Papers, June 18, 1824. For an account of the murder case that lay behind this statement, see Elizabeth A. Fenn, " 'A Perfect Equality Seemed to Reign': Slave Society and Jonkonnu," *North Carolina Historical Review,* 65 (Apr. 1988), 127–153. Compare Judge Ruffin's decision in the Boyce case: "It would really be a source of regret, if, contrary to common custom, it were denied to slaves, in the intervals between their toils, to indulge in mirthful pastimes, or if it were unlawful for the master to permit them among his slaves, or to admit to the social enjoyment the slaves of others, by their consent. . . . We may let them make the most of their idle hours, and may well make allowances for the noisy outpourings of glad hearts, which providence bestows as a blessing on corporeal vigor united to a vacant mind. . . ." (Catterall, *Cases Concerning Slavery,* II, 139–141; several passages from this quotation are taken from the version that appears in Johnson, *Ante-Bellum North Carolina,* 555.)

44. *Fithian Journals,* 52–53.

45. Thorpe, "Cotton," 460–461.

46. Julia Peterkin, in Charlmae Rollins, ed., *Christmas Gif'; an anthology of Christmas poems, songs, and stories, written by and about Negroes* (Chicago: Follett, [1963]), 33; Smedes, *Southern Planter,* 162; see also Blow, Memoir; Cooke, "Christmas Time in Old Virginia," 458; Folsom, "Christmas at Brockton Plantation," 486 (this involved whites only); Joel Chandler Harris, "Something about 'Sandy Claus,' " in his *On the Plantation: A Story of a Georgia Boy's Adventures During the War* (New York, 1892), 116; Johnson, *Ante-Bellum North Carolina,* 552.

47. James Bolton, in Killion and Waller, *Slavery Time,* 25; see also Blow, Memoir.

48. Harris, "Something About 'Sandy Claus,' " 116; Rollins, *Christmas Gif'!,* 35 (Hurston story). In some places this "game" lasted into the twentieth century. See Harnett T. Kane, ibid., 16. Zora Neale Hurston told a story of a black man who hid behind a stump one Christmas and took God Almighty by surprise with the cry "Christmas gift!" (ibid., 35). There is even a reference to this ritual in William Faulkner's novel *The Sound and the Fury.* As young Quentin Compson leaves Harvard College in despair and arrives by train in Mississippi on December 25, the first thing that happens to him when he steps off the train—it is what makes him realize he has arrived "home"—is that he is approached by a Negro beggar who accosts him with the words "Christmas gift."

49. Page, *Social Life,* 96; Baird, *Edmonds,* 9–10 (1857 entry), 177 (1863 entry). See also William Gilmore Simms, *The Golden Christmas: A Chronicle of St. John's, Berkeley* (Charleston, S.C., 1852), 143–145.

50. Edmonds married only in 1870, at the age of 30. One young Virginia married woman claimed the perquisites of both roles: "We [she and her husband] have invitation to a dinner on Wednesday . . . , and I am invited among the young people to an evening party on Friday—so you perceive I have [both] married *and* single privileges" (Tyler ms., Swem Library, College of William and Mary).

51. Smedes, *Southern Planter,* 162.

52. Stampp, *Peculiar Institution,* 366 ("best rigging": quoted from John W. Brown diary, Dec. 25, 1853); Cameron, "Christmas on an Old Plantation."

53. Thorpe, "Cotton," 460 ("drop their plantation names"); Mary A. Livermore, *The Story of My Life* (Hartford, 1897), 210 ("almost a burlesque").

54. Thorpe, "Cotton," 460.

55. Henry, "Yankee Schoolmistress," 129–130 Bayard Hall reported that slaves mimicked the idiosyncrasies of the whites' dialogue and mannerisms (Hall, *Frank Freeman,* 109–110).

56. Quoted Johnson, *Ante-Bellum North Carolina,* 145.

57. *Liberator* 8 (May 26, 1837, 85. The writer acknowledged that "very few of the blacks were at church," and added that "the distant sounds of Cooner reached even there."

58. Johnson, *Ante-Bellum North Carolina,* 552–553 (quoted from ms. in N.C. Legislative Papers, June 18, 1824). For an account of the incident behind this statement—the killing of a white man by a John Canoer—see Fenn, " 'A Perfect Equality Seemed to Reign,' " 127–153. See also Edward Warren, *A Doctor's Experiences in Three Continents* (Baltimore, 1885), 198–203.

59. James Norcom to his daughter Mary Matilda Norcom, Jan. 13, 1838; quoted by Jean Fagan Yellin in Jacobs, *Incidents,* 277. See also Edward Warren, *A Doctor's Experiences in Three Continents* (Baltimore, 1885), 198–203.

60. Jacobs, *Incidents,* 180.

61. Ibid., 179–180.

62. Dougald MacMillan, "John Kuners," *Journal of American Folklore* 39 (1926), 53–57. This verse is quoted by Lawrence Levine, who writes that it was sung by the John Canoe band to "those whites who did not respond to their offerings with generosity." Levine, *Black Culture and Black Consciousness: Afro-American Folk Thought from Slavery to Freedom* (New York: Oxford University Press, 1977), 13. I have found one other (rather inoffensive) fragment of a begging song, recalled years later by a white woman who was raised in the area: "C'ris'mas comes but once er yeah, / An' ev'y po niggiah arter have 'e sha' " (Folsom, "Christmas at Brockton Plantation," 485).

63. Jean Fagan Yellin quotes from a letter from John W. Nunley to Jean Fagan Yellin suggesting that John Canoe was "a creolized masquerade tradition that has incorporated African and English traditions of masking. . . . The penchant for rum and the collecting of money by the maskers is also a shared trans-Atlantic tradition" (Jacobs, *Incidents,* 278–279n.). Frederick G. Cassidy claims that the ceremony comes from the "Gold Coast," though it was widely observed in the New World: Frederick G. Cassidy, " 'Hipsaw' and 'John Canoe,' " *American Speech* 41 (1966), 45–51. On "John Canoe" in North Carolina, see Fenn, " 'A Perfect Equality' "; Richard Walser, "His Worshipful John Kuner," *North Carolina Folklore* 19 (1971), 160–172; and Nancy Ping, "Black Musical Activities in Antebellum Wilmington, North Carolina," *The Black Perspective in Music* 8 (1980), 139–160. As far as the ridiculing song, Dena Epstein notes that "the parallel with African songs of derision is evident" (Epstein, *Sinful Tunes and Spirituals* [Urbana: University of Illinois Press, 1977], 131). The song quoted by Lawrence Levine is taken from Dougald MacMillan, "John Kuners," *Journal of American Folklore* 39 (1926), 53–57. See also Levine, *Black Culture and Black Consciousness*), 12. Ira de A. Reid, "The John Canoe Festival: A New World Africanism," *Phylon* 3 (1942), 349–370, argues for the English origin of the ritual. Martha Warren Beckwith, *Black Roadways: A Study of Jamaican Folk Life* (Chapel Hill, 1929), gives evidence from the 1920s that Shakespearean plays were being used by the John Canoers. (See also the same author's *Christmas Mummings in Jamaica* (Pubs. of the Folklore Foundation: Vassar College, 1923).

64. Epstein, *Sinful Tunes,* 131.

65. For an instance, see Catterall, *Cases Concerning Slavery,* vol. 2, 536: Tennessee cases: "*Bowling v. Statton and Swann,* . . . December 1847. '[A]ction . . . for the loss of a negro man . . . hired . . . and never returned.' "

66. Dan T. Carter, "The Anatomy of Fear: The Christmas Day Insurrection Scare of 1865," in *Journal of Southern History* 42 (1976), 345–364; "nearly one-third the rumors" is

on p. 358. Joel Williamson also notes that in South Carolina "[t]he Fourth of July . . . and Christmas or New Year's Day had marked a large number of insurrections or planned insurrections." Joel Williamson, *After Slavery: The Negro in South Carolina During Reconstruction, 1861–1877* (Chapel Hill: University of North Carolina Press, 1965), 250. For a report of an 1835 slave revolt in Louisiana that was planned for Christmas, see Joe Gray Taylor, *Negro Slavery in Louisiana* (New York, 1963), 218–220. The South Carolina report is from Frederick Law Olmstead, *A Journey Through the Back Country* (London, 1860), 203; quoted in Joseph Cephas Carroll, *Slave Insurrections in the United States, 1800–1865* (Boston, 1938), 176. For the 1856 reports, see Herbert Aptheker, *American Negro Slave Revolts* (New York: Columbia University Press, 1943), 347–350. On December 24, 1856, one Virginia slave was discovered carrying a letter concerning an imminent "meeting" that would lead to "freedom"; the letter claimed that soon "the country is ours certain" (quoted ibid., 350). Some revolts were timed for July 4, the other major slave holiday, and one that was also charged with a powerful symbolism of liberation. Nat Turner, for example, originally intended his 1831 rebellion to begin on July 4.

67. See William McFeely, *Yankee Stepfather: General O. O. Howard and the Freedmen* (New Haven: Yale University Press, 1968); Eric Foner, *Reconstruction America's Unfinished Revolution, 1863–1877* (New York: Harper & Row, 1988); Carter, "Anatomy of Fear"; William C. Harris, *Presidential Reconstruction in Mississippi* (Baton Rouge: Louisiana State University Press, 1967), 88–89; Claude F. Oubre, *Forty Acres and a Mule: The Freedmen's Bureau and Black Land Ownership* (Baton Rouge: Louisiana State University Press, 1978), esp. pp. 1–89. The Civil War origins of a potential land-reform policy are discussed in LaWanda Cox, "The Promise of Land for the Freedmen," *Mississippi Valley Historical Review* 45 (1958), 413–440.

68. Henry Watson to his daughter Julia Watson, Dec. 16, 1865, ms. in Frost Library, Amherst College. This letter was brought to my attention by Wesley Borucki. Watson added that "The [black] women say that they never mean to do any more outdoor work, that *white men* support *their* wives and they mean that *their* husbands shall support *them.*" Such hopes to abandon "outdoor work" suggest intriguingly that these freedwomen harbored bourgeois aspirations—i.e., to work in the home and be supported by their husbands.

69. Carter, "Anatomy of Fear," associates the "Christmas Riots of 1865" with the long history of rowdy behavior on this holiday but does not go on to associate the holiday with gestures of paternalist largesse on the part of whites.

70. *Texas State Gazette* [Austin], quoted in *The Daily Picayune* [New Orleans], Nov. 21, 1865 ("waiting for the jubilee"—the writer had traveled through Georgia, Alabama, Mississippi, and Louisiana); *Daily Picayune,* Dec. 27, 1865 ("their old masters").

71. Henry Watson to Julia Watson, Dec. 16, 1865. "As for work," one South Carolina planter told a visiting reporter, "[T]he freedmen were doing absolutely nothing. He had overheard one of his girls saying that she hadn't seen any freedom yet, she had to work just as hard as ever. And that was the feeling of a great many of them. Then, as he had said, they were waiting for January, and nothing could be done with them till they became convinced that they must work for wages" (*The Nation* I [1865], 651).

72. For example, the provisional governor of South Carolina, James Lawrence Orr, wrote: "[During] Christmas week, which has always been a holiday for the negroes they will congregate in large numbers in the villages and towns where they will get liquor and while under its influence I fear that collisions will occur between them and the whites. When once commenced no one can tell where the conflict will end" (Orr to Gen. Daniel Sickles, Dec. 13, 1865; quoted in Carter, "Anatomy of Fear," 358n).

73. *Atlanta Daily Intelligencer,* Dec. 21, 1865; quoted in Carter, "Anatomy of Fear," 358); *The Nation* I (1865), 651.

74. *Shreveport Gazette,* reprinted in *Cincinnati Daily Enquirer,* Nov. 23, 1865 ("growing more insolent"); ibid., Nov. 24, 1865. For other reports, see the following (all 1865); ibid., Nov. 28 (Louisiana, Texas); ibid., Nov. 30 (Georgia); ibid., Dec. 23 (Texas, citing *San Antonio Gazette*); ibid., Dec. 23 (Virginia); *National Intelligencer* [Washington], Nov. 29 (Mississippi); *Washington Evening Star,* Dec. 26 (Mississippi, citing the *Vicksburg Journal*); *Cincinnati Enquirer,* Nov. 28 (Texas).

75. New Orleans *True Delta,* Dec. 15, 1865, reprinted in *National Intelligencer* [Washington, D.C.], Dec. 30, 1865.

76. *The Daily Picayune* [New Orleans], Nov. 14, 1865.

77. General Howard's address to the freedmen was printed in the New Orleans *Times,* Dec. 10, 1865, and quoted in Carter, "Anatomy of Fear," 360. McFeely, *Yankee Stepfather,* 105, quotes "a la mode Santa Claus." Colonel Strong's speech was quoted in *The Daily Picayune* [New Orleans], Nov. 28, 1865. (Colonel Strong was General Howard's inspector general; he had been sent to Texas by Howard himself.) Not all agents of the Freedmen's Bureau were willing to do this dirty work. At least one, Thomas Conway of the New Orleans office, continued into the fall to advise freedmen that they could apply for free land through the end of December (McFeely, *Yankee Stepfather,* 179; Oubre, *Forty Acres,* 34). And another, General Edgar Gregory—formerly a radical abolitionist—was reported to have given a somewhat incendiary speech to Texas freedmen, telling them that they were entitled to free land and urging them not to sign unfavorable labor contracts (*The Daily Picayune* [New Orleans], Nov. 28, 1865). It was agents such as these that the Southern press regarded as the "bad white men" who were corrupting the black population. For the official mission of the Freedmen's Bureau, see Carter, "Anatomy of Fear," 360.

78. *Columbus* [*Miss.*] *Sentinel,* reprinted in New Orleans *Daily Picayune,* Nov. 28, 1865. See also ms. letter of Henry Watson to Julia Watson, Dec. 16, 1865, Amherst College Archives.

79. John S. Garvin to Governor Parsons; quoted Carter, "Anatomy of Fear," 361. Many blacks were arrested and otherwise harassed during the weeks before Christmas.

80. Unpublished memoir of Sally Elmore Taylor, quoted in Joel Williamson, *After Slavery,* 249–250. For another expression of white fear, see ibid., 251 (a white planter, watching his former slaves slaughtering a hog on December 4, "shuddered . . . to see the fiendish eagerness in some of them to stab & kill, the delight in the suffering of others").

81. *National Intelligencer* [Washington, D.C.], Dec. 30, 1865.

82. *Alexandria Gazette,* Dec. 28, 1865 ("too much whiskey"); *Washington Star,* Dec. 30, 1865 ("much bad whiskey"); *Richmond Daily Whig,* Dec. 29, 1865 ("some colored men"); *National Intelligencer* [Washington, D.C.], Dec. 28, 1865 ("no political significance").

83. *Richmond Daily Whig,* Dec. 27, 1865.

84. *The Daily Picayune,* Dec. 31, 1865.

85. Ibid., Dec. 27, 1865. In any case, the *Picayune* noted, readers could take heart from the knowledge that "the negro population will be found, as it has always been found in the South, to be docile."

86. *Richmond Daily Whig,* Dec. 25, 1865.

Epilogue

1. Booker T. Washington, *Up from Slavery: An Autobiography* (New York, 1901), 133. (He added, referring to the turn of the century, "This custom prevails throughout this portion of the South to-day.") The following material appears ibid., 133–136.

2. This paragraph and the following ones are from Ira de A. Reid, "The John Canoe Festival: A New World Africanism," *Phylon* 3 (1942), 349–370; see also Lawrence

Levine, *Black Culture and Black Consciousness: Afro-American Folk Thought from Slavery to Freedom* (New York: Oxford University Press, 1977), 150 (it is Levine who explains the term *dicty*).

3. William Carleton, "The Midnight Mass," in his *Traits and Stories of the Irish Peasantry* (2 vols., Philadelphia, 1834), I, 13–102 (esp. 46–54).

4. Cited in Kevin Danaher, *The Year in Ireland* (Cork: Mercier Press, 1972), 241–242.

5. Mr. and Mrs. S. C. Hall, *Ireland, Its Scenery, Character, etc.* (3 vols., London, 1861–63 [orig. published in 1841], vol. 1, 23–25. The Halls refer to this as "the only Christmas gambol remaining in Ireland of the many that in the middle ages were so numerous and so dangerous as to call for the imposition of the law, and the strong arm of magisterial authority" (ibid., 25).

6. Colm Kerrigan, *Father Mathew and the Irish Temperance Movement, 1838–1849* (Cork: Cork University Press, 1992), passim (the pledge figure is from p. 82).

7. Ibid., 76–77 (social advancement), 107–127 (repeal).

8. See entry of Dec. 23, 1842, where he "[gave] audience to half the world, some humbly begging for a little help, some asking merely for a loan. . . ." David Thomson, with Moyra McGusty, eds., *The Irish Journals of Elizabeth Smith, 1840–1850: A Selection* (New York: Oxford University Press, 1980), 59.

9. Ibid., 25. (Dec. 25–26, 1840). Two years later, on New Year's Eve, 1842, Mrs. Smith wrote that she and her husband would "drink it [the old year] out in negus upstairs and punch below" (ibid., 60).

10. [New York] *Irish World*, Dec. 28, 1872. For a different reading of temperance, see Paul Johnson, *A Shopkeeper's Millennium: Society and Revivals in Rochester, New York, 1815–1837* (New York: Hill and Wang, 1978); and, of working-class immigrants and the reform of holiday celebrations, see Roy Rozenzweig, *Eight Hours for What We Will: Workers and Leisure in an Industrial City, 1870–1920* (Cambridge and New York, 1983), 65–92, 153–170.

11. These dates appear in James H. Barnett, *The American Christmas: A Study in National Culture* (New York: Macmillan, 1954), 20.

12. *Acts and Resolves Passed by the General Court of Massachusetts, in the Year 1855*, ch. 91, 549; *Acts and Resolves Passed by the General Court of Massachusetts, in the Year 1856*, ch. 113, 59–60.

13. John R. Mulkern, *The Know-Nothing Party in Massachusetts: The Rise and Fall of a People's Movement* (Boston: Northeastern University Press, 1990), 79, 89–90, 101, 108–11 (the quotation is on p. 108). The Know-Nothings lost control of the state legislature in the 1856 elections. See also Ronald P. Formisano, *The Transformation of Political Culture: Massachusetts Parties, 1790s–1840s* (New York: Oxford University Press, 1983).

14. *Boston Daily Bee*, Feb. 8, 1856; see also *Boston Courier*, Feb. 8, 1856, for a letter pointing to the financial effects of the bill. (While Rep. Vose was a Know-Nothing, he was also a leader of the *opposition* to the temperance legislation that had passed the previous year.)

15. This point is made in William B. Waits, *The Modern Christmas in America: A Cultural History of Gift Giving* (New York: New York University Press, 1993), 8.

16. Interview recorded by Alan Lomax, on "Leadbelly: Go Down with Aunt Hannah" (The Library of Congress Recordings, vol. 6; reissued by Rounder Records, 1994: CD 1099).

17. "I begin to whoopie" is from Peetie Wheatstraw, "Santa Claus Blues" (1935), *Peetie Wheatstraw (1930–1941)*, da Music, CD 3541-2; "New Year's Blues" is from Tampa Red, "Christmas and New Year's Blues" (1934), from *Complete Works, vol. 6, 1934–35;* Document Records DOCD-5206; "Valentine's Day" is from Walter Davis, "New Santa Claus"

(1941), from *Complete Works, vol. 7, 1940–46;* on Document Records DOCD-5286. One blues song that does deal with children and presents (sung from a woman's perspective, it is about a man who has abandoned his woman and children during Christmas week) ends by reporting happily that another man has entered the singer's life—"there's a big fat Santy [Santa] walkin' in my front door." See Victoria Spivey, "Christmas Without Santa Claus" (1961) on *Woman Blues* (text by Victoria Spivey: Prestige / Bluesville Records BV-1054. For another Christmas-reunion blues, see Floyd McDaniel, "Christmas Blues" (1992), *The Stars of Rhythm 'n' Blues,* CMA Music Productions CD, CM-10007.

18. Robert Johnson, "Hellhound on My Trail" (1937: from *The Complete Recordings,* Columbia C2K-46222; 1991) [King of Spades Music, 1990]; "Every day is Christmas" is from Joe Turner, "*Christmas Date Boogie*" (1948 / 9: from *Tell Me Pretty Baby,* Arhoolie CD 333 (1992) [text by Joe Turner]; "like a rooster" is from Champion Jack Dupree, "Santa Claus Blues," from *The Joe Davis Sessions, 1945–46* (Flyright FLY CD 22, 1990). The term *Christmas* could actually become a euphemism for sex, as in the blues song "Merry Christmas, Baby." After an opening verse that makes the association between Christmas and sex—by repeating the words of the title and adding, "you sure did treat me nice"—the second verse opens with a line in which the very term *Christmas* has come to mean "sex": "I'm comin' home, comin' home for Christmas right now." By the end of the song we have come to hear the repeated refrain "Merry Christmas, Baby" to mean simply *Thanks for the great sex, baby.* See Luther "Guitar Junior" Johnson, "Merry Christmas, Baby" (1991) on *I Want to Groove with You,* Bullseye Blues/Rounder Records CD BB 9506 [text by L. Baxter and J. Moore: St. Louis Music Corp., 1948]. The association of Christmas with leisure in African-American rural culture has remained so strong that the idea of *working* on Christmas Day is powerfully symbolic. In Howlin' Wolf's "Sittin' on Top of the World," for example, the singer suggests how hard his lot is by simply noting that he spent Christmas Day in his "overalls" [text by Chester Burnett, Arc Music Corp., BMI].

19. "Dresser drawers" is from Sonny Boy Williamson, "Santa Claus" (1960), [text by Rice Miller] *Bummer Road* (Chess/MCA CHD-9324, 1991); "this very Christmas night" is from Charley Jordan and Verdi Lee, "Christmas Tree Blues," in *Charley Jordan: Complete Recorded Works,* vol. 3 (1935–37), Document Records CD, DOCD-5099; "back-door Santa" is from Clarence Carter, "Backdoor Santa" (1960), from *Snatching It Back: The Best of Clarence Carter* Rhino/Atlantic CD (1992), R2-70286 [text by Clarence Carter Carter and Marcus McDaniel: Screen Gems-EMI, BMI]; "even if my whiskers is white" is from Blind Lemon Jefferson, "Christmas Eve Blues" (1928: *Complete Recorded Works,* vol. 3: Document Records DOCD 5019); "hang your stocking by the head of the bed" is from Charley Jordan and Verdi Lee, "Christmas Tree Blues" (cited above); "on your Christmas tree" is from Peetie Wheatstraw, "Santa Claus Blues" (cited above, note 14): the same image is used in Charley Jordan, "Santa Claus Blues" (1931), on *Complete Recorded Works,* vol. 2: Document Records DODC-5098. Other Christmas blues include: Bessie Smith, "At the Christmas Ball" (1925: *Complete Recordings,* vol. 2); Will Weldon, "Christmas Tree Blues" (1937), on *Will Weldon as Casey Bill: The Hawaiian Guitar Wizard, 1935–38;* Blues Collection/EPM, 1994" by W. Weldon; Sonny Boy Williamson [John Lee Williamson], "Christmas Morning Blues" (1938: *Complete Recorded Works,* vol. 2: Document Records, DOCD-5056); Lightnin' Hopkins, "Santa," on *Mojo Hand,* Golden Classics CD (Collectible Records Corp., Narbeth, Penn., CD-5111; Walter Davis, "Santa Claus Blues," from *Complete Works,* vol. 6); Charlie Johnson, "Santa Claus Blues," from *Complete Works,* vol. 2 (1931–34); and Freddie King, "Christmas Tears" (from *17 Hits*).

20. Mikhail Bakhtin, *Rabelais and His World* (Cambridge: MIT, 1968), 4–18, 145–154. For ongoing vestiges of carnival, see Peter Stallybrass and Allon White, *The Politics and Poetics of Transgression* (London: Methuen, 1986), 171–190.

21. But it appears that in many places Thanksgiving itself came to take on some of the aspects of carnival. For an account of this development, see Harriet Beecher Stowe's historical novel *Oldtown Folks* (Boston, 1869), ch. 27: "How We Kept Thanksgiving." For

a contemporaneous perspective, in 1818 the *Farmer's Cabinet* (an Amherst, N.H., newspaper) printed an article lamenting the "frolicks of Thanksgiving" and wishing that "the period annually set apart as a season of devout thanksgiving . . . were in reality a season of heart-felt and religious gratitude . . . when the *heart* and not the *appetite* should be the source of thanksgiving." The same editorial suggested that Thanksgiving had also become at least semi-commercialized, a time when "farmers and merchants make their calculations to profit by its return, in the disposal of their various articles." (*Farmer's Cabinet*, Dec. 26, 1818; reprinted from the *New Hampshire Patriot*).

22. "Hanukkah was probably attached to a solstice feast already celebrated in Jerusalem by Jews friendly to Greece." Martin Hengel, *Judaism and Hellenism: Studies in Their Encounter in Palestine During the Early Hellenistic Period* (translated from the German; 2 vols., Philadelphia: Fortress Press, 1974), I, 235; see also ibid., 303.

23. Israel Abrahams, *Jewish Life in the Middle Ages* (New York, 1896), 389–398 (Chanukah exception is on p. 396).

24. Increase Mather, *A Testimony Against Several Prophane and Superstitious Customs, Now Practiced by Some in New-England* (London, 1687), 41–42.

25. See, for example, Michael Strassfeld, *The Jewish Holidays, A Guide and Commentary* (New York: Harper and Row, 1985), 187–196. This chapter bears the title "Purim: Self-Mockery and Masquerade." See also Francis Spufford, "Pleasures and Perils of Purim," in *Times Literary Supplement*, June 5, 1992. Spufford terms Purim "a carnival as Bakhtin described carnivals."

26. Daniel Miller, "A Theory of Christmas," in Daniel Miller, ed., *Unwrapping Christmas* (Oxford: Clarendon Press, 1993), 3.

Acknowledgments

I WROTE this book in the course of three nonconsecutive years (and an additional summer) during which I lived away from my Amherst, Massachusetts, home. Serious work began in 1989–90, when I was James P. Harrison Professor of History at The College of William and Mary. That appointment included the services of a helpful research assistant, Nigel Alderman, as well as the obligation to deliver several public lectures that managed to transform my Christmas project from a minor arrow in my scholarly quiver into a serious endeavor. John Selby of William and Mary's History Department helped set up those lectures (and my entire year); Marianne Brink, Ann and Bob Gross, and Chandos Bown helped make the year both intellectually and socially memorable.

Much of the book was researched and written during the 1991–92 academic year, when I held a residential fellowship (funded by the National Endowment for the Humanities) at the American Antiquarian Society. But the AAS was more than a wonderful library. It has long been my second home, and the members of its staff are like family. Nancy Burkett (now the AAS librarian) and Joanne Chaison (now reference librarian) were each head of readers' services when I first came to know them. Today Marie Lamareaux occupies that position. All three wore themselves out on my behalf, and without ever losing the graciousness that has long been a hallmark of the AAS. Laura Wascowicz spent hours of what seemed to be her own time hunting down children's literature for me, and her cataloguing skills enabled me to locate items I would never have encountered on my own. Dennis Laurie went beyond the call of any possible duty several times, doing research in newspapers I had not even asked to see. Tom Knoles always made the imposing AAS manuscript division user-friendly. Georgia Barnhill sprang into action whenever she found a picture she thought I might be able to use. Although John B. Hench worked in an office across the street, he was always a benevolent force and a supportive presence. Finally, there were the rewarding conversations with fellow readers at the AAS, readers who included Robert Arner, Catherine Brekus, Nym Cooke, Cornelia Dayton, Alice Fahs, Billy G. Smith, and Ann Fairfax Withington.

In the summer of 1993 I held an Andrew W. Mellon fellowship at the Massachusetts Historical Society. My work there was enhanced by the careful cataloguing of the voluminous Sedgwick family papers (which would otherwise have been impenetrable). I would especially like to thank Peter Drummey, Edward W. Hanson, Richard A. Ryerson, Virginia H. Smith, and Conrad E. Wright—and to remember the Thursday lunches and the conversations with Charles Capper.

Finally, in 1994–95 I finished the book at Harvard University's Charles Warren Center for Studies in American History, a fellowship stay that was made more than pleasant by the center's able and amiable administrator, Susan G. Hunt, and by its present and former directors, Ernest May and Bernard Bailyn, respectively, and by Donald Fleming, who organized our seminars and directed my attention to Charles Loring Brace. Warren Center colleagues who offered support and assistance included Stephen Alter, Mia Bay, Steven Biel, Allen Guelzo, and Laura Kalman. During my year at Harvard I was fortunate enough to live (and eat) at Eliot House, courtesy of its co-masters, Stephen A. Mitchell and Kristine Forsgard, and with the support of its former master (and my one-time teacher) Alan Heimert. Karl and Anita Teeter and Seth Rice provided encouragement and hospitality during my Harvard stay (Seth also helped out by reading German materials for me).

Then there is my first academic home, the University of Massachusetts at Amherst. None of my leaves of absence would have been possible without the assistance of UMass. I would especially like to thank Deans Murray M. Schwartz and Lee Edwards, and History Department chairs Robert Jones, Roland Sarti, and Bruce Laurie, for their unhesitating and consistent support of this project in a time of serious fiscal duress.

UMass has also helped by sending me students from whom I have learned. I always like to teach what I'm studying about, and this project was no exception. In what I hope (and believe) was a mutually beneficial arrangement, many of the students in my three Christmas seminars, both undergraduates and graduates, in the process of fulfilling their own course requirements unearthed material that found its way into this book. These students include Wesley Borucki, Shelley Freitag, Richard Gassan, Carrie Giard, Kevin Gilbert, Bill Hodkinson, Susan Ouellette, and Melissa Vogel; as well as Patrick Breen and Sandra D. Hayslette (at The College of William and Mary). To these and other students I owe a gargantuan debt.

And also to colleagues. Writing this book has reaffirmed my faith that a community of scholarly inquiry does indeed exist. In the process of pursuing their own projects, other scholars have occasionally come across Christmas materials, and when they became aware of my project these scholars were generous in giving or sending me the citations—unsolicited mail I was always overjoyed to receive. These colleagues include Robert Arner, Burton Bledstein, Richard D. Brown, Martha Burns, Milton Cantor, Barbara Charles, Patricia Crain, John Engstrom, William Freehling, David Glassberg, Jayne Gordon, Charles Hanson, Barry Levy, Conrad Wright, and Ron and Mary Zboray. Finally there is Dale Cockrell of William and Mary's Music Department, who has been doing splendidly exciting work along a parallel track (I look forward to his forthcoming book on blackface minstrelsy). Helpful ideas came from Burt Bledstein, Dick Brown, Sue Marchand, and Michael Winship. It was my mother, Claire Willner Nissenbaum, who named for me the meter in which Clement Moore composed "A Visit from St. Nicholas"; her scrupulous concern for and delight in language have affected me even more than she may know.

Other colleagues did other forms of service. Ronald P. Formisano, James A. Henretta, and Laurel Thatcher Ulrich wrote letters that helped me receive the fellowship support which made it possible for me to write this book. James Henretta also brought this project to the attention of Jane N. Garrett, who became my editor at Knopf. I thank all of these people for their early faith, and I thank Jane for her great and continuing enthusiasm; I am proud to be counted among her authors. And speaking of Knopf, let me also thank two painstaking proofreaders, Eleanor Mikucki and Teddy Rosenbaum, and, most of all, Melvin Rosenthal, whose unerring eye and endless patience have made this book more accurate as well as more readable.

It is the mark of a good friend to be willing to say critical things. Christopher Clark and Robert A. Gross, who read my draft manuscript in its entirety, were such good friends (they also happen to be remarkably good historians). Chris Clark persuaded me to redo Chapter 6—and showed me how. Bob Gross has been on intimate terms with this project from the beginning, and a trusted and valued friend for much, much longer. (It was Bob, loyal as always, who first suggested the possibility of my going to William and Mary for a year.) R. Jackson Wilson made several characteristically shrewd (and simple) suggestions when this book was in its formative stages. Jack has been true for more than thirty years. I will never attain the purity of his literary style, but I value his friendship even more. Finally, although David Tebaldi has never read a word of this manuscript, his presence informs it nonetheless. As executive director of the Massachusetts Foundation for the Humanities (which I once served as president), David has been a tireless example to the people of Massachusetts—and to me personally—of how scholars and non-scholars together can confront intellectually serious issues. Like Jack Wilson, Bob Gross, and my old collaborator Paul Boyer, David Tebaldi has been a model for my most important commitment as a writer and teacher: that complex ideas do not need to be expressed in complicated language.

Dona Brown knows more than I do about history and other things that matter. It was she, at the very beginning, who helped me see how "The Night Before Christmas" played a complex riff on the larger ritual of the carnival Christmas, and she who continued at each step to make better sense of what I was thinking (even though she invariably insisted that she was simply repeating what I had just said). All the while, she made sure I used the writing of this book as a way to keep exploring my own sense of what it means to be Jewish. Dona, you are my muse, and my darling.

Index

373

A Note About the Author

Stephen Nissenbaum received his A.B. from Harvard College in 1961, his M.A. from Columbia University in 1963, and his Ph.D. from the University of Wisconsin in 1968. He has taught at the University of Massachusetts, Amherst, since 1968 and is currently professor of history there. He has been the recipient of fellowships from the National Endowment for the Humanities, the American Council of Learned Societies, the American Antiquarian Society, the Massachusetts Historical Society, and the Charles Warren Center at Harvard. In addition, he was James P. Harrison Professor of History at the College of William and Mary, 1989–90. He is the author of *Salem Possessed* (with Paul Boyer); *Sex, Diet and Debility in Jacksonian America*; *Sylvester Graham and Health Reform*; *The Pursuit of Liberty* (with others); and *All over the Map: Rethinking American Regions* (with Edward L. Ayers, Patricia Nelson Limerick, and Peter S. Onuf); and the editor of *The Great Awakening at Yale College*, *Salem-Village Witchcraft* (with Paul Boyer), *The Salem Witchcraft Papers* (with Paul Boyer), and *The Scarlet Letter and Selected Writings*. Active in the public humanities, he has served as member and president of the Massachusetts Foundation for the Humanities, and as historical adviser for several film productions.

This book was set in Caslon, a typeface named after William Caslon (1692–1766). The first of a famous English family of type designers and founders, he was originally an apprentice to an engraver of gunlocks and gun barrels in London. In 1716 he opened his own shop, for silver chasing and making bookbinders' stamps. The printers John Watts and William Bowyer, admirers of his skill in cutting ornaments and letters, advanced him money to equip himself for typefounding, which he began in 1720. The fonts he cut in 1722 for Bowyer's sumptuous folio edition of John Selden, published in 1726, excited great interest. A specimen sheet of typefaces, issued in 1734, established Caslon's superiority to all other letter cutters of the time, English or Dutch, and soon his types, or types modeled on his style, were being used by most English printers, supplanting the Dutch types that had formerly prevailed. In style, Caslon was a reversion to earlier type styles. Its characteristics are remarkable regularity and symmetry, and beauty in the shape and proportion of the letters; its general effect is clear and open but not weak or delicate. For uniformity, clearness, and readability it has perhaps never been surpassed. After Caslon's death his eldest son, also named William (1720–1778), carried on the business successfully. A period of neglect followed which lasted almost fifty years. In 1843 Caslon type was revived by the firm Caslon for William Pickering and has since been one of the most widely used of all type designs in English and American printing.

Composed by North Market Street Graphics
Lancaster, Pennsylvania
Printed and bound by Quebecor Printing,
Martinsburg, West Virginia
Designed by Cassandra J. Pappas